COLLECTED STUDIES SERIES

Medieval Aristotelianism
and its Limits

Cary J. Nederman

Medieval Aristotelianism
and its Limits

Classical Traditions in Moral and
Political Philosophy, 12th–15th Centuries

VARIORUM
1997

Published by VARIORUM
Ashgate Publishing Limited
Gower House, Croft Road,
Aldershot, Hampshire GU11 3HR
Great Britain

Ashgate Publishing Company
Old Post Road,
Brookfield, Vermont 05036
USA

ISBN 0–86078–622–6

British Library CIP Data
Nederman, Cary J.
Medieval Aristotelianism and its Limits: Classical Traditions
in Moral and Political Philosophy, 12th–15th Centuries.
(Variorum Collected Studies Series; CS565).
1. Philosophy, Medieval. 2. Ethics, Medieval. 3. Philosophy,
Ancient–Influence.
I. Title.
189

US Library of Congress CIP Data
Nederman, Cary J.
Medieval Aristotelianism and its Limits: Classical Traditions in
Moral and Political Philosophy, 12th–15th Centuries/Cary J. Nederman.
p. cm. – (Variorum Collected Studies Series; CS565).
Includes bibliographical references and index.
1. Aristotle–Contributions in political science. 2. Aristotle–Ethics.
3. Political science–History. 4. Philosophy, Medieval.
I. Title. II. Series: Collected Studies; CS565.
JC71. A7N43   1997   96–48557
320' .01' 1--dc21   CIP

The paper used in this publication meets the minimum requirements of the
American National Standard for Information Sciences – Permanence of Paper
for Printed Library Materials, ANSI Z39.48–1984. ∞ ™

Printed by Galliard (Printers) Ltd., Great Yarmouth, Norfolk, Great Britain.

COLLECTED STUDIES SERIES C565

CONTENTS

vii

This volume contains xiv + 334 pages

PUBLISHER'S NOTE

The articles in this volume, as in all others in the Collected Studies Series, have not been given a new, continuous pagination. In order to avoid confusion, and to facilitate their use where these same studies have been referred to elsewhere, the original pagination has been maintained wherever possible.

Each article has been given a Roman number in order of appearance, as listed in the Contents. This number is repeated on each page and is quoted in the index entries.

INTRODUCTION

The story of the development of Western medieval moral and political philosophy cannot accurately be recounted in isolation from a second, more complex and far-reaching narrative about the ways in which classical ideas were disseminated, appropriated, and/or subtly revised during the Latin Middle Ages. This proposition forms the guiding thread of the studies contained in the present volume, all of which in some manner consider how the philosophies of Greek and Roman antiquity shaped--and were also profoundly reformulated by--the work of medieval ethical and political theorists. The enterprise collectively represented by these essays teaches an underlying methodological lesson as well: the intellectual intricacies occasioned by the circulation of classical texts and doctrines may never properly be reduced to a "grand scheme" of explanation, whether it be the commanding influence of Aristotle or the liberating impact of Renaissance humanism. Many of the studies below testify to the failure of such "grand schemes" to account very satisfactorily for the sheer diversity and diffuseness of medieval thought between the twelfth and fifteenth centuries.

Aristotle was perhaps the single most decisive classical figure in medieval moral and political philosophy. Whereas Plato's major writings (most importantly, the *Republic*) only became available during the Renaissance, virtually all of the Aristotelian corpus had been translated into Latin by the middle of the thirteenth century. The rapid introduction and circulation of Aristotle's works led an earlier generation of scholars to speak of an "Aristotelian revolution" in medieval thought, characterized by a fundamental reorientation in the philosophical framework of the Middle Ages. But such a "revolution" has proven to be a scholarly chimera. Many of the fundamental tenets of Aristotle's ethics (**I**) and politics (**II**) were already known and employed by medieval authors well before the translation of the *Nicomachean Ethics* or the *Politics*, often through intermediary sources such as Cicero and Boethius as well as by way of Aristotle's previously translated logical writings such as the *Categories* and *Topics*. Aristotelianism blended readily into the philosophical concerns of numerous twelfth-century moral theorists (**III**), generating creative and sophisticated discussions of the acquisition and practice of human virtue. Indeed, the fact that Aristotle's ethics and politics created so small a stir among wary ecclesiastical officials in the thirteenth century--the reading of the *Ethics* and *Politics* was never prohibited, as occurred in the case of the Aristotelian *libri naturales*--seems to confirm to prior familiarity with and acceptance of his views on these subjects.

One of the most significant exponents of twelfth-century moral and political thought was John of Salisbury, who followed a dual career (not unusual for his day) as scholar and active churchman. Sometimes described as the pinnacle of twelfth-century humanist thought, his work weaves his extensive academic training into the daily affairs occasioned by ecclesiastical administration. Thus, lessons derived from his Parisian education in the classics are regularly integrated into the advice John imparts to other churchmen caught up in the volatile events of mid-twelfth-century Church politics (**X**), especially those involving the stormy relationship between the English crown and the archepiscopal court of Canterbury (**IV**), with which he was associated for much of his career. A tireless advocate of an Aristotelian conception of the golden mean (**VIII**), John extended this principle to the criticism of important secular political figures of his day, such as King Stephen (**V**), and even to his former teachers at Paris, whose methods he ridiculed as violating Aristotle's counsels about the proper route to achieving wisdom and virtue (**XI**). John's career thereby deserves to be regarded as a realization of the spirit of Aristotelian "practical philosophy," according to which a virtuous (and happy) life must be attained through the active use of the virtues of the soul.

Ironically, because of John of Salisbury's vast (for its day) classical education, however, his philosophical writings (most notably, his *magnum opus*, the *Policraticus*) have sometimes been accused of lack of originality or rigor. Rather, scholars have interpreted John as producing little more than a pastiche, arranging and stringing together long quotes from Latin texts (Christian as well as pagan) without regard for coherent theoretical argumentation. It seems true that the *Policraticus* was composed over a period of several years, often in the few quiet moments permitted to its author by the whirlwind of politics at Canterbury. But John was no mere *redactor* or parrot of his classical sources. On the contrary, some of his boldest ideas prove to be the creation of his own innovative intellect, even while they are wrapped up in the veneer of classical authority. Perhaps the most famous case is his concept of the body politic, an image on which he draws extensively in the *Policraticus*. Long supposed to be a simple adaptation of the pseudo-Plutarchian *Letter of Instruction to Trajan*--a work now certainly identified as a forgery perpetrated by John himself--the so-called organic metaphor of the *Policraticus* goes far beyond ancient pagan (Plato, Aristotle, Cicero) and Christian (St. Paul) analogies between the living body and the political system (**VI**). On John's account, the organic metaphor emerges as a theory of social cooperation and inclusion unprecedented in medieval thought and destined to exercise a wide influence during the later Middle Ages. In turn, John employed the conception of the body politic to lend a firm foundation to his somewhat notorious justification of the admissibility of tyrannicide (**VII**), a doctrine which has often been called theoretically unprincipled but which in fact flows quite reasonably from the organic precepts adopted in the *Policraticus*.

One intriguing aspect of medieval Aristotelianism is the elasticity with which it was applied to a range of moral and political frameworks. This is not to say that the term "Aristotelian" may appropriately be used to describe any text in which citation of Aristotle occurred in order to bolster the authority of the doctrines proposed therein. Medieval Aristotelianism required, at minimum, a discernable commitment to Aristotle's fundamental epistemic principles, in particular his conception of moral and political knowledge as "practical" in bearing. Yet some works, such as the *De legibus et consuetudinibus Angliae* attributed (for the most part mistakenly) to the thirteenth-century jurist Henry de Bracton (**XIII**), were heavily indebted to an Aristotelian perspective even when their authors evinced no direct familiarity with the writings of Aristotle himself. Drawing on elements of Roman law teachings about justice and its relation to the royal will, "Bracton" constructed a theory of kingship that embraced Aristotelian moral theory filtered through intermediate civilian sources. In other cases, Aristotle's doctrines were expanded to address contemporary political circumstances well beyond the historical reach of the Philosopher himself. Walter Burley's widely disseminated fourteenth-century commentary on Aristotle's *Politics*, for instance, dispensed with ancient Greek examples of political systems and institutions in favor of references to current affairs and leaders, even adapting Aristotle in order to explain the role played by Parliament in the operation of English government (**XIV**). Nor did medieval authors find it necessary to confine themselves to Aristotle's overtly moral and political teachings. Time and again, precepts drawn from Aristotelian natural philosophy, logic, and technical rhetoric emerged as the cornerstones of significant theoretical insights (**VX**). Although by no means infinitely capacious, medieval Aristotelianism never depended upon strict adherence to a fixed and established body of philosophical doctrine.

Among the unfortunate side-effects of the considerable attention paid by scholars to Aristotle's place in medieval thought has been a tendency to disregard or denigrate the contributions of other classical authors. Aristotelianism was, as Antony Black has lately taken to stressing, merely one moral and political discourse among several available to medieval theorists. Another framework, equally rich and complex, often employed during the Middle Ages is due to Cicero, many of whose works on philosophy and rhetoric enjoyed a readership rivalling that of Aristotle. Unlike the Aristotelian corpus, the bulk of Cicero's work was known throughout the Middle Ages, and it sometimes provided a source of ideas that scholars have otherwise regarded to be of distinctively Aristotelian provenance, such as the "naturalness" of social and political life for human beings (**XI**). Yet Cicero's philosophy--a distinctive amalgamation of various trends within Hellenic and Hellenistic thought--was not limited to reproducing Aristotle's teachings. The Ciceronian preference for the active virtue of justice over contemplative wisdom (proposed in his immensely popular *De officiis*, among other writings) staked a unique ground on the medieval intellectual terrain. Even scholastic authors (such as John of Paris and Marsiglio of Padua) who were fully familiar with Aristotle's opposed position on this and related issues cited Cicero's views and showed a marked predilection for them. Consequently, Cicero's importance did not simply wane or diminish once the Aristotelian corpus had become a staple of medieval thought.

The persistent interest in Cicero also suggests the inaccuracy of one of the supposed points of intellectual demarcation between the Middle Ages and the Renaissance. Scholars have often regarded the later medieval period as a time of arid, Aristotelian scholasticism, in contrast with the Cicero-inspired emphasis on eloquence and the *vita activa* typical of the Renaissance. But careful investigation of medieval texts reveals instead an unbroken continuity from the twelfth to the fifteenth century in this connection. For the medieval rhetorician or schoolman, as for the Renaissance humanist, Cicero's work afforded a compelling picture of the wise and eloquent orator as a model of political leadership (**XII**). Nor did Renaissance humanists invariably find in Cicero's writings a prototype for the republican form of government which so many of them advocated. Ciceronianism proved as capacious as Aristotelianism, permitting so distinguished a humanist as Aeneas Sylvius Piccolomini to adapt Cicero's principles in order to defend universal imperial monarchy (**XVII**).

In other ways, however, the period from 1100 to 1500 ought not to be treated as a period of continuous and uniform intellectual development. There has been a pronounced tendency in recent scholarship (represented most notably by Brian Tierney and Francis Oakley) to locate the roots of modern constitutional doctrines in medieval writings proposing the supremacy of the General Council of the Church over the pope and the ecclesiastical hierarchy. While certain resemblances between medieval conciliar ecclesiology and modern secular constitutionalism are clearly evident, the trend to equate the two requires us to overlook the salient assumptions that conciliarists shared with the philosophical and theological principles of thinkers not at all inclined to claim institutional and legal protection for the rights of individuals (**XVI**). Medieval political authors of all orientations, right up to the time of Jean Gerson and Nicholas of Cusa, upheld an organic conception of political community and a belief in the centrality of the personal moral character of the ruler's will--doctrines anathema to modern constitutionalism, with its stress on the fundamentally prepolitical rights of human beings and on the impersonal limitation of governmental power. A profound danger lurks behind the attempt to equate "family resemblances" between ideas with an established paternity caused by direct influence.

The studies gathered together in the present volume were originally published in a disparate array of journals: some in the field of medieval studies, some in history, still others in political science. It is a frustration of the author--due to my unique personal predicament of writing about the history of medieval moral and political philosophy while teaching in the discipline of political science--that many readers familiar with some of the essays republished here will be utterly unaware of others simply because of the disciplinary nature of academic publication. Taken individually, each of these articles makes a specific contribution to one or another particular field of intellectual endeavor; taken as a whole, they represent an effort to achieve a cross-disciplinary perspective on the infiltration and diffusion of classical learning during the Latin Middle Ages. One of my main goals in reprinting the essays contained herein is to promote a heightened consciousness on the part of scholars that research of immediate interest and significance to them may appear in many far-flung locations. Perhaps in the future, given the advent of new information technologies and electronic data bases, the artificial disciplinary narrowness of academic publishing will form less of a barrier to scholarly dialogue.

CARY J. NEDERMAN

University of Arizona
June 1996

ACKNOWLEDGEMENTS

Grateful acknowledgment is made to the following persons and publishers for their kind permission to reproduce the studies contained in this volume: Dr. Diane Speed, editor of *Parergon*, and the Australian and New Zealand Association of Medieval and Renaissance Studies (**I**); Professor Donald R. Kelley, editor of *The Journal of the History of Ideas*, and Johns Hopkins University Press (**II, XI**); the editors of *Traditio* and Fordham University Press (**III**); Duke University Press (**IV**); Professor M.C.E. Jones, editor of *Nottingham Medieval Studies* (**V**); Professor Janet Coleman, Coeditor of *History of Political Thought*, and Imprint Academic (**VI, XIII**); Professor Walter Nicgorki, editor of *The Review of Politics* (**VII**); E.J. Brill (**VIII**); Pontifical Institute of Mediaeval Studies (**IX**); Dr. Mary Rouse, Managing Editor of *Viator*, and the Regents of the University of California (**X**); Professor Malcolm Barber, editor of *The Journal of Medieval History*, and Elsevier Science (**XII**); Professor Michael J. Moore, editor of *Albion* (**XIV**); Elsevier Science (**XV, XVI**); and Professor Jonathan Steinberg, Coeditor of *The Historical Journal*, and Cambridge University Press (**XVII**). In addition, thanks are due to my colleague, Professor Heiko Oberman, for his initial suggestion of the viability of this project; to John Smedley of Variorum for his support through the publication process; and to Allison Hinson for her careful preparation of the index.

I

Aristotelian Ethics before the *Nicomachean Ethics:* Alternate Sources of Aristotle's Concept of Virtue in the Twelfth Century*

I

Among the myriad of classical influences exercised upon the intellecual life of the Latin Middle Ages, perhaps the most pronounced and dramatic impression was left by Aristotle.[1] During the twelfth and thirteenth centuries almost the entirety of the Aristotelian corpus returned to circulation in the West after an absence of more than five hundred years. But not all of Aristotle's writings were afforded the same reception. Some of his treatises, like those comprising the *Organon*, were readily and uncontentiously embraced by the mainstream of the Christian tradition.[2] Other texts, such as the *libri naturales* (which may have been construed broadly to include *De anima* and perhaps the *Metaphysics*, as well as more strictly naturalistic tracts), were repeatedly condemned and prohibited by ecclesiastical statute.[3] In short, the reception of Aristotle's philosophical system by the Western Middle Ages was not uniform and thereby resists

*An earlier version of the present essay was read at the Ninth Conference of Australian Historians of Medieval and Early Modern Europe, held at the University of Auckland, 24-29 August 1987.

[1]Dante's judgment that Aristotle was 'maestre di color che sanno' expressed most eloquently the sentiments of the whole medieval period (*Inferno*, ed. J.D. Sinclair, Oxford, 1961, Canto IV, 1, 131). More recently, P.O Kristeller has explained the unique nature of the Aristotelian contribution in the following terms: 'Aristotle was not studied as a "great book", but as a textbook that was the starting point for commentaries and questions and supplied a frame of reference for all trained philosophical thinkers even when they ventured to reinterpret him, or to depart from his doctrine, according to their own opinions. The Aristotelianism of the later Middle Ages was characterized not so much by a common system of ideas as by a common source material, a common terminology, a common set of definitions and problems, and a common method of discussing these problems', *Renaissance Thought: The Classical, Scholastic and Humanist Strains*, New York 1961, 31-32.

[2]Aristotle's role at the centre of the discipline of logic during the Middle Ages is examined by M. Heren, *Medieval Thought*, Basingstoke, 1985, 88-90, and S. Ebbeson, Ancient Scholastic Logic as the Source of Medieval Scholastic Logic, in N. Kretzmann, A. Kenny and J. Pinborg, eds., *The Cambridge History of Later Mediaeval Philosophy*, Cambridge, 1982, 101-27.

[3]For the circumstances surrounding the prohibition of the *libri naturales*, see F. van Steenberghen, *Aristotle in the West*, trans. L. Johnson, Louvain, 1955, 66-77. The inclusion of the *Metaphysics* among the *libri naturales* is defended by G. Leff, *Paris and Oxford Universities in the Thirteenth and Fourteenth Centuries*, Huntington, New York, 1975, 195. The texts of the 1210 and 1215 condemnations at Paris have been translated in L. Thorndike, ed., *University Records and Life in the Middle Ages*, New York, 1944, 26-30.

generalizations.[4] Different works (and categories of works) followed divergent patterns of diffusion, contingent upon an array of circumstances.

When we approach the transmissional history of the *Nicomachean Ethics*, therefore, we must be sensitive to the unique path of its dissemination during the Middle Ages. This route was characterized, in particular, by reversal. Initially, the *Nicomachean Ethics* was accepted and integrated into the body of medieval Christian learning; only much later did some of its central doctrines stir controversy. Scholars presently believe that the earliest Latin version of the *Ethics* was the so-called '*ethica vetus*', translated anonymously during the twelfth century.[5] More precise dating of the *ethica vetus* has thus far proved impossible. Minio-Paluello has identified a manuscript of the *ethica vetus* bound into several Aristotelian texts which are known to be the work of the early twelfth-century translator James the Greek (Iacobus Graecus, fl. 1125-1150).[6] But no moralist of the twelfth century makes direct reference to the *Nicomachean Ethics*, including John of Salisbury, who is exceptional in his familiarity with current translations.[7] Moreover, the text of the *vetus* version by no means includes the whole of the *Ethics;* it is composed of the second and third books only. Another edition of the *Nicomachean Ethics*, known as the *ethica nova*, seems to have been available only after 1200, though how far into the thirteenth century is itself a point of dispute.[8] The first evidence of a course

---

[4] As a consequence, exception must be taken with the claim of R.R. Bolgar that the whole of the Aristotelian corpus (and indeed the remainder of recovered classical treatises) followed the same three stages of transmission during the Middle Ages; Bolgar's tri-partite scheme is valid only if it is applied in the most general fashion, in which case it becomes simply unhelpful. Cf. *The Classical Heritage and its Beneficiaries*, Cambridge, 1954, 182-83.

[5] A thorough examination of the Latin transmission of the *Nicomachean Ethics*, containing the most recent scholarly appraisal of the known versions and texts, is given by R.A. Gauthier in his edition of the *Ethica Nicomachea* (*Aristoteles Latinus*, vol. 26, pts 1-3, Leiden, 1972-1974), pt. 1, xvi-cli.

[6] L. Minio-Paluello, Iacobus Venetius Graecus: Canonist and Translator of Aristotle, *Traditio* 8, 1952, 293-94.

[7] John's efforts to expand his knowledge of Aristotle are attested to by a letter to Richard l'Evêque, dating to perhaps 1167, which requests a copy 'of the books of Aristotle which you have' (Letter 201, in W.J. Miller and C.N.L. Brooke, eds., *The Letters of John of Salisbury*, vol. 2, Oxford, 1979, 295). If John in fact received a copy of the *ethica vetus* from Richard -- who, indeed, might have had access to it, if we accept the inferences of Minio-Paluello, *op.cit.*, 293 – he demonstrates no evidence of it in his later letters; his major philosophical writings, the *Policraticus* and *Metalogicon*, had been written long before, during the 1150s.

[8] As it was circulated, the *ethica nova* contains only Book I of the *Ethics* and fragments of the other books, but scholars are now satisfied that a full translation must have existed originally. See B.G. Dod, Aristoteles Latinus, in Kretzmann et al, eds., *The Cambridge History of Later Medieval Philosophy*, 49. Further details

of lectures on the *Nicomachean Ethics* dates to 1235-1240 at Paris.[9] Commentaries on the available sections of the text were probably not composed much before that period.[10] Even then, it was only after the middle of the century, once Robert Grosseteste's definitive Latin version of the *Nicomachean Ethics* appeared, that Aristotle's moral philosophy gained a controversial status comparable to that of the *libri naturales*. The *Ethics* may have been the source of some of the conflict leading up to the 1255 proclamation of the University of Paris Arts Faculty curriculum.[11] It certainly loomed large in the work of 'Averroistic' or 'radical' Aristotelianism and many ideas associated with it were among the 219 propositions condemned by the Bishop of Paris, Etienne Tempier, in 1277.[12] In other words, nearly one hundred years intervened between the initial introduction of the *Nicomachean Ethics* into the West and any suggestion that its doctrines represented a threat to Christian orthodoxy. And the controversy which surrounded the *Ethics* was short-lived; the text itself was never prohibited, so that during the fourteenth and fifteenth centuries it came to be widely quoted and was the object of numerous commentaries.[13]

This evidence points to another significant aspect of the transmission of the *Nicomachean Ethics* to the Middle Ages, namely, the slow pace of the text's dissemination. In spite of the fact that forty-eight copies of the *ethica vetus* are known to exist, relatively few date to the twelfth century.[14] A still smaller number of manuscripts of the *ethica nova* have been discovered.[15] Perhaps more pertinently, commentaries on the *Nicomachean Ethics* are extremely rare

regarding this version are supplied by Gauthier's Preface to the *Ethica Nicomachea*, cxlii-cxlvii.

[9]Published by R.A. Gauthier, Le cours sur l'*Ethica nova* d'un maitre des arts de Paris (1235-1240), *Archives d'Histoire Doctrinale et Littéraire du Moyen Age* 42, 1975, 71-141. An extensive analysis of the place of the *Ethics* in the Paris curriculum is given by M. Grabmann, Das Studium der aristotelischen Ethik an der Artistenfakultat der Universität Paris in der ersten Hälfe des 13. Jahrhunderts, *Philosophisches Jahrbuch der Görres-Gesellschaft* 55, 1940, 339-54 and O. Lottin, *Psychologie et Morale au XIIe et XIIIe Siècles*, vol.1, Gembloux, 1942, 505-34.

[10]See the commentaries listed by G. Wieland, The Reception and Interpretation of Aristotle's *Ethics*, in Kretzmann et al., eds., *The Cambridge History of Later Medieval Philosophy*, 658.

[11]As has been suggested by C.H. Lohr, The Medieval Interpretation of Aristotle, in *ibid.*, 87.

[12]On the relation between the radical Aristotelians and the *Nicomachean Ethics*, see G. Wieland, Happiness: The Perfection of Man, in *ibid.*, 680-83. Among the propositions denounced by Tempier which were related to the *Ethics* are Nos. 22, 144, 157, 168, 176, 177, 191; the complete list was translated by E.L. Fortin and P.D. O'Neill in R. Lerner and M. Mahdi, eds., *Medieval Political Philosophy: A Sourcebook*, Ithaca, 1972, 338-54. For the context of the radical Aristotelian view and its prohibition, see Leff, *Paris and Oxford Universities*, 222-40.

[13]Wieland, Reception and Interpretation, 657.

[14]Dod, Aristoteles Latinus, 48, 52-53.

[15]*Ibid.*, 77

58

until the middle of the thirteenth century – the time of Grosseteste's translation – while after c. 1250 there is a relative avalanche of textual analysis.[16] Moreover, one seldom encounters explicit references to the *Nicomachean Ethics* in works of philosophy and theology composed prior to the mid-1200s.[17] These facts are particularly startling when placed in a comparative context. Twelfth-century translations of Aristotle's major and minor treatises on natural philosophy, in spite of repeated prohibition, survive in large numbers. For example, 139 manuscripts of the *Physics* and 144 of *De anima* in the James of Venice versions have been identified, with similar numbers for less significant works.[18] Knowledge of the *libri naturales* was disseminated accordingly. Aristotle's theories of nature were certainly taught at Paris prior to 1210, and at other schools as well.[19] In addition, by 1200 commentators had commenced dissecting the various texts containing Aristotelian natural philosophy.

The intellectual historian is confronted, then, with a paradoxical situation. For it would seem that, while Aristotelian works which were deemed harmful to the faith flourished in the late twelfth- and early thirteenth-century classroom and library, the *Nicomachean Ethics*, which was not proscribed, languished until at least the second quarter of the 1200s. Were the masters and students of the time perverse in their preference for heresy? Or did they regard the problems arising from natural philosophy to be intellectually superior to those connected with moral theory? The evidence suggests that an affirmative answer to neither question is appropriate. But the paradox which leads us to raise such queries is a perplexing and disturbing one. Our trouble stems from the incongruity between the absence of impediments to the dissemination of the *Ethics* and the palpable lack of interest on the part of medieval thinkers (at least prior to c. 1250) in exploring Aristotelian moral doctrines. Can this dissonance be explained in coherent historical terms?

The purpose of the present essay is to provide a plausible account of why medieval philosophers and theologians directed little attention to the translated editions of the *Nicomachean Ethics* in the early stages of the process of recovery. In particular, it will be argued that the manifest apathy evinced by schoolmen towards Aristotelian moral theory between c. 1175 and 1225 cannot be taken at face value. Rather, the absence of a dramatic reaction was a function of a prior

---

[16]Wieland, Reception and Interpretation, 659-72.
[17]Dod, Aristotles Latinus, 72.
[18]*Ibid.*, 75-76.
[19]The University of Toulouse proudly advertised that 'those who wish to scrutinize nature's bosom to the marrow may there hear the books of nature which are prohibited at Paris' (in Thorndike, ed., *University Records and Life in the Middle Ages*, 32-35). The early reception of the *libri naturales* at the University of Oxford is addressed by Leff, *Paris and Oxford Universities*, 272-73. On the initial teaching of these texts at Paris, see Dod, Aristotles Latinus, 70.

familiarity with, and acceptance of, many of Aristotle's most important ethical ideas. This is not to speculate, however, that texts associated with Aristotelian social philosophy were in wide circulation well before the usual dating of the first Latin version of the *Ethics*.[20]

The point is instead that twelfth-century authors and masters were more aware than scholars have allowed of Aristotle's moral thought by means of an alternate set of sources which had already become integrated into the main intellectual currents of the Western Middle Ages prior to 1175 or so. In sum, there was in the twelfth century a pre-existing body of source-materials for an understanding of a number of Aristotle's moral ideas – materials which owed nothing to the discovery and dissemination of the *Nicomachean Ethics*. At best, the recovered text of the *Ethics* only confirmed and reinforced concepts that had become commonplace at an earlier date.

II

But how was it possible for such a large stock of Aristotle's ethical precepts to be available during the Middle Ages in the absence of the *Nicomachean Ethics*, not to mention other sources of his social philosophy like the *Politics* and *Eudemian Ethics*?[21] The answer lies in part with the range of intermediary sources accessible to medieval men which drew upon and applied moral doctrines of an inarguably Aristotelian provenance. Such indirect authorities could be pagan (like Cicero) or Christian (as in the case of Boethius); what they shared, however, was an unquestionably intimate knowledge of Aristotle's writings. Because of this knowledge, they performed the function of transmitting Aristotelian concepts to the twelfth century. Yet these intermediary sources were by themselves insufficient to convey the main body of Aristotle's moral philosophy, since their references tended to be partial and fragmentary. We may only plausibly speak of twelfth-century familiarity with Aristotelian ethical precepts insofar as that awareness emerged from the works of Aristotle himself already available in Latin.

Such a claim may appear odd. After all, while Aristotle's thought had come to constitute the indispensable foundation of scholastic studies by about the middle of the twelfth century, this influence was based solely upon his logical writings. The so-called '*logica vetus*', comprising the *Categories* and *De Interpretations*, formed a well-worn feature of the intellectual landscape

---

[20] A hypothesis that has lately been entertained – on no particularly compelling evidence – by M. Wilks, John of Salisbury and the Tyranny of Nonsense, in Wilks, ed., *The World of John of Salisbury*, Oxford, 1984, 280.

[21] The text of the *Politics* was not translated until c. 1260, while the *Eudemian Ethics* was only known by means of a mid-thirteenth century treatise called *De Bona Fortuna*, which comprised a chapter each drawn from the *Eudemian Ethics* and the *Magna Moralia*. See Dod, Aristotles Latinus, 77-8.

throughout the Latin Middle Ages, almost as much a part of the medieval tradition as the Fathers or Cicero. During the early part of the twelfth century interest in the *logica vetus* was reinforced by the recovery of the remaining works of the *Organon*. By 1159, it is clear that the West enjoyed full access to the logical system of Aristotle.[22] The significance of this development for the transmission of Aristotle's ethical doctrines, while perhaps not immediately obvious, is pivotal. For it is too seldom appreciated that a considerable number of ideas found in the *Nicomachean Ethics* also received treatment in various locations throughout the *Organon*, especially in the *Categories* and *Topics*. As a consequence, prior direct knowledge of Aristotle's moral theory via the *Organon* can help us to explain the unique pattern through which the dissemination of the *Nicomachean Ethics* was to occur after c. 1175.

To illustrate fully the thesis of a pre-existing appreciation of the contents of the *Nicomachean Ethics* would require a study of considerable length. For the present, we may pursue the more modest goal of demonstrating how a single crucial aspect of Aristotle's moral theory was transmitted to a medieval audience before the recovery of the *Nicomachean Ethics*. One doctrine which recommends itself is the Aristotelian definition of virtue proposed at *Nicomachean Ethics* 1106b36-1107a2: 'Virtue (ἀρετή, *arete*) is a disposition (ἕξις, *hexis*) to choose (προαιρετική, *prohairetike*), lying in the mean (ἐν μεσότητι, *en mesoteti*) relative to us, as determined by reason (λόγος, *logos*) and what the prudent man (φρόνος, *phronos*) would do'.[23] The defense and development of this claim forms the bulk of the second and third books of the *Nicomachean Ethics* (coextensive with the medieval *ethica vetus*) and represents a major facet of the Aristotelian contribution to moral philosophy. In particular, Aristotle's definition of virtue contains three component claims: 1. virtue is a disposition to choose; 2. virtuous choice is based on a mean; and 3. the standard of virtue is determined by reference to a rational principle. These themes would certainly have been encountered by any well-read person of the twelfth century, even prior to the translation contained in the *vetus* edition. For the *Organon*, especially when taken in conjunction with other widely known Latin sources, provided a formidable body of evidence attesting to the three main elements of the

[22]Our evidence for this is John of Salisbury's *Metalogion*, finished in 1159, which demonstrates a complete knowledge of all the works of the *Organon*. For a careful estimation of John's familiarity with Aristotle, see E. Jeauneau, Jean de Salisbury et la lécture des philosophes, in Wilks, ed., *The World of John of Salisbury*, 90-2, 96-108.

[23]All citations from the *Nicomachean Ethics* will be drawn from the edition by H. Rackham, Cambridge, Mass., 1934; English translations, while based on Rackham, have been substantially revised by the present author. In future references, the title of the work will be abbreviated to *NE*. After this initial citation all Greek terms are transliterated.

Aristotelian definition of virtue. Still, we may wonder how profound or extensive could be any understanding of the conception of virtue proffered by the *Nicomachean Ethics* if it were based simply on miscellaneous references spread throughout the *Organon* and intermediary sources. The short answer is that the main features of Aristotle's idea of virtue receive a surprisingly detailed and elaborate presentation within these treatises. To evaluate the total extent of the availability of the Aristotelian definition of virtue prior to the *ethica vetus*, however, we must proceed with a thorough examination of the initial transmission of the three doctrines we have identified.

1. Aristotle's concept of virtue pertains in the first instance to the deliberate commission of morally assessable behaviour. In other words, moral actions must be the product of a determination to act, the source of which is to be found in the agent himself. Thus, the choice of an action (*prohairesis*) depends upon deliberation (*bouleuesthai*); insofar as '*prohairesis* involves reasoning (*logos*) and thought processes', it must be 'preceded by deliberation' (*NE* 1112a15-17). In particular, Aristotle insists that 'we deliberate about matters that are in our control and are attainable by action' (*NE* 1112a29-30), that is, we deliberate only about those issues which fall within the realm of possible human choice. To deliberate in this sense is to apply general rules to specific situations; it is to determine how we ought to act in light of our moral knowledge, or what aspect of our moral knowledge is relevant in a given situation (*NE* 1112b8-12). And once we have deliberated – once we have traced a course of action back to ourselves – we thereby initiate action, in the sense that we choose (*NE* 1113b2-7). *Prohairesis* is rational willing, volition performed under the direction (and indeed compulsion) of reason. Consequently, Aristotle declares, 'Man is the origin of his actions, and the province of deliberation is to discover which actions are within our power to perform' (*NE* 1112b32-34). The voluntary aspect of human conduct (as Aristotle understood it) requires that choice occur after and be guided by deliberation.

Yet none of this is to explain the foundation which underpins deliberation and, ultimately, choice. Whence come the rules and knowledge on the basis of which we deliberate and choose? It is in reply to such a question that the *Nicomachean Ethics* argues against the confusion of virtue itself with mere morally correct action. To be virtuous, Aristotle asserts, is not merely to do what is good, but to do so as the result of a well-formed moral character or set of moral habits (*ethos*) (*NE* 1103a17-24). In other words, morally significant actions are rooted in more permanent principles or traits which regulate the behaviour of the agent, so that *bouleuesthai* and *prohairesis* are always in accordance with the character of the agent who deliberates and chooses. Without the doctine of *ethos*, Aristotle could never claim that 'the good man judges

I

everything correctly', since 'what chiefly distinguishes the good man is that he sees the truth of each matter' (*NE* 1113a29-30, 1113a32-33). The good man is so thoroughly imbued with virtue, Aristotle seeks to maintain, that he may be regarded as the 'standard and measure' against which all conduct may be gauged.

Yet regardless of the permanence and stability Aristotle attributes to *ethos*, he does not wish to claim that moral traits are natural. Nature bestows upon man only a capacity (*dynamis*) to be good or evil. The capacity must still be actualized by the process of moral education (*NE* 1103a24-31). Thus, virtue cannot merely be described as a capacity to act in accordance with goodness, since *dynamis* is by definition outside of our control and hence something for which we cannot be held responsible (*NE* 1106a7-14). Rather, Aristotle insists that virtue must be a *hexis*, a state or disposition of the soul. As a general concept in Aristotelian philosophy, *hexis* denotes a type of quality, that is, a way in which a qualitative property may be ascribed to a subject or substance. Specifically, *hexis* is the term employed by Aristotle to denote those qualities which become so firmly rooted in that which they qualify as to form virtually a 'second nature'. Accordingly, *hexeis* are difficult (if not impossible) to alter.

When Aristotle maintains that '*hexis* is the genus of virtue' and 'the virtues are *hexeis*' (*NE* 1106a14, 1143b24-25), he means to convey thereby that moral action arises from a character which is 'something permanent and not easily subject to change' (*NE* 1100b2). By addressing virtue in terms of *hexis*, Aristotle constructs the foundations for the relative stability and longevity of moral qualities without recourse to arguments from nature. The appeal to *hexis* permits him to assert that the virtues are acquired by exposure to and practice of virtuous conduct; performing virtuous acts so as to ingrain a course of action constitutes the basis for a correct moral education (*NE* 1103a31-33, 1103b1-3). For evolving the right moral habits, and becoming good thereby, is a matter of moulding one's *hexeis*, since '*hexeis* develop from corresponding activities' and 'the quality of our *hexeis* depends upon what we do' (*NE* 1103b22-24). The regular practice of morally significant actions forms our ethical dispositions, with the eventual consequence that sufficient training yields 'a firm and unchangeable character' (*NE* 1105a35-b1). In turn, a man whose *hexeis* are inclinded towards good conduct will choose what is virtuous constantly and consistently, as a matter of policy. The *hexeis* he has developed will, in effect, prohibit him from the commission of uncharacteristic acts on purpose. This last qualification is important. Aristotle would not deny, of course, that a good man might occasionally commit an evil action. There are various sorts of reasons why he might do so, such as ignorance, faulty cognition, and the like. Aristotle's point, instead, is that the bad act commited by the good man can never have been done deliberately, that is, on the basis of choice in conformity with his *hexis*. Only the individual whose moral habits are ill-formed truly does

I

evil, since his bad acts issue from the application of his vicious character to the process of ethical decision-making. Virtue and vice cannot be ascribed in isolation from the qualities of the people who perform moral action.

The central themes associated with the treatment of deliberate choice in accordance with moral character were also given expression by Aristotle within the works comprising the *Organon*.[24] In *De Interpretatione*, for example, Aristotle attempts to demonstrate that the world is not governed acording to strict necessity. If this were so, he declares, 'there would be no need for human deliberation (*bouleuesthai*)', for the necessary results of our actions would always be apparent and the correct course would always be adopted (*De Int* 18b31-32). But experience demonstrates that this is not the case: 'We see that both *bouleuesthai* and actions (*praxai*) are causes of future events and that, to speak more generally, in those things that are not continually actual there is a potentiality in either direction' (*De Int* 19a9-11). In other words, deliberation and action are voluntary in the sense that no necessity may be attributed to them in advance.[25] Every deliberation and every action must be treated afresh, as a novel application of thought and choice. Does this imply that Aristotle has shifted his ground to a more purely voluntaristic doctrine? Indeed not, for he acknowledges that in 'some cases things incline or generally tend in one or another direction'; he simply stresses that 'they may issue exceptionally in the opposite direction' (*De Int* 19a21-23). The argument of *De Interpretatione* corresponds to that of the *Nicomachean Ethics* in the sense that the relationship between character and choice is not strictly one of cause and effect. Rather, the fact that deliberation precedes action means that an act may be committed which is incompatible with character (uncharacteristic) because of some fault in the deliberative process itself. We can always say what the good man in a given situation *would* or *should* do, but never what he will actually do.

Aristotle returns to this issue more explicitly in the *Topics*. He stresses that the appropriate objects of praise and approval by human beings include 'that which the prudent man (*phronos*) or the good man (*agathos*) would prefer' (*Topics* 116a14). The chosen actions of the good man always point in the direction of goodness itself, and hence embody a stable orientation against which the choices of others may be measured. Conversely, Aristotle insists that the conduct 'which a bad character would prefer' ought to be shunned and avoided (*Topics* 160b 20). It is the sort of person who acts that constitutes the real

[24]References to the *Organon* will be in all instances derived from the Loeb edition, in the case of *De Interpretatione* (hereafter, *De Int*) and the *Categories* (hereafter, *Cat*) edited by H.P. Cooke, Cambridge, Mass, 1938, and in the case of the *Topics* edited by E. Forster, Cambridge, Mass., 1960. Once again, the translations, while based on these versions, have been revised.

[25]For more thorough analysis of the significance of this passage, see W.R.F. Hardie *Aristotle's Ethical Theory*, 2nd ed., Oxford, 1980, 33, 178, 383-4.

concern of ethical evaluation. Thus, Aristotle posits a firm distinction between evil actions and evil men: 'Even God and the good man are capable of doing bad deeds, but God and such men are not of that type; for the wicked are always so called because of their deliberate choice (*prohairesin*) of evil' (*Topics* 126a34-36). Men always retain the capacity for evil, in the sense that they are by nature capable of committing vicious acts. But those actions that can legitimately be praised or blamed arise from the acquired moral traits of the agent. The *Topics* accordingly argues against the ethical significance of *dynamis*:: 'A just man is he who deliberately chooses (*prohairoumenos*) to distribute what is equal rather than he who has a capacity (*dynamenon*) for doing so. Justice could not be a capacity for distributing what is equal, for then a man would be most just who has the greatest capacity for distributing what is equal' (*Topics* 145b36-146a3). Virtue must be something active rather than passive, a feature of what we do, but still in such a fashion that it is an ingrained characteristic. Moral choice, in other words, is necessarily rooted in firm traits which are demonstrably the products of our own activity.

It should cause little surprise, then, that the *Organon* also invokes the Aristotelian doctrine of *hexis*. Indeed, one encounters repeatedly the contention that '*hexis* is the genus of virtue' or '*hexis* indicates the essence of virtue'.[26] If this was the extent of Aristotle's discussion of *hexis* in the *Organon*, the significance of the concept would remain obscured. But the *Categories* provides a quite precise analysis of the claim that virtue pertains to *hexis*. In general, Aristotle says, *hexis* differs from other qualities 'in being more long lasting and stable', so that should some property eventually 'become through length of time part of man's nature and irremediable or hard to change, one would perhaps call this a *hexis*' (*Cat* 8b28, 9a2-4). When we 'hold of the virtues, justice and temperance and the like' that they are *hexeis*, then, we mean to convey that they are 'not easily changed or dislodged' (*Cat* 8b33-35). The goodness of the virtuous man is relatively permanent: its status as *hexis* ensures that virtue will last over time and will thus provide a stable foundation for moral choice. Yet the *Categories* is quick to emphasize that *hexis* cannot be assimilated to a natural capacity. Rather, *hexeis* must be acquired through a lengthy and difficult process of moral education typified by the gradual inculcation of goodness through practice and experience.[27] The achievement of the sort of relative permanence that Aristotle regards to be the mark of *hexis* demands that the individual become accustomed to certain modes of conduct and thought to such an extent that they are completely ingrained within him. Only when the moral agent has undergone such rigorous training is it possible to speak of him making choices based upon

---

[26]*Topics* 144a16-18; see also *Cat* 8b29 and *Topics* 121b37-39.
[27]*Cat* 13a23-31 presents the most extensive discussion in the whole Aristotelian corpus of the way in which *hexeis* are shaped and transformed.

a stable ethical disposition. But once *hexeis* are fixed, all instances of deliberate choice will issue out of a fully formed moral character whose essential features are constancy and consistency. An important lesson to be drawn from the *Organon*, no less than from the *Nicomachean Ethics*, is that the truly good man can never choose to act except in accordance with a truly good character which he as acquired by his own efforts.

Aristotle's doctrine of moral character enjoyed a considerable following among Latin authors. For example, Cicero's early treatise on rhetoric, *De Inventione*, which discusses problems of argumentation in a fashion similar to the *Topics*, appeals to the Aristotelian doctrine of *hexis* (translated into Latin as *habitus*) in reference to the rules for oratorical practice. Cicero says that in attributing 'qualities of mind and body', it is necessary to distinguish between those 'bestowed by nature' and those 'acquired by one's own industry, which pertains to *habitus*'.[28] The distinction between *natura* and *habitus* is not one of permanence: like nature, '*habitus* consists in a perfect and constant condition of the mind or body' (*De Inv* II. ix. 30). Rather, the difference is one of source. Whereas qualities of nature are inborn, qualities of *habitus* are acquired: 'What we call *habitus* is the realization of something constant and absolute in mind or body, such as virtue ... not given naturally, but achieved by study and industry' (*De Inv* I. xxv. 36). Thus Cicero insists that when we evaluate the moral character of a person – whether he is honourable or not – we must make reference not to his actions *per se* but to the *habitus* which underlies his conduct. Virtue is primarily a matter of a 'mental disposition' from which particular acts of a given kind proceed (*De Inv* II. liii. 160). Consequently, we cannot consider specific instances of ethical behaviour in isolation; we must know what state of mind produced the action and, by extension, whether the given act was consistent with the agent's general disposition. Nor was Cicero alone in propounding this view. In the Christian era, Boethius was similarly concerned that judgments about action must take into account the attributes of the person acting, which encompasses *habitus*.[29] Boethius thereby reiterated the definition that 'virtue is a *habitus* of a well-ordered mind'.[30] So by the twelfth century, a wide range of sources were available to convey the Aristotelian doctrine that virtuous action proceeds from an indelible but neverthelesss acquired moral character.

2. The second component of Aristotle's definition of virtue is the claim that the absolutely virtuous soul is characterised by the inculcation of the virtues in their proper measure. Thus, the *Nicomachean Ethics* describes the various

---

[28]Cicero, *De Inventione*, ed. H.M. Hubbell, Cambridge, Mass., 1949, I. xxiv. 35 (hereafter, *De Inv*); all translations from Cicero are mine.
[29]Boethius, *De Topicis Differentiis*, trans. E. Stump, Ithaca, 1978, 89.
[30]*Ibid.*, 51.

specific forms of moral goodness as mean points because excess and deficiency. To be good is to locate a middle way which is neither 'too much' nor 'too little'; divergence from the mean in either direction entails the performance of vicious acts (*NE* 1107a32-b1). 'Whereas the vices either fall short of or exceed what is right in feelings and actions, virtue ascertains and adopts the mean' (*NE* 1107a4-6). Goodness in human action is located in hitting the mark between excess and deficiency. Evil, on the other hand, occurs when the agent misses the mark in either direction, when, for example, he is either cowardly or foolhardy instead of courageous, or profligate or insensible rather than temperate. The good man, therefore, not only chooses in accordance with a fixed character, but also chooses those particular acts which fall within the mean.

Aristotle's doctrine of the mean suggests two further conclusions. First, the mean or moderate course ought not to be confused with temperance or self-control. The latter is a specific virtue concerned with the soul's relation to pleasure and pain: temperance is the virtue pertaining to the sensuous aspect of human existence (*NE* 1117b24-1119b19). Moderation, on the other hand, is characteristic of all the virtues without ever being construed as a virtue in itself. To follow the mean in one's conduct is a percept which applies across the board, regardless of which particular virtue is under consideration. A second corollary of Aristotle's emphasis on the mean is that the ordinary language opposition between good and evil is deceptive. It is true that good and evil are, in absolute terms, contraries. But in particular cases, that which is good must be juxtaposed to two sorts of evil, both of which are in turn contrary to one another (*NE* 1108b11-35). Hence, moral discourse is considerably more complex than is commonly conceived, for in many instances the possession of 'too much' of a virtue is as dangerous (if not more so) than the possession of 'too little'. In this way, Aristotle cautions his reader to exercise care lest fanatical virtuosity lapse into the commission of clearly vicious acts.

It is the potential for logical and linguistic confusion, engendered by the moderate nature of the virtues, that leads Aristotle to turn to the theme of the mean in some of the works of the *Organon*. In the first place, Aristotle is concerned that the mean be understood as one manner in which goodness may be ascribed to a subject. 'Often, too, the word "good" is applied to that which is moderate (*to metrion*) for that which is moderate, too, is called good' (*Topics* 107a11-13). Thus, to speak of a man as good may signify that he adopts the virtuous mean, rather than that he is skilled, or useful, or whatever. But Aristotle's primary reason for addressing the mean in the *Organon* is to explain an important exception to many of the rules governing the correct usage of contraries. Generally speaking, Aristotle asserts, good and evil are contrasting terms, neither of which admits of degree. A tailor, for instance, cannot be 'too good'. In matters of virtue, however, the situation is not so simple. As

Aristotle observes in the *Categories*, 'what is contrary to badness is sometimes good but sometimes bad. For excess, which is itself bad, is contrary to deficiency, which is bad; yet the mean (*mesotes*) is contrary to both and is good' (*Cat* 14a2-6). The attribution of goodness in the sense of virtue is thereby logically peculiar: it requires that we designate as good a middle term which is opposed to two forms of extremes even as each of the extremes are also opposed to each other. This implies that calling someone 'bad' (in the moral connotation of that word) is imprecise; we must further specify whether the evil involved is one of excess or defect. Yet, by the same token, both forms of moral extreme are more or less equally vicious, insofar as Aristotle emphasises that 'defect and excess are in the same genus – for both are in the genus of evil – whereas what is moderate (*to de metrion*), which is intermediate between them, is not in the genus of evil but of good' (*Topics* 123b27-30). No one can escape culpability by claiming that either excess or defect is 'less evil' in some instance. Both fall into the classification of badness and are thus also absolutely contrary to whatever is good.

Once again we find confirmation and additional articulation of the basic terms of the Aristotelian doctrine of the mean in Cicero's writings. As early as *De Inventione*, Cicero demonstrates a thorough appreciation of the intricacies of Aristotle's moral theory. In particular, Cicero questions the convention of associating every virtue with a single opposing vice, such as courage with cowardice or liberality with cheapness. Instead, *De Inventione* points out, 'Each virtue will be found to have a vice bordering upon it, either one to which a definite name has become attached, as temerity borders on courage ... or one without any definite name. All of these as well as the opposites of good qualities will be classed among things to be avoided' (*De Inv* II.liv.165). Cicero returns to the same theme of moderate conduct as the key to virtue in his mature treatise on moral instruction, *De Officiis* . To the man who wishes to behave in accordance with ethical rectitude, Cicero repeatedly counsels that 'the rule of the golden mean is best'.[31] *De Officiis* furthermore explains that this 'happy mean which lies between excess and defect' has a very definite origin: it is 'the doctrine of the mean ... approved by the Peripatetics' (*De Officiis* II. 89). Thus, Cicero's work not only captures the crucial facets of Aristotle's account of the mean, but also attributes the doctrine explicitly to an Artistotelian source. Twelfth-century readers of Cicero, as well as of the *Organon*, could hardly have failed to grasp the full significance of the Aristotelian equation of virtue with moderation.

---

[31]Cicero, *De Officiis*, ed. W. Miller, Cambridge, Mass., 1913, II. 59; cf. I. 130 and II. 66.

I

3. To understand how the good man becomes so (the training of *hexeis*) and what manner of behaviour he will choose (the virtuous mean) is not yet to comprehend the basis upon which goodness itself subsists. Why can the *agathos* claim the absolute moral superiority ascribed to him by Aristotle? What distinguishes the ethical knowledge enjoyed by the good man from that possessed by other persons? These questions point in the direction of the third component of the Aristotelian definition of virtue, namely, that moral goodness pertains to a rational principle according to which particular acts and characters can be judged. Aristotle's association of virtue with *logos* is a complex affair. But for the present we may concentrate our attention on one aspect of this relationship: how does the rationality of virtue shape differences in conduct between the truly good man and other sorts of persons? Thus far we have only been concerned with action as deliberative choice, viz., the selection of that specific act or course of conduct which will most effectively accomplish our goal. *Prohairesis* is thus rational in a purely instrumental sense: it selects the correct means to an end (*NE* 1113a13-14, 1113a5-7). By extension, the *phronos*, the man of practional wisdom (*phronesis*), is he whose character best equips him to perform particular virtuous acts in a given circumstance. The *phronos* is the person whose deliberate choices are in accordance with a good character (*NE* 1140a24-31, 1140b20-21).

At the same time, however, the virtuous man also controls the conditions under which deliberate choices are made, that is, he fixes his own ends and goals as well as the means to those ultimate purposes. It is in this sense that the inherent rationality of goodness becomes relevant. According to Aristotle's moral theory, all human action aims at the good.[32] We may understand this statement to mean simply that, whenever an agent fixes an end, an ultimate goal of action, he imputes the quality of goodness (according to some conception of the good) to that end. Aristotle contends that no one ever intends to do what is bad, because we all want what is good. (This is not to say, of course, that people do not do evil voluntarily, the Socratic view criticised by Aristotle; cf. *NE* 1145b21-31.) Consequently, Artistotle claims that all ethical conduct is characterized precisely by a desire for the good. The factor of desire (*orexis*) is significant here, for it is desire that renders moral determinations practical: desiring an end at the same time connotes the beginning of our efforts to realize that end. To select an end without desiring it would be to treat the practical virtues as though they were intellectual virtues,[33] which Aristotle would regard as simply incoherent. Moral goals must have practical force, and it is desire which translates the good into *praxis*.

[32]This is the famous claim with which the text of the *Ethics* begins; *NE* 1094a1-3.
[33]The distinction between practical and intellectual virtues is established at *NE* 1103a4-10 and 1103b26-32.

Still, we should not think that all desires are on an equal footing. Sometimes our desires fall within the sphere of 'appetite' (*epithymia*). An appetite constitutes a sort of irrational desire, insofar as irrational animals are said to have appetites (*NE* 1111b13-14). By contrast, other of our desires may be classified as 'wishes' (*bouleseis*). *Boulesis* denotes rational desire, that is, *orexis* insofar as it is connected with thought (*NE* 1139a36-37). More specifically, Aristotle says that *boulesis* is the rational desire of an end: 'We wish rather for ends than for means, but choose (*prohairesis*) the means to our ends. For example, we wish to be healthy, but choose things that make us healthy' (*NE* 1111b27-28). *Boulesis* thereby signifies the rational desire for a good (in the sense of proper and appropriate, as well as morally correct) *telos*. This is not to imply, however, that the application of *boulesis* is limited to men of virtue. Rather, because all actions aim at the good, rational conduct in general depends upon *boulesis*.

This poses a philosophical dilemma for Aristotle. On the one hand, it would seem that if men wish only for the truly good, then 'what a man who selects his end wrongly wishes for is not really wished for at all; since if it is to be wished for it must be demonstrably good, whereas in this case it may happen that a man may wish for something (in truth) bad' (*NE* 1113a17-20). If, for instance, I wish for physical pleasure in the (mistaken) belief that it is a worthy end, then I cannot be said to have wished at all, because the end was not actually a good one. But if evil is not wished for, then it cannot be voluntary; and that conflicts with Aristotle's insistence that men are equally responsible for both virtuous and vicious conduct (*NE* 1113b3-8). Yet, on the other hand, *boulesis* cannot merely refer to a wish for any end whatsoever as it appears to the individual agent. The relativism implied in the denial of truth or falsity to ends generates a contradiction, according to Aristotle. Insofar as 'different and perhaps opposite things appear good to different people', the ascription of goodness itself loses any definite meaning. What is truly 'good' can be both *a* and not-*a* depending upon the agent, whereas if something is morally good for one then it must be so for all.

Aristotle can envisage only one solution which will allow him to maintain the voluntary status of moral action while simultaneously distinguishing between genuine and apparent goods. He asserts that 'what is wished for in the true and unqualified sense is the good, but what appears good to each person is wished for by him; the good man wishes for what is truly wished for, and the bad man wishes for anything at all' (*NE* 1113a23-26). All men wish for the good as it appears to them. The good for which the *agathos* wishes, however, is identical with the genuine good. By contrast, the good for which the vicious person wishes, although it appears good to him, is not truly so. The wish of the good man is consequently characterized by the rational desire for a *rational* end. The ends sought by others are, conversely, irrational since they do not correspond to the real principle of goodness.

If only because the imputation of motives and reasons for behaviour plays such a large role in argumentation, Aristotle is compelled to address the rationalistic premises of moral psychology in the *Organon*. As in the *Nicomachean Ethics*, he posits a clearly delineated distinction between means and end. We desire actions, he asserts, insofar as they are conducive to ends, whereas the ends are sought for their own sake. In this sense, the desire to take medicine has a qualitatively different status from the desire to be healthy; the former is a *telos*, the latter a means to that *telos* (*Topics* 110b18-20, 110b35-111a4). Thus, Aristotle acknowledges the dual manner in which human action is purposive. Not only are specific actions the result of *prohairesis*, and thus done with a purpose; but deliberate choices are themselves means to ultimate goals which we desire to fulfil, and are hence connected to a higher purpose. Aristotle explains that 'the *telos* in a given instance is what is best or that for the sake of which all else exists' (*Topics* 146b10-11). Consequently, Aristotle asserts that 'everything aims at the good (*agathon*)' in the sense that the good 'is what everybody or all things would prefer' (*Topics* 116a19-20). In turn, our ability to attain the good depends upon our desire of a specific good. The end is fixed by desire, and indeed by desire of a particular sort; Aristotle says that we must describe 'wish (*boulesin*) as a desire of the good (*orexin agathon*)' (*Topics* 146b6-7). What we deem to be good is rendered practical – in the sense that it may be achieved through deliberate choice – only when we wish for that good. The *Organon* also gives clear definition to the sense in which *boulesis* is a type of desire. Unlike *epithymia*, which is identified with desire of the pleasant (*Topics* 146b12-13), *boulesis* seeks ends in a rational fashion. Aristotle insists that if anything falls within 'the appetitive faculty (*epithymetikon*), it cannot be a kind of wish (*boulesis*). *Boulesis* is always in the rational faculty (*logistikon*)' (*Topics* 126a13-14). So *boulesis* connotes the desire of an end in accordance with reason, specifically, the rational desire of a definite good.

Aristotle recognized, however, that it is insufficient to speak of a good as though its substance were universally self-evident. Certainly, all rational action aims at the good, but most agents are bound to fall short of the mark since their conception of the good itself is faulty. The *Topics* demonstrates an acute awareness of this problem. Considering both the major species of *orexis* – namely *boulesis* and *epithymia* – Aristotle warns that we commonly neglect 'to add the qualification "apparent"; for example in the definitions "wish is a desire for the good" or "appetite is a desire for the pleasant". For those who feel desire often fail to perceive what is good or pleasant, so that the object of their desire is not necessarily good or pleasant, but only apparently so (*Topics* 146b37-147a4). In other words, we must always take special care to distinguish between the wish for an end or good and the claim that the *telos* wished for is actually good. Everyone aims to do the good, but many people, because of their moral condition, do not wish for the truly or absolutely good.

We cannot detour around this difficulty by asserting that our wish is for a merely apparent good instead of the true good, that is, by appeal to the relativist position. Aristotle claims that such a view entails an insurmountable conceptual problem: 'Absolute appetite is for the absolutely pleasant and absolute wish for the absolutely good, and so they are not for the apparently good or the apparently pleasant, for it is absurd to suppose that an absolutely-apparently-good or pleasant can exist' (*Topics* 147a8-11). Since we do in fact wish for the good *per se*, rather than simply for what *seems* good, it must be the case that some people's wishes for the actual good are vindicated. Meanwhile, other individuals prove incapable of achieving the true goodness for which they wish because the specific *telos* they desire is incompatible with or inappropriate to the genuine or absolute good. It is the difference between the good man, who wishes aright for the absolute good, and the evil man, whose conception of the (true) good is only a chimera, that underpins the rational principle contained within Aristotle's definition of virtue. The good man is rational in a double sense. First, his desire for the good is a function of *boulesis*, the application of reason to the question of ends. But second, the good wished for by the *agathos* is also the genuine good, or to state matters more accurately, the good which appears to the good man is in fact truly good. That both aspects of this doctrine are recounted in the *Organon* means that the third major element in the Aristotelian definition of virtue was also indisputably present to a medieval audience prior to the earliest transmission of the text of the *Nicomachean Ethics*.

III

It ought not to be supposed that the only substantive precept of Aristotelian moral philosphy given expression in the *Organon* and/or intermediate sources was the conception of virtue. For example, Aristotle's logical writings touch upon numerous other themes central to his ethical thought, such as the meanings of the term 'good',[34] the idea of *akrasia* (incontinence),[35] the relationship of the virtues to happiness,[36] and so on. But the point of the present essay is not to reconstruct the text of the *Nicomachean Ethics* from fragments of the *Organon* in conjunction with Latin treatises. Instead, I have sought to demonstrate that the comparatively smooth assimilation of the *Nicomachean Ethics* into the mainstream of medieval philosophy, as well as the relative lack of interest from schoolmen in the *ethica vetus* and *ethica nova*,

---

[34]Compare *Topics* 107a5-13 with *NE* 1096a24-38.
[35]Compare *Topics* 146a25-27 with *NE* 1147b20-1148a12.
[36]Compare *Topics* 117a23-24 and 116b36 with *NE* 1098b9-1099a31.

may coherently be explained as a function of an awareness of Aristotelian ethical concepts by medieval thinkers before textual transmission had commenced. The theories of the *Nicomachean Ethics* would not have shocked or surprised or disconcerted any moderately well-read man of the late twelfth or early thirteenth century.

In part, this thesis was previously proposed by Georg Wieland, who has argued that 'the reception of the Aristotelian concept of virtue was not a revolutionary step' insofar as the notion of 'natural' or 'acquired' virtue 'was already present in twelfth-century theology'.[37] It needs to be stressed, however, that much of the reason Aristotle's moral philosophy exercised no revolutionising impact upon Christian ethical teaching circa 1200 was the pre-existing stock of specifically Aristotelian ideas that had been disseminated and adopted over the course of the previous century. It is simply an error to impute to the periods before and after 1200 respectively a profound division in moral perspective such as is implied in Paul Oskar Kristeller's remark that 'prior to the thirteenth century, writings on moral subjects were largely influenced by Cicero, Seneca and Boethius; by theological conceptions; and by popular codes of conduct such as those of chivalry. With the rise of scholasticism and of the universities during the thirteenth century, moral philosophy became a formal academic discipline for the first time in the West, based on Aristotle's *Nicomachean Ethics*'.[38] We have seen, however, that the presence in the medieval West of Aristotle's moral philosophy may be detected far earlier and more broadly than Kristeller and others allow. As the absence of a conservative backlash against the translation of the *Nicomachean Ethics* indicates, the decades around 1200 were no watershed in the history of ethical thought. To the contrary, the *Nicomachean Ethics* merely affirmed and expanded upon ideas which medieval schoolmen already knew and widely accepted.

It might still be objected that the case made in the present paper is entirely indirect. That is to say, we have shown how a studious reader of Aristotle's *Organon* and Latin intermediaries could have been exposed to elements of Aristotelian moral philosophy. But we have not provided any evidence that various twelfth-century authors actually appropriated and applied ethical doctrines deriving from Aristotle. In matter of fact, this poses no great difficulty. A recent series of articles have revealed the vast influence which Aristotelian moral theories exercised over the mid-twelfth century philosopher John of Salisbury.[39]

[37]Wieland, Reception and Interpretation, 657.
[38]P.O. Kristeller, *Renaissance Thought and Its Sources*, New York, 1979, 128.
[39]See C.J. Nederman and J. Brückmann, Aristotelianism in John of Salisbury's *Policraticus, Journal of the History of Philosophy* 21, 1983, 203-29; C.J. Nederman, The Aristotelian Doctrine of the Mean and John of Salisbury's Concept of Liberty, *Vivarium* 24, 1986, 128-42; *idem*, Aristotelian Ethics and John of Salisbury's Letters, *Viator* 18, 1987, 161-73; *idem*, Knowledge, Virtue and the

And it is similarly possible to show that whole range of early and middle twelfth-century thinkers – ranging from the School of Anselm of Laon to Peter Abelard to Alan of Lille – were also indebted to Aristotle's ethical ideas by way of the *Organon* and Roman sources.[40]

Yet even if this spade work had not been accomplished, the objection that the present argument is wholly indirect would nevertheless be frivolous. For all the writings which we have cited – namely, the *Organon*, Cicero's *De Inventione* and *De Officiis*, and Boethius's *De Topiciis Differentis* – numbered among the standard texts of a basic theological and philosophical education in the High Middle Ages. The great minds of the twelfth century knew and revered these works, as did many minds less well furnished. And this meant that the *Organon* and the Latin sources were afforded that rigorous, detailed and painstaking study which typified medieval textual interpretation.[41] One can be sure that the elements of the Aristotelian definition of virtue would have been pondered, debated and thoroughly analyzed in due course by the twelfth-century student of logic and rhetoric. When these same minds encountered the text of the *Nicomachean Ethics* itself (especially in its *vetus* version, containing an elaborate treatment of the Aristotelian definition of virtue) there would have been little new to stimulate their imaginations or to alter their preconceived ideas about moral goodness. The *Nicomachean Ethics* was no doubt largely regarded with a sense of *déjà vu*; here were ideas that seemed to be familiar old friends, well-worn concepts dressed up on a different guise. No wonder that the *Nicomachean Ethics* was effortlessly and uncontroversially incorporated into the medieval canon. And no wonder, too, that its readership was so limited and slow to materialise. For the very absence of any novelty normally associated with the Latin edition of the *Nicomachean Ethics* would have discouraged schoolmen from penetrating very deeply into its arguments.

These factors pose a new sort of problem to the historian of medieval ideas. Given that the *Nicomachean Ethics* was readily acceptable to the Latin Middle Ages, why did the mid-thirteenth century see a change in outlook towards Aristotle's moral philosophy? In other words, why did doctrines that had been uncontentious but relatively unexplored for perhaps 150 years quite suddenly become an important object of investigation and discussion in the latter half of the thirteenth century? The events of the mid-1200s, insofar as they fomented an interpretation of the *Nicomachean Ethics* that culminated in the condemnation of 1277, represent a definitive break with a long-standing tradition of moral thought

Path to Wisdom: the Unexamined Aristotelianism of John of Salisbury's *Metalogicon*, *Mediaeval Studies* 51 (forthcoming 1989).

[40]See C.J. Nederman, Nature, Ethics and the Doctrine of Habitus: Aristotelian Moral Psychology in the Twelfth Century, *Traditio* (forthcoming 1989).

[41]For a brief account of the methods employed in the study of Aristotle's thought during the Middle Ages, see Dod, *Aristoteles Latinus*, 72-3.

that was nevertheless Aristotelian in its provenance. It was the work of Grosseteste and Albertus Magnus, Aquinas and Boethius of Dacia, rather than the simple transmission of the text of the *Ethics*, that constituted the true 'rediscovery' of Aristotle's moral philosophy.[42] For their interpretations led in novel and uncharted directions that would have been utterly anathema to scholars and churchmen before c.1250. In this sense, the considerable growth of interest at mid-century in moral philosophy generally, and in the *Nicomachean Ethics* more specifically, was a function not of the mere presence of Aristotelian ethical learning, but rather the product of a dramatic shift in the treatment and understanding of ideas which had been available to and circulating among medieval thinkers for many decades. However we ultimately account for this transformation in perspective – and that is a matter far beyond the scope of the current inquiry – it must be done solely by reference to factors endogenous to the intellectual traditions of medieval Christianity, instead of in relation to the extraneous exigencies of textual dissemination.

There is one further lesson to be drawn from our reflections on the transmissional history of Aristotle's moral thought in the Latin Middle Ages. I have written previously about an 'underground tradition' of Aristotelian social philosophy extant in the Middle Ages prior to the availability of the texts of the *Nicomachean Ethics, Politics* and similar works.[43] This notion of an 'underground tradition' – a phrase suggested by the late Professor Brückmann, my one-time collaborator – has never been adequately defined, however, with the result that certain confusions about its application have arisen. It is perhaps appropriate to attempt a clarification at present.[44] As should be obvious from the case of the *Nicomachean Ethics*, the study of the patterns according to which classical thought was transmitted and received during the Middle Ages has normally stressed the major themes of a given text or group of texts. Thus scholars maintain that the *Organon* disseminated Aristotelian concepts of language and logic, that the *libri naturales* spread Aristotle's physical and metaphysical doctrines, and so forth. But as we have seen – and this holds true

---

[42] I count as part of this mid-thirteenth century 'discovery' of Aristotelian moral philosophy Grosseteste's decision to undertake a full translation of the *Nicomachean Ethics* and simultaneously to translate a number of commentaries on that work from Greek. A recent appreciation of Grosseteste's contribution to Aristotelian scholarship has been offered by R. Southern, *Robert Grosseteste: The Growth of an English Mind in Medieval Europe*, Oxford, 1986.

[43] In particular, see discussion of this theme in Nederman and Brückmann, Aristotelianism in John of Salisbury's *Policraticus*, 227-9; C.J. Nederman, Bracton on Kingship Revisited, *History of Political Thought* 5, 1984, 76; *idem*, Knowledge, Virtue and the Path to Wisdom.

[44] The notion of an 'underground' Aristotelian tradition is in some ways analogous to R. Klibansky's argument in *The Continuity of the Platonic Tradition during the Middle Ages*, London, 1939.

for Latin authors as well as for Aristotle – the actual subject matter of a given text was not so rigidly divided and narrowly delimited as modern scholars have implied.[45] Treatises on rhetoric or logic might well contain substantial arguments drawn from classical moral philosophy, and as such they transmitted to the Middle Ages many important ideas that were not strictly related to the main topic of the text.[46] It is in this sense that we may speak of an 'underground tradition' of Aristotelian moral theory: even when textual evidence of Aristotle's contribution as a moral philosopher was completely unknown among medieval men, there nevertheless existed a considerable body of literature attesting to the substance of his ethical doctrines. Indeed, it is by no means clear that some authors of the twelfth century who were heavily indebted to Aristotelian moral concepts would have regarded themselves as particularly 'Aristotelian' at all.

The point, then, is that direct textual access is not the sole criterion of intellectual influence. All manner of alternate sources may be equally effective in conveying the theories whcih we would normally associate with a particular text.[47] In its current state, the historical study of medieval ideas tends to saddle the works of Aristotle and other classical authors with specialized categories or labels that may serve to hide the actual content of a text. So long as artifical classifications continue to be imposed upon the materials through which classical thought was transmitted to the Latin Middle Ages, it will be necessary to speak of 'underground traditions' of learning. The notion of an 'underground tradition' only ceases to have meaning once the full impact of classical texts upon medieval thought is accorded recognition and the full range of classical ideas available to the Middle Ages is thereby permitted expression.

[45] An excellent analysis of another such case of 'indirect' or unintentional transmission is offered by P.E. Dutton, *Illustre Civitatis et Populi Exemplum*: Plato's *Timaeus* and the transmission from Calcidius to the end of the twelfth century of a tripartite scheme of society, *Mediaeval Studies* 45, 1983, 79-119.

[46] A fact neglected, for example, by M. Grabmann, Aristoteles im 12. Jahrhundert, *Mediaeval Studies* 12, 1950, 123-62.

[47] A similar case of a set of alternative sources transmitting a doctrine ordinarily associated with Aristotle has been carefully documented by G. Post, The Naturalness of State and Society, in *Studies in Medieval Legal Thought: Public Law and the State, 1100-1322*, Princeton, 1964, 494-561 and C.J. Nederman, Nature, Sin and the Origins of Society: the Ciceronian Tradition in Medieval Political Thought, *Journal of the History of Ideas* 49, Jan.-March 1988, 3-26.

II

Aristotelianism and the Origins of "Political Science" in the Twelfth Century

It used to be fashionable among historians of medieval thought to posit the occurrence of an intellectual revolution around the year 1250 associated with the translation and transmission of Aristotle's *Nicomachean Ethics* and *Politics*. Indeed, some scholars went so far as to impute a sort of "epistemological break" between the pre- and post-Aristotelian periods. A classic proponent of this view was the late Walter Ullmann, who unreservedly proclaimed, "The influence of Aristotle from the second half of the thirteenth century onwards wrought a transmutation in thought that amounts to a conceptual revolution. In fact and in theory the Aristotelian avalanche in the thirteenth century marks the watershed between the Middle Ages and the modern period."[1] Other prominent and influential scholars have been equally prepared to see the recovered *Ethics* and *Politics* as bearers of a complete transformation of the medieval mindset. For instance, Paul O. Kristeller found in the two treatises the basis for the creation of an entirely fresh approach to moral philosophy (broadly construed),[2] while Michael Wilks spoke of "a philosophical revolution" within social thought which "occurred during the thirteenth century with the rediscovery of many of the lost works of Aristotle."[3] Examples of similar remarks could be multiplied *ad infinitum*. In short, the ascription of an "Aristotelian revolution" in ethics and politics to circa 1250 constituted one of the cherished interpretive canons of medieval intellectual historiography.

---

[1] Walter Ullmann, *Medieval Political Thought* (Harmondsworth, Middlesex, 1975), 159. A more extensive defense of this position by Ullmann is presented in *Principles of Government and Politics in the Middle Ages* (London, 1961), 231-43.

[2] Paul O. Kristeller, *Renaissance Thought and Its Sources*, ed. M. Mooney (New York, 1979), 128.

[3] Michael Wilks, *The Problem of Sovereignty in the Later Middle Ages* (Cambridge, 1963), 84.

This thesis has been slowly disintegrating during the past few years, however, as the result of important developments in the understanding of twelfth-century ideas and their place within the contours of medieval thought. In the field of ethics, for example, it has become clear that significant features of Aristotle's moral philosophy—including his theory of the virtues and vices, his doctrine of the mean, his moral psychology, and his conception of ethics as a practical science—were widely known and well utilized for perhaps 150 years before a complete Latin version of the *Nicomachean Ethics* was available.[4] For this reason, as Georg Wieland observes, "the reception of the Aristotelian concept of virtue was not a revolutionary step."[5] Rather, key elements of Aristotle's moral system entered into general circulation by means of "underground" or indirect sources: intermediary transmitters like Cicero and Boethius, as well as fragmentary references to moral and social questions in Aristotle's own *Organon,* provided to the twelfth century the substance of numerous Aristotelian doctrines.[6] Thus, when Latin versions of the *Ethics* became available during the early and middle 1200s,[7] they largely reinforced already familiar, even traditional, moral teachings.

It is also possible to observe a similar erosion of confidence in the transformative power of Aristotle's *Politics.* At one time scholarship took entirely for granted that so-called political naturalism—that is, the doctrine that political association arises directly out of the requirements

---

[4] This work was pioneered by Philippe Delhaye in a series of studies, especially "La Place de l'éthique parmi des disciplines scientifiques au XIIe siècle," *Miscellanea Moralia in Honorem eximii domini Arthur Janssen* (2 vols.; Leuven, 1948), I, 29-44; "L'Enseignement de la philosophie morale au XIIe siècle," *Mediaeval Studies,* 11 (1949), 277-99, and " 'Grammatica' et 'Ethica' au XIIe Siècle," *Recherches de théologie ancienne et médiévale,* 25 (1958), 59-110. More recently, some of Delhaye's insights have been developed by Georg Wieland, *Ethica—Scientia Practica* (Munich, 1981), and "The Reception and Interpretation of Aristotle's *Ethics,*" N. Kretzmann, A. Kenny and J. Pinborg (eds.), *The Cambridge History of Later Medieval Philosophy* (Cambridge, 1982), 657-72; by Cary J. Nederman and J. Brückmann, "Aristotelianism in John of Salisbury's *Policraticus,*" *Journal of the History of Philosophy,* 21 (1983), 203-29; and by Cary J. Nederman, "Bracton on Kingship Revisited," *History of Political Thought,* 5 (1984), 61-77; "The Aristotelian Doctrine of the Mean and John of Salisbury's Concept of Liberty," *Vivarium,* 24 (1986), 128-42; "Aristotelian Ethics and John of Salisbury's Letters," *Viator,* 18 (1987), 161-73; "Knowledge, Virtue and the Path to Wisdom: The Unexamined Aristotelianism of John of Salisbury's *Metalogicon,*" *Mediaeval Studies,* 51 (1989), 268-86; and "Nature, Morals and the Doctrine of *Habitus*: Aristotelian Ethics in the Twelfth Century," *Traditio,* 45 (1989/1990).

[5] Wieland, "The Reception and Interpretation of Aristotle's *Ethics,*" 657.

[6] I have attempted to trace elements of this intermediary tradition in "Aristotelian Ethics Before the *Nicomachean Ethics*: Sources of Aristotle's Concept of Virtue in the Twelfth Century," *Parergon,* N.S., 7 (1989), 55-75.

[7] The history of the translation of the *Ethics* is described in detail by R. A. Gauthier in the first volume of his edition of the *Ethica Nicomachea (Aristoteles Latinus,* 24.1-3) (Leiden, 1974).

of human nature instead of divine inspiration or convention—was only introduced into medieval thought with the recovery of the *Politics*.[8] But scholars have lately stressed the plethora of sources for such naturalism to which medieval authors enjoyed access. In the works of Cicero, Seneca, Lactantius, Macrobius, and other widely read Latin authors, we may detect considerable appreciation of the naturalistic origins of human social and political association.[9] Moreover, these alternate sources exercised a great influence upon political texts and arguments both before and after the *Politics* returned to circulation.[10] It seems clear, then, that the political naturalism derived from the *Politics* supplemented rather than supplanted preexisting traditions of thought.

The task of displacing the "Aristotelian revolution" thesis with a more gradualist interpretation of the processes through which the West encountered Aristotle's moral and political ideas is by no means finished, however. In ethics far greater documentation is required for the varied applications of Aristotelian moral concepts by twelfth- and early thirteenth-century authors. The situation with regard to politics is more dire still. Beyond disposing of the claim that political naturalism was a wholly Aristotelian phenomenon, the scholarly literature has investigated little more of the prehistory of Aristotelianism in political thought prior to the return of the *Politics*. This gap in scholarship has permitted some commentators to continue advocating a revised version of the "Aristotelian revolution" thesis. According to the recycled account of Aristotle's impact, the *Politics* occasioned a radical step forward in medieval political theory by giving identity and definition to the realm of "the political" as a distinct mode of experience worthy of study; politics was thereafter a separate branch of knowledge, conceptually independent of law, theology, ethics (narrowly defined), and all similar extrinsic considerations. As Brian Tierney argues, "The *Politics*, one of the last of Aristotle's works to be translated, opened up a new world of thought to medieval men. It showed them that political theory need not be merely a branch of jurisprudence; it could be an autonomous science in its own right."[11] This point is echoed by Joseph Canning, who stresses that "the very idea of

---

[8] Proponents of this view are enumerated by Gaines Post, "The Naturalness of Society and the State," *Studies in Medieval Legal Thought: Public Law and the State, 1100-1322* (Princeton, 1964), 496-98; to Post's list may be added Wilks, *The Problem of Sovereignty in the Later Middle Ages*, 86.

[9] Post, "The Naturalness of Society and the State," 499-512, and Cary J. Nederman, "Nature, Sin and the Origins of Society: The Ciceronian Tradition in Medieval Political Thought," *JHI*, 49 (1988), 3-26.

[10] One example of this is analyzed by Cary J. Nederman, "Nature, Justice and Duty in the *Defensor Pacis*: Marsiglio of Padua's Ciceronian Impulse," *Political Theory*, 18 (1990), 615-37.

[11] Brian Tierney, *Religion, Law, and the Growth of Constitutional Thought, 1100-1600* (Cambridge, 1982), 29.

political science as an autonomous discipline and the notion of the political as a distinct category of human activity and relationships were the product of . . . the rediscovery of Aristotle's *Politics* and *Ethics*." Such a recognition of the unique identity of politics, Canning notes, pervades a host of political tracts composed after the middle of the thirteenth century.[12] And Quentin Skinner finds in the *Politics*-induced claim of the autonomy of the political realm a watershed between medieval and modern thought every bit as pronounced as that once posited by Ullmann: "Any attempt to excavate the foundations of modern political thought needs to begin with the recovery and translation of Aristotle's *Politics*, and the consequent re-emergence of the idea that political philosophy constitutes an independent discipline worthy of study in its own right."[13] In sum, the scholarly literature on medieval political thought, having been deprived of naturalism as the key to the "revolutionary" character of the *Politics*, seems now to have turned its focus to the differentiation of politics from other realms of experience and investigation.

The identification of the "autonomy of politics" as the salient contribution of Aristotle's *Politics* to the Latin Middle Ages is no more warranted, however, than the doctrine of political naturalism. For it is possible to discover already in medieval texts dating to the beginning and middle of the twelfth century a coherent account of the place of politics within the general system of human knowledge—an account which is substantially indebted to a specifically Aristotelian conception of the differentiation of the "sciences." Very exceptionally, this fact has received some attention in the scholarly literature. But its significance is normally diminished or belittled on the grounds that, in the absence of "classic" philosophical text books or authorities (such as Aristotle's *Politics*), it failed to generate any creative political philosophy.[14] Yet such a claim is not strictly true. Not only did many twelfth-century authors realize that politics was a separate and distinct subject matter for inquiry but they also sometimes attempted to speculate more generally on the nature of the political realm itself, the purpose and function of politics, and the relationship between politics and other forms of "practical" knowledge. In sum, it is possible to detect a subterranean tradition of thought in the twelfth century whose contributors had already begun to engage in the sort of philosophical discussion of "the political" and its study that scholars currently claim

---

[12] Joseph P. Canning, "Introduction: Politics, Institutions and Ideas," J. H. Burns (ed.), *The Cambridge History of Medieval Political Thought* (Cambridge, 1988), 360.

[13] Quentin Skinner, *The Foundations of Modern Political Thought* (2 vols.; Cambridge, 1978), II, 349.

[14] For example, D. E. Luscombe, "Introduction: The Formation of Political Thought in the West," Burns (ed.), *The Cambridge History of Medieval Political Thought*, 169, and Nicolai Rubinstein, "The History of the Word *Politicus* in Early-Modern Europe," A. Pagden (ed.), *The Languages of Political Theory in Early-Modern Europe* (Cambridge, 1987), 41-42.

was only possible after the recovery of the *Politics*. Within this tradition may be included some of the most prominent names of twelfth-century thought, such as Hugh of St. Victor, William of Conches, Dominicus Gundisalvi, and John of Salisbury. To the extent that these figures embraced such a shared perspective, we must once again reject attempts to claim for the revived *Politics* a "revolutionary" status. As in the case of the *Nicomachean Ethics*, the process of the transmission and diffusion of Aristotelian ideas occurred at a slower and more evolutionary pace than scholars might lead us to imagine.

One of the chief features of twelfth-century thought was its passion for the systematic organization of knowledge. Inspired by such diverse factors as the recovery of Roman Law and the renewal of interest in Aristotelian logic, this general mania for systematization led to recurring debate about the proper classification of the disciplines which composed philosophy or "the sciences." Two models were widely available to the twelfth century for the arrangement of human knowledge. The first approach, derived from St. Augustine's reading of Plato, divided philosophy into three fields of study: logic, ethics, and physics. According to this tripartite scheme, physics pertains to the realm of contemplation, ethics to that of action, and logic to both contemplation and action (with an inclination towards the former).[15] Augustine clearly construes the "practical" discipline of moral philosophy in quite narrow terms: it concerns the appropriate end of individual action, personal virtue.[16] The political or public realm receives no mention in this context. The Platonic-Augustinian account of the divisions of philosophy was widely disseminated in the Middle Ages, both through *The City of God* itself and by way of such intermediary sources as Isidore of Seville's well-known *Etymologies*.[17] Moreover, early medieval thinkers such as Alcuin incorporated the tripartite classification into their systematizations of human knowledge.[18]

It is also possible to identify a second, and equally popular, classificatory structure present within medieval thought which arose from an alternate tradition. This conception of philosophy, derived directly from Aristotle, also began with a distinction between "contemplative" inquiry (devoted to inquiry into pure truth) and "active" or "practical" disciplines (aiming at the correct conduct of life). Aristotle had observed in the *Eudemian Ethics* that "the theoretical sciences . . . [like] astronomy and natural science and geometry have no other end except to get to know and to contemplate the nature of things that are the subjects of the

---

[15] St. Augustine, *De Civitas Dei*, ed. D. S. Wiesen (Cambridge, Mass., 1968), 8.4.
[16] *Ibid.*, 8.8.
[17] Isidore of Seville, *Etymologiae*, ed. W. M. Lindsay (Oxford, 1911), 2.24.
[18] Delhaye, "La Place de l'éthique parmi les disciplines scientiques au XIIe siècle," 30-31.

sciences"; by contrast, "the end of the productive sciences is something different from science and knowledge, for example . . . the end of political science is good order."[19] Such "productive" sciences are practical insofar as they aim at a good action or a result rather than at knowledge for its own sake.[20] This basic division of knowledge placed the investigation of such topics as physics, mathematics, and metaphysics (or "theology") into the field of *theoria* (contemplation) and of ethics, economics, and politics into the category of *praxis*.[21] Aristotle specifies that the categories of practical knowledge are themselves clearly drawn, if still interrelated. The art of politics ("statesmanship") is not premised directly on individual virtue,[22] nor is it simply an extension of the skills required for the efficient management of the household.[23] Thus, the Aristotelian method of classification, unlike the Platonic-Augustinian one, explicitly embraced the concept of politics as a proper and distinct subject for philosophical inquiry.[24] Indeed, Aristotle pronounces politics to be the "master science of the good," that is, the supreme field of study within the sphere of practical knowledge.[25]

Of course, twelfth-century authors did not enjoy direct access to the texts in which Aristotle examined the systematic classification of the sciences and the place of political inquiry within it. But numerous intermediary sources also propounded the Aristotelian scheme, among them Boethius's *Commentary on Porphyry's Isagoge* and Cassiodorus's *Institutes* as well as Isidore's *Etymologies*.[26] These works were among the most widely disseminated treatises of the High Middle Ages, so we can be assured that Aristotle's categorization of the forms of philosophical knowledge would have been a familiar feature of medieval learning.

It is generally agreed that the first thinker of the twelfth century to make thorough use of the Aristotelian division of the philosophical disciplines was the monk Hugh of St. Victor.[27] In his *Didascalion*, which dates to the late 1120s, Hugh argued for a four-fold division of the sciences

[19] Aristotle, *Eudemian Ethics*, tr. H. Rackham (Cambridge, Mass., 1952), 1216b11-18; see also Aristotle, *Nicomachean Ethics*, tr. H. Rackham (Cambridge, Mass., 1934), 1177a12-1178a23.

[20] Aristotle, *Eudemian Ethics*, 1218b1-8.

[21] See *ibid.*, 1218b13-14.

[22] Aristotle, *Politics*, tr. H. Rackham (Cambridge, Mass., 1932), 1276b16-1277b33.

[23] *Ibid.*, 1252a7-23.

[24] For a more extensive discussion of the role of politics in the Aristotelian system of philosophy, see Richard Mulgan, *Aristotle's Political Theory* (Oxford, 1977), 8-9.

[25] Aristotle, *Nicomachean Ethics*, 1094a18-1094b11.

[26] See Boethius, *Commentaria in Prophyrium*, 1.3 (*Patrologia Latina*, LXIV, cols. 11-12); Cassiodorus, *Institutiones*, ed. R. A. B. Mynors (Oxford, 1937), 2.3.7; and Isidore, *Etymologiae*, 2.24.16.

[27] For Hugh's contributions, see R. R. Bolgar, *The Classical Heritage and Its Beneficiaries* (Cambridge, 1954), 231-32; Frederick Copleston, *Medieval Philosophy* (London, 1952), 57-58; and Wieland, *Ethica—Scientia Practia*, 23-25.

into the contemplative, practical, logical, and mechanical realms.[28] His analysis of these fields of knowledge is clearly indebted to the Aristotelian tradition.[29] This is especially evident in the case of his discussion of "practical" philosophy:

The practical may be divided into the solitary, the private and the public; or put otherwise, into the ethical, the economic and the political; or again, into the moral, the administrative [*dispensativam*] and the civil. . . . The solitary is thus that which, by bringing forth care for oneself, encourages, exalts and extols all the virtues in combination. . . . The private is that which assigns domestic duties, arranging affairs through moderate administration. The public is that which looks towards the care of the republic. . . . Therefore, the solitary is appropriate for individuals, the private for heads of families, and the political for governors of cities [*urbium*].[30]

In Aristotelian fashion Hugh acknowledges that the distinction between politics and the other forms of practical knowledge is qualitative: where ethics treats of personal virtue and economics of the material circumstances of the household, politics is concerned with its own special end, namely, the good of the public sphere. The study of politics thus requires different principles and yields different sorts of conclusions than the "sciences" of morality or household management. Hugh thereby lays the groundwork for the unique identity of political experience as a subject requiring specialized investigation.

One of the most striking elements of Hugh's discussion is the connection he draws between politics and the rule of cities. Aristotle had insisted that it was the *polis* specifically which constituted the highest form of human association.[31] Yet medieval thinkers, faced with the predominance of geographically larger political arrangements such as empires and kingdoms, often ignored this crucial aspect of Aristotelian teaching. Instead, they attempted to apply Aristotle's conclusions about small, self-governing urban bodies to the institutions of medieval monarchy.[32] By contrast, Hugh follows Aristotle more closely in asserting that the knowledge generated by political science is specifically useful in the governance of urban communities. Whether this means that "statesmanship" is wholly inappropriate for kings and emperors remains unclear. But Hugh seems

---

[28] Hugh of St. Victor, *Didascalion*, ed. C. H. Buttimer (Washington, D.C., 1933), 131. A full schematization of Hugh's system of knowledge is constructed by Gérard Paré, Adrien Brunet and Pierre Tremblay, *La Renaissance du XIIe siècle* (Paris, 1933), 100.

[29] Michael Haren, *Medieval Thought* (Basingstoke, Hampshire, 1985), 112.

[30] Hugh of St. Victor, *Didascalion*, 37; all Latin translations in the present paper are the author's.

[31] Aristotle, *Politics*, 1252b28-1253a20.

[32] The extent of this departure is treated by Jean Dunbabin, "Aristotle in the Schools," B. Smalley (ed.) *Trends in Medieval Political Thought* (New York, 1965), 65-85, and Thomas J. Renna, "Aristotle and the French Monarchy, 1260-1303," *Viator*, 9 (1978), 309-24.

to regard the rule of the city as the appropriate and particular domain of political science, and this places him firmly within the tradition of Aristotle (if at a distance from medieval realities).

Although Hugh was perhaps the most prominent thinker in the twelfth century to articulate the Aristotelian conception of politics and its place within the system of knowledge, he was by no means alone. Indeed, many of the themes touched on by Hugh were extended and elaborated by his successors. A case in point is William of Conches, a noted philosopher and teacher, and a contemporary of Hugh. In the prologue to his commentary on Plato's *Timaeus*, William reproduces the basic features of the Aristotelian division of knowledge, but unlike Hugh he does not add the further classifications of the logical and the mechanical sciences. Thus, according to William,

> There are two species [of philosophy]: the practical and the contemplative. There are three practical forms: ethics for the instruction of morals, since "ethics" means the same as "moral character"; economics for household administration [*dispensativa*], which teaches everyone how they should administer their own family affairs, since a steward [*echonomus*] is a household administrator; and politics for civil affairs, which teaches how the republic is to be managed, since the city [*civitas*] is the *polis*.[33]

William touches here upon a number of familiar themes. But he also adds a new dimension to the understanding of politics by equating the *polis* with the *civitas*. For by means of this equation, William makes more explicit the connection assumed by Hugh between "political science" and the governance of cities. Since, as William points out, the *polis* is identical to the *civitas* and the term "political" is derived from the *polis*, we are led to conclude that the study of politics is especially concerned with urban forms of community. Again, this is to make an essentially Aristotelian point; but to do so both overtly and by means of the citation of Greek vocabulary which, outside of the field of logic, was seldom invoked in the early twelfth century.

William also contributes to the expansion of thinking about politics by beginning to establish an order of value or priority among the various forms of knowledge. In his commentary on Boethius's *De Trinitate* he argues that there is a definite hierarchical arrangement of knowledge which should determine the ordering of one's studies should one wish to master philosophy. Generally speaking, one ought to ascend from the practical fields of inquiry to the contemplative, rather than the reverse. There is also a hierarchy which pertains among the practical disciplines themselves: "A man is first to be instructed in moral matters by ethics, then in the management of one's own family affairs by economics, and

---

[33] The text of this prologue is edited by Delhaye as Appendix A to "L'Enseignement de la philosophie morale au XIIe siècle," 96.

thereafter in the governance [*gubernatio*] of affairs by politics. Then, when he has been trained in these to perfection, he should pass on to contemplation. . . ."[34] This ordering within the realm of practical knowledge reproduces the sense of Aristotle's own insistence that politics is the master science of the good, subsuming all other practical sciences under it because its ends are superior to ethics and economics. That William was directly aware that he was adopting an Aristotelian viewpoint with regard to the superiority of political science seems unlikely. Yet even if his inspiration did not stem from Aristotle, his ability to draw Aristotelian conclusions from the basic categories of practical knowledge demonstrates the extent to which twelfth-century thinkers had begun to explore the foundations of political inquiry.

Other authors took the Aristotelian framework pioneered by Hugh in directions more congruent with the medieval context. For instance, in the *Microcosmus* of the late twelfth-century Parisian master of theology, Geoffrey of St. Victor, we find an attempt to extend the application of an Aristotelian conception of politics beyond a strictly urban context. After identifying the three species of practical knowledge, Geoffrey explains that "through the first, everyone is prepared for suitable social intercourse by instructing them commendably in outward action; through the second, the household is well ordered in the eyes of men outside of it; through the third, a subject people is laudably molded by its prince, as though a fruit-bearing tree was made to grow in our native land [*terram nostram*]."[35] Geoffrey goes on to praise recent writings on ethics, economics, politics, and public and private law, which he says will stimulate the process of legal innovation, on the analogy of the planting of new trees which produce all manner of fruits and fragrant smells.[36] The value of political science, presumably, is in the postulation of novel doctrines for the promotion of the public welfare; Geoffrey's king would seem here to be coextensive with the Aristotelian statesman. In this way Geoffrey, writing near the close of the twelfth century, presages the royalist readings which will be imposed on Aristotle's *Politics* after its recovery. For him the study of politics constitutes the path by means of which monarchs can command the loyalty of their subjects and improve the conditions which exist in their realms through legislative enactments.

Among the most intriguing applications of the Aristotelian analysis of politics during the twelfth century is to be found in the *De Divisione*

---

[34] William of Conches, *In Boethium de Trinitate*, edited by C. Jourdain, "Des Commentaries inédits de Guillaume de Conches et de Nicolas Triveth sur la Consolation de la Philosophie de Boèce," *Notices et extraits des manuscrits de la Bibliothèque Nationale*, 20 (1862), 74.

[35] Geoffrey's text may be found in Appendix B of Delhaye, "L'Enseignement de la philosophie morale au XIIe siècle," 96-97.

[36] *Ibid.*, 97.

Philosophiae of Dominicus Gundisalvi. Gundisalvi was a mid-twelfth-century Spaniard who is best known for his translations of Aristotelian and Islamic works.[37] Around 1150 he composed a treatise on the elements of philosophy which suggested a deep interest in politics along with a knowledge of Aristotle which was unprecedented in the West.[38] Gundisalvi's unique awareness of Aristotelian thought was probably a function of his familiarity with the work of the Islamic philosopher Alfarabi.[39] Given the far greater attention to political inquiry typical of medieval Islam, this Arabic influence helps to explain the extensive role assigned to the political realm in *De Divisione Philosophiae*.

The framework for Gundisalvi's discussion of the categories of philosophy is essentially that which we have already encountered in earlier texts. He distinguishes theoretical from practical knowledge and identifies the latter as "the science of what ought to be done."[40] Moreover, he discerns within the practical sphere the three concerns of the individual, the household, and society at large, corresponding to ethics, economics, and politics.[41] Gundisalvi's special contribution is that he articulates the features of each of these fields in much more complete fashion than his Latin predecessors. This is to be expected given the theme of his treatise; where the classification of the subject matter of philosophy was still of somewhat ancillary interest to previous thinkers, it constituted the central point of *De Divisione Philosophiae*, demanding a full and detailed account of all the forms of philosophical knowledge.

Gundisalvi's discussion of political science flows from the general aim of his treatise. He regards political science, construed in its broadest terms, as "the science of arranging one's social intercourse with all men."[42] This fixes the more general character of political knowledge in comparison with ethics and economics; where ethics concerns the relation between individual action and inward disposition and economics treats of "discipline and caring and instruction within the family,"[43] politics seeks to regulate the proper actions and aims of mankind as a whole. It is in light of this more universal purpose that Gundisalvi examines "the science of governing cities, which is called political or civil reason."[44] In a passage

---

[37] For a fuller account of Gundisalvi's career, see Manuel Alonso Alonso, "Notas sobre los traductores toledanos Domingo Gundisalvo y Juan Hispano," *Al-Andalus*, 8 (1943), 155-88, and "Traducciones del arcediano Domingo Gundisalvi," *Al-Andalus*, 12 (1947), 295-338.

[38] A modern edition of *De Divisione Philosophiae* has been prepared by Ludwig Baur (Munich, 1903).

[39] A suggestion supported by Wieland, *Ethica—Scientia Practica*, 26.

[40] Dominicus Gundisalvi, *De Divisione Philosophiae*, 11.

[41] *Ibid.*, 16.

[42] *Ibid.*

[43] *Ibid.*, 16, 139.

[44] *Ibid.*, 134.

meant to capture the breadth of the subject-matter addressed by political science, he proclaims that a knowledge of politics by governors is the ultimate guarantee of human goodness and happiness.

> Civil science inquires into the categories of action, and the habits of creatures who will [*voluntariorum*], and into the dispositions and morals and deeds from which proceed such habitual actions; and into the ends for which such actions are performed; and it teaches how these ought to exist in man and in what way they are to be grasped and fashioned in him. . . . It discriminates among the various actions which are performed and by means of it is calculated and demonstrated which actions make for true happiness and which do not make for happiness. And it is proclaimed that true happiness cannot be possessed in the present world but only in the future.[45]

In sum, the good life on earth and the possibility of an eternal life thereafter depend upon the existence of political order. Thus, Gundisalvi views the ruler as a sort of moral and religious educator, dedicated to promoting virtue and faith among members of the civic body. The clear implication is that political science is the master science of the good, inasmuch as the ends of ethics and economics are subordinate because they are realized only when a well governed polity exists to regulate them. That Gundisalvi imposes upon this essentially Aristotelian lesson a Christian cast which stresses the ultimately supernatural goal of human existence does not diminish his achievement. For even the most radical Aristotelians of the late Middle Ages did not deny that salvation was the highest aim of mankind and that politics played a crucial role in attaining it.[46] Rather, Gundisalvi is one with succeeding Aristotelians in insisting that political science, through its judgments about the ordering of human relations, is necessarily conducive to human happiness even in its final heavenly form.

While *De Divisione Philosophiae* tackles many of the same problems which challenged later authors who enjoyed full access to the *Politics*, this fact may not reflect simply the foresight of Gundisalvi. There is reason to believe that he was far more conscious than his contemporaries of the actual content of Aristotle's political doctrines. For in concluding his discussion of political knowledge, he explains that the basis of civil "science is contained in the book of Aristotle which is called the *Politics* and which is part of the *Ethics*."[47] So far as I can detect, Gundisalvi does not quote directly from the text of the *Politics*, and he may never have enjoyed first-hand exposure to it. But he clearly knew of its existence a full century before its translation into Latin, which is startling in itself given the ordinary presumption of complete ignorance about the *Politics* prior to

[45] *Ibid.*

[46] For example, see the arguments of the fourteenth-century anti-papalist Marsilio of Padua, *Defensor Pacis*, ed. C. W. Previté-Orton (Cambridge, 1928), 1.4.3-4.

[47] Gundisalvi, *De Divisione Philosophiae*, 136.

the 1250s.[48] More importantly, however, Gundisalvi's reference to the *Politics* suggests that his treatment of political science as distinct from and superior to ethics and economics represented an attempt to reproduce what he regarded as Aristotle's own position. With Gundisalvi, one might say, the "underground tradition" of Aristotelian political science begins to surface, to acknowledge explicitly its debt to Aristotle. No longer are authors employing ideas of Aristotelian provenance without a clear appreciation of their textual source (or perhaps even of their derivation from Aristotle). Instead, we confront the glimmerings of that consciousness of the actual teachings of the *Politics* which would culminate in William of Moerbeke's mid-thirteenth-century translation.

It seems indisputable that politics enjoyed a fixed place as a topic of philosophical discussion from the 1120s onwards. But we may still wonder whether interest in a separate and distinct political realm was not limited to a small circle of schoolmen who addressed it in merely formal fashion as part of a broader philosophical exercise. To what extent did the language and concepts of Aristotelian political science form the basis for more thorough investigations of political questions?

Perhaps the best indication of the ability of twelfth-century authors to engage in the process of political inquiry along the lines set out by the Aristotelian categorization of philosophy may be found in John of Salisbury's *Policraticus*, completed in 1159. The *Policraticus* does not make reference either to the distinction between theoretical and practical knowledge or to the tripartite classification of practical knowledge itself. But John, who received an excellent philosophical training in Paris during the 1130s and 1140s (including a period of study with William of Conches),[49] seems to take this systematic arrangement of philosophy largely for granted in his approach to public affairs. Indeed, one of the central assumptions of the *Policraticus* is that political questions may be treated in separation from moral and theological issues, even if there exists an ultimate interconnection among them. Consequently, John comfortably integrates political language into his thought, employing "politics" to denote the secular community in which individuals associate with one another according to human laws and temporal rulers. When he cites

[48] See the remark of James Schmidt, "A Raven with a Halo: The Translation of Aristotle's *Politics*," *History of Political Thought*, 7 (1986), 298: "There is passing reference to the *Politics* in the second century AD, another comment on it in the fifth century, and then nothing until the thirteenth century when the text, miraculously recovered, made its debut in Latin." For the research on which this observation is based, see Schmidt's note 9 on 298.

[49] John relates his educational experiences, and his association with William of Conches, in his *Metalogicon*, eds. J. B. Hall and K. S. B. Keats-Rohan (Oxford, 1991), 2.10. Of William, John says: "I studied under him for three years, during which I learned a great deal, and I will never regret the time spent thereby."

from Roman Law texts the blessings which are gained from submission to law, for example, he concludes that "it is proper for everyone who dwells within the community of political affairs [*in politicae rei universitate*] to live according to [law]."[50] For John, politics most essentially refers to the presence and maintenance of human bonds on earth; political affairs, in turn, pertain to the best and most appropriate methods for organizing communal institutions.

As a result of this conception of the political realm, John is able to recommend consultation with pagan sources in order to learn about politics. The *Policraticus* does not regard the pursuit of political inquiry to be possible only in a Christian society or to be a monopoly of Christian authors.

The gentile philosophers, teaching the principles and conduct [*moribus*] associated with that form of justice which is called "political," by whose benefit human republics subsist and grow, determined that each person is to be content with his own goods and endeavors, prescribing for urban and suburban dwellers, coloni or rustics, their own place and proper endeavour. [By means of political justice] individuals and totality would all serve the public utility with care. Every person will receive the fruits of nature, labour and industry strictly according to merit.[51]

Thus, "political justice" for John is coextensive with what Aristotle calls "distributive justice"; it involves the correct assignment of responsibilities and rewards within the civic unit, so as to ensure that everyone acts for the good of the whole.[52] Inasmuch as he mentions non-Christian authorities, John conveys a belief that such justice can exist independent from a religious context. Indeed, he affirms precisely this point when he remarks that "Justice is one matter, piety is another."[53] Although any truly pious community would necessarily be a politically just one, justice may still be a feature of social arrangements whose members are ignorant of the Christian faith. For this reason, John does not regard it as detrimental to religion to extract from the lessons of pagan philosophers knowledge about politics and how the good republic should be ordered.

The most obvious illustration of John's understanding of politics as a fundamentally secular enterprise stems from his famed use of organic imagery both to identify and to describe the cooperation between the functional parts of the public body.[54] He claims to derive this organic metaphor from an explicitly pagan source: a treatise he calls the *Institutio Traiani* by Plutarch. Although no such work is extant, and it may well

---

[50] John of Salisbury, *Policraticus*, ed. C. C. J. Webb (2 vols.; Oxford, 1919), 4.2, 515a.
[51] *Ibid.*, 1.3, 390a-b.
[52] Aristotle, *Nicomachean Ethics*, 1131a10-33 and *Politics,* 1282b14-1283a23.
[53] John of Salisbury, *Policraticus*, 4.8, 530c.
[54] For a survey of John's organic argument and the scholarly interpretation of it, see Cary J. Nederman, "The Physiological Significance of the Organic Metaphor in John of Salisbury's *Policraticus*," *History of Political Thought*, 8 (1987), 211-23.

have been a fabrication on John's part,[55] the ascription of the source of his own theory of political society to a non-Christian authority who was addressing a pagan (if virtuous) prince underscores his view that political inquiry may legitimately be conducted without direct reference to religion. This is reinforced by his repeated portrayal of the "Plutarchian" public organism as a *politica constitutio*, a political arrangement or order.[56] The significance of this phrase may be deduced from the features of the *Policraticus* we have already examined. Insofar as the analogy between body and community provides a graphic representation of the place and duties of each member within the whole, it realizes precisely the principle of political justice articulated by "gentile philosophers." The *Policraticus* hence insists that the very existence of the public organism depends upon its functioning in accordance with the dictates of justice.[57] Since political justice has an essentially temporal bearing, its expression by means of the organic metaphor assumes the validity of a secular political realm, knowledge of the inner workings of which is equally accessible to individuals regardless of their religious beliefs. The indispensability of earthly, distributive justice to the good order of the public body defines the "political" character of John's organic depiction of the community. The political realm is where determinations are made about the good of the totality in relation to the capacities and needs of its parts. Thus, logically speaking, John's theory of the body politic would lack an adequate philosophical grounding in the absence of an idea of politics organized according to its own unique and internally assessed standards.

The *Policraticus* in this way begins to elaborate the theoretical consequences of the Aristotelian approach to the classification of knowledge. We need not speculate, as Michael Wilks has done, that John enjoyed access to an early Latin version of the *Politics*.[58] Instead, John, who in other respects demonstrated a remarkable facility to draw fruitful conclusions from the meager twelfth-century stock of Aristotelian ideas,[59] seems simply to have extended the logic of contemporary discussions of

---

[55] The arguments about John's authorship of the *Institutio Traiani* have been examined most recently by Janet Martin, "John of Salisbury as Classical Scholar," M. Wilks (ed.), *The World of John of Salisbury* (Oxford, 1984), 179-201, and Max Kerner, "Randbemerkungen zur *Institutio Traiani*," *ibid.*, 203-6.

[56] See John of Salisbury, *Policraticus*, 5.1, 539d; 5.2, 540a. References to "politica" and terms deriving therefrom may be found throughout the *Policraticus*. For example, speaks of "virum politicum" at 6.24, 622d; "res politica" at 6.25, 626b; and "politicorum" at 7.17, 676a.

[57] This identification of the good of the body with the performance of justice is documented by Nederman, "The Physiological Significance of the Organic Metaphor in John of Salisbury's *Policraticus*," 219-22.

[58] Michael Wilks, "John of Salisbury and the Tyranny of Nonsense," in M. Wilks (ed.), *The World of John of Salisbury*, 280-81.

[59] See the studies of the Aristotelian components of John's thought by the present author listed in note 4 above.

scientia politica. Where other authors merely identified politics as a sepa-rate field of inquiry, fixing its place within the system of human knowl-edge, John initiated the process of specialized investigation into the sub-stantive issues posed by political experience. The difference is between the methodologist and the practitioner. In contrast to his predecessors, who concentrated mainly on the terms under which political science should be conducted, John applied their methodological strictures to the creation of a coherent account of politics. It is therefore not entirely anachronistic to claim that the *Policraticus*, no less than the treatises composed after the recovery of Aristotle's *Politics*, embraced the notion that political science is an autonomous discipline and sought to conceptualize political affairs accordingly.

The discovery that politics constituted an important category of philo-sophical analysis throughout the twelfth century both challenges and confirms conventional wisdom about medieval political theory. On the one hand, the present research substantiates the claim that the emergence of the basic conceptual and linguistic building blocks of political theory during the Latin Middle Ages was heavily indebted to an Aristotelian source. Medieval political philosophy may be said to have proceeded along a path mapped by Aristotle's definitions of politics and political science. In particular, his stress on the independence and superiority of politics in relation to other sorts of human activity and his concomitant insistence that political science is the master science of the good seem to form salient assumptions of medieval speculation about public affairs from the twelfth century onwards. Once these Aristotelian premises were disseminated and accepted, theoretical debate about purely temporal political issues and questions commenced, generating some of the philosophical underpin-nings for an idea of the secular state. In sum, we must reaffirm the view that Aristotle was a primary influence upon the formation of the central features of the medieval tradition of political theory.

Yet the ordinary understanding of the nature and extent of this influ-ence needs to be redefined. First and most obviously, the presence of a significant Aristotelian component in medieval political thought did not depend upon the availability of Aristotle's *Politics*. As was so often the case during the Middle Ages, familiarity with specific teachings was not strictly tied to the accessibility of a given text; rather, a wealth of interme-diary and indirect sources could be knitted together in order to recreate Aristotelian doctrines whose textual origins were otherwise unknown. Thus, Aristotle's *Politics* cannot be seen as the revolutionary document so commonly portrayed by scholars.[60] Yet the effect of this conclusion is

---

[60] An important exception to this rule must be noted. In an often ignored remark in his article on "Some Medieval Commentaries on Aristotle's *Politics*," *History*, 36 (1951), 29-30, Conor Martin observes, "The 'fact' of the *Politics* did not come as a surprise to the men of the later thirteenth century. In the first place, the Aristotelian idea that the study

194

to enhance, if also to complicate, Aristotle's contribution to the history of medieval political ideas. For we must assert that Aristotle's thought exercised a far more pervasive influence upon philosophical inquiry into politics during the Middle Ages than has hitherto been suspected. This means, for instance, that it may be possible to speak of a wider range of philosophers and texts as meaningfully Aristotelian in their outlook, even in the absence of the *Politics*. We may also explain thereby the relative ease with which the lessons of the *Politics* were integrated into main stream political thought following the circulation of William of Moerbeke's Latin translation: Aristotle's text was not assailing common beliefs about public life but merely reinforcing and elaborating upon a conception of politics and its study which by 1260 had become traditional and uncontroversial. Because the *Politics* was not a source of contention—for example, its doctrines avoided condemnation from ecclesiastical authorities[61]—it could be rapidly assimilated and applied by medieval authors of highly divergent intellectual and polemical inclinations.

Much of the complexity arising from this interpretation stems from the fact that it makes the task of the researcher more difficult. For in order to establish how Aristotelian political ideas were disseminated and utilized, we are compelled to wade through a vast body of literature, some of which is not specifically political in its bearing. Yet only by casting our net in such broad fashion, as well a widening our scope to include the twelfth century, does it become possible to illuminate fully the process by which politics emerged as a central subject of philosophical discourse, as a science which yields knowledge crucial to human goodness and happiness.[62]

---

of the state was a branch of the scheme of the sciences was known to the middle ages from the very beginning. . . . Furthermore, in the twelfth century, Gundissalinus gathered from the work of the Arab Alfarabi that Aristotle has actually written a book about the state. Before the end of the fourties of the thirteenth century, numerous clear references to that book were given to the scientific world by Robert Grosseteste's Latin translation of the *Nicomachean Ethics* and of Greek commentaries on it."

[61] For instance, the ideas of the *Politics* did not figure at all in the famous 1277 condemnation of 219 "Aristotelian" propositions by the Bishop of Paris; see the text of the condemnation, edited and translated by E. L. Fortin and P. D. O'Neill, in R. Lerner and M. Mahdi (eds.), *Medieval Political Philosophy* (Ithaca, 1972), 335-54.

[62] An earlier version of this essay was presented to the XVth Conference of the Australia and New Zealand Association of Medieval and Renaissance Studies, Dunedin, New Zealand, 1990. Thanks are due to Prof. John O. Ward and Ms. Allison Holcraft for their helpful comments and suggestions. Professor Herbert A. Deane read this paper for *JHI* and recommended many refinements; his contributions to scholarship and support for young colleagues will be greatly missed. I dedicate this essay to his memory.

III

NATURE, ETHICS, AND THE DOCTRINE OF 'HABITUS': ARISTOTELIAN MORAL PSYCHOLOGY IN THE TWELFTH CENTURY

Among the range of moral concepts that the Middle Ages derived from Aristotle, few exercised greater influence than the doctrine of *habitus* (a term ordinarily translated as 'habit,' but more properly meaning 'state' or 'condition').[1] In the thirteenth century, such prominent thinkers as Thomas Aquinas, Godfrey of Fontaines, Duns Scotus, and William of Ockham placed *habitus* (derived from the Greek term ἕξις) near the heart of their studies of ethics.[2] It is largely possible to explain thirteenth-century interest in the concept of *habitus* on the basis of the appearance of Robert Grosseteste's full translation of Aristotle's *Nicomachean Ethics*. Grosseteste's Latin version, taken in conjunction with a growing interest in the field of ethics among arts masters,[3] rendered the technical vocabulary of Aristotelian moral thought into a commonplace of scholastic philosophy.

The intense debate about *habitus* evident during the thirteenth century was not, however, a wholly novel development. As Odon Lottin demonstrates in his survey of the moral theories of the High Middle Ages, the language and concepts associated with *habitus* were already in wide circulation by the early twelfth century. Yet this is not to suggest a continuity between twelfth- and thirteenth-century uses of the idea of *habitus*. Lottin clearly shows how the specific application of *habitus* which typified ethical discussion in the 1100s largely broke down and had to be resuscitated again in the following century.[4]

What was the appeal to twelfth-century moral thinkers of the notion of *habitus*? Lottin and Georg Wieland have attempted to link early references to

---

[1] An earlier version of this paper was presented at the Fourteenth Australia–New Zealand Association of Medieval and Renaissance Studies Conference held at the University of Sydney. Thanks are due to Paul O. Kristeller, Elizabeth A. R. Brown, Allison Holcroft, and Constant Mews for suggestions which improved the content and composition of the text.

[2] These later medieval treatments of *habitus* are surveyed in O. Fuchs, *The Psychology of Habit According to William of Ockham* (St. Bonaventure 1952); for bibliography see xii.

[3] On the institutional context for the thirteenth-century study of ethics, see R.-A. Gauthier, 'Le cours sur l'*Ethica nova* d'un maître ès arts de Paris (1235–1240),' *Archives d'histoire doctrinale et littéraire du moyen âge* 42 (1975) 71–141; M. Grabmann, 'Das Studium der aristotelischen Ethik an der Artistenfakultät der Universität Paris in der ersten Hälfte des 13. Jahrhunderts,' *Philosophisches Jahrbuch der Görres-Gesellschaft* 55 (1940) 339–54; and O. Lottin, *Psychologie et morale aux xii⁰ et xiii⁰ siècles* (Louvain 1948–60) I 505–34.

[4] *Ibid.* III² 99–104 and 142–50.

habitus to the development of a distinction in scholastic ethics between 'natural' and 'supernatural' virtues — a distinction that has traditionally been ascribed to the thirteenth century, after the recovery of the *Nicomachean Ethics*.[5] As Wieland argues, the principle that 'virtue, or good human character, can be rationally discussed without recourse to theology' was in circulation among medieval thinkers long before the *Nicomachean Ethics* was disseminated. Because 'the conception of a natural virtue ... was already present in twelfth-century theology,' Wieland concludes that 'the reception of the Aristotelian concept of virtue was not a revolutionary step.'[6] Wieland regards the plausibility of this claim to rest, at least partially, upon the presence of *habitus* as an alternative foundation for 'natural' moral qualities, quite apart from revelation.[7] For Wieland, as for Lottin before him,[8] twelfth-century reliance on *habitus* reflects an increasing differentiation between philosophy and theology as regards ethical issues.

But the effort to explain twelfth-century discussions of *habitus* by invoking the emerging distinction between natural and supernatural virtue has so far not been matched by a detailed analysis of the specific philosophical functions that the concept was made to perform. In the present paper, I argue that close study of several major twelfth-century treatments of the Aristotelian doctrine of *habitus* suggests that no simple dichotomy between 'natural' and 'supernatural' virtue can be sustained. The philosophers who used *habitus* did so not for the general reason that they wished to exclude theological considerations from ethics, but instead because they sought to articulate a fundamentally anthropocentric perspective on moral theory. That is to say, the introduction of *habitus* into medieval ethical discourse, while it indeed formed the groundwork for a non-theological conception of human virtues and vices, simultaneously separated moral conduct from any wholly naturalistic foundations. *Habitus* allowed authors to distinguish the specifically acquired features unique to moral character from all qualities outside of human control — those stemming from an innate or otherwise natural source, as well as from supernatural infusion. What these early proponents of *habitus* sought was to identify a special realm for a peculiarly human conception of ethics, a realm in which

---

[5] See P. O. Kristeller, *Renaissance Thought and its Sources* (New York 1979) 128; R. Southern, *Medieval Humanism* (Oxford 1970) 55–56; and M. Haren, *Medieval Thought* (London 1985) 189–90.

[6] G. Wieland, 'The Reception and Interpretation of Aristotle's *Ethics*,' in *The Cambridge History of Later Medieval Philosophy* (edd. N. Kretzmann, A. Kenny, and J. Pinborg; Cambridge 1982) 657.

[7] G. Wieland, *Ethica — Scientia Practica: Die Anfänge der philosophischen Ethik im 13. Jahrhundert* (Münster 1981) 222–29.

[8] 'Nous sommes ici sur un terrain purement philosophique': Lottin, *Psychologie et morale* III² 103.

virtue and vice were the products neither of revelatory experience nor of naturalistic determination, but rather of man's own activity and deliberation. Appeal to the doctrine of *habitus* reflected an embryonic confidence in the ability of men to become good (or evil) *on their own* and *by themselves*, without either direct divine guidance or unconscious natural impulse.

Lottin's *Psychologie et morale* documents the vast extent to which *habitus* was present in moral tracts of the 1100s. Possibly as early as the School of Anselm of Laon (ca. 1100), but certainly by the middle of the twelfth century, *habitus* was a basic feature of the moral vocabulary used by many thinkers: it looms large in the work of Peter Abelard and his disciples, in ethical treatises like the *Ysagoge in theologiam* and the *Moralium dogma philosophorum,* and in the writings of John of Salisbury.[9] The variety of sources within which *habitus* played a role should not, however, obscure the important stages through which the doctrine evolved during the course of the twelfth century. There were three steps in the articulation of an anthropocentric moral theory rooted in an Aristotelian conception of *habitus.* The first was Abelard's early attempt to define virtue in terms of *habitus.* The second was John of Salisbury's more refined application of *habitus* to moral matters. The third was the systematic analysis of *habitus* as an ethical construct by Alan of Lille and Simon of Tournai. These authors were not the sole contributors to twelfth-century discussions of *habitus.* But they indicate how an anthropocentric strain in moral theory developed — a strain that was profoundly indebted to Aristotelian ethical thought well before the arrival of the *Nicomachean Ethics* in any of its versions.[10]

*
*   *

A central question emerges from this hypothesis. Did twelfth-century authors enjoy access to a substantial body of Aristotelian moral philosophy associated with the term *habitus* prior to the transmission of Aristotle's ethical *opera*? The fact is that an abundance of sources presented a clear and detailed picture of the moral significance of the concept of ἕξις as it was articulated in

---

[9] For the influence of the doctrine of *habitus,* see *ibid.* III² 103–15. Lottin also shows (125–42) how the concept of *habitus* became enmeshed in and central to twelfth-century discussions of baptism, particularly such questions as whether the sacrament of baptism conveys virtue and the condition of the infant prior to baptism. Similarly, *caritas* was commonly construed in the theological literature as a *habitus*: see A. M. Landgraf, *Einführung in die Geschichte der theologischen Literatur der Frühscholastik, unter dem Gesichtspunkte der Schulenbildung* (Regensburg 1948).

[10] On the recovery of the *Nicomachean Ethics,* see R.-A. Gauthier's introduction to his edition of the Latin *Ethica Nicomachea* (*Aristoteles Latinus* XXVI, i–iii; Leiden 1971–74) I xvi–cxlvii.

the *Ethics*. These sources included some of the texts of Aristotle himself that circulated in twelfth-century Europe, as well as Roman pagan and Christian authorities. To judge the extent to which these intermediary texts faithfully and fully portrayed Aristotle's original doctrine of ἕξις, however, we must turn initially to the *Nicomachean Ethics* itself.[11]

The *Nicomachean Ethics* contends that virtue *per se* ought not to be confused with specific morally correct acts. To be virtuous, Aristotle asserts, is not merely to do what is good, but to do so as the result of a well-formed moral character or set of moral habits.[12] In other words, morally significant actions are rooted in more permanent principles or traits that regulate the behaviour of the agent. Aristotle does not, however, construe the permanence and stability of moral character as the product of an in-bred or natural inheritance. Nature bestows upon man only a capacity (δύναμις) to be good or evil. The capacity must be actualized by moral education.[13] Thus virtue cannot merely be described as a capacity to act in accordance with goodness, since δύναμις is outside of human control and hence something for which human beings cannot be held responsible.[14] Rather, Aristotle insists that virtue is a ἕξις, a state or condition of the soul. According to Aristotle, ἕξις denotes a type of quality, that is, a way in which a qualitative property may be ascribed to a subject or substance. Specifically, Aristotle employs the term to denote those qualities which become so firmly rooted in that which they qualify as to form virtually a 'second nature.' Accordingly, ἕξεις are difficult (if not impossible) to alter.

When Aristotle maintains that 'ἕξις is the genus of virtue' and 'the virtues are ἕξεις,'[15] he means to convey thereby that moral action arises from a character which is 'something permanent and not easily subject to change.'[16] By addressing virtue in terms of ἕξις, Aristotle constructs the foundations for the relative stability and longevity of moral qualities without direct reference to innate qualities. Thus, the moral virtues are acquired by exposure to and practice of virtuous conduct; performing virtuous acts so as to render a course of action habitual constitutes the basis for correct moral education.[17] Evolving the right moral habits and becoming good thereby is a matter of moulding one's ἕξεις, since 'ἕξεις develop from corresponding activities' and 'the quality

---

[11] Citations from the *Nicomachean Ethics* are taken from the edition by H. Rackham (Cambridge, Mass. 1934); my translations are based on Rackham.

[12] *Nicomachean Ethics*, II.i.1103a17–24.

[13] *Ibid.* II.vi.1106a24–31.

[14] *Ibid.* II.v.1106a7–14.

[15] *Ibid.* II.v.1106a14, VI.xii.1143b24–25.

[16] *Ibid.* I.x.1100b2.

[17] *Ibid.* II.i.1103a31–33, 1103b1–3.

of our ἕξεις depends upon what we do.'[18] The regular practice of morally
significant actions forms our ethical dispositions; thus, sufficient training
yields 'a firm and unchangeable character.'[19] In turn, a man whose ἕξεις are
inclined towards good conduct will choose what is virtuous, constantly and
consistently, as a matter of policy. The ἕξεις such a man has developed will
prohibit him from committing uncharacteristic (and evil) acts *on purpose*. This
last qualification is important. Aristotle would not deny that a good man
might occasionally do evil. He might do so through ignorance or faulty
cognition. Aristotle's point, instead, is that the bad act committed by the good
man can never have been done deliberately, on the basis of choice that
conforms with his ἕξις. Only the individual whose moral habits are ill-formed
deliberately does evil, since his bad acts issue from the application of his
vicious character to the process of ethical decision-making. Virtue and vice are
ascribed less to isolated acts than to the qualities of the people who perform
them.

In Aristotle's appeal to ἕξις, then, three features stand out. First, moral
qualities are not a function of natural inheritance or infusion. Rather, ethical
precepts can only be acquired through education and training. Moral character
ultimately rests upon what men do and how they live. Yet the denial of a purely
natural basis for ethical attributes does not render men fickle or unpredictable in
their moral conduct. Permanence, on the contrary, is to be found in the acquisition
of ἕξις, because it is an ingrained condition of the soul that cannot normally be
altered or eradicated once it exists. So the man whose ἕξις is fully formed acts
consistently, according to his character. The third crucial aspect of the moral
psychology of ἕξις pertains to its symmetry. Good ἕξεις and bad both result
from the individual's conduct and are equally permanent. Just as the truly
virtuous man is forever good because he has acquired ἕξεις in accordance with
virtue, so the vicious man is characteristically evil, since he is unable to act
except by reference to his vicious ἕξεις. Vice is as difficult to eradicate as
virtue — for the same reason.

Numerous sources widely accessible during the twelfth century contain
discussions of ἕξις (or *habitus*) in general and its ethical connotations in
particular. Foremost among such sources is Aristotle's *Organon*, especially the
Categories and *Topics*.[20] These treatises often voice the contention that 'ἕξις is

---

[18] *Ibid.* II.i.1103b22–24.
[19] *Ibid.* II.iv.1105a35–b1.
[20] References to the *Organon* are to the Loeb edition; the *Categories* is edited by H. P. Cooke
(Cambridge, Mass. 1938) and the *Topics* by E. S. Forster (Cambridge, Mass. 1960). My
translations are based on these versions. Latin translations of Aristotle given in the notes are
from the contemporary version of the text given in the *Aristoteles Latinus* edition; the
Categories is edited by L. Minio-Paluello in *Aristoteles Latinus* (Bruges–Paris 1961) I i–v and
the *Topics* also by Minio-Paluello in *Aristoteles Latinus* (Leiden 1969) V i–iii.

the genus of virtue' and that '*ἕξις* indicates the essence of virtue.'[21] Nor does Aristotle allow such references to go unexplained. He says in the *Categories* that *ἕξις* is a special sort of quality. It is differentiated from other qualities, like *διάθεσις*, 'in being more long-lasting and stable,' so that, should some property eventually 'become through length of time part of man's nature and irremediable or hard to change, one would perhaps call this a *ἕξις*.'[22] When we 'hold of the virtues — justice and temperance and the like' — that they are *ἕξεις*, we mean to convey that they are 'not easily changed or dislodged.'[23] Thus Aristotle explicitly invokes the claim that the goodness of the virtuous man is relatively permanent: its status as *ἕξις* ensures that virtue will last over time and will provide a stable foundation for moral choice.

Yet the *Categories* simultaneously emphasizes that *ἕξις* cannot simply be seen as a natural capacity. Whereas nature bestows 'an inborn capacity to do something easily,'[24] *ἕξεις* must be acquired through a long and difficult process in which moral qualities are gradually inculcated through practice and experience. Aristotle also stresses that the formation of *ἕξεις* pertains both to the virtues and to the vices. He insists that vice is not simply the 'privation' or 'absence' of virtue.[25] Rather, the good and the bad person become equally accustomed to specific 'habits of living and reasoning.'[26] Aristotle reports that 'when this process [of moral training] continues occurring, it will at great length bring him over into the contrary *ἕξις* [of goodness or badness], provided that time permits.'[27] Aristotle's lesson is that virtue and vice enjoy equal standing with regard to *ἕξις*. The evil man no less than the good is possessed of a set of moral properties which he will find exceedingly hard and perhaps impossible to change or reform after they have been implanted.

These themes from the *Organon* were also expounded by Latin authors. For example, Cicero's early treatise on rhetoric, *De inventione*, appeals to Aristotle's

---

[21] '... habitus genus virtutis ... Amplius habitus quidem quid est significat virtus...': *Topics* VI.vi.144a16–18. See also *Categories* VIII.8b29, and *Topics* IV.ii.121b37–39.

[22] 'Differt autem habitus affectione quod permanentior et diuturnior.... Similiter autem et in aliis, nisi forte in his quoque contingit per temporis longitudinem in naturam cuiusque translata et insanabilis vel difficile mobilis, quam iam quilibet habitudinem vocet': *Categories* VIII.8b28 and 9a2–4.

[23] 'Similiter autem et virtus, et iustitia vel castitas et singula talium non videtur facile posse moveri neque facile permutari': *ibid.* VIII.8b33–35.

[24] 'Non enim quoniam sunt affecti aliquo modo, unumquodque huiusmodi dicitur, sed quod habeant potentiam naturalem vel facere quid facile vel nihil pati': *ibid.* VIII.9a16–18. For elaboration of this position, see 9a14–17.

[25] For Aristotle's explanation of the sense in which virtue and vice, because they are contraries, cannot be 'possessive' and 'privative,' see *ibid.* X. 13a17–36.

[26] '... consuetudinem sermonemque...': *ibid.* X.13a23.

[27] '... et hoc saepius factum perfecte in contrariam habitudinem consistere, nisi tempore prohibeatur': *ibid.* X.13a29–31.

notion of ἕξις when discussing rules for oratorical practice. Cicero says that
when an orator attributes 'qualities of mind and body,' those 'bestowed by
nature' must be distinguished from those 'acquired by one's own industry,
which pertains to *habitus*.'[28] The distinction between *natura* and *habitus* is not
one of permanence: like nature, '*habitus* consists in a perfect and constant
condition of the mind or body.'[29] Rather, the difference is one of source.
Whereas qualities of nature are inborn, qualities of *habitus* are acquired.
'What we call *habitus* is the realization of something constant and absolute in
mind or body, such as virtue ... not given naturally, but achieved by study
and industry.'[30] Thus, Cicero insists that when the moral character of a person
is evaluated — whether he is honourable or not — reference must be made not
simply to his actions but to the *habitus* which underlies his conduct. Virtue is
primarily a matter of a '*habitus animi*' from which particular acts of a given
kind proceed.[31] Consequently, specific instances of ethical behaviour should
not be considered in isolation; we must know what state of mind produced the
action and, by extension, whether the act was consistent with the agent's
general inclinations. For Cicero as for Aristotle, judgements about action must
take into account the attributes of the person who is acting. A good man who
erroneously commits an evil act is not to be condemned or reviled in the same
way as a characteristically dishonourable man.

Boethius evinced a similar interest in the Aristotelian conception of *habitus*.
Throughout his writings appears the formula (which enjoyed considerable
popularity during the Middle Ages) that 'virtue is a *habitus* of a well-ordered
mind.' Sometimes, as in the *De topicis differentiis*, the phrase appears without
any explanation or elaboration.[32] But elsewhere, as in his commentary on
Aristotle's *Categories,* Boethius makes very clear what is meant by the
ascription of *habitus* to virtue: 'Nothing is a virtue unless it is difficult to
change. For neither he who is judged just in appearance is truly just, nor he
who seems to commit adultery is truly an adulterer, except when his will and

---

[28] 'Et omnino quae a natura dantur animo et corpori considerabuntur. Nam quae industria
comparantur, ad habitum pertinent, de quo posterius est dicendum': Cicero, *De inventione*
(ed. H. M. Hubbell; Cambridge, Mass. 1949) I.xxiv.35; my translations from Cicero are based
on Hubbell's rendering.

[29] 'Habitus autem, quoniam in aliqua perfecta et constanti animi aut corporis absolutione
consistit, quo in genere est virtus, scientia et quae contraria sunt': *ibid.* II.xx.30.

[30] 'Habitum autem appellemus animi aut corporis constantem et absolutam aliqua in re
perfectionem, et virtutis aut artis alicuius perceptionem aut quamvis scientiam et item
corporis aliquam commoditatem non natura datam, sed studio et industria partam': *ibid.*
I.xxv.36.

[31] *Ibid.* II.liii.160.

[32] Boethius, *De topicis differentiis* (trans. E. Stump; Ithaca 1987) 51, 89.

deliberation is permanent.'[33] Boethius thus reiterates some of Aristotle's basic conclusions about *habitus*. He regards virtue as fixed and virtually inalterable; for one's actions to be susceptible to moral analysis one must have an ingrained set of ethical characteristics. Likewise, Boethius acknowledges the symmetrical character of the moral qualities rooted in *habitus*. Vices, like virtues, entail a permanent cast of mind, since this is the mark of a morally mature and competent person.

* * *

A well-educated twelfth-century cleric would have had at his disposal a vast array of sources on the basis of which he could recount the doctrine of ἕξις as it appeared in the *Nicomachean Ethics*. It is impossible, however, to gauge with much accuracy the precise date at which an essentially Aristotelian understanding of *habitus* entered the vocabulary of ethical debate. The *Liber Pancrisis* attributes to the school of Anselm of Laon the claim that 'virtue is a *habitus* of a well-ordered mind, and vice is a *habitus* of a badly-ordered mind.'[34] But the text in question delves no further into the specifically Aristotelian connotations of *habitus*, turning instead to a discussion of sin and penitence which owes nothing to Aristotle. It would seem, then, that not before Peter Abelard was there a full awareness of the ethical aspects of *habitus* and their application to a conception of temporal virtue. Abelard appeals to *habitus* extensively in both the *Ethica* and the *Dialogus inter Philosophum, Judaeum et Christianum*, the latter of which Constant Mews has recently dated to 1125/26.[35] Consequently, Abelard seems to be a seminal figure in the presentation of an account of moral character founded on precepts derived from Aristotle. This accords with Abelard's general philosophical outlook, which stressed the relative independence of the powers of reason from the direct control of faith,[36] a perspective which surely encouraged a distinction between supernatural and earthly goods.[37]

---

[33] 'Virtus enim nisi difficile mutabilis non est. Neque enim qui semel iuste iudicat, iustus est, neque qui semel adulterium faciat, est adulter, sed cum ista voluntas cogitatioque permanserit': Boethius, *In Aristoteles Categoriae commenta* (PL 64) 242b.

[34] 'Virtus est habitus mentis bene constitute, et vicium habitus est mentis male constitute': given in Lottin, *Psychologie et morale* V 59.

[35] For this proposed chronology of Abelard's works, see C. Mews, 'On Dating the Works of Peter Abelard,' *Archives d'histoire doctrinale et littéraire du moyen âge* 52 (1985) 73–134, esp. 122–26.

[36] This view Abelard expresses in the *Dialogus inter Philosophum, Judaeum et Christianum* (ed. R. Thomas; Stuttgart 1970), 1341–42, and the prologue to *Sic et Non* (edd. B. B. Boyer and R. McKeon; Chicago 1974).

[37] D. E. Luscombe, 'The *Ethics* of Abelard: Some Further Considerations,' in *Peter Abelard* (ed. E. M. Buytaert; Leuven – The Hague 1974) 71.

Yet Abelard's references to *habitus* were designed less to justify a distinction between eternal and temporal ethics than to explain why nature *per se* is an insufficient basis for the formation of human moral qualities. In the *Dialogus,* for example, *habitus* is only introduced after the interlocutors have jointly admitted a distinction between the Supreme Good (God) and the highest human good (*summum hominis bonum*), that is, between ultimate universal goodness and goodness as it exists specifically for man.[38] Such a differentiation depends upon the conviction that special human goodness can be conceived as subsisting apart from the supreme good. Abelard's Philosopher holds that because human beings possess qualities which, while they owe nothing immediately to God, are nonetheless recognized as good, we may speak of a proper and sufficient sphere for the realization of a distinctive human goodness (or for that matter, badness).[39] In sum, virtue and vice should not be construed as synonyms for faithfulness and sin, but as parallel temporal terms. Being good in an absolute sense is related to being virtuous, but each has its own designated properties and features.

How, then, are the qualities associated with the highest human good of virtue constituted? Whence do they arise? Abelard's Philosopher responds with the claim that 'virtue is the best *habitus* of the soul; and on the contrary vice is thought to be the worst *habitus* of the soul.'[40] In other words, men achieve supreme earthly good (or evil) insofar as they are characteristically virtuous (or vicious). The effect of this definition is to demonstrate that specifically human goodness is distinguished by its source; it results from the qualities which men acquire by themselves, rather than from forces or powers outside their control. Abelard contends that this criterion is not met if virtue is treated as a natural or inherent property of a person: 'Hence we do not count among the virtues that so-called natural chastity due to frigidity or some other complexion of the body, which never has to fight or overcome desire and which has no merit.'[41] Virtue is something which is necessarily the product of human effort. Where there is no struggle, no active process by which moral character is shaped — where the inclination to act is purely natural or instinctual — merit cannot be assigned and virtue cannot be ascribed. For if the highest

---

[38] Abelard, *Dialogus* 1936–63. Abelard's familiarity with *habitus* extended beyond ethical concerns to his logic; see his *Dialectica* (ed. L. M. de Rijk; Assen 1956) 93–95, 101–2, and *passim.*

[39] Abelard, *Dialogus* 1971–75.

[40] 'Virtus, inquiunt, est habitus animi optimus; sic e contrario vitium arbitror esse habitum animi pessimum': *ibid.* 1987–88. The translations from this text are mine.

[41] 'Unde hanc, quam naturalem in quibusdam castitatem nominant ex corporis videlicet frigiditate vel alique complexione nature, que nullam umquam concupiscentie pugnam sustinet, de qua triumphet, nec meritum optinet, nequaquam virtutibus connumeramus': *ibid.* 1992–96.

human good is uniquely *human*, then it must arise from those aspects of life which are within our direct power. Thus, in order to qualify for this highest human good, we must deserve our reward by earning it; we must have attained through our own deeds a particular moral condition. We cannot rightfully claim credit for those things, like natural propensities, over which we have exercised no control. By contrast, as Abelard points out in the *Ethica*, the individual who develops a character contrary to his nature — a person who, for example, is naturally disposed to anger or luxury, but who overcomes this inherent trait by his own efforts — is precisely the person who may be credited with virtue.[42] Active formation of moral character is the indispensable key to the *summum hominis bonum* (and presumably also to its opposite).

This is the point at which *habitus* achieves special relevance for Abelard. The Aristotelian notion of *habitus* afforded Abelard a basis for the formation of moral character which looked beyond nature towards human industry. Explicitly citing Aristotle's *Categories*,[43] the *Dialogus* explains that '*habitus* is a quality which does not inhere naturally in a thing, but is acquired through careful study or deliberation and is difficult to change.'[44] A *habitus* can be said to exist only when someone has actively formed it. This process of training removes virtue from a purely naturalistic context and renders it a distinctively human trait. As Abelard proclaims elsewhere in the *Dialogus*, 'virtue is a *habitus* of the soul which, in order to make evident its excellence, possesses stability through application and study more than by nature.'[45] In a sense, then, *habitus* is the means by which nature is overcome, whether by altering innate qualities or by developing new sorts of attributes with which we would not otherwise be endowed. It is through the formation of *habitus* that men become human. Although Abelard is vague about precisely how study actually yields a *habitus* and whether the learning process must necessarily be conscious, his central contention is that men become most fully themselves — attain the *summum hominis bonum* — when their own ethical qualities are fashioned apart from and occasionally in opposition to natural propensities.

Yet, like natural qualities, *habitus* is to all intents and purposes inalterable, or at least not subject to rapid fluctuations. Thus, although human virtue is not a natural endowment, it is still marked by a high degree of consistency and predictability. Abelard stresses throughout the *Dialogus* that 'all the virtues

---

[42] Abelard, *Ethica* (ed. D. E. Luscombe; Oxford 1970) 4. Translations from this text have occasionally been revised.

[43] Abelard, *Dialogus* 1988.

[44] 'Est igitur habitus qualitas rei non naturaliter insita, sed studio ac deliberatione conquisita et difficile mobilis': *ibid.* 1990–92.

[45] '... virtus habitus sit animi, quem, ut ex superioribus liquet, per applicationem vel studium magis quam per naturam haberi constat': *ibid.* 2164–66.

are difficult to change'[46] and that virtue is absent 'wherever qualities of the soul are easily changed.'[47] The basis for his statements is the stability which he believes *habitus* affords to an acquired property. Abelard most clearly addresses this quasi-natural aspect of *habitus* in the *Ethica*, when he contrasts human virtue with the 'goods that merit beatitude, which consist in the good of obedience.'[48] The will to obey God is not immediately comparable to virtue, Abelard argues, since the obedient 'will sometimes will be able to exist if, at the time it is possessed, it is not so firm and difficult to change that it can be called a virtue.'[49] A person who is basically inclined to obey God may nevertheless occasionally sin without surrendering a will oriented towards obedience.

Virtue is profoundly different: to have a virtue means to act according to its dictates without exception or fail. That such a stable propensity is possible for men, Abelard explains, is directly attributable to *habitus*:

> The philosophers have agreed that virtue is by no means said to be in us unless it is a *habitus* of the best mind or a *habitus* of the well-ordered mind. Now, what they call *habitus* or *dispositio*, Aristotle diligently distinguished in the first species of quality, that is, teaching that those qualities which do not inhere naturally in us, but arrive by our application, are designated *habitus* or *disposiciones*. They are called *habitus* if they are difficult to change — such are, he says, knowledge and the virtues; by contrast, they are called *disposiciones* if they are easily changed.[50]

What especially characterizes a *habitus* is a resistence to alteration, a regularity which assures that a quality will remain firmly attached to whatever it qualifies. In the case of virtue, this means that a moral property, once acquired, will generate consistent conduct which cannot be deflected, at least not without the greatest effort. Abelard's conclusion is appropriate to the quasi-natural feature of immobility associated with *habitus*: 'Therefore, according to this, if any virtue of ours is called a *habitus*, it does not appear absurd that the will ready to obey God, when it is easy to change, should in no

---

[46] '...virtutem omnem difficile mobilem...': *ibid.* 2005.

[47] '...quecunque animi qualitates facile sunt mobiles': *ibid.* 1996–97.

[48] '...beatitudinem promeremur bonis, que in bono consistunt obediencie': Abelard, *Ethica* 128.

[49] 'Que fortassis voluntas nonnunquam esse poterit, si ad tempus habita nondum ita firma sit ac difficile mobilis, ut virtus dici possit': *ibid.* 128.

[50] 'Ut enim philosophis placuit, nequaquam virtus in nobis dicenda est, nisi sit habitus mentis optimus, sive habitus bene constitute mentis. Quid vero habitum vel dispositionem dixerint, Aristoteles in prima specie qualitatis diligenter distinxit, docendo videlicet eas qualitates que non naturaliter nobis insunt, set [sed] per applicationem nostram veniunt, habitus vel disposiciones vocari. Habitus quidem, si sint difficile mobiles, quales, inquit, sunt sciencie vel virtutes. Disposiciones vero, si e contra fuerint facile mobiles': *ibid.* 128.

way be called a virtue before it becomes firm, just as it is not a *habitus*.'[51] Yet this is not an adequate reason to consign to eternal damnation the soul still weak in the face of sin and temptation. Few men are saints or martyrs, and singleness of mind cannot be a satisfactory criterion for salvation.[52] Nevertheless Abelard is prepared to ascribe virtue only to those persons in whom moral qualities endure without variation or mutation. Although it does not arise from nature, virtue takes on a quasi-natural quality of permanence because true moral goodness must be rooted in *habitus*.

The work of Abelard contains most of the essential ingredients of Aristotelian moral psychology. Admittedly, Abelard's account is deficient in some respects. For example, he does not move beyond vague phrases like 'application' in explaining the process by which moral qualities are acquired. Nor does he adhere strictly to the Aristotelian principle of the symmetry of virtue and vice. Abelard sometimes implies that 'nature itself or the bodily constitution' renders people prone to vice, as in the case of luxury or anger. In short, he seems to be unsure about whether vice, like virtue, is entirely a product of human activity.[53] Yet the manner in which Abelard assembles the salient elements of the Aristotelian conception of *habitus* is still remarkable. Upon an Aristotelian foundation he constructs an ethical theory which avoids traditional theological ideas of moral goodness without indulging in an unalloyed naturalism which denigrates the contribution made by human effort. The removal of both naturalistic and supernatural bases for moral character need not imply, however, that human goodness and happiness are merely transitory, arbitrary, or fickle. Rather, the Aristotelian moral psychology of *habitus* guarantees that the traits of virtue which men evolve will neither perish nor diminish. Indeed, Abelard's own view would seem to be close to that of the Philosopher in the *Dialogus*: 'What is truly best is a *habitus* of the soul, which shapes us for the merit of true happiness (*vere beatitudinis*).'[54] Man's ultimate allegiance may be to God, yet it remains possible for him to achieve through his own work, unaided by external forces, a measure of temporal excellence and satisfaction.

*
*   *

Perhaps the most remarkable lacuna in Lottin's survey of twelfth-century discussions of *habitus* is the absence of any reference to John of Salisbury. Yet

---

[51] 'Si ergo secundum hoc habitus sit dicenda quelibet virtus nostra, non absurde videtur nonnunquam voluntas ad obediendum parata, cum sit facile mobilis, antequam firmetur nequaquam dicenda virtus, sicut nec habitus': *ibid*. 128.

[52] See *ibid*. 128–30.

[53] *Ibid*. 4. See also Luscombe's n. 1 for further references.

[54] 'Optimus vero est ille animi habitus, qui ad vere beatitudinis meritum nos informat': Abelard, *Dialogus* 2012–13.

as several recent studies have demonstrated,[55] John often cites the basic elements of Aristotelian moral psychology. As a student of Abelard[56] and a man of considerable familiarity with current Aristotelian learning,[57] John could reasonably be expected to rely upon *habitus*. Yet John's position as a scholastically-trained ecclesiastical administrator meant that his use of the Aristotelian account of *habitus* would be different from Abelard's.[58] John often employed Aristotle's concepts as tools to evaluate the personalities and courses of action with which he was immediately confronted. Thus Aristotelian doctrines are as much in evidence in John's correspondence as in his philosophical tracts.[59] John appreciated that Aristotle's moral thought had a practical dimension which could aid the politically-active cleric in advising and counseling his superiors.

The practical impulse behind much of John's writing hence frequently converged with his philosophical outlook. Nowhere is this convergence more evident than in his attack in the *Metalogicon* on the so-called 'Cornificians.'[60] According to John, 'Cornificius' and his followers believe that the qualities and powers with which men are born constitute the limits of their knowledge and faculties. This implies that human beings are incapable of altering their lot or condition in life; it is grace, rather than the improvement of their minds and skills, that earns them happiness and salvation.[61] John takes extreme

---

[55] See C. J. Nederman and J. Brückmann, 'Aristotelianism in John of Salisbury's *Policraticus*,' *Journal of the History of Philosophy* 21 (1983) 203–29; C. J. Nederman, 'Aristotelian Ethics and John of Salisbury's Letters,' *Viator* 18 (1987) 161–73; and idem, 'Knowledge, Virtue and the Path to Wisdom: The Unexamined Aristotelianism of John of Salisbury's *Metalogicon*,' *Mediaeval Studies* 51 (1989), 268–86.

[56] John describes his association with Abelard in the *Metalogicon* (ed. C. C. J. Webb; Oxford 1929) 867b. Translations from this text are based on the translation by D. D. McGarry (Berkeley 1955).

[57] John's awareness of the process of transmission is witnessed by a letter to Richard l'Évêque, ca. 1167, which requests a copy 'of the books of Aristotle which you have': Letter 201, in *The Letters of John of Salisbury* (edd. W. J. Millor and C. N. L. Brooke; Oxford 1979), II 295. John's own testimony in *Metalogicon* 902c–d shows that he was among the first in Western Europe to possess a complete Latin text of Aristotle's *Topics*.

[58] For a detailed account of John's career and its implications for his thought, see K. Guth, *Johannes von Salisbury (1115/20–1180): Studien zur Kirchen-, Kultur- und Sozialgeschichte Westeuropas im 12. Jahrhundert* (St. Ottilien 1978) and K. L. Forhan, 'The Twelfth-Century "Bureaucrat" and the Life of the Mind: John of Salisbury's *Policraticus*' (diss. Johns Hopkins University 1986).

[59] See Nederman, 'Aristotelian Ethics' 172–73.

[60] For recent reflections on the identity of 'Cornificus,' see R. B. Tobin, 'The Cornifician Motif in John of Salisbury's *Metalogicon*,' *History of Education* 13 (1984) 1–16 and E. Tacchella, 'Giovanni di Salisbury e i Cornificiani,' *Sandalion* 3 (1980) 273–313.

[61] For further discussion of the philosophical precepts of the Cornificians and of John's response, see Nederman, 'Knowledge, Virtue and the Path to Wisdom' (n. 55, *supra*) and 'Nature, Sin and the Origins of Society: The Ciceronian Tradition in Medieval Political Thought,' *Journal of the History of Ideas* 49 (1988) 11–14.

exception with this view. In the *Metalogicon* he maintains that nature cedes to man certain capacities which are only realized through the formation of a second, acquired nature. John teaches that our knowledge and skills depend upon what we do: 'Assiduous application ... smooths the way for understanding.'[62] The ignorant or incompetent man becomes accustomed to false or incorrect precepts because his actions are improper. Likewise, the well-educated individual repeatedly practices the behaviour which accords with true knowledge of a discipline or skill. John observes that 'art, which becomes firmly established by use and practice, yields a faculty of accomplishing those things that are proper to it.'[63] Competence in any field of study is assured only to those who train carefully and regularly over a long period of time. In a passage which echoes *Categories* 13a23–31, John remarks that 'what is difficult when we first try it, becomes easier after assiduous practice, and once the rules for doing it are mastered, very easy, unless languor creeps in, through lack of use or carelessness, and impedes our efficiency.'[64] Repeated activity familiarizes man with the knowledge or talent he seeks to acquire: he learns by doing.

In order to defend this position, John appeals to the essentially Aristotelian doctrine that *habitus*, determined by usage, provides the basis for the possession of any knowledge or skill. John declares that mastery of the principles of a discipline can only be ascribed once 'the *habitus* of employing them is firmly fixed by practice and exercise.'[65] *Habitus* is the criterion for the completion of education. When a particular object of knowledge becomes so characteristically a part of an individual that it is virtually insusceptible to change, then the person has been successfully educated. John explicitly refers in this regard to the Aristotelian distinction between διάθεσις (*dispositio*) and ἕξις (*habitus*): '[theoretical principles] must be consolidated by practice and exercise, except perhaps where a disposition has already been transformed into a *habitus*.'[66] The end of all instruction is the formation of a 'second nature,' an irresistible but acquired inclination to behave in accordance with definite precepts. Such a 'second nature' is present only when a *habitus* has been engendered, that is, only when a quality becomes so thoroughly a part of a

---

[62] 'Operis scilicet assiduitas ... vias tamen parat intelligentiae': John of Salisbury, *Metalogicon* 835b.

[63] 'Arte, quae usu et exercitatione firmata est, provenit facultas exequendi ea, quae ex arte gerenda sunt': *ibid*. 853a.

[64] 'Quod difficile fuerat in prima agitatione, ab assiduitate usus reddatur facilius; et cum regulas hoc faciendi deprehenderit, fiat, nisi desuetudinis et negligentiae torpor obsistat, facillimum': *ibid*. 838c.

[65] 'His enim perfecte cognitis, et habitu eorum per usum et exercitium roboratis': *ibid*. 902b.

[66] '... si non usu et exercitio assiduo roboretur: nisi forte in habitum transierit dispositio': *ibid*. 932c.

person that it inheres in him. By conceiving of the goal of all education as the creation of a *habitus*, John responds to and deflects the naturalistic over-determination of the 'Cornificians.'

John's general reluctance to adopt a wholly naturalistic perspective and his reliance upon the doctrine of *habitus* in order to bolster his position significantly affect his moral philosophy. For like his master Abelard John rejects the claim that the virtues and vices are purely natural in foundation and owe nothing to active human participation. But at the same time the anthropocentric perspective implied in supplanting nature by *habitus* is elaborated by John in such fashion that some of the gaps in Abelard's account are filled. John evinces an understanding of how moral states are acquired and investigates the symmetry of the virtues and the vices; both of these features move him closer to Aristotle's own thought. Hence John's treatment of moral character cannot fairly be regarded as merely derivative from Abelard. John expands and clarifies the insights of his teacher and thereby contributes to the emerging Aristotelianism of twelfth-century moral psychology.

The fullest exposition of John's adaptation of the doctrine of *habitus* to specifically ethical matters is found in the fifth book of the *Policraticus*, which contains a discussion of the possible reasons why a person might deserve to be respected or obeyed. Among the grounds elucidated — and explicitly distinguished from nature[67] — is moral character. John explains that 'character (*mos*) is a *mentis habitus* from which particular acts proceed assiduously.'[68] In other words, to possess a moral quality is to have a *habitus* on the basis of which one will inevitably and predictably act. *Habitus* is present when there exists a permanent and stable foundation for ethical action. This much accords with Abelard and with John's own observations in the *Metalogicon*. But John goes on to describe the process by which such a moral *habitus* is acquired. In Aristotelian fashion, John reports that if an act 'is done once or more often, it does not immediately become part of character, unless by assiduous practice it passes into usage (*usum*).'[69] When a certain sort of action is constantly repeated — when it becomes a regular feature of one's conduct — then and only then may a moral *habitus* be attributed to an individual.

Once the training has been completed, the character of the person will henceforth enjoin him to act strictly in accordance with the specific quality he has acquired. As John remarks in a letter of 1168, the possession of a friendly

---

[67] John of Salisbury, *Policraticus* (ed. C. C. J. Webb; Oxford 1909 rpt. 1965) 544a. All translations are from my forthcoming English translation of the *Policraticus*, to be published by Cambridge University Press.

[68] 'Mos autem mentis habitus ex quo singulorum operum assiduitas manat': *ibid.* 544d.

[69] 'Non enim si quid fit semel aut amplius, statim moribus aggregatur, nisi assiduitate faciendi vertatur in usum': *ibid.* 544d–45a.

character depends upon practice from an early age: 'Assiduousness in friendship has conferred on me an *usus,* and use rendered into *habitus* compels me to be friendly even to the unfriendly.'[70] The acquisition of a *habitus,* John stresses throughout his writings, is effectively the formation of a kind of *altera natura,* a second nature distinct from the *primitiva natura* with which men are born.[71] Unlike their inherited nature, the second nature which men possess is a creation and reflection of their own experiences and modes of life. *Habitus* emerges from long usage, and once fixed it generates an uninterrupted flow of similar actions. Even in the face of adversity, *habitus* ensures that men are able to follow a particular course of conduct because of their moral education.

John recognizes that implicit in his account of moral character is a potential ambiguity. He notes that his presentation of *habitus* would seem to apply without variation to both well-formed and ill-formed characters: 'usage includes both virtues and vices.' Yet at the same time, in ordinary discussions of the topic 'the vices are not included in character, to which the vices are usually opposed.'[72] That is to say, the term *mores* has both a neutral and a prescriptive sense. In its neutral connotation, the word indicates qualities of character regardless of whether they are virtuous or vicious. John observes that 'we sometimes speak of good and bad *mores* to distinguish the vices and the virtues.'[73] But in its prescriptive meaning, character is limited to the realm of moral goodness: 'Only the virtues are included under the name of *mores.*... Thus we use character in its good sense when we speak of "people of character".'[74] This ambiguity directly affects John's treatment of *habitus.* He explains in the *Policraticus* that whereas in the immediate discussion permanence of character refers only to those qualities of virtue worthy of respect and reverence — wisdom, bravery, temperance, and justice — it is nevertheless true that the same account of *habitus* equally applies to *mores* broadly construed. The process by which moral qualities are acquired is symmetrical: vices no less than virtues are the product of assiduous practice over a long period of time. And indeed John does refer elsewhere in the *Policraticus* to one vice, *iniustitia,* as a *'mentis habitus* which exterminates equity from the region of character.'[75] If it occasionally appears that the moral

---

[70] 'Assiduitas ergo amandi et obsequendi contulit usum, et ille versus in habitum me semper amare compellit etiam non amantes': *Letters of John of Salisbury* II 512.

[71] The notion of an *altera natura* is discussed at *Policraticus* 489b and in *Letters* II 144.

[72] 'Hic autem virtutes et vitia aeque complectitur, licet vitia non mores esse sed a plerisque dicantur moribus obviare': *Policraticus* 545a.

[73] 'Bonus tamen aut malos dicimus mores, vitia distinguimus et virtutes': *ibid.* 545a.

[74] 'In quo planum est solas virtutes censeri nomine morum.... Unde *moratos* a bono sive *morigeros*': *ibid.* 545a.

[75] '...iniustitia mentis habitus quae a regione morum exterminat aequitatem': *ibid.* 537c.

psychology of *habitus* is asymmetrical, pertaining only to virtue, then this is merely the result of an ambiguity in a common usage of moral language.

John's presentation of *habitus* improves in important ways upon the treatment found in Abelard. Yet John's investigations do not represent the pinnacle of twelfth-century thought about *habitus*. John's conception of *habitus* is neither systematic nor rigorous. He takes for granted the answers to a wide range of philosophical questions about the relationship between *habitus* and nature which later thinkers felt compelled to address. Perhaps this lack of interest in a full philosophical treatment of *habitus* resulted from his primarily practical interest in the concept. But this left the way open for significant elaboration and examination of Aristotle's theory of moral character.

*
* *

By the last third of the twelfth century, the dominant definition of moral properties (and especially of virtue) involved reference to *habitus*. As Lottin has shown, even the proponents of essentially theological ideas of ethics had by the late 1100s accepted terminology associated with Aristotelian moral psychology.[76] But the extent to which the doctrine of *habitus* influenced twelfth-century moral thought can perhaps best be judged from the level of sophistication with which it was applied to the analysis of ethical problems. The later 1100s saw efforts to clarify and refine a *habitus*-based approach to morals, so as to generate a systematic account of ethical experience and conduct along fundamentally Aristotelian lines. This entailed both deepening the appreciation of *habitus* itself and delineating the relationship between *habitus* and other issues within moral theory. It was simple enough to define virtue as the *habitus* of a well-ordered soul or mind, a formula to which many twelfth-century authors subscribed. It was far more difficult to undertake a philosophical exploration of the significance of this definition, as Simon of Tournai and Alan of Lille attempted ca. 1170. In his so-called *Tractatus de virtutibus et de vitiis et de donis Spiritus Sancti*, Alan initiated a comprehensive review of current moral ideas with the apparent goal of reconciling discordant views.[77] Many of Alan's conclusions were echoed and amplified in a disputation by Simon on the foundations of virtue.[78] Taken together, these works

---

[76] Lottin, *Psychologie et morale* III ii 105 and n. 5.

[77] The full text of the *Tractatus* is edited in Lottin, *Psychologie et morale* VI 45–92. Translations from this text are mine. On the *Tractatus* and its place in twelfth-century ethics, see P. Delhaye, 'La vertu et les vertus dans les œuvres d'Alain de Lille,' *Cahiers de civilisation médiévale x^e–xiie siècles* 6 (1963) 13–25.

[78] For Simon's disputation, see Lottin, *Psychologie et morale* III ii 106–9. The translation is mine.

testify to the thorough understanding of *habitus* that had emerged in moral philosophy before the close of the twelfth century.

The desire of both Alan and Simon to elucidate virtue in terms of *habitus* drove them back to the *Organon* and to the other available sources of the doctrine. These authors concentrated upon Aristotle's categorization of the genus of *habitus* as quality. Since virtue falls within the genus of *habitus* and *habitus* is a type of quality, Alan and Simon stress that ultimately 'the genus of virtue is the category of quality.'[79] This claim is significant in helping to determine when virtue can properly be ascribed to an agent. Simon explains that a quality (such as *dispositio*) 'that is easily moved over a length of time is not called virtue, unless it is changed into a tenacious *habitus*. So virtue does not seem to be changeable, but is durable.'[80] The attribution of a *habitus* is thereby impossible 'when, in the use of a quality over time, a man fluctuates perpetually between the use of the quality or not; this quality is called disposition; when one assents constantly to the use of the quality of the soul, this is called a tenacious *habitus*, even though a quality is not used perpetually but only at times.'[81] Anything less than complete constancy and regularity of conduct means that a *habitus* cannot be assigned to an individual. The *intention* to act in a certain fashion is not a sufficient criterion for the possession of a *habitus* (and thus a moral quality). To illustrate this point, Alan cites St. Paul's remark in Romans (7.18) that ' "although the will to do good is there, the performance is not"; such a disposition is not *habitus* and therefore it is not virtue. But when the person has the will to persevere efficaciously, so that he has the will in no way to retreat from what is willed, then in that instance, it is not a disposition but a *habitus* and therefore a virtue.'[82] To have a *habitus* is not merely to have the will or desire to perform a particular kind of act, but it is actually to do so. The possession of *habitus* can be ascribed solely to that person whose will to act in a given fashion is unfailing and unflagging.

Hence, as Simon insists, the existence of a *habitus* places an individual beyond susceptibility to external influences and contraints. Indeed, Simon

---

[79] 'Est enim qualitas genere predicamenti': *ibid.* 107. For similar statements, see *ibid.* 106 and Alan, *Tractatus* 47, 49.

[80] 'Que qualitas quamdiu est dispositio facile mobilis non dicitur virtus, sed tunc demum cum versa est in tenacem habitum. Unde virtus non videtur momentanea, sed diuturna': Simon of Tournai (n. 78, *supra*) 106.

[81] 'Quamdiu enim homo fluctuat utrum qualitate perpetuo utatur vel non, cum ad tempus utatur qualitate, qualitas dicitur dispositio; cum vero constanter assentit ut utatur illa qualitate animi, dicitur tenax habitus, quamvis tamen perpetuo non utatur sed ad tempus': *ibid.* 106–7.

[82] 'De qua voluntate dicitur ab Apostolo: *velle adiacet michi, perficere autem bonum non invenio* [Rom. 7.18]; talis dispositio non est habitus, et ideo non est virtus; sed quando habet voluntatem efficaciter perseverandi ita ut habeat voluntatem nullo modo recedendi ab hac voluntate, tunc non est ibi dispositio, sed habitus, et tunc est virtus': Alan, *Tractatus* 49.

says that only when one is indifferent to the conditions and consequences of one's conduct is 'the mind . . . well-ordered towards the sequence of acts which virtue requires.... Yet if a mind is in such good order that, if adversity or prosperity occurs, it is neither weakened by adversity nor exalted by prosperity, then it is said to possess the *habitus* of fortitude. The same judment holds of the other virtues.'[83] The man of real virtue cannot avoid doing as virtue itself demands; he is undeterred in the face of circumstance. The reason for this is that his moral character is rooted in *habitus,* which determines a wholly consistent pattern of conduct.

For all the permanence and stability with which *habitus* endows ethical attributes, it still may be objected that the virtues and vices lack substance, as medieval authors used that word. If moral predicates merely denote acquired qualities, then it is not necessary — but accidental — that human beings have any ethical properties whatsoever. By contrast, if virtue is treated as a natural attribute, moral qualities gain substance, since it is necessary for men to have *some* ethical properties, whatever they may be. An example may help to clarify this distinction. Such qualities as color and texture pertain to the substance of the human body, not in the sense that the body must be one or another color or texture, but that it must have some color or texture. It would be impossible to talk of a human body which had no color or texture whatsoever. On the other hand, it is accidental whether or not a human being possesses the quality of mathematical knowledge or of competency in horseback riding. In other words, just because someone does not know how to add and subtract or to ride a horse does not make that person any less human, because such qualities are not necessary features of man's substance.

In view of the doctrine of *habitus* thus far elucidated, moral qualities would seem to be accidental. The virtues and vices are acquired traits, properties with which humans are not born but which they must learn (and which they may fail to learn) through practical application. This is the way Simon views the matter: 'Virtue is accidental; when it first orders the mind to carry out a required duty with a required end, virtue begins to exist; when the order ceases, virtue is extinguished.... Because virtue sometimes begins to exist and sometimes is extinguished, virtue may therefore be called accidental since it may disappear or appear in formation.'[84] The problem here is that the

---

[83] '... quando mens bene constituta est ad exsequendum quod virtus exigit.... Si tamen mens bona constitutione habilis est ut, si emergat adversitas vel prosperitas, nec frangatur adversis nec extollatur prosperis, dicitur habitu habere fortitudinem. Idem iudicium de ceteris': Simon of Tournai (n. 78, *supra*) 108.

[84] 'Virtus ex accidente; cum enim primo mentem constituit ad exsequendum debitum officium fine debito, incipit esse virtus; cum vero cessat constituere, desinit esse virtus ... quia modo incipit esse virtus, modo desinit esse virtus, ideo virtus dicitur abesse et adesse more accidentis': *ibid.* 107–8.

possession of moral character, if it is purely accidental, loses any connection to what Abelard had earlier termed the 'supreme human good' and the 'supreme human evil.' If men are not ethical creatures *ex natura*, then moral life cannot logically be the route through which they realise their highest and truest earthly end.

Both Alan and Simon seek to respond to this potential objection. Simon proposes the principle that whereas the possession of virtue by particular persons at particular times is indeed accidental, there is still another sense in which virtue is a natural quality, and therefore substantial: 'Nature as a quality of all virtue... is an inborn inclination (*natum aptum*).'[85] Reason provides the model for Simon's identification of the natural aspect of virtue: 'If rationality is of the human substance even though men do not sometimes use reason, then still their inborn inclination is towards the use of reason.'[86] A person does not cease to have the quality of reason even if that quality is seldom or never in evidence. Reason is necessary to being human, regardless of whether any particular man actually employs the reasoning faculty. Indeed, all existing human beings could presumably cease to employ reason simultaneously without altering its ascription as a quality natural to man. Like color, which remains a property of men even if it cannot be seen, the manifestation of reason ought not to be confused with its status as a property of the human substance. And what is true of reason, Simon contends, is equally true of virtue; the qualities of virtue are further instances of *aptum natum*.

Does this mean that resistance to a purely naturalistic account of ethics, observed already in Abelard and John, has been reversed? Indeed not. Rather, Simon's notion of *aptum natum* appears to embrace the full range of moral traits, encompassing vices as well as virtues. Simon's point is not that human beings are by nature either good or evil: 'who has one [moral quality] by nature has all by nature, all good ones as well as all bad ones.'[87] Simon's conclusion is that men must, by their nature, have *some* moral attributes — they necessarily become either virtuous or vicious. But at the same time, which route they follow is an accidental matter. This position alone justifies Simon's declaration that the virtues 'are natural and immobile qualities of man and yet the virtues are accidental.'[88] It is man's nature — hence necessary to him — to be a *moral* agent, although the specific quality of his ethical character (that is, whether his *habitus* is good or bad) is a matter of

---

[85] 'Natura, qualiter omnis virtus habetur ab omni rationali, quia rationale aptum natum est': *ibid.* 108.

[86] 'Si enim rationalitas est homini substantialis licet homo quandoque ratione non utatur, quia tamen aptus natus est ad utendum ratione': *ibid.* 107.

[87] 'Qui ergo habet unam natura, et omnes natura, ut omnes tam boni quam mali': *ibid.* 108–9.

[88] '... esse naturales qualitates homini et immobiles et ex accidenti esse virtutes': *ibid.* 108.

accident, since it is natural neither that man be good nor that he be evil, but simply that his behavior have a moral dimension.

Alan's discussion of the same problem delves deeper into the relationship between nature and *habitus*. Alan begins with two ostensibly contrasting and perhaps incongruent views about virtue: that virtue is a quality, as asserted by Aristotle, and that virtue is natural, as held by Cicero (and derived from the Stoics). Alan asks: is there any possible interpretation of these positions that renders them consistent? He responds by suggesting that quality itself be reconsidered: 'Virtue must be conferred on the soul by creation, not such that what is conferred is virtue, but quality. Virtues are accidental to one, but quality is substantial.'[89] Alan claims that men are not born with any particular moral traits. Instead, they all naturally possess a receptivity to the acquisition of *some* ethical characteristics. It is this receptivity that constitutes man's inborn quality: men have an inclination to be virtuous in the sense that they are by nature capable of or suited to virtue. This is a point that Aristotle had originally stressed, when he said that men are born with a natural capacity ($\delta\acute{v}\nu\alpha\mu\iota\varsigma$) for virtue. Alan's term for such a natural predisposition is 'potentiality': 'Virtues are natural potentials of rational creatures introduced by creation. Just as the ability to walk or to be rational is a human potential introduced by creation, so the potential of men not to be exalted in prosperity or to weaken in adversity, and the potential to return to others what belongs to them, is given to men by creation.'[90] But Alan emphasises that the possession of a potential to be virtuous is not to be confused with the possession of the virtue itself. All men enjoy their potential because they are natural creatures, but the potential within them must still be realised. Thus, an individual is never called 'brave' or 'temperate' or 'just' *by nature*, 'although a man by nature has the potential' to be any of these things. For a man's moral condition 'to be designated as courageous, just, or temperate, ... such designations should pertain to the use of the potential rather than to the potential itself.'[91] Alan introduces here a distinction of considerable importance in contending that the ascription of virtue can be made only when there is evidence of its exercise. For that can never be left to nature alone.

---

[89] 'A creatione confertur anime virtus; non tamen quod confertur est virtus, sed qualitas. Accidentale est enim ei esse virtutem, sed substantiale est esse qualitatem': Alan, *Tractatus* 47.

[90] 'Sunt enim virtutes naturales potentie rationali creature a creatione indite. Sicut enim gressibilitas vel rationalitas est potentia homini indita a creatione, ita potentia non elevandi prosperis vel frangendi adversis, potentia reddendi quod suum est, est homini a creatione indite': *ibid.* 47.

[91] 'Sed quamvis homo a natura habeat has potentias, tamen adveniente etate non denominatur ab eis fortis, iustus, temperatus, quia huiusmodi denominationes potius sumuntur ab usu potentie quam a potentia': *ibid.* 48.

When individuals are said to possess 'virtue,' Alan comments, 'this should predicate the use of potential rather than the potential use.'[92] Every human being is by nature potentially virtuous or capable of virtue, but whether someone is actually virtuous can be judged only from particular actions.

For this reason *habitus* plays a pivotal role in the formation of moral character. As that specific type of quality which ensures the permanence and regularity of action, *habitus* represents a mediating force so that 'the potentiality may become virtue'; it stands midway between *natura* and *usus*.[93] By the formation of *habitus*, the potential which is within all human natures is brought to fruition according to the sort of education received. A properly educated soul will realise its potential for goodness by performing virtuous acts; likewise, a poorly fashioned psyche will generate vicious behavior.[94] Alan clearly acknowledges the centrality of the educative process in the transformation of natural potential into moral action:

> A man should be called courageous not from the potential with which he is born to do this or that, but from the use of the potential; and when he reaches the age of discretion, if a man uses well his potential called courage or prudence, then he is said to be courageous or prudent. And before the age of discretion, a man is not said to have virtues, as he has them not as virtues but as potentials.[95]

The sense in which we may speak of moral qualities as 'natural,' according to Alan, is narrowly limited to a passive receptivity of the soul to training and formation. Men are by nature ethical because they cannot avoid acquiring some set of moral traits — whether good or bad. But while men cannot prevent their moral life from taking shape, the particular direction that the process follows is contingent upon the formation of *habitus*, and thereby accidental. Human beings actively determine for themselves the general pattern of their moral character.

The positions adopted by Alan and Simon do not diverge from the basic insights of predecessors like Abelard and John of Salisbury. Despite their references to 'natural virtue,' Alan and Simon both ultimately maintain an anthropocentric perspective in which men are active participants in their own moral growth. But these later twelfth-century figures contribute a philosophical sophistication to the basic Aristotelian doctrine of *habitus* which was

---

[92] 'Ista enim potius predicant usum potentiarum quam poɩentias usuum': *ibid.* 48.

[93] 'Videamus ergo que concurrunt ad hoc ut potentia virtus sit': *ibid.* 48.

[94] See *ibid.* 50.

[95] 'Homo non dicitur fortis a potentia illa qua aptus est ad hoc vel illud faciendum, sed potius ab usu potentie; unde, cum ventum est ad annos discretionis, si homo utitur illa potentia bene que dicitur fortitudo vel illa que dicitur prudentia, fortis vel prudens dicitur. Unde ante annos discretionis, virtutes homo habere non dicitur, cum non habeat eas ut virtutes, sed ut potentias': *ibid.* 48.

previously not so evident. For them the notion of *habitus,* when set within the broader perspective afforded by considerations of nature and action, becomes a lively and valuable concept, instead of merely part of a formulaic definition of virtue. In the works of Simon and Alan the Aristotelian tradition of *habitus* achieved maturity.

*
*   *

Scholars have generally overlooked the fact that *habitus* and a wide range of other concepts associated with Aristotelian moral philosophy[96] were available to authors before the recovery of the Nicomachean Ethics. They have consequently failed to appreciate the extent and depth of Aristotle's influence on twelfth-century ethics. When viewed from the perspective of conventional historical wisdom, the dissemination of the doctrine of *habitus,* a moral idea of demonstrably Aristotelian provenance, between the 1120s and the 1170s could not occur. In this sense, the presence of an Aristotelian component in twelfth-century ethical philosophy represents a sort of 'underground' tradition of learning. This is not to say that the medieval adherents to the tradition in question were unaware of their intellectual debt. As I have tried to show, Aristotle is explicitly cited as the primary authority on matters touching on the relation between *habitus* and virtue (although the impact of intermediary figures such as Boethius and Cicero is also evident). Rather, by referring to an 'underground' tradition of Aristotelian moral thought in the twelfth century, I maintain that the availability of Aristotle's ethical writings is not the sole criterion for detecting the presence of his ethical doctrines.

Strange as it may seem to speak about an 'underground' tradition, the need for such a term arises from assumptions generally shared by intellectual historians. Scholars are inclined to presume an intimate connection between the availability of certain texts and the awareness of specific ideas. Thus it is assumed that medieval thinkers required access to Aristotle's *Organon* before they could be familiar with the principles of his logic and to the *Nicomachean Ethics* before they could know the outlines of his moral philosophy. Yet as the case of Aristotle's moral psychology illustrates, medieval authors were able to reconstruct large parts of his moral thought in the absence of any direct access to the ethical treatises within his *corpus.* By assembling together and drawing deductions from available texts they managed to recover a significant body of supposedly inaccessible Aristotelian concepts. The rationale for talking in terms of an 'underground' tradition is thus to stress the need for a more sensitive approach to the treatment of the dissemination of ideas during the Middle Ages.

---

[96] See C. J. Nederman, 'Aristotelian Ethics before the *Nicomachean Ethics:* Sources of Aristotle's Concept of Virtue in the Twelfth Century,' *Parergon* N.S. 5 (1989) 55–75.

110

One would never deny that the reception of the complete text of the *Nicomachean Ethics* was the ultimate prerequisite for the emergence of a full range of Aristotelian jargon in moral studies. The most significant accomplishment of twelfth-century thinkers was to translate the meagre Aristotelian materials which they knew into a comprehensive account of how men as temporal creatures acquire and employ their moral traits apart from God and nature. The striking anthropocentrism which characterises the adaptation of Aristotle's idea of *habitus* by these authors reflects the sophistication with which they drew from and built upon many aspects of classical learning.

IV

To the court and back again: the origins and dating of the *Entheticus de Dogmate Philosophorum* of John of Salisbury

CARY J. NEDERMAN and ARLENE FELDWICK

I

John of Salisbury's 1852-line satirical and philosophical poem, the *Entheticus de Dogmate Philosophorum* (or *Entheticus Maior*) must surely rank among the most closely studied texts in recent scholarship on the twelfth century. No fewer than six critical editions of this work were produced in the period from 1954 to 1987, the latest and definitive version consisting of three volumes of text, critical apparatus, commentary, and translation.[1] One might assume that such careful attention would have generated a great amount of knowledge about the nature of the poem and the circumstances of its composition. Yet in many ways we are still as uncertain about these aspects of the *Entheticus Maior* as we have ever been.

The persisting problems posed by the *Entheticus Maior* are of two sorts. First, there has been little effort to delineate the purpose for which the poem was composed. The question raised by Rodney Thomson at the 1980 John of Salisbury conference—"What is the *Enthet-*

---

1. These are Christopher Elrington, "John of Salisbury's *Entheticus de dogmate philosophorum*: The Light It Throws on the Educational Background of the Twelfth Century" (unpublished thesis, University of London, 1954); Phyllis Barzillay, "The *Entheticus de dogmate philosophorum* of John of Salisbury: An Analysis and Translation" (unpublished thesis, Hunter College, 1959); Samuel Buckley, "*Entheticus de dogmate philosophorum* of John of Salisbury: A Translation and Critical Study" (unpublished thesis, Tulane University, 1965); Daniel Sheerin, "John of Salisbury's *Entheticus de dogmate philosophorum*: Critical Text and Introduction" (unpublished thesis, University of North Carolina at Chapel Hill, 1969); Ronald E. Pepin, "The *Entheticus* of John of Salisbury: A Critical Edition and Commentary" (unpublished thesis, Fordham University, 1973) (the critical text prepared by Pepin was published in *Traditio* 31 [1975]: 127–93 and was emended by J. B. Hall, "Notes on the *Entheticus* of John of Salisbury," *Traditio* 39 [1983]: 444–47, while Pepin's translation and commentary were published in *Allegorica* 9 [Winter 1987]: 7–133); and Jan van Laarhoven, *John of Salisbury's "Entheticus maior and minor,"* 3 vols. (Leiden: E. J. Brill, 1987).

icus?"–is really no closer to receiving a final or satisfactory solution.[2] Second, a precise and plausible dating of the text remains elusive. While scholars have proposed various chronologies, there is no general agreement about when John in fact wrote the work.

The present paper seeks to address these problems by arguing that the dating and purpose of the *Entheticus* are interlinked. First, we claim that the poem in its extant version was completed prior to John's famous disgrace at the court of Henry II (in later 1156 and 1157), and therefore in no way reflects the experiences that were to shape his composition of the *Policraticus* and *Metalogicon*. Instead, the entire *Entheticus* constitutes John's articulation of a code of conduct, a kind of courtly *De officiis*,[3] addressed to Thomas Becket in particular. Second, we wish to defend the more specific view that the completion of the *Entheticus* occurred in the period between the appointment of Becket as royal chancellor (December 1154) and Easter of the following year, that is, during a period when the expectations of John and his Canterbury colleagues for Becket's adherence to the cause of Archbishop Theobald were at their highest. Insofar as this narrower frame of composition can be established, the *Entheticus* may be viewed quite concretely as a farewell gift and instructional manual for Becket as he undertook his new responsibilities at Henry's court. The first thesis is based on a combination of internal and external evidence; the second depends wholly on the interpretive clues contained within the text itself.

II

A broad array of suggestions has been made for the dating of the *Entheticus*, often without especially persuasive evidence. Traditionally, the text has been dated to 1159, roughly contemporaneous with the known year of completion of the *Policraticus* and *Metalogicon*.[4] Occasionally, however, a somewhat earlier date has been proposed: Hans Liebeschütz initially accepted autumn 1158 but later adopted the

2. Rodney Thomson, "What is the *Entheticus?*" in M. Wilks, ed., *The World of John of Salisbury* (Oxford: Basil Blackwell, 1984), 287–301.

3. To adopt Thomson's description, ibid., 295.

4. Clement C. J. Webb, *John of Salisbury* (London: Methuen, 1932), 100; C. N. L. Brooke, introduction to W. J. Millor, H. E. Butler and C. N. L. Brooke, eds., *The Letters of John of Salisbury*, vol. 1 (London: Thomas Nelson, 1955), xlix; and Phyllis Barzillay, "The *Entheticus de dogmate philosophorum* of John of Salisbury," *Medievalia et Humanistica* 16 (1964): 19–20.

hypothesis of autumn 1155 suggested by Christopher Elrington.[5] In fact, looking solely at the internal evidence, the text could have been completed at any time between Becket's appointment as chancellor and the death of Theobald.[6] But two crucial pieces of evidence, either unknown or unconsidered by prior commentators, have come to be taken into account in the most recent literature. First, because of Giles Constable's reliable redating of John's period of disgrace from 1159–60 to 1156–57, as well as some careful textual criticism on the part of Max Kerner, we now have a more accurate picture of John's circumstances in the second half of the 1150s.[7] Second, current scholarship rejects the premise that the entire *Entheticus* was composed at a single time, asserting rather that it was written over a long span of time, although principally during two periods. As Thomson has observed, the first and second sections, containing theological and philosophical reflections, have a markedly different tone and style from the third and fourth parts, which address the moral dangers of court and public life.[8] Thomson ascribes this to a temporal disparity in their composition— the first written during 1155 (or possibly even earlier), the second during the disgrace of 1156–57.[9] Van Laarhoven adopts essentially the same position, but defends the plausibility of the claim that "large portions, at least of Parts I and II, were conceived and written not in England, but already in France, and not by a busy secretary, but by a diligent senior student or *repetitor*," that is, in the early 1140s, prior to John's entry into Theobald's service.[10]

These two factors taken together effectively eliminate the possibility that the *Entheticus* as we have it was written in whole or in part during the final third of the 1150s. But we maintain that even the *terminus a quo* of the disgrace (late 1156 or early 1157) is subject to challenge. Thomson's rationale for this *terminus a quo* is that John's disgrace itself

---

5. Hans Liebeschütz, *Mediaeval Humanism in the Life and Writings of John of Salisbury* (London: The Warburg Institute, 1950), 22; Elrington, "John of Salisbury's *Entheticus de dogmate philosophorum*," 83; Liebeschütz, "Chartres und Bologna: Naturbegriff und Staatsidee bei Johannes von Salisbury," *Archiv für Kulturgeschichte* 50 (1968): 10.

6. As pointed out by van Laarhoven, *Entheticus*, 48.

7. Giles Constable, "The Alleged Disgrace of John of Salisbury in 1159," *English Historical Review* 69 (1954): 67–76; Max Kerner, *Johannes von Salisbury und die logische Struktur seines Policraticus* (Wiesbaden: Franz Steiner, 1977), 114–16 and passim.

8. Thomson, "What is the *Entheticus?*" 294–95; van Laarhoven, *Entheticus*, 50–51.

9. Thomson, "What is the *Entheticus?*" 295.

10. Van Laarhoven, *Entheticus*, 51.

"lies behind the change of tone between section II and III of the *Entheticus.* . . . As a consequence, the *Entheticus*, which was begun as an exhortation to public men to regulate their actions according to the precepts of the ancient philosophers, ended as a semi-private statement of John's own philosophic principles, and at his bitterness at his—and their—rejection by the court."[11] While, in our view, Thomson is correct to emphasize the differences that divide the various sections of the poem, his dating of the third and fourth parts to 1156–57 cannot be sustained. Rather, when judged on the basis of the available historical and literary evidence, the text in its extant version seems more likely to have been completed prior to the disgrace, that is, before the middle of 1156.

To understand this assertion, it is necessary first of all to appreciate the *Entheticus* in the context of some of the salient experiences of its author and the Canterbury court generally during the latter half of the 1150s. This is particularly relevant insofar as the poem is primarily (if perhaps not exclusively) addressed to Thomas Becket at the time he served Henry II.[12] The importance of Becket to the poem can be established quite independently of the addition to the *explicit* of the exemplar manuscript British Library, Royal 13 D. IV, which reads "editus ad Thomam cancellarium postea Cantuariensem archiepiscopum," or "written for Thomas the chancellor, later archbishop of Canterbury" (an emendation made in another hand, probably between 1162 and 1170).[13] For reference is made to Becket in undisguised or thinly veiled terms throughout the text, especially in section 3, where the chancellor is described as the commissioner and "patron" of the poem.[14] Thus the relations between the Canterbury and royal courts, and between John and Becket, are crucial to locating the *Entheticus* both temporally and intellectually.

Becket's appointment as royal chancellor soon after Henry II's coronation was quite clearly engineered by Archbishop Theobald, probably as recompense for the support of Canterbury for the Angevin cause in the later stages of the war against King Stephen.[15] Theobald was anxious that the new king should be more respectful of the liberties

11. Thomson, "What is the *Entheticus?*" 295.

12. Van Laarhoven, *Entheticus*, 48–49, 51–52.

13. Cited by Thomson, "What is the *Entheticus?*" 290.

14. *Entheticus*, ll. 1291, 1459, 1515, and 1531; this text will be cited from van Laarhoven's critical edition. Translations are also van Laarhoven's.

15. Avrom Saltman, *Theobald, Archbishop of Canterbury* (London: The Athlone Press, 1956), 168.

of the church and of the archiepiscopacy than had been his predecessor.[16] As an especially capable and loyal servant of Canterbury, Becket no doubt seemed ideal to Theobald as an advocate of ecclesiastical prerogatives and metropolitan rights.

Yet, as scholars today generally attest, Becket's arrival at Henry's court occasioned a rapid transformation both in the churchman's personal habits and in his political allegiances.[17] Beyond the new chancellor's sudden taste for luxurious apparel and grooming, three events during his initial eighteen months in office suggest the frustration of Theobald's hopes. First, Becket served his royal master faithfully in the early stage of the conflict between Hilary, Bishop of Chichester, and Battle Abbey over the authenticity of the abbey's royal charters. Although the controversy was to reach a climax in 1157, it originated in Henry's decision during Lent 1155 first to confirm, then to deny, and finally to confirm once again the clearly fraudulent charters in spite of Theobald's strenuous objections.[18] Becket followed Henry's orders precisely and without question, showing no inclination to influence the king or to use the uncertainties of the situation in support of Canterbury's position. A similar failure to rally to the cause of Canterbury may be observed in the scutage of early 1156. Henry ordered a special tax to finance the armed suppression of his brother, Geoffrey, and commanded its application to ecclesiastical as well as secular properties. Theobald complained loudly about the infringement of church liberties entailed by this scutage, but to no avail.[19] While we do not know the extent of Becket's involvement in levying the tax,[20] he certainly did nothing to change Henry's mind about the imposition; and we are reliably informed that Becket was active in promoting and conducting the campaign against Geoffrey.[21] A final reason for Theobald's rapid disenchantment with the chancellor was afforded by the so-called second aid controversy. Sometime in mid-1156, Thomas, in his unrelinquished role as archdeacon of Canterbury, apparently announced a tax on the churches of the diocese to be imposed on top of Theobald's own exaction. Since the only motive for

16. David Knowles, *Thomas Becket* (London: Adam and Charles Black, 1970), 27–29.
17. Ibid., 39–42; Christopher Brooke, "Thomas Becket," in idem, *Medieval Church and Society: Collected Essays* (London: Sidgwick and Jackson, 1971), 124–25; and Frank Barlow, *Thomas Becket* (London: Weidenfeld and Nicolson, 1982), 44–45.
18. Barlow, *Thomas Becket*, 49–50.
19. Saltman, *Theobald*, 43–44.
20. Knowles, *Thomas Becket*, 46.
21. Ibid., 37.

this levy was personal enrichment, Theobald prohibited its collection and virtually accused the chancellor of placing desire for material wealth above concern for eternal salvation.[22] In sum, by mid-1156 Theobald had considerable reason to doubt the trustworthiness of Becket in matters pertaining to the interests of the archiepiscopacy and the church.

To these considerations should be appended the evidence of the more personal relations between John and Thomas. Scholars have too often been tempted to postulate a close friendship between the two men because of their nearness of age, their almost simultaneous studies in Paris and employment at Canterbury, and their later association in the time of Becket's archiepiscopacy.[23] But little documentary evidence exists for such a relationship.[24] Even if John and Thomas knew each other well in Paris and maintained this friendship during their years of service to Theobald,[25] there is reason to suppose that feelings cooled during the early years of Becket's chancellorship. After 1155, Becket was almost constantly in the king's company, which kept him away from England from January 1156 to April 1157 and again after August 1158.[26] This distance doubtless contributed to a lack of intimacy which was felt, for instance, in John's attitude towards Thomas at the time of his disgrace. In spite of the chancellor's powerful influence with the king, John declined to approach Thomas directly for assistance in assuaging Henry. Rather, John pleaded with Becket's secretary, Ernulf, to intercede with his master.[27] Nor may any special relationship be inferred from Thomas's eventual treatment of John upon his accession to the see of Canterbury. John's role in Theobald's household, which had been greatly increased as the archbishop's illness became more debilitating during the late 1150s,[28] was indeed diminished upon Becket's election. Thomas seems to have favored his more recent intimates

22. See *The Letters of John of Salisbury*, Ep. 22; this should be compared with John's private reassurances to Becket about his own noncomplicity at Ep. 28.

23. For example, Mario dal Pra, *Giovanni di Salisbury* (Milan: Fratelli Bocca, 1951), 16; also J. J. N. McGurk, "John of Salisbury," *History Today* 25 (1975): 46.

24. Knowles, *Thomas Becket*, 27.

25. Ibid., 47–48; Barlow, *Thomas Becket*, 20, 32–33.

26. Ibid., 48.

27. *The Letters of John of Salisbury*, Ep. 28; on this incident, see Barlow, *Thomas Becket*, 49.

28. John of Salisbury, *Metalogicon*, ed. C. C. J. Webb (Oxford: Clarendon Press, 1929), IV.42: "Siquidem pater meus et dominus, immo et tuus, venerabilis Teobaldus, Cantuariensis archiepiscopu in egritudinem incidit, ut incertum sit quid sperare, quid timere opporteat. Negotiis more solito superesse non potest; iniunxitque michi provinciam duram, et importabile onus imposuit, omnium ecclesiasticorum sollicitudinem."

over close associates of Theobald such as John.[29] On the whole, the judgment of van Laarhoven must be sustained: "We ought not to repeat the anachronism of so many authors, medieval as well as modern, who refer the future to the past and relocate John's later relations with Thomas to a time when the latter was mostly abroad with his king and the former at his desk in the archbishop's house or journeying to the papal curia."[30] And even such later relations were themselves more tenuous than is often supposed; John was comparatively slow to identify himself fully with the cause of Becket in the 1160s.[31]

These historical factors point to the distancing of the members of the Canterbury curia from Becket in the months prior to John's disgrace. Yet the *Entheticus* reflects little sense of such estrangement. On the contrary, the poem consistently suggests that the chancellor is on the very best terms with his metropolitan, and indeed is serving more or less directly as an agent of Theobald's interests. This is expressed most clearly in John's introductory remarks to part 3:

> Qui iubet, ut scribas, solet idem scripta fovere,
>   quaeque semel recipit nomina, clara facit.
> Ille Theobaldus, qui Christi praesidet aulae,
>   quam fidei matrem Cantia nostra colit,
> hunc successurum sibi sperat, et orat, ut idem
>   praesulis officium muniat atque locum.
> Hic est, carnificium qui ius cancellat iniquum,
>   quos habuit reges Anglia capta diu. . . .
>
> (ll. 1291-98)

> He who orders you to write, the same one is wont to encourage
>   writings, and once he receives names, he makes them famous.
> That Theobald who presides in the court of Christ
>   which our Kent honours as the mother of faith,
> hopes that this man will succeed him and he prays that the same
>   will strengthen the office and position of bishop.
> He is the one who cancels the unjust law of the butchers
>   whom captive England has for a long time had as kings. . . .

29. Anne Duggan, "John of Salisbury and Thomas Becket," in Wilks, ed., *The World of John of Salisbury*, 428.
30. Van Laarhoven, *Entheticus*, 49.
31. See the careful analysis by John McLoughlin, "The Language of Persecution: John of Salisbury and the Early Phase of the Becket Dispute (1163-66)," *Studies in Church History* 21 (1984): 73-87.

That the chancellor (*cancellarius*) is meant here is evident from the pun on the "cancellation" of iniquitous rights. Becket is identified by John as Theobald's heir apparent, the person who may be counted upon to defend and protect the see and its authority within the realm. John's reference to "ius iniquum" in the context of the passage implies that Thomas is restoring specifically those ecclesiastical rights which had been eroded under Stephen. Indeed, this represents the fulfillment of Henry's promise in his coronation charter to abolish the evil customs that had been instituted under his predecessor.[32] Although John believes that Becket may be "frustra" in his efforts to defend the rights of the kingdom, he nevertheless asserts that "cancellarius instet, ut mutet mores aula superba suos" (the chancellor is striving that the proud court should change its customs; ll. 1485–86). This is the sort of conduct one would expect of Theobald's designated successor, not the faithful royal servant that Becket had certainly become by 1156.

In general, the claims of the *Entheticus* about Becket grow increasingly implausible the later the date one ascribes to the text. For example, John views Thomas as ingratiating himself into the royal court in order to further Canterbury's goals:

> Tristior haec cernit iuris defensor, et artem,
>   qua ferat auxilium consiliumque, parat.
> Ut furor illorum mitescat, dissimulare
>   multa solet, simulat, quod sit et ipse furens;
> omnibus omnia fit; specietenus induit hostem,
>   ut paribus studiis discat amare Deum. . . .
> Hac igitur ratione tui mens sana patroni,
>   ut patienter eum perferat aula furens,
> conciliare studet sibi conviventis amorem
>   turbae, ne peragat ebria mortis iter.
>
>   (ll. 1435–40, 1459–62)

> Very sadly the defender of law perceives these things, and he
>   plans a method by which he may bring help and advice.
> In order that their savageness may grow more gentle, he usually
>   feigns many things, he simulates that he himself is also
>   savage;

32. William Stubbs, ed., *Select Charters and Other Illustrations of English Constitutional History*, 9th ed. (Oxford: Clarendon, 1913), 158.

> he becomes all things to all people; in appearance only he
>   assumes the role
> of the enemy, in order that he may learn with equal zeal
>   how to love God. . . .
> In this manner, then, in order that the mad court may patiently
>   endure
> him, the sound mind of your patron takes
> pains to win over to himself the love of the feasting crowd
>   with whom
>   he lives, so that it may not drunkenly complete the journey
>   of death.

One must resist the temptation to attribute remarkable foresight to John. It is simply anachronistic to read these lines in a hagiographical manner as a rationalization or justification of Becket's behavior prior to his investiture.[33] Rather, John seems to be referring to Becket at a time when his commitments to Henry might still be deemed superficial, that is, when there remained reason to suppose that loyal service to the crown did not reflect the chancellor's genuine sentiments. It is precisely for this reason that John warns against *garrulitas*: he imagines that Becket's ultimate dedication to Theobald and Canterbury may be divulged and his usefulness diminished by loose talk in support of the cause of true religion (ll. 1495–1512). Such concern to hide the chancellor's genuine loyalties points to the earliest period of his career in the king's service, when he was still expected to champion archiepiscopal policies.[34]

Further evidence for an early dating of the *Entheticus* is suggested by its relatively slight attention to the vice of avarice. In the *Policraticus* and *Entheticus Minor*, both of which are also explicitly addressed to Becket, John places special emphasis upon the dangers of avaricious conduct among courtiers and churchmen and warns of the perils that await the greedy.[35] By contrast, as van Laarhoven has observed, the

33. Barlow, *Thomas Becket*, 45.

34. As Brooke, "Thomas Becket," 131 remarks: "At times, it seems, Henry might have been inclined to suspect that Becket was in some measure Theobald's spy in his household. Such was the nature of patronage in the Middle Ages that the suspicion could not be entirely false: the Archbishop had certainly expected help from Becket, who was his archdeacon as well as the King's Chancellor."

35. *Policraticus*, ed. C. C. J. Webb (Oxford: Clarendon, 1919; reprint, Frankfurt am Main: Minerva, 1965), 7.16–17, 7.23, 8.4, 8.13, and passim; *Entheticus in Policraticum*, ll. 263–98.

Entheticus Maior concentrates upon "the vice of 'vainglory' . . . , mainly in connection with ambitious philosophers and idle teachers."[36] Since Becket's reputation for avarice grew markedly in the wake of the "second aids" controversy, one might suppose that any text composed by John for Thomas after 1156 would have paid particular attention to the sin of cupidity. The thematic distance between the *Entheticus Maior* and later writings in this regard hints at the composition of the former before Becket's avaricious traits became clearly apparent.

Thematic analysis of the *Entheticus* indicates the likelihood of its pre-disgrace composition in other ways as well. If Thomson is correct that the differences between the second and third sections reflect John's political disillusionment in the wake of his clash with Henry, then some serious problems are posed. For instance, a post-disgrace dating renders the poem of a piece with the *Policraticus*, which we know was begun in the second half of 1156.[37] If John was hard at work on parts 3 and 4 during the autumn, why did he almost immediately commence the meditations on human fortune that formed the first segments of what would eventually become the *Policraticus*? The *Entheticus* is far less introspective in tone and substance than the *Policraticus*; it is a work of advice to another (or others) rather than of the self-consolation suggested by a concentration on fortune. The *Entheticus* addresses fortune in extended fashion only once, for fourteen lines in part 1 (251–64), which may have been composed as early as the 1140s. Given such a disparity between the two texts, it seems more plausible to posit the experience of disgrace as an intervening factor. The poem's concerns about earthly corruption serve to illuminate its author's moral lessons, not to assuage his private agonies.

Thomson's thesis also leaves unexplained John's prolific output between mid-1156 and late 1159. Apart from the disgrace period itself, John was a busy administrator, increasingly so with Theobald's ill health, and a diplomatic envoy whose time and opportunity for writing were doubtless severely constrained, as he himself reports in the *Policraticus*.[38] To add the *Entheticus Maior* to the already lengthy

---

36. Van Laarhoven, *Entheticus*, 86–87.
37. For a full account of the apparent order of composition of the *Policraticus*, see ibid., 49 n. 52.
38. *Policraticus*, 7, prologue: "Et in his, quae propriae voluntatis et sapientiae instinctu gerenda sunt, michi vix tempus indulgeatur ad pauca. Dies et non necessariis et alienis occupationibus transiguntur ut nec rei familiari curam impendere liceat; et tu hortaris ut scribam?"

list of works composed in the aftermath of the disgrace is to strain credulity.

But perhaps the greatest difficulty arising from a dating after the middle of 1156 is the lingering fascination of the *Entheticus* with the reign of Stephen and its relative lack of commentary on Henry's court. In its one unambiguous reference to the Angevin ruler, the poem warns against the dangers presented by "nova curia rege sub puero" (ll. 1463–64). The use of the term *puer* in and of itself is by no means evidence of the age of Henry or of the date of the text, as van Laarhoven's analysis demonstrates.[39] But the coupling of *puer* with *nova curia* (upon which van Laarhoven makes no remark) erases much of the uncertainty: Henry is clearly in the earliest stages of his reign, when his court had only recently been formed. By contrast, John has much to say about the rule of Stephen, whose identity scholars have consistently detected in the pseudonym of "Hircanus the tyrant."[40] Hircanus himself earns more than fifty lines of poetic condemnation (ll. 1301–54), while his courtiers are reviled to an even greater extent (ll. 1363–1434). In spite of Ronald Pepin's suggestion that "Hircanus" is a pun on "Henricus,"[41] John's pseudonymous character is clearly a king whose reign has ended; the past tense is employed throughout the passage in question. And the description of Hircanus's negligence accords closely with John's description of the chaos of Stephen's reign in the *Policraticus*.[42] That Stephen should be the central target of John's wrath seems strange if the finished *Entheticus* was stimulated by its author's banishment from court. An earlier date of composition, which locates the text in the initial eighteen months of Henry's rule, more adequately explains the focus upon Stephen rather than his successor. The evil customs and policies (especially towards the Church) initiated by Stephen constituted a far more tangible threat in the minds of the Canterbury circle than any potential machinations on the part of the "boy king" whose accession had enjoyed the support of the archbishop and who was presumed to be under the guidance of Theobald's faithful minion, Becket. For John, the situation would have

39. Van Laarhoven, *Entheticus*, 389.
40. Ibid., 377–78; Barzillay, "The *Entheticus de dogmate philosophorum*," 20–21 and n. 77; Liebeschütz, *Mediaeval Humanism*, 21–22.
41. Ronald E. Pepin, "John of Salisbury's *Entheticus* and the Classical Tradition of Satire," *Florilegium* 3 (1981): 221.
42. This has been examined by Cary J. Nederman, "The Changing Face of Tyranny: The Reign of King Stephen in John of Salisbury's Political Thought," *Nottingham Medieval Studies* 33 (1989): 3–20.

140

changed slowly over the course of 1156 and crystallized with the disgrace: thereafter Henry and his court could no longer be trusted to act in the interests of the Church and its loyal servants. Only if we accept the *Entheticus* as a work of 1155 or early 1156 can large segments of the text be understood in a historically coherent manner.

III

There are two features of the *Entheticus* that mark it as a coherent poetical work: one is stylistic, the other narrative. Its unifying stylistic thread stems from a technique (pioneered by Ovid) called prosopopeia, through which the author addresses his book as though it were a person. As van Laarhoven remarks, the prosopopeia "provided a good way for an author to shield himself behind such a conversation with his brain child, whilst the identity of the true addressee is kept uncertain, being mentioned at the most by allusions."[43] This device accords with the view that Becket is the primary intended audience for the poem's advice, so that when John speaks to his book, giving it instructions and guidance, his words are meant for Becket. Thus, when the book is told "Memor esto tui" (Be mindful of yourself; l. 1851), its author employs a piece of advice identical to that he has already offered to Becket directly (ll. 1515–16), and which he would again offer to him in other writings.[44] And more overtly still, John lectures his text:

> Pontificum regumque parens te Cantia fovit,
> hospitiumque tibi praeparat, immo domum.
> Haec petit, ut redeas et in illa sede quiescas,
> quae caput est regni iustitiaeque domus.
> Parebis matri praesertim recta monenti,
> quaeque tuos tendit perpetuare dies.
>
> (ll. 1637–42)

> Kent, mother of bishops and of kings, has fostered you
> and prepares a hospice for you, or rather a home.
> She asks you to return and to rest in that place
> which is the head of the kingdom and the home of justice.

43. Van Laarhoven, *Entheticus*, 48.
44. See van Laarhoven, *Entheticus*, 423.

You have to obey a mother especially when she admonishes
  right things,
  and who aims to perpetuate your days.

When read in conjunction with the previous remark that Becket was
Theobald's heir apparent, John's application of the prosopopeia technique in this passage is especially transparent. It becomes impossible to
distinguish between the identities of the poem and the chancellor.

The second connecting thread within the *Entheticus* is its recurrent
use of the motif of the journey. This aspect is closely related to the
prosopopeia device, insofar as John couches much of his advice to his
book in terms of guidance to a traveler. In particular, John recommends to his poem the safest mode of conduct while away from home
and warns it about the dangers both of the trip and of the destination.
The travel theme is introduced almost immediately in the prologue:

> Aula novis gaudet, veteres fastidit amicos,
>   sola voluptatis causa lucrique placent.
> Quis venias? quae causa viae? quo tendis? et unde?
>   forsitan inquiret. Pauca, libelle, refer.
>
> (ll. 7–10)

The court delights in new friends and despises its old ones;
  only the cause of pleasure and profit is pleasing.
"Who are you that come, what is the reason for the journey,
  where are you
  going, and whence?" perhaps it will thus inquire. Reply
  briefly, little book.

John then proceeds to discuss the doctrines of truth and virtue that
form the substance of parts 1 and 2. But in parts 3 and 4, the motif of
the book as traveler returns. John first explains to the poem what perils
await it among courtiers, counseling it most especially not to speak
indiscriminately or rashly:

> Aut taceas prorsus, aut pauca loquaris in aula,
>   aut quaeras, in quo rure latere queas;
> nam si non parcis verbis, nemo tibi parcet,
>   praevenietque dies impia turba tuos.
>
> (ll. 1509–12)

142

> Either be utterly silent or speak little at court,
> or find out in what farm you can hide;
> for if you are not sparing in your words, no one will spare you
> and the impious mob will overtake your days.[45]

Dissemblance is promoted as the best course of action for the *Entheticus* until it can have a private word with its patron (who is also engaging in pious dissimulation) and return home to Canterbury (ll. 1513–32). But the journey back will itself be fraught with the temptations of the flesh, which take particular root in those who frequent inns and roadhouses (ll. 1533–1635). The safest place is back home among like-minded men of virtue and wisdom—cloistered but preferably not cowled (ll. 1643–81). Although not even the monastery is entirely free of bad types, it is still more conducive to the health of the soul than any secular court. Finally, having summarized his advice for a safe trip, John sets his poem on its way:

> Sed quid multa moror? properas exire. Videto,
> quid facias; coeptum perfice cautus iter.
>
> (ll. 1849–50)

> But why do I delay longer? you are in a hurry to go. Watch out
> what you may do; carefully complete the journey once
> started.

From virtually beginning to end, the book is portrayed as in the final stages of preparation for its journey. It awaits only John's instructions before its departure.

The convergence of the prosopopeia technique with the traveler motif is highly suggestive for the problem of the dating of the *Entheticus*. For if the book stands in for the chancellor as the recipient of John's advice, and if that advice is couched as guidance for the uninitiated traveler to court (the *novum amico* of John's prologue, l. 7), then attribution of the completion of the *Entheticus* to the period soon after Thomas's departure for court (that is, during Christmastide 1154 or early in the New Year 1155) seems warranted. Indeed, we might speculate that the *Entheticus* was a sort of parting gift to Becket: John was counseling Thomas about how to behave at court so as to advance

---

45. We have slightly altered van Laarhoven's translation.

Canterbury's interests and reminding him that his true home was back among his old circle in the archbishop's household. The poem was thus following in its patron's footsteps (a favorite Salisburian metaphor) along the route to court, but was also mapping out the path for the return journey to Canterbury (possibly as Theobald's successor). It is unreasonable to attribute to John any prescience in the latter regard. Becket's eventual return to Canterbury occurred under quite different circumstances and possibly did not meet with John's wholehearted approval at the time. Rather, the *Entheticus* is best read as John's travel guidebook to the alien world of secular political affairs and a reminder that Becket was not ultimately a member of the temporal realm but instead belonged in the spiritual sphere. That Thomas did not heed this advice, preferring to plunge headlong into the moral corruption of the court, perhaps points to John's sensitivity towards the flaws in his colleague's character.

IV

Regardless of whether one accepts the stronger or the weaker version of our argument, the redating and reinterpretation of the *Entheticus Maior* in the preceding fashion permits us to draw several general conclusions about the career of John of Salisbury. First, we may speak more confidently about the course of John's intellectual development than was possible in the past. Establishing the *Entheticus* as a work of a youthful or innocent period—a period during which John had not yet personally confronted the dangers of courtly intrigue—lends perspective to the process by which its author was eventually to formulate the doctrines of the *Policraticus* and *Metalogicon*. We can begin to appreciate why it became clear to John that a moralistic critique of court and school (such as is offered in the *Entheticus Maior*) was insufficient to counteract the sources of tyrannical and impious attitudes and conduct: what was required was a full-scale blueprint for the renovation of political society and the reform of the curriculum according to which courtly servants such as himself were educated. These needs were fulfilled in John's mature writings, the *Policraticus* and *Metalogicon*. The *Entheticus* thus provides a reliable baseline for judging the direction and extent of the subsequent progress of John's thought.

Our approach to the *Entheticus* also permits us to chart with greater accuracy the course of the relations between John and Becket over two decades. While it may be tempting to depict John as an unwavering supporter of Becket, in the manner of his *Vita Sancti Thomae*,[46] the truth about their relationship seems far more complex. The *Entheticus* demonstrates a confidence in Thomas's loyalty to Canterbury that later events would not bear out. By contrast, John's tone in the *Policraticus* is more reproachful, and he apparently continued to remain skeptical about Becket until well into the 1160s.[47] Only in the later moments of the Becket conflict does John seem to have shrugged off his ambivalence and supported his archbishop without qualification.[48] Thomas's failure to live up to the initial hopes expressed in the *Entheticus* may indeed suggest part of the explanation of why John was so slow to lend Becket his full backing.

Finally, inasmuch as our interpretation of the circumstances surrounding the composition of the *Entheticus*, especially when taken in conjunction with other information about John's attitude towards Thomas, casts doubt upon a close or deep friendship between the pair, we may also draw some more definite conclusions about the nature of John's genuine intellectual commitments. It would appear to be the welfare of Canterbury, rather than any bonds of personal attachment, that stimulated John's advice about courtly conduct in the *Entheticus*. John addresses his counsel to Becket as Theobald's specially selected agent within the royal household and as the designated heir of the archbishop. By contrast, concern on John's part for Thomas's personal well-being is less evident, even at this uncontentious stage in their relationship. The centrality of Canterbury for John is signaled by the very structure of the *Entheticus*: the book, presumably like its patron, is to travel to court and then back again. The return segment of the journey in the traveler motif is invariably the more important one. The prospect of the return to Canterbury—the spiritual home of the English

46. John's hagiographical work has been edited by J. C. Robertson in *Materials for the History of Thomas Becket, Archbishop of Canterbury* (London: Longman, 1870), 2:299–352.

47. This is stressed by both Duggan, "John of Salisbury and Thomas Becket," and McLoughlin, "The Language of Persecution."

48. Even Brooke, who posits a close personal relationship between John and Becket, acknowledges that "John did not wholly trust his old friend" and "felt a deep suspicion about Becket's state of mind" ("Thomas Becket," 131). It is interesting that John expressed his misgivings in his correspondence in terms of the Aristotelian moral doctrines he had articultaed in the *Policraticus*; see Cary J. Nederman, "Aristotelian Ethics and John of Salisbury's Letters," *Viator* 18 (1987): 171–72.

church and of Becket—looms as a constant reminder of the true duties and responsibilities of the chancellor. John of Salisbury's devotion to Canterbury and its circle, which has been so well documented in biographical terms,[49] may consequently be treated as the primary impetus behind his composition of the *Entheticus Maior* as well.[50]

49. In particular, see Klaus Guth, *Johannes von Salisbury (1115/20–1180)* (St. Ottilien: Eos, 1978) and Janet Martin, "Uses of Tradition: Gellius, Petronius, and John of Salisbury," *Viator* 10 (1979): 67-68, 73-76.

50. In a private communication, Rodney Thomson has drawn attention to the "messiness" of the exemplar manuscript as further evidence for our thesis that the *Entheticus Maior* was composed somewhat hurriedly as a parting gift to Becket. Thomson comments: "John, with limited time, packaged up some philosophical verse he'd written in the Schools, with some advice and satire, tying it all together with the 'viator' and 'prosopopeia' motifs. Much later he tinkered with the text again, as witnessed by the annotations in the St. Albans MS." We wish to thank Dr. Thomson for this observation, as well as for many other generous suggestions regarding a draft of the present essay.

V

The Changing Face of Tyranny:
The Reign of King Stephen in John of Salisbury's
Political Thought*

I

Not so many years ago, it was fashionable to treat the writings of John of Salisbury as works unrelated to their place and time, as the anachronistic products of a classical mind whose intellectual connections with his own age were tenuous at best.[1] Fortunately, the scholarly tide seems to have turned definitively since the Second World War, due in large measure to a better understanding of John's intellectual and political career,[2] the immediate circumstances in which he wrote,[3] the potential audience for his compositions,[4] and the nature of the sources to which he had access and upon which he relied.[5] None of this is to dismiss or trivialize the importance of John's vast (for its day) classical knowledge. On the contrary, it is to recognise that John, so far from pursuing classical learning for its own sake, studied the wisdom of the ancients as a key to unlock solutions to the political and intellectual controversies which engulfed the twelfth century.

---

* An earlier version of this essay was presented to the Twelfth International Conference on Patristic, Medieval and Renaissance Studies, Villanova University, October 1987. It has benefited from suggestions made by Professors Conal Condren and Kate Forhan, as well as by the readers for the present journal.

[1] Among the proponents of this interpretation may be counted R. L. Poole, *Illustrations of the History of Medieval Thought and Learning* (London, 1920), pp. 191–2 and C. H. Haskins, *The Renaissance of the Twelfth Century* (Cambridge, Mass., 1927), pp. 359–60.

[2] K. Guth, *Johannes von Salisbury (1115/1120–1180): Studien zur Kirchen-, Kultur- und Sozialgeschichte Westeuropas im 12. Jahrhunderts* (St. Ottilien, 1978).

[3] G. Constable, 'The Alleged Disgrace of John of Salisbury in 1159,' *EHR*, lxix (1954), 67–76 and M. Kerner, *Johannes von Salisbury und die logische Structur seines Policraticus* (Weisbaden, 1977).

[4] E. Turk, *Nugae Curialium: Le règne d'Henri Plantagenêt et l'ethique politique* (Geneva/Paris, 1977).

[5] J. Martin, 'John of Salisbury's Manuscripts of Frontinus and of Gellius,' *Journal of the Warburg and Courtauld Institutes*, xl (1977), 1–26; Martin, 'Uses of Tradition: Gellius, Petronius and John of Salisbury,' *Viator*, x (1979), 57–76; Martin, 'John of Salisbury as Classical Scholar,' in *The World of John of Salisbury*, ed. M. Wilks (Oxford, 1984), pp. 179–201; and C. J. Nederman and J. Brückmann, 'Aristotelianism in John of Salisbury's Policraticus,' *Journal of the History of Philosophy*, xxi (1983), 203–29.

One of the clearest examples of John's desire to turn his erudition to practical ends is offered by his interest in recent and current English events. In particular, the social and political unrest that characterised the rule of King Stephen of England provided an important focus for the concerns and problems addressed by John.[6] As Hans Liebeschütz long ago observed, 'the experience of the church in Stephen's anarchical reign is at the back of [John's] mind'.[7] The chronology of John's career as an ecclesiastical administrator lends prima facie support to the claim that Stephen's years on the English throne left a deep impression. John joined the court of Archbishop Theobald of Canterbury in 1147,[8] and thus participated actively and at close quarters in the events of Stephen's closing years. John was certainly present at and party to the dramatic appearance of Theobald at the Council of Rheims called by Pope Eugenius III, where the Archbishop defended Stephen's claim to the throne and pleaded with the pope not to excommunicate the king.[9] John also seems to have witnessed Henry of York's unsuccessful 1151 appeal to Eugenius to legitimize the rights of Stephen's progeny to the English crown in perpetuity.[10] Hence, John had considerable direct experience of the conditions of England's church, as fashioned and dictated by politics, during the reign of Stephen. And we might well believe that the anarchy of the period—with consequent attacks upon ecclesiastical persons and possessions, in brief, the *libertas ecclesiae*—was a matter of prime concern to a politically active churchman like John.

John's earliest known effort to confront and analyse the conditions within twelfth-century England is to be found in his satirical and political poem, the *Entheticus de Dogmate Philosophorum.*[11] Probably written in the mid-1150s,[12] the

---

[6] See H. Liebeschütz, 'John of Salisbury and Pseudo-Plutarch,' *Journal of the Warburg and Courtauld Institutes*, vi (1943), 34; Liebeschütz, *Mediaeval Humanism in the Life and Writings of John of Salisbury* (London, 1950), pp. 6, 20–2, 45–6, 52–3 and passim; Liebeschütz, 'Chartres und Bologna: Naturbegriff und Staatsidee bei Johannes von Salisbury,' *Archiv für Kulturgeschichte*, l (1968), 23; P. von Sivers, 'John of Salisbury: Königtum und Kirche in England,' in *Republica Christiana*, ed. P. von Sivers (Munich, 1969), pp. 47–70; Turk, *Nugae Curialium*, pp. 74, 83; P. Barzillay, 'The *Entheticus de dogmate philosophorum* of John of Salisbury,' *Mediaevalia et Humanistica*, xvi (1964), 19–21; and R. R. Bezzola, *Les origines et la formation de la littérature courtoise en occident (500–1200)*, 3 vols (Paris, 1963), 3, pt. 1, 23.

[7] Liebeschütz, *Mediaeval Humanism in the Life and Writings of John of Salisbury*, p. 48.

[8] A. Saltman, *Theobald, Archbishop of Canterbury* (London, 1956), pp. 169–75.

[9] As recorded by John of Salisbury in his *Historia Pontificalis*, ed. M. Chibnall (London, 1956), pp. 6–8.

[10] *Ibid.*, pp. 83–6. Much of the rest of the *Historia Pontificalis* also deals with events of Stephen's reign touching upon the church, as well.

[11] Citations from the *Entheticus* in the present essay are derived from the new edition

Entheticus applies lessons drawn from John's scholastic education to the evaluation of the personalities and forms of conduct he encountered as a court bureaucrat. The motives for John's composition of the *Entheticus* remain unclear; perhaps he intended to counsel his friend Becket,[13] possibly he was advising a young protegé in the wicked ways of the world.[14] But John's technique is unmistakable: he creates a gallery of heroes and villains, of kings and tyrants, philosophers and flatterers. In constructing this typology of the admirable and the abominable, John addresses or at least touches upon many of the themes that were to become characteristic of his writing. He recounts the wisdom of the ancients but insists upon the ultimate supremacy of theology; he praises true eloquence and condemns the decay of linguistic skills; he proclaims the inviolability of the *libertas ecclesiae* and denounces rulers who abuse or deny it; and he enumerates the sins of courtiers while specifying the qualities which typify true counsellors. John is perfectly happy to name those (like Theobald and Becket[15]) whom he regards to be blameless and upstanding. But he is more cautious when it comes to rulers, officials and churchmen whose conduct he reviles. The rogue's gallery of the *Entheticus* is populated by individuals whose actual identities are masked by classical pseudonyms.[16]

It is one such pseudonym—King Hircanus—that is generally believed to represent King Stephen.[17] If this is so, then the attitude towards Stephen enunciated in the *Entheticus* can be accorded a major role in the formation of John's political thought. For the text describes Hircanus as a 'tyrant,' that

prepared by J. van Laarhoven, *John of Salisbury's Entheticus Maior and Minor*, 3 vols. (Leiden, 1987); van Laarhoven's text is published in the first volume. Translations are my own.

[12] R. Thomson, 'What is the *Entheticus*?', in *The World of John of Salisbury*, p. 295. Thomson's dating is largely confirmed by van Laarhoven (i. 15–16), although the latter does propose the intriguing suggestion that sections of the *Entheticus* may have been drafted already in the early 1140s (i. 501).

[13] Barzillay, 'The *Entheticus de dogmate philosophorum* of John of Salisbury,' pp. 19–20.

[14] The conclusion formed by C. R. Elrington, John of Salisbury's *Entheticus de Dogmate Philosophorum*: The Light it Throws on the Educational Background of the Twelfth Century, Unpublished M. A. Thesis, University of London, 1954.

[15] See *Entheticus* 1291–1300 and 1636–1652.

[16] Some instances of such veiled references may be found at *Entheticus* 1559–1596.

[17] A view defended by Liebeschütz, *Mediaeval Humanism in the Life and Writings of John of Salisbury*, pp. 20–2; Barzillay, 'The *Entheticus de dogmate philosophorum* of John of Salisbury,' p. 20, note 77; Turk, *Nugae Curialium*, p. 83; and van Laarhoven, *John of Salisbury's Entheticus*, i. 55 and ii. 377–8.

especially evil sort of ruler of whom John throughout his career was to be an implacable foe. Hircanus is encountered immediately following the lament of the *Entheticus* about the villains 'whom captive England had as its kings for a long time, thinking them to be kings whom it suffered as tyrants.'[18] Foremost among these tyrannical rulers was Hircanus, whom John depicts by extended reference to animalistic imagery: Hircanus was a wild beast, or really, an amalgam of all the worst features of many creatures.[19] John regards Hircanus not as a king at all, but as 'a public enemy with the title of king... The pursuit of peace gave him pleasure, but in the way of a tyrant so that he might see all things subject at his feet.'[20] Under the rule of Hircanus, justice was sold, the good man perished, and the guilty went unpunished.[21] In sum, the reign of Hircanus was characterised not by reason and law, but by passion and will.[22] John leaves no doubt about the traits which earned Hircanus the epithet 'tyrant.'

The *Entheticus* then proceeds to extrapolate from the conduct of Hircanus to the more general features of tyranny. Like the legitimate monarch, the tyrant seeks to impose peace upon his subjects. But there is a difference. Where the true king brings concord to his people by means of law and justice, the 'peace of tyrants exists so that no one may protest whatever they do: they can do everything and the laws nothing. Justice is absent... They institute what they desire in place of justice.'[23] Tyrannical rule is thereby arbitrary in the sense that it reflects merely the personal wishes of the monarch and neglects all standards of government external to his private will. The tyrant is, in the worst possible sense, his 'own man.' The consequence for subjects is the complete denial of their liberty: they become enslaved, their own judgement rendered subservient to the desires of the tyrant. The *Entheticus* declares that 'this is the liberty of the people under the domination of a tyrant, that everyone chooses what he is told to do.'[24] The discretion that typifies human choice, the ability to decide matters freely for oneself, is incompatible with the tyrant's insistence that his will alone shall determine the conduct of subjects. Hence, submission to the peace and tranquility of the tyrant occurs at the price of human liberty: subjects obey him not because they freely acknowledge the justice he embodies but because they have no other option.

---

[18] *Entheticus* 1298–1299.
[19] *Entheticus* 1303–1309.
[20] *Entheticus* 1310, 1313–1314.
[21] *Entheticus* 1315–1338.
[22] *Entheticus* 1302: 'Libitum pro ratione fuit.'
[23] *Entheticus* 1341–1344.
[24] *Entheticus* 1347–1348.

JOHN OF SALISBURY'S POLITICAL THOUGHT

V

Unfortunately, the political ideas of the *Entheticus* are developed little further. John does condemn those proponents of tyranny who serve a monarchic master in order to gratify their own perverted desires for glory and wealth.[25] This section, too, is characterised by the use of classical pseudonyms—Mandrogerus, Antipater and Sporus—to obscure references to historical figures, in particular, Stephen's servants Robert of Leicester, Richard de Lucy and Richard de Hommet.[26] What all these characters are said to have in common is a hatred of liberty (especially the *libertas ecclesiae*), law and virtue; like Hircanus, they confuse public power with private gain and equate 'what is permitted and what is pleasing.'[27] This merely confirms the fundamental conception of tyranny that John had already advanced with regard to Hircanus. The key political lesson of the *Entheticus* is that good government must be government consistent with the liberty of the populace, rule which does not mistake any public order whatsoever with just and lawful order.

It may be our initial impulse to doubt the attribution of the historical identity of Hircanus the tyrant to Stephen the king. After all, even commentators who have accepted that John's Hircanus was a thinly-veiled sketch of Stephen have remarked on the lack of correspondence between the conduct ascribed to the poetic tyrant and the actual behaviour of the historical king.[28] Yet this absence of parallels may be explained by reference to John's highly conventionalized use of the term 'tyrant' in the *Entheticus*. Since at least the time of Isidore of Seville's *Etymologies*, the Latin Christian tradition had construed tyranny as a term which encompassed all of the various manifestations of wicked public power.[29] In the classical statement of the matter, Isidore had remarked that 'in common usage those who come to be called tyrants are the very worst and most vile kings, dominated by a passion for luxuries and exercising domination of the cruelest sort over their peoples.'[30] This definition led to the postulation of a simple dichotomy between the king and the tyrant, according to which the latter ruled contrary to justice and law, enslaved his subjects, and pursued his own personal vices. The

---

[25] This discussion is contained in *Entheticus* 1363–1474.
[26] See D. Luscombe, 'John of Salisbury in Recent Scholarship,' in *The World of John of Salisbury*, p. 29 and Turk, *Nugae Curialium*, p. 83.
[27] *Entheticus* 1375–1376: 'Factio Mandrogeri licitum libitumque coaequat, /Quodque semel placuit, praedicat esse bonum.'
[28] Barzillay, 'The *Entheticus de dogmate philosophorum* of John of Salisbury,' p. 20 note 77.
[29] A review of the primary contributions to this tradition prior to John is provided by W. Parsons, 'The Mediaeval Theory of the Tyrant,' *Review of Politics*, iv (1942), 129–39.
[30] Isidore of Seville, *Etymologies*, ix, 3 (in *PL* lxxxii).

6

king, by contrast, was said to rule well, in the sense that he respected divine dictates, promoted the liberty of his subjects, and cultivated virtue. When the *Entheticus* proclaimed Hircanus to be a tyrant, then, it was merely invoking a commonplace, short-hand description for an evil ruler who affronted God and His people. In traditional terms, tyranny and bad government were synonyms. The very fact that Stephen (cum Hircanus) failed to exercise his powers of office to their full extent was sufficient to earn him the epithet of 'tyrant.'

II

The *Entheticus* by no means reflected John's final word on either the reign of Stephen or the idea of tyranny. The question thus logically arises: did John's later work, in particular the *Policraticus*, merely confirm his previous opinions? Or did John develop or alter his views about Stephen or regarding tyranny? Liebeschütz long ago contended that between the *Entheticus* and the *Policraticus* there is a measurable decline of interest in the problems posed by Stephen's rule.[31] Similarly, Rodney Thomson has lately argued that the *Policraticus* represented a considerable evolution of thought in relation to the *Entheticus*: 'By the late 1150s John found himself less of a philosophical poet and more of a political philosopher than he had been even five years earlier... Above all he wished to analyse political systems, not merely to satirise the political scene.'[32] This intellectual development from the *Entheticus* to the *Policraticus* is evident in two ways relevant to our present concerns. First, John's conception of the tyrant matured into a better defined and delineated tool of inquiry. Second, John's judgement of King Stephen—while still thoroughly negative—shifted in conjunction with the notion of tyranny, so that the label of 'tyrant' ceased to apply with accuracy to the English monarch. In short, if Stephen was John's prototypical tyrant in the *Entheticus*, he could no longer play that role by the time of the *Policraticus* in view of refinements to the theoretical understanding which lay behind the application of the term.

On the face of it, John's statement of the idea of tyranny in the *Policraticus* seems little different from the version of the *Entheticus*.[33] In perhaps its most

---

[31] Liebeschütz, *Mediaeval Humanism in the Life and Writings of John of Salisbury*, pp. 21–2.

[32] Thomson, 'What is the *Entheticus*?', p. 301.

[33] Citations of the *Policraticus* will be from the edition by C. C. J. Webb (1909; reprinted Frankfurt a.M., 1965), 2 vols. Translations will be based upon the standard renderings by J. Dickinson (*The Statesman's Book*, (New York, 1927) and J. B. Pike (*The Frivolities of Courtiers and the Footprints of Philosophers* (Minneapolis, 1938)), although they have been heavily revised by the present author. In future references, the critical edition will

famous discussion of the theme, John posits a definition of the tyrant in terms explicitly derived from traditional sources: 'A tyrant, as depicted by the philosophers, is one who oppresses the people by rulership based on force... The tyrant thinks nothing done unless he brings the law to nought and reduces the people to slavery.'[34] The tyrant is the enemy of law and justice; he compels his subjects to act as he would have them, regardless of their own wills. As in the *Entheticus*, the *Policraticus* equates tyranny with the denial of any meaningful liberty to those whom the tyrant rules.

Yet the *Policraticus* introduces important clarifications of and elaborations upon this position which modify its significance. Specifically, John poses the question: How is it that some persons become tyrants? John's answer begins with the postulate that all men seek to acquire and maintain their own liberty. That is, they aim to make their own independent choices. According to John, 'Liberty judges freely in accordance with individual judgement.'[35] The *Policraticus* insists that such liberty is the absolute prerequisite for the acquisition of virtue: the morally good man must be free to choose for himself the correct course of conduct as the circumstances dictate.[36] This is not to say that the free man will always make the right decision; but no morally defensible choice whatsoever is possible in the absence of liberty.[37] Thus, liberty is incompatible with slavish submission to the will of another.

Yet, at the same time, liberty necessarily involves a measure of obedience, in the sense that it is connected to the pursuit of virtue and the (self-imposed) obligation to strive to perform good deeds.[38] In other words, liberty is not coextensive with doing just whatever one wishes or desires; liberty is not license. John fears that men are too often ignorant of the distinction between the two: they do not know that liberty is a matter of self-control, limitation and moderation, whereas license entails no such restraint. In particular, license does not take note of the circumstances under which given acts are chosen; license is utterly willful, in the negative connotation of that term. The person who confuses liberty with

---

be abbreviated as *P*, *The Statesman's Book* as *S*, and *The Frivolities of Courtiers* as *F*.

[34] *P* 777d (*S*, p. 335).

[35] *P* 705c (*S*, p. 323).

[36] The intimate relationship between virtue and liberty is explained by John at *P* 400a and 705d.

[37] Thus, John asserts: 'etenim quid opus est libertate si volentibus luxu perire non licet?' (*P* 741c).

[38] For a more thorough discussion of the issues addressed in the present paragraph, see C. J. Nederman, 'The Aristotelian Doctrine of the Mean and John of Salisbury's Concept of Liberty,' *Vivarium*, 24 (November 1986), 128–42.

license 'affects a kind of fictitious liberty, so that he can live without fear and do with impunity whatever pleases him, and somehow be just like God; not, however, that he wishes to imitate divine goodness, but rather to incline God to favour his evil will by granting him immunity from punishment.'[39] License is a sort of self-deification in which man fails to distinguish between the arbitrary pursuit of desires and the divinely granted freedom to make moral choices. The man of license wishes to conform God's will to his own, thereby equating whatever he chooses with what God had ordained. On 'the pretext of liberty,'[40] license releases men from their duties and inverts their proper relationship with God.

To enjoy liberty, of course, one must have the conditions which permit its efficacious exercise. Slavery, as one might surmise, renders liberty impossible because it denies to men the power to will anything at all according to their own discretion. The slave is unfree because he is in the power of another.[41] So power is a concept intimately associated with liberty: to have true liberty one must have the power to put free determinations into action. John remarks that 'there is no one who does not take joy in liberty, and who does not desire the strength with which to preserve it.'[42] John's concern is that those men who confuse liberty with license are incapable of knowing what limit to place on the quest for power; their pursuit of unbounded liberty is simultaneously ambition for the power through which their license can be realized and their wills gratified. Ambition is understood by John in more a classical than a modern sense; it is an excessive grasping for the power to realise one's own desires. License (ignorance of the true nature of liberty) requires ambition, and ambition (if realised) in turn produces tyranny.[43] For the *Policraticus* redefines the tyrant as one whose license is rendered efficacious by means of the acquisition of power: 'When such a man does attain to power, he exalts himself into a tyrant, and, spurning equity, does not scruple in the sight of God to oppress the equals of his nature and rank.'[44] In other words, the tyrant is someone who, lacking discretion in his decisions, chooses anything he

---

[39] *P* 675c (*S*, p. 282).

[40] *P* 706b (*S*, p. 324).

[41] It perhaps needs to be pointed out that John does not object to power *per se*, which he regards as a divinely-granted gift; rather, we are addressing ourselves solely to the abuse of power: 'Omnis autem potestas bona, quoniam ab eo est a quo solo omnia et sola sunt bona. Utenti tamen interdum bona non est aut patienti sed mala, licet quod ad universitatem sit bona, illo faciente qui bene utitur malis nostris' (p 785d).

[42] *P* 675c (*S*, p. 282).

[43] *P* 676a (*S*, p. 283): 'Dum ergo ambitio invalescit, calcata aequitate procedit iniustitia et, tirannidis procurans ortum, omnia quibus illa crescit exequitur.'

[44] *P* 675d (*S*, p. 282).

desires in the name of freedom and possesses the power to realize his will. Tyranny is license put into practice.

In consequence of this argument, we must recognise that tyranny is not, at least in the first instance, a political concept or category. John speaks in the *Policraticus* of several species of tyrant: the private tyrant and the ecclesiastical tyrant, as well as the public or monarchic tyrant.[45] The present analysis of generic tyranny should make it obvious how this is possible. Anyone who takes liberty to excess and has the power to effect his license may be classified as a tyrant. John indeed explicitly admits that his notion of tyranny deviates considerably from the ordinary usage of that term:

> Although it is not possible for all men to get hold of rulership or kingdoms, still men are either rarely or never immune from tyranny. It is said that the tyrant is one who oppresses a people by forceful domination; but it is not solely over a people that he exercises his tyranny, but he can do so from the lowest position. For if not over a people, still he will lord over (*dominatur*) whomever he can... Who is it who does not wish to come before some other one if he might be subdued?[46]

What especially distinguishes John's concept of tyranny is the universality of its application. Any immoderate use of power, any attempt to exceed the proper bounds of liberty, qualifies as a case of tyranny, regardless of whether it occurs within the household, the manor, the shire, or the kingdom.[47] Tyranny is the peculiar vice of those who use to excess any power with which they are endowed, and who thus further their own interests at the expense of the liberty of others.

This also gives us a clue to the triadic relationship between tyranny, enslavement and liberty. Insofar as tyranny is understood as the excessive application of power, that power must be used over someone else; it entails compelling another person to conform to one's desires or wishes regardless of his own determinations. Any instance of the employment of power in accordance with license must simultaneously be the denial of freedom to at least one other individual. The surfeit of liberty is only coherent in a relational context, where

---

[45] K. L. Forhan has addressed at length this multiplicity of tyrants in her recent dissertation, *The Twelfth-Century Bureaucrat and the Life of the Mind: The Political Thought of John of Salisbury*, Unpublished Ph.D. thesis, Johns Hopkins University, 1987.
[46] *P* 675d–676a (*S*, pp. 282–3).
[47] *P* 786a: 'Patet ergo non in solis principibus esse tirannidem, sed omnes esse tirannos qui concessa desuper potestate in subditis abutuntur.'

there is a concomitant deficit in liberty elsewhere. Consequently, tyranny is not only vicious in itself, but is also dangerous because it denies the possibility of virtue to those enslaved by it. Since virtue is necessarily voluntary—free choice in accordance with right—slavish (hence involuntary) action can by definition never be virtuous. When John describes slavery as 'the image of death' or 'the yoke of vice,'[48] he means to convey that the slave has lost all possibility of living a truly virtuous or faithful life.[49] Even if his behaviour is to all external standards good, the slave will never retain virtue, insofar as he has not acted freely in accordance with his own circumstantial determinations.

By contrast, the situation in which there is no tyranny will be a condition in which there is no slavery, that is, in which liberty exists in perfect equilibrium. In the tyrantless world, each person will be free to act virtuously without hindrance or interference from any of his virtuous fellows. John proclaims that 'it is part of the best and wisest man to give a free reign to liberty and to accept with patience freely spoken words, whatever they may be. Nor does he oppose himself to its works so long as these do not involve the casting away of virtue.'[50] Minor faults and errors will be tolerated in the name of defending the liberty of individuals to form, and to behave in accordance with, their own discretionary judgements. Only severe threats to religion or good morals would be deemed worthy of correction and punishment in the genuinely free community. Is it any wonder that John so effusively praises tolerance as a quality of the well-ordered society?[51] Toleration alone is regarded by the *Policraticus* as the touchstone of the harmonious pursuit of liberty. In a tolerant community, neither tyrants nor slaves can subsist at any level.

John is not, of course, optimistic about the realization of a temporal polity founded on the twin principles of liberty and toleration. He regards licentiousness, ambition and their offspring, tyranny, to be far too widespread to be easily rooted out. But the *Policraticus* does give some consideration to the prerequisites for the free and tolerant society. In particular, John holds that it pertains to the prince, the supreme public power in the realm, to ensure the liberty of those over whom he reigns. This is why the problem of liberty is especially important when considering the nature of government. John in fact considers the legitimacy of rulership to turn on the existence of liberty in the community at

---

[48] These phrases appear, for instance at *P* 765c and 675c (*F*, p. 365 and *S*, p. 282).

[49] Thus, John regards 'virtue' to be 'quae singularis vivendi causa est' (*P* 705c).

[50] *P* 706b (*S*, p. 324).

[51] John explains his doctrine of tolerance at *P* 629a-c (*S*, pp. 264–5) and *P* 708d and 710a-b (*S*, pp. 329, 330–1).

large. By definition, 'the prince fights for the laws and liberty of the people.'[52] In view of John's stipulation that good laws were 'introduced for the sake of liberty,'[53] we may conclude that the preservation of the liberty of subjects is the prime function of kingship. This is perhaps an element of what the *Policraticus* seeks to convey when it declares that within the body politic, 'an injury to the head... is brought home to all the members.'[54] For no liberty is possible where the political organism is disordered: because the prince assures that his subjects 'have peace and practice justice and abstain from falsehood and perjury,' only through his rule will they 'enjoy liberty and peace in such fullness that nothing can in the least disturb them.'[55] The intimacy which obtains between the political body and its royal head arises from an organization of society in which each is free to choose his own course of action in accordance with the dictates of right.[56] Under such a harmonious order, none need fear enslavement and those who desire more than their proper sphere of liberty—in sum, who attempt to tyrannize—will be kept in check.

As a consequence, the prince occupies a very special and sensitive place in the network of liberty. If the ruler is good, he will respect the freedom of his subjects and will eradicate threats to it; if he is evil, then the distribution of liberty among members of the community will become unbalanced. The realization of a polity characterized by freedom is hence heavily dependent upon the moral character of the prince. A virtuous prince is the best guarantee of a free kingdom. The connection here between royal virtue and public liberty is clearly mediated through John's Aristotelian definition of virtue itself as a mean between excess and deficiency.[57] When applied to the king, this notion of virtue leads John to conclude that the ruler must neither allow his subjects too much liberty nor control them too closely. Rather, the hallmark of good rule is moderation: 'With how much care should the prince moderate his acts, now with the strictness of justice, and now

---

[52] *P* 777d (*S*, p. 335).
[53] *P* 705d (*S*, p. 323).
[54] *P* 626c (*S*, p. 259).
[55] *P* 536b-c (*S*, p. 54).
[56] This accords with the general features of John's account of the organic metaphor, according to which each part of the political body must be free to serve the common good as it sees fit. See C. J. Nederman, 'The Physiological Significance of the Organic Metaphor in John of Salisbury's *Policraticus*,' *History of Political Thought*, viii (1987), 211–23.
[57] See for example, *P* 480d: 'Qui si modum excesserit, vergit ad culpam. Omnis enim virtus suis finibus limitatur et in modo consistit; si excesseris, in invio es et non in via.' For the Aristotelian origins of this doctrine, see Nederman, 'The Aristotelian Doctrine of the Mean and John of Salisbury's Concept of Liberty,' pp. 130–3.

with the leniency of mercy, to the end that he may make his subjects all be of one mind in one house, and thus as it were out of discordant dispositions bring to pass one great perfect harmony?'[58] The prince must exercise his own moral liberty to make determinations as circumstances dictate so as to promote mutual respect and charity among his subjects. This requires that the ruler never overlook or encourage moral error within the community, yet also never punish those evils (stemming from the bad choices which free persons sometimes make) that do not endanger public order or religious orthodoxy. On the one hand, the king should suppress those 'flagrant outrages' which 'it is not permissible to tolerate or which cannot be tolerated in good conscience.'[59] Yet, on the other hand, the *Policraticus* objects to the ruler 'who is ready to fault his subjects, and take revenge on them for their faults.'[60] Like all other good men, the prince is expected to use his power moderately in accordance with the nature of virtue. But unlike anyone else within his society, the ruler's failure to conform to the dictates of the virtuous mean will necessarily result in disorder and loss of liberty for the rest of the community.

We are thereby led to conclude from the account of the *Policraticus* that political disorder and unfreedom are the inevitable consequences of the immoderate conduct of government. In line with John's adherence to the Aristotelian definition of virtue as a mean, the absence of moderate rule will be characterized by one of two possible types of regimes. If the ruler seeks for himself excessive liberty, if he attempts to use his power to dominate the community, then he is what John calls a 'public tyrant.' That is, the public tyrant is a person of tyrannical character whose ambition for the supreme governmental office has been fulfilled. What renders him a public tyrant is strictly speaking neither his moral qualities nor the power he possesses, but the conjunction and combination of the two. The result of public tyranny is the disruption of the properly ordered community in the face of demands for the slavish obedience of subjects. There can be no liberty among members of the polity when a tyrant rules. A public tyrant claims a monopoly of discretionary authority over all those under his control, so that the maintenance of his full license requires the absence of true freedom on the part of any other. The *Policraticus* insists that 'as long as all, collectively and individually, are borne along at the will of a single head, they are deprived of their own free will.'[61] Nor does John believe that the victim of the public tyrant ought 'to make a virtue of necessity by uniting consent and necessity

---

[58] *P* 530b (*S*, p. 39).
[59] *P* 629b (*S*, p. 265).
[60] *P* 531d (*S*, p. 43).
[61] *P* 496c (*F*, p. 184).

and by gracefully embracing that which is incumbent upon him.' To pretend that one wishes what one has not freely chosen is to preserve 'the semblance of liberty' only, without retaining 'any measure of real and pure liberty.'[62] John instead advocates positive measures to protect the community from its tyrant—in the last instance, tyrannicide.[63] For since public tyranny creates an enslaved populace, and inevitably destroys the possibility of virtue, the ruler is never free to abrogate the legitimate liberty of subjects. Only when private citizens themselves become tyrants is the royal power of correction and punishment legitimately employed.

Yet John realizes that evil rulership is not wholly coextensive with tyranny. Rather, the disturbance and disarray of the community can also be achieved by a ruler who pays too little attention to his duties and responsibilities. Such a monarch, regardless of whether he acts out of indulgence or incompetence, is possessed of what John calls a 'slavish character' (*moribus servilibus*).[64] This is not to say that the ruler in question (whom we may label the 'pseudo-prince') is himself in a condition of coercive subjection to another. On the contrary, John distinguishes between 'slavery of the person' (which 'may seem at times the more to be pitied') and 'slavery to the vices' (which 'is ever far the more wretched').[65] The former in the product of tyranny, the denial of liberty to some person(s) as the result of the license of another. But slavery to vice is self-imposed, and leads to a general lethargy instead of to ambition. The slavish personality—for whom John's archetype is the Epicurean[66] —seeks only the satisfaction of private pleasure to the neglect of the offices and obligations with which he has been charged. As a slavish character raised to the mantle of public power, the pseudo-prince is typically regarded to be the weak ruler.

John's model of the pseudo-prince is perhaps the Virgilian Dido, ruler of Carthage. As John describes her, Dido was careless and irresponsible, preferring her passion for Aeneas to her duties as monarch of her city. Thus, by setting 'luxuriae' ahead of public welfare, Dido caused the harmonious cooperation present in the Carthage of former times to disintegrate into self-indulgence and eventually into the destruction of the city itself.[67] The moral which John derives

---

[62] *P* 496d (*F*, p. 184).

[63] It is for the sake of the common liberty of the body politic, and of each of its members, John insists, that justice condones the slaying of the tyrant; see C. J. Nederman, 'A Duty to Kill: John of Salisbury's Theory of Tyrannicide,' *Review of Politics*, 1 (1988), 365–89.

[64] *P* 706b.

[65] *P* 705d (*S*, p. 323).

[66] Thus, John remarks of 'Epicureorum' that 'nam ad eorum sectam indubitanter pertinere noscuntur qui in omnibus propriae serviunt voluntati' (*P* 711a).

[67] For John's recounting of the story of Dido and Aeneas, see *P* 621c–622a

V

14

from the story of Dido is that 'the happiness of the republic does not last unless the head looks out for the safety of the whole body.'[68] Because she was a slave to her own vices, Dido was unable to enforce and maintain the order required for liberty to flourish. Her weakness allowed her subjects too great a measure of personal freedom and ultimately they could not unite when a common enemy threatened them. (Indeed, Dido was so besotted that she could not even recognize her enemy.) In the extreme, such slavish attitudes on the part of the ruler make it possible for tyranny to emerge among members of the citizen body itself. Without the regulation and supervision of freedom by the prince, individuals will find themselves able to exceed the bounds of liberty, to combine license with power, and thus to tyrannize their fellows with impunity. Rulers who are 'sapped by luxury' cannot prevent such 'destruction and dissolution' from overtaking their realms; 'a government corrupted by luxury cannot long stand, or if it stands, it will regurgitate through God's judgement whatever it has swallowed with immoderate luxury.'[69] John often describes the pseudo-prince in misogynistic terms: it is 'effeminacy' or 'womanish weakness' that characterizes the behaviour of the slavish monarch and makes it impossible for him to impose limits upon the conduct of subjects.[70] John's message, then, is clear. The slavish prince, who either refuses or lacks the strength to perform his duties, poses an equal if conceptually distinct danger to the kingdom in comparison with the public tyrant. Both types of vicious rulership will result in a populace deprived of its own appropriate liberty. And if subjects have no freedom, then virtue also will be absent. Good government, typified by rule in accordance with the virtuous mean, is regarded by the *Policraticus* to be the sole guarantee that moral goodness shall predominate within a society.

---

[68] *P* 621c (*S*, p. 247).

[69] *P* 610c and 610a-b (*S*, pp. 223, 222): 'Et praecedentium quidem regum robur a luxuria emollitum est, deinde per singulos quasi per gradus invalescente mollitia in hoc tandem effeminatum fractum et comminutum est... Principatus vero quem corrumpit luxuria, diu stare non potest aut, si steterit, opprimente iudicio Dei evomet quicquid immoderatio luxuariae hausit.'

[70] For an analysis of the significance of John's misogynistic attitudes, see C. J. Nederman and N. E. Lawson, 'The Frivolities of Courtiers Follow the Footprints of Women: Historical Women and the Crisis of Virility in John of Salisbury,' in *Ambiguous Realities: Medieval and Renaissance Women*, ed. C. Levin and J. Watson (Detroit, 1987), pp. 82–96.

III

It should be evident that John's account of tyranny in the *Policraticus* represents a considerable development over and departure from the doctrine of the *Entheticus*. As articulated in the *Policraticus*, tyranny is a far more intricate and coherent phenomenon than one might have expected from the *Entheticus*—a theoretical precept rather than an invective. In particular, the 'tyrannology'[71] of the *Policraticus* advances our understanding of tyranny in three ways. First, John demonstrates that tyranny is not purely a public or political affair. Instead, tyrants exist in all facets of human life, since tyranny is simply the conjunction of license and power. Thus, the public tyrant is one species (albeit with distinctive features) among several different types of tyranny. Second, the liberty usurped by the tyrant is not merely coextensive with ecclesiastical liberty. The *Policraticus* is certainly concerned about affronts to the liberty of the church,[72] but John employs a more expansive notion of liberty which encompasses the full range of issues connected with freedom, stretching from personal choice all the way to political and legal prerogatives. The core of this doctrine of liberty is philosophical; it arises from the contention that virtue in all its aspects cannot be realized without free moral will. Whatever is conducive to such freedom (which includes the *libertas ecclesiae*) ought to be maintained and protected; whatever thwarts liberty must be opposed and eliminated. Third, the *Policraticus* challenges the conventional and nearly automatic definition of tyranny as evil rulership or bad government. John rather argues that a ruler may be regarded as bad either by enslaving his people (tyranny) or by renouncing his duties and leaving his subjects to their own devices (the slavish pseudo-prince). In the former case, subjects may themselves usurp power and attempt to tyrannize and enslave one another. The good ruler, by contrast, enforces the conditions under which virtue may flourish and tolerates the minor faults that arise from free choice. The promotion of a properly balanced public order is the prime duty of the true king. Evil rulers can disturb this balance by paying too little regard to the arrangement of the community as well as by compelling the conformity of the society to their own wills. Once again, we confront the irredeemably moderate character of good government as envisaged by the *Policraticus*.

---

[71] A felicitous term coined by J. van Laarhoven, 'Thou Shalt NOT Slay a Tyrant! The So-called Theory of John of Salisbury,' in *The World of John of Salisbury*, p. 329.
[72] For example, John provides an extended defence of the *libertas ecclesiae*, based on secular rather than canon law, at *P* 691–696c.

It is not yet clear, however, how these refinements in the conception of tyranny might have affected John's evaluation of King Stephen and his reign. Fortunately the *Policraticus* addresses explicitly the events of Stephen's time in such fashion that we can specify their relationship to his theoretical doctrines. What is perhaps most immediately striking about the treatment of Stephen in the *Policraticus* is the absence of any direct ascription of tyranny to his rule—and this in spite of John's lack of reluctance to apply the label 'tyrant' to other recent or contemporary figures.[73] At the same time, John leaves no doubt that he regards Stephen as a bad monarch. Stephen is described as 'a despiser of the good and the just, whose counsel was full of folly from the beginning, whose course was founded on iniquity and faithlessness... He did many things ill and few things well.'[74] John is particularly incensed that Stephen usurped the English crown from a legitimate ruler, Matilda, to whom he had previously sworn an oath of allegiance.[75] It was the violation of this promise which, John suggests, assured Stephen an unhappy reign: 'He did not find among his own subjects the loyalty and faith which he had not kept with God and his own earthly lord; for it was meted out to him in the same measure with which he meted it out to others.'[76] But even flagrant usurpation does not earn Stephen the appellation of tyrant. For John does not cite any substantial evidence that Stephen sought to employ his royal power (no matter how ill-gotten) towards the end of subordinating the liberty of his subjects to his own will. The hallmark of Stephen's reign was instead weakness: by concentrating his efforts totally upon retaining the English crown for himself and his posterity, he failed to provide any real governance for the realm at all. Stephen never controlled the throne so completely that the opportunity arose for him to convert royal power to the purposes of tyranny. Thus, Stephen is portrayed by John as entirely consumed with fear that he will lose his crown. We are told that he plotted incessantly against Matilda and her progeny[77] ; he ceased to trust the ecclesiastical and temporal lords, suspecting everyone of treachery, 'so that finally none felt secure in coming to his court.'[78] In short, the Stephen whom John depicts

---

[73] Van Laarhoven has compiled a seemingly complete list of all of John's known uses of the terms 'tyrant' or 'tyranny' in 'Thou Shalt NOT Slay a Tyrant!', pp. 333–41.

[74] *P* 614d and 615b (*S*, pp. 234, 235).

[75] John's sympathy with Matilda's cause is discussed by Nederman and Lawson, 'The Frivolities of Courtiers Follow the Footprints of Women,' pp. 84–6.

[76] *P* 615a-b (*S*, p. 234).

[77] *P* 615a: 'Vicinas studuit corrumpere nationes, cum principibus matrimonia contraxit et amicitias, ne quo Dei beneficio parvulus, qui adhuc vagiebat in cunis, ad petitionem hereditatis posset accedere. Plurima quidem adversus innocentiam machinabantur sed in omnibus his mentita est iniquitas sibi.'

[78] *P* 615b (*S*, p. 235).

is a slave to his own dread of dethronement, an irremediable paranoic, and hence utterly distracted from the tasks of government. We might well conclude from the account of the *Policraticus* that Stephen was a victim of his own usurpation and the mistrust which grew out of it.

The consequence of Stephen's submission to his own fears and suspicions was a weakness which bred public disorder. By his virtual abdication of royal responsibility, Stephen 'neglected discipline to the point that he did not so much reign as arouse and collide with the clergy and people to the extent that all men were provoked to do all things; force was the only measure of right.'[79] John accuses Stephen, because of his political impotence and lethargy, of creating the climate in which his subjects turned upon and terrorised one another. For, finding no royally-enforced barriers to their own ambitions, they appropriated powers to which they where not entitled and oppressed whomever could not resist them. England under Stephen's rule became a land of private tyrants, unencumbered by the moderating effects of a superior public power. In this connection, the *Policraticus* cites a litany of English nobles who followed the path of tyranny (to a bad end) during Stephen's time:

> To speak of our own land, where now are Geoffrey, Milo, Ranulf, Alan, Simon, Gilbert—men who were not so much earls of the kingdom as public enemies? Where is William of Salisbury? Where is Marmion?... Their malice is indeed notable, their infamy famous, and their unhappy endings a thing whereof the present age cannot be ignorant. If therefore a man is not acquainted with ancient history,... if he does not recollect the mischances and downfalls of bygone tyrants, let him attend to that which is forced upon his unwilling eyes, and he will see more clearly than the light of day that all tyrants are miserable.[80]

John's immediate point is to underscore the punishment which inevitably accompanies tyranny. But his list is indicative of his attitude towards Stephen's reign. The tyranny rampant during the period was of an essentially private nature, the result of an absence of strictures or limits upon the use of power in accordance with license. All men were free to do as they willed without danger of punishment or opposition by a supreme temporal authority. England was thus populated with tyrants who pillaged and looted the realm (and especially churches)[81] with

---

[79] *P* 614d–615a (*S*, p. 234).
[80] *P* 807a-b (*S*, p. 393).
[81] That John is greatly concerned about attacks upon clerical properties is clear from his remarks about the Danegeld and the conduct of Stephen's son, Eustace, at *P* 806c–807a.

impunity because no public power existed to restrict their behaviour. Had the laws of the kingdom been executed in accordance with royal judgment, however, such tyrannical brigandage would have been suppressed and the realm saved from enslavement.

The contention that the word 'tyranny' could more properly be applied during Stephen's reign to the magnates of the kingdom than to the king was a feature of John's thought which he shared with many of his contemporaries in the English church. Edmund King has lately documented a number of passages in texts dating to the 1130s and 1140s in which the vocabulary of tyranny was employed to describe the wielding of arbitrary power by members of the English nobility. In particular, King points out, the attribution of such tyrannical conduct was associated with the construction of unlicensed castles and the exaction of unauthorized taxes.[82] Yet all of the documents cited by King are strictly concerned with the treatment of the church and its servants by the great men of England. By contrast, the *Policraticus* opens up the field of application of the term 'tyrant' to include those who suppress any legitimate liberty—ecclesiastical as well as secular. Thus, John adds a more abstract, theoretical dimension to the use of the word than may be found in other mid twelfth-century documents which address the anarchy.

Yet, by inference, contemporary English churchmen would be inclined to agree with what appears to be the ultimate conclusion of John's appraisal of Stephen's reign when taken in conjunction with the theory of tyranny in the *Policraticus*: that Stephen himself was a pseudo-prince whose failure to impose law and order over England permitted others to exercise personal license. The evil of Stephen's rule was one of defect, not of excess; it was reflected in the withdrawal of virtually all public protection and safeguards of liberty, rather than in the unlimited use of royal power. This is surely the reason that John, in either the *Policraticus* or thereafter, never labels Stephen a tyrant.[83] Given the more sophisticated and complex conception of tyranny itself articulated in the *Policraticus*, Stephen simply ceased to qualify as a tyrant because he did not meet

Also as H. A. Cronne, *The Reign of Stephen* (London, 1970), p. 2 points out, 'In John of Salisbury's well-known list of public enemies, all have one thing in common. These men were, whatever their other crimes, violators of churches.'

[82] Edmund King, 'The Anarchy of King Stephen's Reign,' *Transactions of the Royal Historical Society*, 5th ser., xxxiv (1984), 135–6.

[83] Yet John continued in his correspondence to describe as a tyrant the infamous Flemish mercenary, William of Ypres, who was in Stephen's employ (documented by Van Laarhoven, 'Thou Shalt NOT Slay a Tyrant!', p. 339). Evidently, John did not regard Stephen to be sufficiently authoritative even over his own paid troops to be held responsible for their actions.

the criteria set down by John. Stephen was indeed a bad ruler, but his real crime was to abrogate his public duties and so to create the conditions whereby individual subjects could enslave one another. For this Stephen is soundly reprimanded by John; but it does not transform the failed and incompetent king into a tyrant.

Assuming that the evaluation of Stephen in the *Policraticus* represents a changed perspective from the *Entheticus*, we may yet wonder why John felt the need to reconsider his initial opinion. In part, the answer may have to do with John's intellectual growth. In the process of thinking afresh about the themes he originally treated in the *Entheticus*—and perhaps doing so after exposure to newly discovered texts[84] —John doubtless arrived at a deeper understanding of the intricacies of human morals and politics. The doctrine of tyranny in the *Policraticus* is thereby the fruit of philosophical maturation on the part of John. And as a direct function of this development, John would have been compelled to reexamine and revise his estimation of Stephen and his reign.

At the same time, there is certainly also an historical dimension to the evolution of John's thought. Scholars have never ceased to emphasize that the *Policraticus* in many ways reflects John's experiences during the early years of Henry II's rule. In contrast with its vilification of Stephen, the *Policraticus* speaks approvingly and enthusiastically of Henry's pacification of the kingdom.[85] Yet John had been an early victim of Henry's wrath.[86] This personal experience, combined with the king's evident desire to consolidate and expand his powers of taxation over church and laity alike,[87] convinced John that he was confronted with a monarch whose traits were in most ways the opposite of Stephen's. Where Stephen was weak and indecisive, Henry was strong and sure; where Stephen never really controlled England and its populace, Henry sought to refashion the inhabitants of the island in his own image. In later years, John never hesitated to apply the label of tyrant to Henry—as well as to other important European monarchs.[88] It may be that the new ruler's style of government so contrasted with

[84] In particular, one might cite Aristotle's *Topics*—the primary bearer of the Aristotelian doctrine of the mean as John knew it—which John only seems to have read in the very late 1150s, judging from his remark in the *Metalogicon* that he had only recently encountered the work for the first time. See Nederman and Brückman, 'Aristotelianism in John of Salisbury's *Policraticus*,' p. 204.

[85] John's discussion of Anglo-Norman history reserves praise only for Henry I and his grandson among recent kings, although it is clear that Henry II is primarily valued for his military prowess; see *P* 614c-d and 615c–616b.

[86] Constable, 'The Alleged Disgrace of John of Salisbury in 1159,' pp. 74–6.

[87] Cf. J. A. Green, 'The Last Century of Danegeld,' EHR, xcvi (1981), 251–8.

[88] Besides Henry II, John applied the label 'tyrant' to Frederick Barbarossa, William

that of Stephen that John sensed a need to distinguish in qualitative, theoretical terms between the two. In many ways, John's understanding of tyranny, as it emerged within the *Policraticus*, had already begun to frame some of the issues over which Henry and Becket would ultimately clash.

As a consequence, it seems most sensible to reaffirm the view suggested by Liebeschütz that the theories of the *Policraticus* were more or less equally 'determined by the experiences of two periods,' namely, the anarchy under Stephen and the Angevin monarchy of Henry.[89] For, on the one side, John could appreciate the destructive tendencies within a polity in which no law was executed and men were abandoned to their own wills. But John also recognized that a strong ruler, anxious to replace public liberty with deference to his will, constituted a grave threat to the proper order of the community. We may therefore view John's doctrine of moderate government (and perhaps in addition his unique version of the organic metaphor of the body politic)[90] as a response to the historical conditions he confronted at mid-century. This is not an implausible conclusion. As we saw at the outset of the present essay, John always sought to render philosophy into a practical discipline, to adapt it to the needs of time and place.[91] The conceptual evolution of John's political theory in relation to the historical situation of medieval English government appears to represent yet another instance of John's remarkably flexible and nondogmatic intellect.

Rufus and Roger of Sicily; see van Laarhoven, 'Thou Shalt NOT Slay a Tyrant!', pp. 339–41.

[89] Liebeschütz, *Mediaeval Humanism in the Life and Writings of John of Salisbury*, p. 45.

[90] See Nederman, 'The Physiological Significance of the Organic Metaphor in John of Salisbury's *Policraticus*,' pp. 222–3.

[91] More thorough discussions of John's metaphilosophy may be found in C. J. Nederman, 'Aristotelian Ethics and John of Salisbury's Letters,' *Viator*, xviii (1987), 172–3 and 'Knowledge, Virtue and the Path to Wisdom: The Unexamined Aristotelianism of John of Salisbury's *Metalogicon*,' *Mediaeval Studies*, li (Forthcoming 1989).

VI

THE PHYSIOLOGICAL SIGNIFICANCE OF THE ORGANIC METAPHOR IN JOHN OF SALISBURY'S *POLICRATICUS**

Political theory no less than other modes of expression and argumentation has thrived throughout its history on metaphor.[1] But particular styles of metaphorical discourse about politics have enjoyed popularity according to the demands of historical circumstance and intellectual tradition. The ancient Greek fondness for metaphors of *technē* has correctly been taken as a peculiar characteristic of its political culture.[2] Likewise, one of the most enduring metaphors in the political thought of the Latin Middle Ages was the likening of politics or society to a living (generally human) body. Following the lead of Calcidius' commentary on Plato's *Timaeus*, early medieval authors commonly compared the operation of the city to bodily parts and functions.[3] As political institutions and patterns of life became richer over the course of the Middle Ages, so did the organic analogy evolve in its intricacy and breadth of application.[4] At the close of the medieval period, the metaphor of the body was still widely employed to describe all manner of human institutions and forms of government.[5] Indeed, only a few scripturally derived metaphors

* An early version of this essay was presented to the Medieval and Renaissance Guild of the University of Alberta; I wish to thank the members of that Guild, as well as my former colleague Professor Jeremy Paltiel, for helpful comments. Dr Janet Coleman and an anonymous reader for the present journal have also provided insightful suggestions. Research for this paper was supported by the Mactaggart Fellowship of the University of Alberta.

[1] For a discussion of the uses of metaphor in political texts, see Wayne C. Booth, 'Metaphor as Rhetoric: The Problem of Evaluation', in *On Metaphor*, ed. S. Sacks (Chicago, 1979), pp. 47–70.

[2] A survey of the prominence of *technē*-analogies in Greek thought is included in Terence Irwin, *Plato's Moral Theory* (Oxford, 1977), pp. 24–8, 71–7 and *passim*.

[3] This has been thoroughly documented by Paul Edward Dutton, '*Illustre civitatis et populi exemplum*: Plato's *Timaeus* and the Transmission from Calcidius to the End of the Twelfth Century of a Tripartite Scheme of Society', *Mediaeval Studies*, 45 (1983), pp. 79–119.

[4] The broader development of the organic metaphor in the Middle Ages is described in considerable detail by Tilman Struve, *Die Entwicklung der Organologischen Staatsauffassung im Mittelalter* (Stuttgart, 1978).

[5] On the persistence of the bodily analogy through the sixteenth century, see Ernst H. Kantorowicz, *The King's Two Bodies: A Study in Medieval Political Theology* (Princeton, 1957), pp. 447–8 and *passim*. A clear example of the appeal of organic ideas in the fifteenth century is provided by Sir John Fortescue's *De laudibus legum anglie* (ed. S.B. Chrimes (Cambridge, 1949)), in which the qualities of the 'naturali corpore' are compared to the 'corpore politico' in order to establish that 'in corpore politico intencio populi primum vivens est, habens in se sanguinem, videlicet, provisionem politicam utilitatis populi illius, quam in caput et in omnia membra eiusdem corporis ipsa transmittit, quo porpus illus alitur et vegitatur' (sec. 13).

(such as Peter and the keys) seem to have rivalled the body in appeal to political authors.

Yet if there was a regularity to the use of organic imagery among political thinkers during the Middle Ages, then there were also certain important benchmarks, certain texts that broadened the dimensions and applicability of the metaphor. By general agreement, one such benchmark was John of Salisbury's *Policraticus*, an advice book for princes and courtiers completed in 1159, which has been praised for its advanced conception of the body politic. Books Five and Six, comprising some one hundred and seventy five pages in the critical edition of the *Policraticus*,[6] are in fact wholly devoted to a microscopic dissection of the 'parts' of the polity employing terminology drawn from the model of the human organism. The commonwealth, John states flatly, 'is a certain body endowed with life'.[7] Like all bodies, it is animated by a soul which guides its activities: 'those who preside over the practice of religion should be looked up to and venerated as the soul of the body'.[8] But the clerics who enjoy the place of the soul in the polity are not, strictly speaking, 'members of the commonwealth,'[9] just as the eternal soul itself does not exist coextensively with the physical organism in which it resides. Thus, despite John's reference to the soul as 'the prince of the body',[10] his organic metaphor expresses a primarily secular political theory which excludes religious offices from a place within the organism itself. The body politic *per se* is ruled by the prince, who 'holds the place of the head',[11] and thus 'who rightly deserves to be preferred before others'.[12] At the heart of the commonwealth lies the senate, that body of counsellors upon whose wisdom the ruler draws.[13] The senses correspond to

[6] The standard critical edition is that by C.C.J. Webb (1909; 2 vols., reprinted Frankfurt am Main, 1965). The *Policraticus* has been translated into English in two separate volumes, one by John Dickinson containing the 'political' chapters under the title *The Statesman's Book* (New York, 1927), the other by J.B. Pike containing the 'courtly' sections under the title *Frivolities of Courtiers and Footprints of Philosophers* (Minneapolis, 1938). For the convenience of non-specialists, citations in the present paper will be given to the existing translated version (with occasional revision); corresponding quotations from the Latin text, using the marginal numeration of the Webb edition, will be provided in the notes. In further references, the Latin edition will be abbreviated as *P* and *The Statesman's Book* as *S*.

[7] *S*, p. 64; *P* 540a: '. . . corpus quoddam . . . animatur . . .'.

[8] *S*, p. 64; *P* 540b: 'Illos vero, qui religionis cultui praesunt, quasi animam corporis suspicere et venerari oportet'.

[9] *S*, p. 83; *P* 548d: '. . . membris rei publicae . . .'. This is confirmed by the wording in the final paragraph of the chapter immediately preceding; cf. *S*, p. 82; *P* 548d.

[10] *S*, p. 64; *P* 540b: 'anima totius habet corporis principatum'.

[11] *S*, p. 83; *P* 548d: 'principem locum obtinere capitis'.

[12] *S*, p. 107; *P* 560b: '. . . merito praefertur aliis . . .'.

[13] *S*, p. 108; *P* 560b–d.

the royal judges and local agents (sheriffs and bailiffs) who exercise jurisdiction in the king's name.[14] The county financial officers constitute the stomach and intestines of the body,[15] while the hands are formed by the tax-collector and the soldier respectively.[16] Finally, the feet John compares to the peasantry 'who raise, sustain and move forward the weight of the entire body'.[17] It is on the basis of this arrangement of the body politic that John produces the lengthy exegesis contained within the fifth and sixth books of the *Policraticus*.

If only because of the extent to which John depicts the intricacies of the political organism, scholars have been impressed by the qualities of its presentation in the *Policraticus*. Over a century ago, Otto Gierke observed that 'John of Salisbury made the first attempt to find some member of the natural body which would correspond to each portion of the State'.[18] Gierke's remark is essentially confirmed by Hans Liebeschütz's assertion that 'John's comparison between State and body, which led some critics to consider the author as an early representative of the organic doctrine of the State, has a very restricted meaning, although it contains more details of State administration than older examples of its kind. John's point is to emphasize the importance of the differentiation of human tasks.'[19] And quite recently, Janet Martin has reiterated that the organic analogy allows John to describe 'in turn the duties of each member of the commonwealth, descending from head to feet. His theme is that if the body is to be healthy, each member must perform its own duty properly and not try to usurp the functions of the other members'.[20] In short, the predominant line of interpretation running from Gierke to Martin — and encompassing many others besides[21] — emphasizes the body as a metaphor for a richly differentiated but strictly ordered political system; John's organic

---

[14] *S*, pp. 123, 145; *P* 567c, 576c–d.

[15] *S*, p. 65; *P* 540c.

[16] *S*, p. 173; *P* 589a–b.

[17] *S*, p. 65; *P* 540d: '. . . qui totius corporis erigunt sustinent et promovent molem'.

[18] Otto Gierke, *Political Theories of the Middle Ages*, trans. F.W. Maitland (Cambridge, 1900), p. 24.

[19] Hans Liebeschütz, *Mediaeval Humanism in the Life and Writings of John of Salisbury* (London, 1950), p. 45.

[20] Janet Martin, 'The Uses of Tradition: Gelius, Petronius and John of Salisbury', *Viator*, 10 (1979), p. 62.

[21] Among the others who adhere, in whole or in part, to this view are: W. Stürner, *Natur und Gesellschaft im Denken des Hoch- und Spätmittelalters* (Stuttgart, 1975), pp. 120–30; Georges Duby, *The Three Orders: Feudal Society Imagined*, trans. A. Goldhammer (Chicago 1980), pp. 264–7; Dutton, '*Illustre civitatis et populi exemplum*', pp. 110–11; Struve, *Die Entwicklung der Organologischen Staatsauffassung im Mittelalter*, p. 125; Tilman Struve, 'The Importance of the Organism in the Political Theory of John Salisbury', in *The World of John of Salisbury*, ed. M.J. Wilks (Oxford, 1984), pp. 303–4, 309; and Bernard Guenée, *States and Rulers in Later Medieval Europe*, trans. J. Vale (Oxford, 1985), pp. 43–4.

account of government and society is of an essentiaily anatomic character. (An 'anatomic' version of the organic analogy is one which concentrates on 'an architecture of parts'.)[22] Thus, John's contribution is seen to be purely quantitative; he articulates in numerically greater detail the elements of the polity in comparison to the parts of the body and hence the ways in which the elements relate to one another. The traditional medieval ordering principle of hierarchy is maintained by John, but more factors are now incorporated within the architectonic which the *Policraticus* designs.[23] One unfortunate analogue to the anatomic reading of John's organic metaphor has been the concentration of scholarship upon the search for his sources and antecedents rather than upon examination of his philosophical originality. Indeed, the larger part of the recent scholarly debate regarding John's conception of the body politic has centred on the range of classical and Christian texts which might have provided him with an archetype for his organic doctrines.[24] This approach stems from the operative assumption within the literature that there exists an essential thematic continuity between John's presentation of the body politic and that of the preceding organic tradition — a continuity constituted by a shared anatomical understanding of the metaphor.

It remains the case, however, that the attribution of strictly anatomic significance to John's bodily imagery has been mainly imputed rather than proven. An important question thereby demands response. Did John of Salisbury fashion his organic analogy in order to convey an anatomic vision of politics? The evidence provided by John himself suggests that a negative answer is appropriate. The present paper aims to demonstrate that John's metaphor of the political body involves a theoretical framework that owes little to the anatomic one advocated by his predecessors. It will be argued, in particular, that John's contribution was to recast the organic metaphor on a physiological model. (The 'physiological' interpretation of the organic analogy stresses 'organs cooperating by virtue of voluntaristic categories such as common purpose'.)[25] Where the anatomic approach emphasizes the diversity

---

[22] Richard Jung, 'A Quarternion of Metaphors for the Hermeneutics of Life', in *Proceedings of the International Conference of the Society for General Systems Research*, Vol. 1, ed. B.H. Banathy (Seaside, CA, 1985), p. 172.

[23] A point made by Beryl Smalley, *The Becket Conflict and the Schools* (Totawa, NJ, 1973), pp. 97–8. As a highly skilled intellectual and a seasoned administrator, John was ideally placed to translate the increased complexity of contemporary government into a much more thorough-going vision of the body politic. For John's career, see Klaus Guth, *Johannes von Salisbury (1115/20– 1180): Studien zur Kirchen- Kultur- und Sozialgeschichte Westeuropas im 12. Jahrhunderts* (St. Ottilien, 1978).

[24] For a brief survey of the literature on this issue, see Max Kerner, 'Randbermerkungen zur *Institutio Traiani*', in *The World of John of Salisbury*, ed. Wilks, pp. 203–6 and notes; to Kerner's list should be added: Janet Martin, 'John of Salisbury as Classical Scholar', in *ibid.*, pp. 179– 201.

[25] Jung, 'A Quarternion of Metaphors', p. 172.

and uniqueness of the parts, the physiological approach actually favoured in the *Policraticus* focuses on the body as a coherent unit all of whose members perform according to a shared principle. Consequently, we may argue that John intended the organic metaphor specifically to be an institutionalized expression of political rule based on *cooperation* between diverse elements of society in order to realize a singular aim. Government is thus not limited to a strict regimen of subordination and rule, but entails the collective activity of the various social components undertaken jointly for a common purpose. In contradistinction to earlier medieval schemes of the body politic, John's version of the organic metaphor requires that individuals and groups have a place within the community only insofar as they collaborate with one another in the governance of their polity. While a measure of hierarchical duty to rulers and superiors is retained, all parts of the body are primarily bound to a collective end which is greater than any of its members and which is equivalent to the good of the whole society.

To speak of a shift from an anatomic to a physiological conception of the body politic involves a bold and profound step forward in medieval political philosophy. In particular, a physiological understanding points towards the doctrine of the absolute precedence of the common good over private interests[26] and ultimately towards the resurgence of the state conceived as an entity whose interests are co-extensive with the highest social good.[27] As a consequence, it may be argued that the *Policraticus* advances the terms of medieval theoretical inquiry, if only by suggesting that responsibility for the creation and perpetuation of a good society does not rest entirely upon the moral credentials of the ruler, but in addition pertains to the conduct of all the other elements of the community. Insofar as this essentially physiological claim was the insight John wished to propound, we may also explain many of the peculiar qualities of the *Policraticus*. For instance, it has been commonly remarked that the *Policraticus* was the first treatise during the Latin Middle Ages to break away from the 'mirror for princes' genre and to address the moral and social behaviour of royal courtiers, counsellors and bureaucrats.[28] That John sought to broaden the scope of his instruction and criticism is arguably a function of

---

[26] For a fourteenth-century statement of this view, see Cary J. Nederman, 'Royal Taxation and the English Church: The Origins of William of Ockham's *An princeps*', *Journal of Ecclesiastical History*, 37 (1986), pp. 377–88.

[27] A process described by Joseph R. Strayer, *On the Medieval Foundations of the Modern State* (Princeton, 1970), pp. 9–10. An account of some of the important conceptual factors in this transformation may be found in Cary J. Nederman, 'Quentin Skinner's State: Historical Method and Traditions of Discourse', *Canadian Journal of Political Science*, 18 (June 1985), pp. 339–52.

[28] See Egbert Turk, *Nugae Curialium: La regne d'Henri Plantagenet et l'éthique politique* (Geneva/Paris, 1977), pp. 17–86; Duby, *The Three Orders*, p. 266; and Kate Langdon Forhan, 'A Twelfth-Century "Bureaucrat" and the Life of the Mind: The Political Thought of John of Salisbury', presented at the Tenth International Conference on Patristic, Medieval and Renaissance Studies, Villanova University, 1985.

VI

216

his physiological interpretation of the body politic. For to conceive of the organic metaphor physiologically implied that the safety and virtue of the polity could no longer be adequately treated as a duty of the ruler alone. John was rather compelled to reflect upon the conduct of the king's servants and even his subjects in order to provide a complete description of the qualities of good government.

How John of Salisbury in fact intended to apply the organic metaphor is perhaps suggested most succinctly by remarks addressed to his regular correspondent and close friend Peter of Celle. In an 1159 letter which apparently accompanied the copy of the *Policraticus* which John presented to Peter, we are confronted with an explicit depiction of the metaphor of the body in unmistakably physiological terms.[29] John observes that the natural world is organized as a totality in which all phenomena 'derive their strength from mutual aid'. The universe, in other words, is structured according to an 'indwelling spirit of unanimity' which 'nurtures the concord of things dissident and the dissidence of things concordant'. Not merely is the physical world a whole, but it is a whole whose dissimilar parts cooperate in order to produce a singular result. This indicates to John that the universe is comparable to the model of the body, insofar as the spirit of unanimity

> arranges the divers parts of the body of the universe as though they were its members, in order that they may be attuned for mutual and reciprocal service. Thus, thus it is that in the human body the members serve each other, and the offices of each are allotted for the benefit of all. There are less of some and more of others according to the size of the body but all of them are united to secure the body's health; they differ in their effects, but, if you consider the health of the body, they are all working for the same end.

John has here stated the salient features of the physiological version of the organic metaphor. First, while the parts of the body are unequal in function, they are not thereby organized in purely hierarchical fashion. The subordination of inferior to superior is not unrestricted. Rather, the parts have a primary duty to cooperate in such a manner as to form a unified and mutually satisfying

---

[29] The quotations in the following paragraph are derived from *The Letters of John of Salisbury*, Vol. 1, ed. W.J. Millor, H.E. Butler and C.N.L. Brooke (London, 1955), p. 181 (Letter 111). The editors have previously dated the letter to autumn 1159, barely after the completion of the *Policraticus*. It is remarkable that no commentator on John's organic metaphor has, to my knowledge, made any reference whatsoever to this epistle. The relevant segment of the letter is as follows: 'Mutuis auxiliis constant omnia, et gravia vicissim levibus temperantur, et profecto ea sic universa procedunt, quod tantam dissidentium concordiam et concordium dissidentiam idem unanimitatis "spiritus intus alit" et, ut sibi invicem vicario quodam ministerio consonent, mundani corporis partes velut membra disponit. Sic sic in humano corpore sibi invicem membra deserviunt et singulorum officia publicis usibus deputantur. Absunt quidem haec magis illa minus pro mole corporis, sed in effectu salutis eius omnia uniuntur; varios habent effectus, sed si usum salutis penses, in idem universa concurrunt'.

totality. Second, the members of the body cohere in this way because they are all operating fundamentally for the good of the whole. John posits an end distinct from the individual benefit of any particular member which animates the cooperative spirit with which the body is imbued. Philosophically, then, John does not employ the comparison with the body after the manner of the Platonic claim that good order stems from doing one's job and minding one's own business.[30] Instead the physiological implications of John's organic metaphor lead to the very opposite conclusion that the true harmony of the parts is a matter of active collaboration rather than strict division.

Admittedly, John's letter to Peter only presents the physiological significance of the bodily analogy in a general way, without any specific reference to the polity. But the themes and language of the document are echoed throughout Books Five and Six of the *Policraticus*, thereby confirming the physiological connotations of the organic metaphor in John's political theory. The most obvious sign that John sought to apply the precepts of physiology to the political community is his repeated use of corporatist terminology. He speaks often of 'totius populi'[31] or 'corpore rei publicae'[32] or even the 'universitatem membrorum'.[33] In the Roman legal tradition, such phrases were employed to convey a fundamental unity of interest among otherwise disparate individuals. Thus, Romanist authors conceived of the community as 'a self-contained body, whose life was regulated by the public legal order'.[34] The presence of corporatist language in the *Policraticus* is hardly surprising in view of John's recognized familiarity with and sympathy for Roman law teachings.[35] It also seems likely that John found corporate sentiment alive in the work of Cicero, of whose thought he enjoyed intimate knowledge. Cicero's famous definition of the *res publica* (of which John was aware through St. Augustine)[36] emphasized that society entailed a fundamental harmony among men constituted 'by a common agreement about law and rights and by the desire to

---

[30] The famous definition of justice in Plato, *Republic* 434d.

[31] *S*, pp. 83, 103; *P* 549a, 560c.

[32] *S*, pp. 67, 91; *P* 541b, 553a.

[33] *S*, p. 259; *P* 626c.

[34] Otto Gierke, *Associations and Law: The Classical and Early Christian Stages*, trans. G. Heiman (Toronto, 1977), p. 122; but cf. also Gierke's remark that 'the idea that the state in its totality could be a living organism . . . did not appear in Roman law' (*ibid.*, p. 104).

[35] For a general review of John's familiarity with Roman legal concepts and texts, see Max Kerner, 'Romisches und Kirchliches Recht im *Policraticus*', in *The World of John of Salisbury*, ed. Wilks, pp. 365–79. John's interest in Roman law is also suggested by his bitter condemnation of King Stephen's prohibition of the teaching of civilian books and by his apparent close association with the Romanist Vacarius (*S*, pp. 396–7; *P* 808d).

[36] See St. Augustine, *City of God*, II.21 and XIX.21, trans. M. Dods (New York, 1950), pp. 61–2, 699.

participate in mutual advantages'.[37] Cicero thereby viewed the common-wealth as a 'natural' evolution out of the impulse to associate which was implicit in the gregariousness of the native human faculties of reason and speech.[38] Indeed, the latter doctrine John expressly adopted in his account of the origins of men's social intercourse in the *Metalogicon*.[39]

In terminology and inspiration, then, John's conception of the community in terms of corporate concord had precedents in Roman sources. But neither classical Roman lawyers nor Cicero had framed a doctrine of human society by reference to the organic metaphor. The *Policraticus* thus entered unexplored territory by animating the body politic with a principle of cooperative harmony through which otherwise disparate individuals and interests are reconciled and bound together. The *Policraticus* insists that 'there can be no faithful and firm cohesion where there is not an enduring union of wills and as it were a cementing together of souls. If this is lacking, it is in vain that the works of men are in harmony, since hollow pretence will develop into open injury, unless the real spirit of helpfulness is present'.[40] All the parts of the body, in other words, must be truly dedicated to a common or public welfare which supercedes the aggregate private goods within the polity. The ruler and magistrates are advised to attend 'to the common utility of all',[41] the lesser elements are counselled 'in all things [to] observe constant reference to the public utility',[42] and in general 'all the members' are expected to 'provide watchfully for the common advantage of all'.[43] John reveres ancient Carthage as the pre-eminent model of political cooperation, since there the inhabitants 'all labored together in common, and none idled'.[44] Of course, in Carthage, just as in the medieval commonwealth, the types of 'labor' might vary considerably among the different parts of society: some orders are charged with leadership and supervision, others with actual implementation.[45] But this by no means

---

[37] Cicero, *De res publica*, trans. G.H. Sabine and S.E. Smith (Indianapolis, 1929), p. 129; '. . . iuris consensu et utilitatis communione sociatus' (ed. C.W. Keyes (Cambridge, Mass., 1928), p. 65).

[38] As Cicero makes clear in *De officiis*, I.11–12, 50, 107, 156; *De inventione*, I.1–3; and *De res publica*, I, 25–6.

[39] John's reliance upon Cicero's naturalistic theory has been more closely examined in Cary J. Nederman, 'Nature, Sin and the Origins of Society: The Ciceronian Tradition in Medieval Political Thought', *Journal of the History of Ideas* (forthcoming).

[40] *S*, p. 95; *P* 554d–555a: 'Coherentia fidelis et firma esse non potest, ubi non est tenax unio voluntatum et quasi ipsarum animarum conglutinatio. Quae si defuerit, hominum frustra sibi congruunt opera, cum dolus in perniciem pergat sine affectu proficiendi'.

[41] *S*, p. 257; *P* 626a: ' . . . omnium utilitatem attende'.

[42] *S*, p. 243; *P* 619b: ' . . . ad publicam utilitatem omnia referantur'.

[43] *S*, p. 256; *P* 625b–c: 'Omnia denique membra publicis invigilant commodis'.

[44] *S*, p. 246; *P* 620d: 'Omnium namque laborem communem agnosces et neminem otiari'.

[45] *S*, p. 258; *P* 626b–c.

denigrates the value of the contribution to the whole made by any segment of the community. Instead, John claims that the unity of the body politic can only be established and maintained by means of a joint commitment to a public good which benefits every part without distinction, so that 'each and all are as it were members of one another by a sort of reciprocity, and each regards his own interest as best served by that which he knows to be most advantageous for the others'.[46] This statement reveals the extent to which an essentially physiological vision of the organic metaphor informs the political theory of the *Policraticus*. John's political body is one in which, beyond all social differentiation, 'mutual charity would reign everywhere',[47] because all wills are attuned to the same precept of an enduring common purpose which encompasses the interests of the whole. Unity follows from cooperation, and cooperation entails the existence of a good shared by the entire community and each of its members.

It may properly be objected that to speak in terms of an amorphous common good does not illuminate or articulate very adequately the actual principle which animates the body politic. Unlike many medieval authors, however, John was careful to identify the character of that common utility whose manifestation he sought in all the parts of the organism. It was John's view that the common good, the overall 'health' of the body politic, was constituted by the realization of justice throughout the organs and members. This equation of the common good with justice need not merely be inferred from the *Policraticus*, for John renders it explicit: 'So long as the duties of each individual are performed with an eye to the welfare of the whole, as long, that is, as justice is practiced, the sweetness of honey pervades the allotted sphere of all'.[48] The purpose common to every organ of the body, then, is the implementation and perpetuation of a polity which exercises justice as a matter of ingrained disposition.[49] All other public goods flow from the presence of justice in the corporate totality, and none of the collateral benefits of human society are possible in the absence of equity.[50] We ought to acknowledge that it is through the identification of justice with public utility that John's physiology of the political organism acquires a spiritual significance. Justice is not solely its own

---

[46] *S*, p. 244; *P* 619c: 'Singula sint quasi aliorum ad invicem membra et in eo sibi quisque maxime credat esse consultum in quo aliis utilius noverit esse prospectum'.

[47] *S*, p. 276; *P* 634a: 'Regnante undique mutua caritate'.

[48] *S* p. 247; *P* 621c: 'Dum sic coluntur officia singulorum ut universitati prospiciatur, dum iustitia colitur, fines omnium mellea dulcedo perfundit'.

[49] On the notion of justice (and indeed, every other virtue) as an 'ingrained disposition' (*habitus*), see Cary J. Nederman and J. Brückmann, 'Aristotelianism in John of Salisbury's *Policraticus*', *Journal of the History of Philosophy*, 21 (April 1983), pp. 216–23.

[50] Throughout the *Policraticus*, John treats *aequitas* as essentially coextensive with *iustitia*, although equity seems to be more directed towards the legal precepts through which just determinations are rendered. See *S*, p. 6; *P* 514c–d.

reward on earth, but it is also a path to otherwordly salvation; those whose wills are just, John remarks in an earlier passage of the *Policraticus*, shall be 'translated from riches to riches, from delights to delights, from things temporal to things eternal'.[51] The common good shared by the members of the political organism is not, broadly speaking, distinct from the religious goals of the body of Christian believers. But it is noteworthy that, at least in Books Five and Six, John seeks to give an account of the advantages of justice within strictly secular confines, based on the temporal needs of a physiologically well-ordered body politic. Where Book Four of the *Policraticus* treated of rulership in more traditional theological terms, John intended his presentation of the organic metaphor 'to shape the prince and the offices of the common-wealth to the practice of justice'[52] without direct reference to the divine system of rewards and punishments.

The *Policraticus* accomplishes this more limited task of equating the secular common good with the exercise of justice by concentrating on the manner in which just deeds are typically to be performed by each of the bodily members. The king is depicted as the chief purveyor of justice, whose will must be unfailingly oriented towards the performance of just acts and the promotion of universal equity through the promulgation of law.[53] Should one wish to know the proper 'formula of ruling', one need only look to 'the example of the just man';[54] the justice of a royal head is readily revealed when the body 'subject to its governance attains thereby to such pleasantness and abundance of fruits and flowers that if one enters therein he rejoices as though he were amid the delights of paradise'.[55] In short, the whole welfare of the community depends heavily upon the justice inhering in the ruler's soul,[56] if only because the king possesses primary responsibility for assuring the well-being of the remaining parts of the body.[57] An unjust head is the surest cause of the degeneration and dissipation of the political organism.

Despite the pre-eminence of the head, John by no means prohibits the other members of the body from playing an essential role in the realization of a just polity. To the contrary, it is John's view that all the offices of government (strictly understood) are direct extensions of the prince in the sense that their

---

[51] *S*, p. 47; *P* 533a: '. . . de divitiis ad divitias, de deliciis ad delicias, de gloria ad gloriam princepes transferantur, de temporalibus ad eterna'.

[52] *S*, p. 66; *P* 541a: '. . . principem et officia rei publicae ad cultum iustitiae informabat'.

[53] The royal function as legislator is most clearly articulated at *S*, p. 7; *P* 515b−c.

[54] *S*, p. 86; *P* 550c−d: 'Ecce regnandi in viro iusto ex magna parte expressa est formula'.

[55] *S*, p. 91; *P* 553a: '. . . subiectus exequitur tanta quidem amenitate florum et fructuum ubertate ut, si quis eum ingreditur, Paradisi de deliciis gaudeat interesse'.

[56] *S*, pp. 266−7; *P* 630b.

[57] *S*, p. 60; *P* 538d. Tilman Struve rightly speaks of the king as the 'coordinator' of the body's efforts to achieve the common utility (Struve, 'The Importance of the Organism', p. 310).

occupants are primarily charged with giving judgment in accordance with equity (albeit within a limited jurisdiction). 'Every magistrate is but the slave of justice', the *Policraticus* declares.[58] Unjust men ought to be excluded from among the counsellors who form the heart, for the king must be advised only by men who place the safety of the commonwealth above their own profit.[59] Likewise, the senses, regardless of whether they perambulate through the countryside or remain fixed in a single locality, are responsible for 'the administration of justice among the provincials'.[60] No less than the king himself, such officials 'are bound to justice by their profession or by an oath'.[61] We must consequently apply the same rigorous standards regarding the performance of justice to these magistrates that have been required of the prince. Any royal servant who prefers his own benefit to the practice of justice entailed by his office should be 'plucked out, cut out and cast away'.[62] Nor are the hands exempted from a duty towards the actualization of justice: while 'the unarmed [hand] is that which administers justice',[63] the armed hand is ordained so that just determinations may be rendered effectual. Soldiers 'execute the judgement that is committed to them to execute . . . in accordance with equity and the public utility . . . As it is for judges to pronounce judgement, so it is for these to perform their office by executing it'.[64] Where the prince is charged with propounding the precepts of justice, and the magistrate with rendering just judgment, the soldier is assigned to maintain the orientation of the body towards what is just by wielding the sword through which the good are protected and the evil punished. The *Policraticus* even accords to the feet a measure of obligation towards the dictates of justice which compose the essence of the common good. The proper health of the body requires that 'the lower [members] respond faithfully . . . to the just demands of their superiors'.[65] The feet ought in no manner to be construed as utterly servile; they are obliged to perform their functions with the proviso that their services accord with the precept of equity. While the feet are hardly qualified for greater duties, they are as much moved to act by the common interest as any other member and, by implication at least, they ought to refuse whatever is unjustly asked of them by the rest of the body.

[58] *S*, p. 126; *P* 569a: 'Omnis etenim magistratus iustitiae famulus est'.

[59] *S*, p. 112; *P* 562b–d.

[60] *S*, p. 123; *P* 567c: ' . . . in iure reddendo provincialibus'.

[61] *S*, p. 166; *P* 588a: ' . . . qui professione aut sacremento iustitiae obligati sunt'.

[62] *S*, p. 265; *P* 629c: ' . . . ervantur abscidantur et procul eiciantur'.

[63] *S*, p. 173; *P* 589a–b: 'Inermis quae iustitiam expedit'.

[64] *S*, pp. 199–200; *P* 600d–601a: ' . . . faciant in eis iudicium conscriptum . . . ex aequitate et publica utilitate . . . sicut iudicum dictare iudicium, ita et istorum faciendo exercere officium est'.

[65] *S*, p. 244; *P* 619c: 'Inferiora superioribus pari iure respondeant.'

From head to toe, the political organism must be disposed to the performance of justice if it is to survive. Justice is the end or purpose which unites the members, the goal which impels disparate organs to collaborate and coordinate their functions. The physiological connotations of John's argument are clear; the organic metaphor represents a careful account of how the cooperation between parts necessary to the physiology of the body is achieved through the disposition of each member towards the practice of justice in itself and in the whole.[66] Thus, we might say that John's intention was not to dissect but to nurture the body politic: the physiologist heals where the anatomist merely examines and differentiates.

In a broader sense, the image of John as a physiologist is a compelling one, for the political circumstances of mid-twelfth-century England had seriously damaged the health of the polity. The ascension of King Stephen, and the ensuing decades of civil disorder, had left deep wounds throughout the island, as John himself had often observed.[67] Moreover, Henry II's early years on the throne, while quelling the strife rampant during Stephen's reign, had already demonstrated to John that a king whose strength was too great could represent as grave a danger as a monarch who was too weak.[68] So the essential lesson of the *Policraticus* is that the healing of the community must occur by means of a thorough and rigorous training of all wills therein to bend to the dictates of justice.[69] Such instruction in justice as the *Policraticus* advocates will mould the various parts — from the prince to the peasant — into peaceable, law-abiding, prosperous and, above all, religious men. It is not enough to educate the ruler, as John's medieval predecessors had supposed; because all the members of the political organism have characteristic duties towards the common interest of the whole, they must each be instructed in the nature of

[66] Might justice thus be the long sought-after theoretical foundation for John's suggestion that rulers who become tyrants are rightfully put to death? Current scholarship seems inclined to reject the view that John had a coherent *theory* or *doctrine* of tyrannicide at all; see Jan van Laarhoven, 'Thou Shalt *Not* Slay a Tyrant! The So-called Theory of John of Salisbury', in *The World of John of Salisbury*, ed. Wilks, pp. 319–41. But this revisionist line contradicts an understanding of the *Policraticus* which has been a settled matter for approximately eight hundred years. I address this problem at greater length in a forthcoming paper entitled 'John of Salisbury and Tyrannicide: In Defense of Orthodoxy'.

[67] Scholars have so far not addressed John's attitudes towards the events of Stephen's reign in very great detail; I plan a careful examination of this topic shortly.

[68] This is amply illustrated by John's own fall from royal grace in 1156–7, which seems to have been the result of Henry II's policies towards the goods and liberties of the Church; full details are provided by Giles Constable, 'The Alleged Disgrace of John of Salisbury in 1159', *English Historical Review*, 69 (1954), pp. 67–76.

[69] Given the twin dangers of royal weakness and royal strength, it is perhaps not coincidental that the *Policraticus* defines justice in Aristotelian terms as a mean between excess and deficiency. On this theme, see Nederman and Brückmann, 'Aristotelianism', pp. 210–6; and Cary J. Nederman, 'The Aristotelian Doctrine of the Mean and John of Salisbury's Concept of Liberty', *Vivarium*, 24 (1986), pp. 128–42.

justice and must eventually practice just deeds until their wills are firmly fixed upon the principle of equity. In sum, John of Salisbury's reliance upon the organic metaphor seems calculated to achieve what Stephen and young Henry had not: reconciliation of the contentious elements of the polity by shaping them into a united whole all of whose parts collaborate out of mutual love and advantage. Insofar as the cooperative spirit exhibited in the *Policraticus* was to become a central theme of governmental practice and political theory alike in medieval England,[70] the physiologically-inspired organic metaphor introduced by John of Salisbury may be characterized as a pioneering model for rulers as well as for philosophers.

---

[70] On the cooperative spirit in thirteenth- and fourteenth-century English authors, see Cary J. Nederman, *State and Political Theory in France and England, 1250–1350* (Toronto, unpublished dissertation, York University, 1983), pp. 245–312.

VII

A Duty to Kill:
John of Salisbury's Theory of Tyrannicide

This article examines the doctrine of tyrannicide in John of Salisbury's mid-twelfth century political treatise, the *Policraticus*, in light of recent scholarly skepticism that John never meant to advocate a theoretical defense of slaying the tyrant. It is argued that John's conception of tyrannicide in fact possesses a philosophical foundation derived from his idea of the state as a political organism in which all the members cooperate actively in the realization of the common utility and justice. When the ruler of this body politic behaves tyrannically, failing to perform his characteristic responsibilities, the other limbs and organs are bound by their duty to the public welfare and God to correct and, ultimately, to slay the tyrant. John illustrates this position by reference to the many historical and scriptural instances of tyrants who have legitimately been killed. Thus, John not only proposes a theory of tyrannicide, but also roots it in a strong positive obligation to raise the sword against tyrannical rulers in the name of public benefit and justice.

I

Among students of Western political philosophy, the name of the mid-twelfth century author John of Salisbury has long been synonymous with (and infamous for) the classic medieval defense of the doctrine of tyrannicide.[1] Textbook accounts commonly attribute to John's major political treatise, the *Policraticus*, the origins of the claim that it is legitimate, at least under certain circumstances, to slay a ruler whose behavior has proved to be irredeemably tyrannical.[2] In turn, John's discussion of tyrannicide has been cited by all manner of later political thinkers and polemicists — from thirteenth-century jurists to sixteenth-century protestants to Fidel Castro[3] — as inspiration or justification for their own theories and strategies. As a consequence, a heavy burden falls on the reputation of John of Salisbury: he is implicated in a long-standing tradition of political violence.

We may well raise the question, however, of whether John's affiliation with this tradition of violence is warranted on the basis of the text of the *Policraticus*. After all, the nature of John's doctrine of tyrannicide is far from self-evident.[4] John never presented a single, coherent treatment of either his idea of tyranny,[5] or his justification of tyrannicide. Rather, discussions of these topics are distributed far and wide throughout the text of the *Policraticus*.[6] The ascription of a theory of tyrannicide to John rests primarily on two pieces of evidence. The first is his insistence (in the context of a discussion of courtly flattery) that it is lawful, right and just to take the life of a tyrant.[7] The second consideration stems from his extensive citation of historical cases of tyrants who, by virtue of their tyrannical conduct, met with painful or violent ends.[8]

A skeptical mind might easily doubt that such evidence could actually amount to a full and proper theory. This is an old suspicion. The prehumanist Coluccio Salutati had already expressed misgivings about John's "theory" in the fourteenth century: "The learned John of Salisbury, ... [who] declares that it is right to kill a tyrant and tries to prove this by a multitude of illustrations, seems to me to reach no result. His illustrations prove, not that the murder of tyrants is right, but that it is frequent."[9] Salutati's reservations, while seldom addressed directly in the intervening centuries, have never been put adequately to rest. Thus, within the last few years, scholars have renewed the challenge to the interpretation of John's writing as a theoretical source of the view that tyrants ought to be slain. For instance, Jan van Laarhoven declares of tyrannicide that "John does not have such a theory, John has a *praxis* . . . and he draws only one conclusion: tyrants come to a miserable end."[10] For van Laarhoven, we ought to drop all discussion of tyrannicide and speak of John's "tyrannology," that is, his account of how tyrants actually live and die.[11] Even if John makes the additional moral judgment that tyrants deserve the end they get, we are still not to impute to the *Policraticus* a theoretical defense of the justifiability of slaying a tyrant.[12] Van Laarhoven represents perhaps a pronounced and radical statement of skepticism about John's adherence to a doctrine of tyrannicide. Yet van Laarhoven is not alone. In varying degrees, many of the authors who have lately written about John's concept of tyrannicide have doubted the extent or sincerity of its intended application.[13]

Before we dismiss John completely as a genuine theorist of tyrannicide, however, we ought perhaps to ask once again whether there is any validity in the textbook interpretation of his conception of tyranny. An honest appraisal indicates, I contend, that there is still some wisdom in the orthodox reading of John's doctrine of tyrannicide. To locate the basis for such an interpretation, we must connect John's discussions of tyrannicide to the political ideas contained in the remainder of the *Policraticus*. When we view the doctrine of tyrannicide as a feature or logical consequence of John's political thought as a whole, it becomes clear that he did mean for his readers

to conclude that — at least under fixed conditions — it is right and
proper to employ force against a tyrant. More specifically, we may
locate the theoretical root of tyrannicide within John's thought in
his unique application of the organic metaphor to depict the political community.[14] For the terms which John employs to describe
the body politic in the *Policraticus* are imbedded in a conceptual structure that logically entails tyrannicide. Nor is this merely to impute
a relationship between John's ideas of the political organism and
of tyrannicide where none was intended. A careful survey of John's
treatment of tyrannicide instead suggests that he meant for the doctrine not to stand on its own, but to be seen as a direct and inescapable corollary of his understanding of the polity as an animate entity. It is this aspect of John's argument that for better or worse
ultimately vindicates his reputation as a theoretician of political
violence.

II

The first intimation of a connection between John's discussion
of tyrannicide and his conception of the body politic appears in Book
Three of the *Policraticus*. As already noted, John's reference to the
doctrine of tyrannicide occurs there within the context of his treatment of flattery. This may seem an odd place to assert the legitimacy
of slaying the tyrant. John's immediate purpose in invoking the idea
is to demonstrate that while flattery is ordinarily evil, it is not always
so. John reasons that so long as some measure of justice is present
at court, the good man has a duty to speak frankly and openly to
the ruler, and even to criticize those royal actions which he regards
as opposed to moral rectitude and orthodox faith. To flatter the king
under such circumstances, rather than to counsel him honestly, is
to place private gain before public welfare.[15] By contrast, John believes the reverse to be true in the case of the tyrant. To flatter a
tyrant is to protect oneself and one's community from the wrath
and vengefulness which might guide the tyrannical ruler's reaction
to honest advice. For if by flattery and dissimulation one may turn
a tyrant away from an evil policy, or at least mitigate the effects
of such evil, then one has a clear obligation to do so, according to
John. After all, John regarded the tyrant to be evil incarnate, the
imago pravitatis, to whom no respect or subservience is owed.[16] Hence,
one must employ for the sake of the whole polity those means to which

one has access, including flattery, in order to deflect the debilitating and sinful consequences of tyrannical rule.[17]

It is as part of his "proof" for the validity of this claim that John cites tyrannicide. John's argument is deceptively simple: "In the secular literature there is a caution that one must live differently with a tyrant than with a friend. It is not lawful to flatter a friend, but it is permitted to flatter (*mulcare*) the ears of a tyrant. For it is lawful to flatter whomever it is lawful to kill. Furthermore, it is not only lawful but equitable and just to kill a tyrant."[18] If we consider this passage carefully, it does not seem to constitute much of a defense of tyrannicide. Rather, as van Laarhoven has correctly pointed out, what John actually presents is a syllogism of which the principle of the propriety of tyrannicide is the minor premise (the major premise is that whoever may be slain may be flattered).[19] The conclusion of the syllogism is that one may flatter a tyrant — precisely what we would expect in the context of the section in which the argument appears. To suppress the syllogistic character of John's remarks, as some scholars have been inclined to do,[20] is to distort seriously the significance of his reference to the legitimacy of slaying a tyrant. In the passage under examination, tyrannicide is merely assumed for the sake of justifying the use of flattery upon the tyrant.

But we ought not to neglect the fact that John does attempt to give some foundation to the minor premise of his syllogism in the same section of Book Three. He goes on to explain that the tyrant whom one may flatter is the usurper, the servant not of God but of his own will.[21] To be a usurper, in this sense, is not merely to ascend to the throne by illegitimate means; it is rather to exercise power in accordance with arbitrary will and caprice.[22] This reflects John's emphasis throughout the *Policraticus* upon the significance of the moral will of the tyrant.[23] Because the tyrant is defined by his characteristic viciousness, he necessarily misuses whatever power he employs, since all authority is from God and therefore good. In consequence, "respect for the right and the just is either not sufficiently present or else wholly wanting from the face of tyrants."[24] John's assertion is obviously unproblematic in the case of so-called private and ecclesiastical tyrants who assail justice and right and must consequently be punished. Such nonpublic tyrants are, of course, restrained within the confines of human laws and institutions. Indeed, it is in order to deter those who prefer their own will to the public good that law is promulgated and enforced by rulers. By contrast, the public tyrant poses a special difficulty. For who may impose upon the vicious ruler the law which it is his duty to proclaim and execute over the whole community?

John evinces a clear awareness of the dimensions of this problem in the passage under discussion. He suggests that we might fruitfully reconceptualize tyranny on the order of the "crime of *majesté*," that is, treasonous behavior against a superior. Under the law pertaining to *majesté*, John remarks, "it is permissible for all to prosecute those charged with the crime of majesty."[25] In stating this, John merely repeats the customary legal precept that anyone (even a woman or a serf) may lay and testify to the charge of treason.[26] But John imparts to this concept new force by adding the proviso that public tyranny ought to be understood as the ultimate treason, a crime against the very body of justice (*corpus iustitiae*). When viewed from this perspective, John argues, "Not only do tyrants commit a crime against the public, but, if it is possible, more than the public."[27] In other words, since justice is ultimately a divinely endowed or inspired gift to a political community,[28] to offend against justice itself (the crime of the tyrant) is to attack God's will as well as to assault the body politic. This imputes to everyone concerned with the performance of justice the authority to act against, to prosecute, the tyrant by the appropriate means. Fear of retribution cannot excuse hesitation: "Truly there will be no one to avenge a public enemy," since the tyrant is the friend of none nor does he enjoy any just claim upon loyalty. In short, the public tyrant must be opposed by all who can do so. Indeed John describes the eradication of the tyrant in terms of a duty, an obligation: "Whoever does not prosecute [the tyrant] sins against himself and against the whole body of the secular republic (*in totum rei publicae mundanae corpus*)."[29] So John does not regard tyrannicide as a matter of choice for the individual; it is instead an obligation which is incumbent upon every member of the community. In turn, those who renounce their duty are accused by John of behaving like accessories to tyranny. This is the sense in which recalcitrant individuals commit a crime against themselves as well as the polity: they affront justice (and thereby God) by refusing to do what right demands of them.

John's argument in the third book of the *Policraticus* goes no further. In particular, he does not articulate any theoretical foundation for the obligation to oppose tyranny that he imputes to all members of the community. But by referring to the corporate "body" of the secular state, and by associating it with the *corpus iustitiae*, John directs his reader's attention to another section of the *Policraticus*, namely, the fifth and sixth books wherein he presents his theory of the body politic in terms of the organic metaphor. The implication is clear: if we seek to understand why every person in the polity is obliged to oppose the tyrant even to the point of slaying the oppressor, then we must turn our attention to the organic conception of the secular community.

III

John has been widely celebrated for his watershed contribution to the tradition of thought that models political organization along organic lines.[30] Although it enjoyed a long history prior to John's lifetime, and was commonly employed throughout the Middle Ages, the organic metaphor was articulated by the *Policraticus* in unprecedented detail and scope. John begins with the simple observation that the commonwealth may be likened to a "body endowed with life."[31] The differentiation of the offices of political society can thus be represented in a manner analogous to the distinction of the parts of the human anatomy. Like all bodies, the commonwealth is animated by a soul which guides its activities; John asserts that the place of the soul belongs to "those who preside over the practice of religion."[32] Yet the clerical soul of the polity is not, strictly speaking, a "member of the commonwealth," just as the eternal soul of man is not coextensive with the mortal physical organism which it directs.[33] The political creature is an essentially secular entity. Thus, the body politic properly speaking is ruled by the prince, who "holds the place of the head,"[34] and who "rightly deserves to be preferred before others."[35] At the heart of the commonwealth lies the senate, composed of the counselors whose wisdom the ruler consults.[36] The senses correspond to the royal judges and local agents such as sheriffs and bailiffs who exercise jurisdiction in the king's name.[37] The financial officers constitute the stomach and intestines of the body,[38] while the two hands are formed by the tax collector and the soldier respectively.[39] Finally, John compares the feet to the artisans and peasants "who raise, sustain and move forward the weight of the entire body."[40] Each of these parts of the organism, according to the *Policraticus*, has its own definite functions and tasks which are fixed by its location within the overall scheme of the body.

But we should not suppose that the point of John's organic depiction of the community was merely to justify hierarchy and division within society. To the contrary, the body politic is invoked in the

Policraticus as the expression of a principle of cooperative harmony through which otherwise disparate individuals and interests are reconciled and bound together. This is a theme that runs throughout John's writings: he recurrently stresses "reciprocity" as the salient characteristic of natural and social systems.[41] In the case of the *Policraticus*, John insists that "there can be no faithful and firm cohesion where there is not an enduring union of wills and as it were a cementing together of souls. If this is lacking, it is in vain that the works of men are in harmony, since hollow pretence will develop into open injury, unless the real spirit of helpfulness is present."[42] All the parts of the body, in other words, must be truly dedicated to a common or public welfare which supersedes the aggregate private goods within the polity. The ruler and magistrates are advised to attend "to the common utility of all,"[43] the lesser parts are counseled "in all things [to] observe constant reference to the public utility,"[44] and in general "all the members" are expected to "provide watchfully for the common advantage of all."[45] John praises ancient Carthage for promoting a spirit of cooperation in which "all labored together in common, and none idled."[46] John claims that the unity of the body politic can only be established and maintained by means of a joint commitment to a public good which benefits every part without distinction, so that "each and all are as it were members of one another by a sort of reciprocity, and each regards his own interest as best served by that which he knows to be most advantageous for the others."[47] John's political body is one in which, beyond all social differentiation, "mutual charity would reign everywhere,"[48] because all wills are attuned to the same precept of an enduring common purpose which encompasses the true interests of the whole. Unity follows from cooperation, and cooperation stems from the existence of a good shared by the entire community and each of its members.

A question remains, however, about what constitutes the substance of the common good of the body politic. How is the public welfare to be realized? In the physical organism, the joint purpose is achieved by the maintenance of the health of the whole body. Analogously, John contends that the "health" of the body politic, the public welfare, is coextensive with the dissemination of justice throughout the organs and members. John's actual definition of the common good in terms of justice is simultaneously imbedded in a recognition of a correlative obligation on the part of all members of the commonwealth: "So long as the duties (*officia*) of each individual are performed with an eye to the advantage of the whole, as long, that is, as justice is practiced, the sweetness of honey pervades the allotted sphere of all."[49] Every organ of the body must conduct itself according to the dictates of justice if the polity is to exist as a corporate unity. All other public goods flow from the presence of justice in the corporate totality, and none of the collateral benefits of human society are possible in the absence of that equity which is the product of the just will.[50]

It may still be unclear why John would make justice the touchstone of the political organism's common good. The answer has much to do with the very manner in which John defines justice. Following Cicero's definition in *De officiis*, the *Policraticus* asserts, "It is agreed that justice consists chiefly of not doing harm and of prohibiting out of duty to humanity those who seek to do harm. When you do harm, you assent to injury. And when you do not impede those who seek to do harm, you then serve injustice."[51] The essence of justice pertains to a responsibility toward others; this responsibility is not simply constituted by a negative obligation to refrain from the commission of injury, but entails a positive duty to protect others from harm as well. To behave in accordance with justice requires one both to ensure that one's own acts do not threaten the good of others and to attend to the injurious actions that other people may commit. Justice is thus inherently productive of social cooperation, whereas injustice necessarily tends to human disharmony and social disintegration. Nor does John believe that justice is a virtue the cultivation of which is best left to a few individuals. Rather, he contends that justice is rooted in the Christian teaching of the golden rule: "justice . . . in all things does to others that which it desires to have others do to it."[52] Any truly faithful Christian is as a consequence obliged to perform just deeds. Yet John's defense of justice as a generalized virtue is not limited solely to a theological context. The *Policraticus* also propounds a secular conception of moral psychology through which John can explain how justice may be acquired by every human soul. According to John, justice is like all other virtues in the sense that it is an ingrained disposition (*habitus*) which is created by assiduous practice.[53] Hence, it is possible for any person to become just by fashioning and shaping one's character in a rigorous fashion.[54] In short, justice in its temporal as well as its heavenly aspect is treated by John as a moral quality for which all persons are equally suited.

John's approach to justice has important repercussions for his theory of the body politic. For since the exercise of justice is the salient characteristic of a polity oriented toward the common good, justice must determine the manner in which each of the bodily members performs its functions. This is obvious in the case of the king, who is regarded to be the chief purveyor of justice. The royal will must be unfailingly oriented toward the performance of just acts and the promotion of universal equity through the promulgation of law.[55] Should one wish to know the proper "formula of ruling," one need only consult "the example of the just man."[56] Yet John's emphasis on the justice of the head by no means precludes the other members of the body from playing a significant role in the actualization of a just polity. It is the dissemination of responsibility for justice that leads John to declare that "every magistrate is but the slave of justice."[57] Unjust men ought to be excluded from among the advisors who form the heart, since the king must be guided only by those who place the safety of the commonwealth above their own profit.[58] Likewise, the senses, composing judicial officials, are expected to be diligent in "the administration of justice among the provincials."[59] No less than the king himself, such magistrates "are bound to justice by their profession or by an oath."[60] We must consequently apply to these public servants the same rigorous standards regarding the performance of justice that were ordinarily imposed upon the prince. Nor are the hands exempted from a duty to realize a just community. John describes the unarmed hand as "that which administers justice,"[61] while he reserves for the armed hand the authority to render just determinations effectual. Soldiers "execute the judgment that is committed to them to execute . . . in accordance with equity and the public utility. . . . As it is for judges to pronounce judgment, so it is for these to perform their office by executing it."[62] Even the feet are accorded a measure of obligation toward fostering the dictates of justice. The proper health of the body requires that the "lower [members] respond faithfully . . . to the just (*iure*) demands of their superiors."[63] The servility of the feet is limited to the performance of their functions consistent with the precept of rectitude that forms the common good. By implication at least, the feet ought to refuse what is unjustly asked of them by the rest of the body.

The effect of John's argument is the wide diffusion of responsibility for the maintenance of justice: all members of the body politic are ultimately charged with guarding and protecting the common good. This represents an important innovation in medieval political thought. John's predecessors (and indeed, many of his successors) had tended to attribute the duty for the promotion of justice wholly to the monarch.[64] The *Policraticus*, on the other hand, describes a commonwealth in which each of the greater and lesser parts cooperates in the dissemination of justice within the total community; none is exempt. In turn, John's refusal to equate the performance of justice with the specialized activity of the monarch has profound implications for his doctrine of tyrannicide. It may be recalled that John had declared in Book Three that failure to prosecute a public tyrant constituted a crime against "the whole body of the secular republic." Viewed in the light of his presentation of the organic metaphor, the full meaning of this statement becomes clear. John contends that since cooperation between the parts of the body is achieved through the disposition of each member toward the practice of justice in the whole, the organs and limbs have an obligation to resist the disease of injustice when it threatens to infect the organism. Ordinarily, the enforcement of justice is achieved through the application of the laws within which the path of equity is found, insofar as tyrants are normally of the private variety.[65] In such cases, the head and members act in concert to render just judgment and its execution. But on some occasions the ruler may be tainted by injustice, revealing himself to possess the moral characteristics of the tyrant instead of the true king. At such times, it becomes impossible to impose the law upon the ruler, because he is himself its source and final judge. Thus, extralegal remedies need to be introduced.

John thereby argues that the public enemy — the foe of that justice which constitutes the health and good order of the political organism — is to be opposed directly by those other parts of the body who share responsibility for the advancement of justice. Note that in virtue of the force of his conception of the body politic, John cannot merely be speaking of a *right* to fight and to slay the tyrant. Rather, he can only mean that an obligation exists which is incumbent upon every office of the body politic that still purports to be performing its duty. To decline to enforce justice against the public tyrant is to implicate oneself in the commission of tyranny. Hence, one sins against oneself (because one's best interests — spiritual and temporal — lie in living a just life) as well as against that political body in which one enjoys membership. In sum, John's contention that the public tyrant is rightfully to be slain may be regarded as a direct logical consequence of his approach to the body politic. The intelligibility of a theory of tyrannicide in the *Policraticus* depends upon its close relationship with the idea that in the political organism all members have definite duties toward serving the common welfare of the whole by promoting justice in each and every sphere of public life. No one who is not himself beyond the bounds of virtue can properly decline responsibility for ending the rule of the tyrant, if necessary by violent means.

IV

Recognition of a cogent theoretical foundation for John's doctrine of tyrannicide does not, however, resolve all outstanding interpretive difficulties. For it might reasonably be asked whether John has consistently or coherently applied this theory in the more substantial discussion of tyranny and tyrannicide contained within seven chapters of Book Eight. Scholars have long pointed out that the purpose of this section was not really to demonstrate the legitimacy of tyranny.[66] Rather, John's aim was to show that all tyrants come to a bad end, and do so at the behest of God Himself. Tyrants may be slain in battle, or struck down by natural disaster, or even die at an old age in bed — but every tyrant can expect punishment of the most horrific sort administered directly by the divine will.[67] In consequence, John regards the killing of a tyrant by one of his subjects to number among several possible fates which may accord with the plan of God's justice. "Wickedness is always punished by the Lord," the *Policraticus* proclaims, "but sometimes it is his own, and at other times it is a human hand, which He employs as a weapon with which to impose punishment upon the unrighteous."[68] Ultimately, John maintains, the way in which the tyrant meets his bad end depends upon the determination of God, although repentance and prayer may hasten the implementation of divine judgment.[69]

The sovereignty of the divine will raises the question of whether any theory of tyrannicide is meaningful when men are viewed merely as God's instruments.[70] For how can there be room left for independent human discretion when all legitimate cases of tyrannicide are seen to be directed by and subject to a divine plan? We must take care not to interpret John's remarks about the instrumentality of human action too literally. The *Policraticus* manifests a highly developed conception of man's liberty and free will.[71] John would seem to believe that God works through human hands when men freely accede to the divine will and serve it accordingly. To understand this perspective, we must acknowledge the dual significance of justice in John's thought. On the one hand, the performance of justice by each member of the political body is vital to the maintenance of the stable reciprocal structure from which all the material and secular benefits of communal life flow. Yet, on the other hand, justice in John's account retains an ultimate spiritual significance. While just deeds have their reward on earth, they are also steps on the path to other worldly salvation. Thus, John advocates what we might term the "unity of justice": those whose wills are just shall be "translated from riches to riches, from delights to delights, from things temporal to things eternal."[72] In other words, justice constitutes both the key to happiness in the present world and the assurance (insofar as true justice is inseparable from faith) of eternal beatitude. The common good shared by members of the political organism is therefore not, broadly speaking, distinct from the religious goals of the body of Christian believers.

The inescapable conclusion of the fundamental unity of justice is that the man who performs just deeds in the context of the commonwealth additionally reserves his place in heaven. This would seem to be the sense in which John remarks that God sometimes employs a human hand in eliminating tyrants: the man who commits tyrannicide does the bidding of God by imitating the divine will in the practice of justice. The secular obligation which members of the body politic acquire to serve the dictates of justice is paralleled by their divinely ordained duty to live in accordance with God's righteous law. When viewed in this manner, John's survey of the final disposition of various tyrants may be regarded as a casebook filled with illustrations of, generally speaking, how divine retribution is the end of tyranny and, more specifically, how parts of the political organism which do their duty according to the requirements of temporal justice also fulfill their responsibilities to God. Where the third book of the *Policraticus* had defended the justifiability of tyrannicide in purely secular terms, John's return in Book Eight to the theme of slaying the tyrant makes explicit reference to the theological context of this theory. The convergence between justice in the polity and divine justice does not negate, but rather reaffirms, his theory of tyrannicide.

That John intended his audience to draw a connection between the purely secular organic metaphor and his theologically informed treatment of the bad ends of tyrants is clear from the text of Book

Eight. At the beginning of his discussion of tyranny, he refers the reader to his previous survey of "the duties of the prince and of the different members of the commonwealth." Review of that passage, John contends, renders it "easier to make known here, and in fewer words, the opposite characteristics of the tyrant."[73] John envisages the qualities of the well-ordered body politic to be the reverse image of the characteristics of the polity ruled by the tyrant. A society which allows a tyrant free reign and affords no resistance to his dictates resembles nothing so much as a deformed and monstrous creature. John refers in this regard to "the commonwealth of the ungodly" which "has also its head and members, and strives to correspond, as it were, to the civil institutions of a legitimate commonwealth. The tyrant who is its head is the likeness of the devil; its soul consists of heretical, schismatic and sacrilegious priests . . . ; its heart of unrighteous counselors is like a senate of iniquity; its eyes, ears, tongue and unarmed hand are unjust judges, lawyers and officials; its armed hand consists of soldiers of violence whom Cicero calls brigands; its feet are those in the humbler walks of life who go against the precepts of the Lord and His lawful institutions."[74] The irreligious polity thus inverts all of the features of the political body ordered according to justice. Where the common utility animates the rightly arranged civil organism, self-interest pervades the deformed body; mutual and reciprocal service is replaced by the gratification of personal pleasures and passions. If the perverted body coheres at all — if, in other words, it does not merely disintegrate from internal conflict — then it does so only because of the superior coercive force of its tyrannical head. For in such a monstrocity there can be no truly shared or unifying principle of communal organization.

John's primary point here is, in effect, that a people gets the ruler it merits.[75] Where the members of the polity are oriented toward the maintenance of the common utility through the performance of appropriate just deeds, no tyrant will arise or, if by unfortuitous accident a tyrant ascends to the throne, he will soon be corrected or removed. John does not believe that a tyrant can corrupt by force a commonwealth whose other parts are thoroughly imbued with a just disposition.[76] Yet an unjust monarch, who seeks to substitute his own lordship in place of his rightful moderating role,[77] may nevertheless destabilize and derange the structure and operation of the whole. Consequently, if the tyrannical ruler of a well-ordered body politic does not "return to the path of righteousness," and instead "persist[s] in malice," then he will surely and justly be destroyed – if not by God directly then by whichever member of the community first succeeds in carrying out his obligation to promote the common welfare.[78]

The situation is fundamentally different in the case of the "commonwealth of the ungodly." For when a tyrant emerges among an essentially wicked populace, we are confronted with God's determination to impose a form of punishment as a penalty for the viciousness of the community. "Tyrants are demanded, introduced and raised to power by sin," John proclaims, and they "were rightly deserved" by societies which resist goodness.[79] It is not John's contention here, of course, that God's will is executed by means of direct intervention in human affairs. Rather, a corrupt people will almost inevitably generate a ruler in its own image – a lesson which Plato had long before taught[80] – who will in turn oppress it and convert it into his own private preserve. And as long as the subjects remain determined to renounce moral and religious precepts, they will (with divine authorization and approval) continue to be commanded by tyrants. The tyrant is both the product of the corrupt body politic and its divinely ordained punishment.

Tyrannicide can thereby be regarded as a viable course of action solely when the tyrant exercises power over a basically just community or when the moral disposition of the populace itself changes. The first case is relatively unproblematic: the members of the body politic are simply fulfilling the obligation imposed upon them to safeguard justice. The second instance is perhaps more troublesome. John insists that as a corollary to their origins in sin, tyrants "are excluded, blotted out and destroyed by repentance."[81] That is, when a people collectively acknowledges the error of its ways and seeks to rededicate itself to the service of divine and secular justice, the *Policraticus* permits the eradication of an unrepentant tyrant. Referring to examples of communal contrition, John asserts that such societies "were allowed to cast off the yoke from their necks by the slaughter of their tyrants; nor is blame attached to any of those by whose valor a penitent and humbled people was thus set free, but their memory is preserved with affection by posterity."[82] The complete restoration of rightful order to the political organism demands the total elimination of injustice from the body. Consequently, the tyrannical head, if he will not repent his crimes, must be removed from office – by means of his death, if necessary.

John's much vaunted plea for patience among the subjects of a tyrant does not mitigate this basic insight.[83] Rather, insofar as the act can be performed "without loss of religion or honor . . . tyrants ought to be removed from our midst."[84] Certainly, one way of ridding the regenerated commonwealth of a tyrant is for its members "to pray devoutly that the scourge with which they are afflicted may be turned aside from them."[85] The reason that this approach is considered preferable is that human judgment, while it may approximate divine justice, is nevertheless potentially fallible in a way that God's will is not.[86] But should the perpetuation of the tyrant's rule endanger the communal welfare, justice (in both its earthly and heavenly aspects) dictates that he be slain. To use John's own phrase, the tyrant has in such circumstances become a "public enemy," an outlaw, who may be killed without hesitation or remorse.[87] Exactly as the outlaw rebels against the just laws of his land, so the tyrant may be understood as "a rebel against God," preferring his own patrimony to "God's Law and His justice."[88] To the extent that this equation is valid, so too is John's conclusion: "If it is lawful to kill a condemned enemy, then it is to kill a tyrant."[89] The tyrant is indeed an enemy on perhaps a grander scale; his offense is not against one or a few laws, but against the very idea of law as a manifestation of justice. In sum, toleration of the tyrant must ultimately be tempered according to the extent of his harmfulness to the political organism. The tyrant should be endured with magnanimity and patience if that is possible without endangering public welfare, but he must be slain as soon as it is apparent that his tyrannical behavior imperils the ability of his subjects to live according to virtue and religion.

To say this is merely to apply a principle which John himself had earlier invoked, namely, that one should refuse to punish "that which can be tolerated honorably and without loss to religion," but that "there are some things which it is not permissible to tolerate or which cannot be tolerated in good conscience."[90] The same formula of justice which John ascribes to the ruler — that no ruler should be "too ready to punish his subjects, and take revenge on them for their faults"[91] — must also be expected of the other members of the commonwealth. In this sense, John is quite consistent in advocating patience where possible, but tyrannicide when necessary. Nor need one fear divine retribution; God surely confirms and even rewards the just determinations of human beings in such matters. For when humans will what is truly just, they reveal themselves to be created in the divine image and are at one with their holy master.

Yet none of this is to explain why John proceeds in Book Eight with the encyclopedic list of examples of tyrannicide, drawn from pagan and Christian sources, that forms a significant portion of the discussion of tyranny. It might be tempting to share Salutati's suspicion that John's copious citations represented an effort to "prove" the legitimacy of tyrannicide by arguing from particular examples to general precepts of rectitude. In fact, however, John presents no such position in the *Policraticus*. At best his examples have rhetorical force only as illustrations, as evidence that his theory has practical implications.[92] That he is so scrupulous in the collection of the *exempla* may further reflect John's acute fear of overt intellectual novelty. As perhaps the best read man of his time,[93] possessing a vast knowledge of the available classical sources,[94] John's intellectual instincts resisted the postulation of innovative ideas unsupported by long-standing tradition. Thus, even in the case of the organic metaphor itself, John did not claim to have created an original theory. Instead, he attributed the entire framework to the almost certainly spurious pseudo-Plutarchian *Institutio Traiani*.[95]

The same attitude toward intellectual novelty seems to explain the multitude of examples of tyrannicide surveyed in the *Policraticus*. John seeks to demonstrate that the obligation imposed by God and commonwealth to kill tyrants is not simply his own farfetched invention, but rather had long been recognized and acted upon by both pagan and Judeo-Christian peoples. Book Eight takes for granted the theoretical validity of the doctrine of tyrannicide, and attempts to establish a pedigree for that doctrine — an authoritative tradition which might remove the taint of originality from the theory. These are certainly the terms under which John himself invokes historical cases. He declares that from the study of history "it will readily appear that it has *always* (*semper*) been lawful to flatter tyrants and an honorable thing to slay them if they can be curbed in no other way. . . . It does not seem beside the point to illustrate what has been said by a few examples."[96] Likewise, the *Policraticus* invokes "the authority of Roman history," as well as "examples drawn from sacred and Christian history," in order to show that "it is *everywhere* (*undique*) obvious . . . that only that power is secure in the long run which places bounds on its own exercise."[97] John hence recommends consultation with "historical writers" to prove not the rectitude of tyrannicide, but the universal acknowledgment of the obligation to slay the tyrant. John's theoretical case for tyrannicide does not stand or fall on his examples from history. Rather, they lend authoritative weight to John's additional claim that, so far from originating the defense of tyrannicide, he has only revived and perpetuated a traditional conviction that members of the body politic have an irrevocable duty to kill the tyrant. Scholars have perhaps not sufficiently appreciated the difference between these two claims. John's normative argument on behalf of tyrannicide is rooted in his version of the organic metaphor, logically independent of the number or antiquity of the historical precedents for the slaying of the tyrant.

The logical independence of the theoretical basis of tyrannicide from the examples John surveys in Book Eight is further confirmed by his conviction that the way in which tyrannicide is practiced must be strictly consistent with the reason for which it is practiced, namely, to promote justice in the community. John insists that the theory thereby specifies the conduct (or range of conduct) acceptable in carrying out the deed. In order to achieve a just goal, in other words, one can only use a just means. Justice is a measuring stick against which may be judged the rectitude of various particular instances of tyrant-slaying. Thus, John asserts that oaths or bonds of fealty claim priority over the duty to slay a tyrannical ruler: "None should undertake the death of a tyrant who is bound to him by an oath or an obligation of fealty."[98] The reason is that such pledges are private covenants vouchsafed before God himself and do not depend upon other considerations for their performance.[99] One is as bound to keep a sworn promise to a wicked man as to a good one. The act of swearing an oath or homage means that one must keep the agreement unless or until the other party has broken it. This is the only principle of promise consistent with justice, and it is one John's contemporaries would well have understood. Thus, the *Policraticus* asserts that "sureties for good behavior are justly given even to a tyrant"; disregard for "the sacred obligation of fealty" will incur God's wrath and constitute a violation of justice even when the aim of the action — to remove the tyrant — is itself just.[100] The guarantee to fulfill an undertaking is contingent only upon the continued fidelity of both parties — and upon no other extraneous factors, tyranny included.

Similar considerations of justice lead John to proscribe the use of poison as a method of slaying the tyrant. It is on this point that the distance between John's theoretical defense of tyrannicide and his historical examples is most apparent. In his litany of the ends of Roman emperors, John mentions several tyrants who died by the poisoner's art.[101] Initially, he passes such information to his reader without additional comment. But he later judges poison to conflict with the terms under which tyrannicide is justly committed: "As for the use of poison, although I see it sometimes wrongfully adopted by infidels, I do not read that it is ever permitted by any law."[102] John's argument is not that the poisoning of tyrants is unprecedented, but that it is unjust. And no matter how many cases can be cited of tyrants murdered by poison, John's judgment is unchanged. Poisoning will always and forever constitute an unjust means of committing tyrannicide. John's rationale for this view, admittedly, is not immediately apparent. Perhaps he believed that poison — unlike the dagger and the sword, about which he manifests no overt reservations — left uncertainties about who assassinated the tyrant, and thus about whether the deed conformed to the precepts of secular and divine justice. Such speculations aside, the implication of John's refusal to sanction poison as a just method of tyrannicide should be clear: the theory itself dictates not only the worthiness of the end, but also the range of means which might appropriately be employed to fulfill the goal. And exactly as the justification of tyrannicide ultimately stems from a theoretical principle, rather than from the number of historical instances in which a tyrant was slain by his subjects, so the rectitude of methods for the accomplishment of tyrannicide cannot be determined merely by a study of previous cases. The requirements of justice are discovered solely through philosophical and moral reflection.

V

There seem to be compelling reasons to accept the conclusion that John of Salisbury richly deserves his traditional reputation as a theorist of tyrannicide. But we may well wonder whether John ever expected his theory to have practical consequences. In other words, was the *Policraticus* seeking to legitimize or to promote the mobilization of actual opposition to a given government? To answer this question thoroughly would of necessity lead us into a new field of investigation. But two observations are germane to the present study. First, John does not appear to have couched his theory of tyrannicide in such terms as to redress specific grievances against a particular tyrant. Despite occasional attempts by scholars to identify John's "perfect" tyrant as some definite historical figure,[103] the *Policraticus* scrupulously avoids citing any contemporary ruler as especially deserving of an early demise. The tyrants of the twelfth century mentioned by John are strictly of a private or quasi-private sort, like King Stephen's son Eustace or the rebellious barons and captains of the period of the anarchy.[104] The restraint of such individuals is mainly the responsibility of the royal head who enforces law and exercises jurisdiction. In short, John's presentation of tyrannicide rebuffs any interpretation which views it as a polemical call to action against a specific monarch. The *Policraticus* instead addresses the slaying of the tyrant from a more properly theoretical stance.

Yet, at the same time, we would also be unjustified in asserting that the conception of tyrannicide in the *Policraticus* was *merely* theoretical, in the sense that it lacked any practical import.[105] As we have seen, John's reference to the historical practice of tyrannicide and his discussion of the relationship between ends and means suggest his approval of actual opposition to tyranny. Perhaps more significantly, the theory itself stipulates the penalties for the refusal to do one's duty: not only does recalcitrance do serious harm to the body politic and to the justice for which it stands, but it is also an implicit affront to God. For to accede to the rule of a tyrant, and thereby to participate in the "commonwealth of the ungodly," is the mark of a weak, sinful and impious people; to seek the tyrant's removal is a sign of righteousness and virtue among the populace. By fashioning his account of tyrannicide in terms of virtue, and by specifying the consequences of declining to act upon one's obligation, John makes abundantly clear his confidence that tyrants will be slain in the future as they have been in the past. The function of John's remarks was not to incite individuals to commit any particular act of tyrannicide, but rather to articulate the theoretical premises of such behavior through the demonstration of a duty to slay a tyrant when circumstances dictate.

Nor would someone familiar with the general tenor of John's career and thought expect a different conclusion. As in so many facets of John's intellectual life, theory and practice ultimately merge. John could not abide dry scholastic exercises any more than the complete absence of philosophical reflection.[106] For him philosophy was only really valuable as a guide to a virtuous and honorable life, as an instrument rather than an end in itself. The case of the doctrine of tyrannicide is illustrative of this general intellectual orientation. Theory is necessary if one is to know how to treat a tyrant consistent with the precepts of justice. But theory is barren except insofar as it eventually intersects with and enriches practice. John of Salisbury's doctrine of tyrannicide is neither mere philosophical fancy nor a vague warning to tyrants. It is instead a challenge to members of the body politic to perform their duty to God and commonwealth when the situation requires it.[107]

NOTES

1. The literature on John's doctrine of tyrannicide is enormous. Among the more significant or substantial studies of the topic are: Richard H. and Mary A. Rouse, "John of Salisbury and the Doctrine of Tyrannicide," *Speculum* 42 (October 1967): 693–709; Johannes Spörl, "Gedanken zum Widerstandsrecht und Tyrannenmord im Mittelalter," in B. Pfister and G. Hildmann, *Widerstandsrecht und Grenzen zur Staatsgewalt* (Berlin: Duncker und Humblot, 1956), pp. 11–32; Gian Carlo Garfagnini, "Legittima 'postestas' e tirranide nel *Policraticus* di Giovanni di Salisbury," *Critica Storia* 14 (1977): 575–610; Peter von Sivers, "John of Salisbury: Königtum und Kirche in England," in *Republica Christiana*, ed. P. von Sivers (Munich: List Verlag, 1969), pp. 47–72; Max Kerner, *Johannes von Salisbury und die logische Struktur seines Policraticus* (Wiesbaden: Franz Steiner Verlag, 1977), pp. 193–203; and Jan van Laarhoven, "Die tirannie verdrijven . . . John of Salisbury als revolutionair?" in *Geloof in revolutie: Kerkhistorische kanttekeningen bij een actueel vraagstuk*, ed. W. F. Dankbar (Amsterdam, 1977), pp. 21–50.
2. For a sampling of surveys of political thought which have propounded this conclusion, see: R. N. Berki, *The History of Political Thought: A Short Introduction* (London: Dent, 1977), p. 104; Jean-Jacques Chevalier, *Histoire de la Pensée Politique*, 2 vols. (Paris: Payet, 1979), 1:172–73; Thomas I. Cook, *History of Political Philosophy from Plato to Burke* (New York: Prentice-Hall, 1937), pp. 215–16; Paul Janet, *Histoire de la Science Politique*, 2 vols., 4th ed. (Paris: Librarie Felix Alcan, 1913), 1:341–44; Robert H. Murray, *The History of Political Science from Plato to the Present* (Cambridge, MA: W. Heffer and Son, 1926), pp. 54–55; Charles H. McIlwain, *The Growth of Political Thought in the West* (New York: Macmillan, 1932), pp. 320–23; and George H. Sabine and Thomas L. Thorson, *A History of Political Theory*, 4th ed. (Hinsdale, IL: Dryden Press, 1973), p. 235.
3. The extent of John's impact may be measured from: Walter Ullmann, "The Influence of John of Salisbury on Medieval Italian Jurists," *English Historical Review* 57 (1944): 384–92; Amnon Linder, "John of Salisbury's *Policraticus* in Thirteenth Century England: The Evidence of Ms Cambridge Corpus Christi College 469," *Journal of the Warburg and Courtauld Institutes* 40 (1977): 276–82; Amnon Linder, "The Knowledge of John of Salisbury in the Late Middle Ages," *Studi medievali*, 3rd ser. 18 (1977): 315/881–366/923; Walter Ullmann, "John of Salisbury's *Policraticus* in the Later Middle Ages," in *Jurisprudence in the Middle Ages* (London: Variorum, 1980); Friedrich Schoenstedt, *Studien zum Begriff des Tyrannen und zum Problem des Tyrannenmordes im Spätmittelalter insbesondere in Frankreich* (Würzburg: Buchdruckerei R. Mayr, 1938); Dorotea C. Macedo de Steffens, "La Doctrina del Tiranicidio: Juan de Salisbury (1115–1180) y Juan de Mariana (1535–1621)," *Annales de Historia Antiqua y Medieval, 1957–1958* (Buenos Aires, 1957), pp. 123–33; Janet, *Histoire de la Science Politique*, 1: 341; and Fidel Castro, *History Will Absolve Me* (New York: Liberal Press, 1959), p. 73.
4. As the Rouses have pointed out, historians of political thought have generally neglected or covered up the ostensive inconsistencies in John's discussion of tyrannicide; "John of Salisbury and the Doctrine of Tyrannicide," pp. 693–94.
5. The various senses of "tyranny" in John's theory have been analyzed by Kate Langdon Forhan, "The Twelfth Century Bureaucrat and the Life of the Mind: The

Political Thought of John of Salisbury" (Ph.D. diss., Johns Hopkins University, 1987).

6. The standard edition is that by C. C. J. Webb (1909: reprinted Frankfurt a.M.: Unveränderter Nachdruck, 1965), 2 vols. (hereafter *P*). The *Policraticus* has been translated into English in two distinct volumes, one by John Dickinson containing the "political" sections under the title *The Statesman's Book* (New York: Knopf, 1927) (hereafter *S*), the other containing moral advice to prince and courtiers by J. B. Pike under the title *Frivolities of Courtiers and Footprints of Philosophers* (Minneapolis: University of Minnesota Press, 1938) (hereafter *F*). For the convenience of nonspecialists, citations in the present article will be given to the existing translated versions (although translations have often been revised); corresponding citations from the Latin text, employing the marginal numeration of the Webb edition, will be provided in the notes.

7. *F*, pp. 211–12; *P* 511b–d.

8. *S*, pp. 335–410; *P* 777c–814d.

9. Coluccio Salutati, "De Tyranno," in *Humanism and Tyranny: Studies in the Italian Trecento*, ed. E. Emerton (Cambridge, MA: Harvard University Press, 1925), p. 90. A discussion of the nature of Salutati's objections may be found in Conal Condren, *The Status and Appraisal of Classic Texts* (Princeton: Princeton University Press, 1985), pp. 278–79.

10. Jan van Laarhoven, "Thou Shall *Not* Slay a Tyrant! The So-called Theory of John of Salisbury," in *The World of John of Salisbury*, ed. M. Wilks (Oxford: Basil Blackwell, 1984), p. 328.

11. *Ibid.*, p. 329.

12. *Ibid.*, p. 328.

13. Among the scholars who seem susceptible to this charge are: Wilhelm Berges, *Die Fürstenspiegel des hohen und späten Mittelalters* (Stuttgart: Hiersemann, 1938), p. 59; Hans Liebeschütz, *Mediaeval Humanism in the Life and Writings of John of Salisbury* (London: The Warburg Institute, 1950), p. 53; Rouse and Rouse, "John of Salisbury and the Doctrine of Tyrannicide," p. 705; Kerner, *Johannes von Salisbury und die logische Struktur seines Policraticus*, pp. 192–93; and Garfagnini, "Legittima 'potestas' e tirannide nel *Policraticus* di Giovanni di Salisbury," pp. 37, 43–44.

14. For a thorough survey of John's conception of the organic metaphor, see Cary J. Nederman, "The Physiological Significance of the Organic Metaphor in John of Salisbury's *Policraticus*," *History of Political Thought* 8 (Spring 1987): 211–23; and Tilman Struve, "The Importance of the Organism in the Political Theory of John of Salisbury," in Wilks, *The World of John of Salisbury*, pp. 303–17.

15. John consequently defends a large measure of free speech and tolerance at *S*, pp. 323–31; *P* 705c–709b.

16. *S*, pp. 335–36; *P* 777d–778a.

17. See also John's defense of the biblical Judith, who engaged in flattery and dissimulation in order to defeat the tyrant Holofernes (*S*, p. 371; *P* 795b).

18. *F*, p. 211; *S* 512c. John's reference to the "secular literature" is apparently to Cicero, *De amicitus*: "Shall we live with a friend upon the same cautious terms we must submit to live with a tyrant?" (ed. J. Warrington [London: Dent, 1966], p. 209).

19. Van Laarhoven, "Thou Shall *Not* Slay a Tyrant!", p. 320.

20. For instance, Pike's translation (p. 211) omits altogether any English equivalent for the sentence "Amico utique adulari non licet, sed aures tiranni mulcere licitum est"; for similar errors, see van Laarhoven, "Thou Shall *Not* Slay a Tyrant!", p. 320, note 3.

21. *F*, p. 211; *P* 512c.

22. These are the terms under which John recurrently defines tyranny: *S*, pp. 351–52, 338 and 381; *P* 785d–786c, 778d and 800b.

23. See Cary J. Nederman and J. Brückmann, "Aristotelianism in John of Salisbury's *Policraticus*," *Journal of the History of Philosophy* 21 (April 1983): 224–27.

24. *S*, p. 338; *P* 778d.

25. *F*, p. 212; *P* 512d.

26. For a more thorough discussion of *majesté*, see *S*, p. 259–60; *P* 626d–627c.

27. *F*, p. 212; *P* 512d.

28. *S*, p. 4; *P* 514a.

29. *F*, p. 212; *P* 512d.

30. See Tilman Stuve, *Die Entwicklung der Organologischen Staatsauffassung im Mittelalter* (Stuttgart: Hiersemann, 1978), pp. 123–48; Paul Edward Dutton, *"Illustre civitatis et populi exemplum*: Plato's *Timaeus* and the Transmission from Calcidius to the End of the Twelfth Century of a Tripartite Scheme of Society," *Mediaeval Studies* 45 (1983): 108–12; and Nederman, "The Physiological Significance of the Organic Metaphor in John of Salisbury's *Policraticus*," pp. 211–16.

31. *S*, p. 64; *P* 540a.

32. *S*, p. 64; *P* 540b.

33. *S*, p. 83; *P* 548d.

34. *S*, p. 83; *P* 548d.

35. *S*, p. 107; *P* 560b.

36. *S*, p. 108; *P* 560b–d.

37. *S*, pp. 123, 145; *P* 567c, 576c–d.

38. *S*, p. 65; *P* 540c.

39. *S*, p. 173; *P* 589a–b.

40. *S*, p. 65; *P* 540d.

41. See W. J. Millor, H. E. Butler and C. N. L. Brooke, eds., *The Letters of John of Salisbury* (London: Thomas Nelson, 1955), 1:181; and John of Salisbury, *Metalogicon*, ed. C. C. J. Webb (Oxford: Oxford University Press, 1929), 825d–827d. I have attempted to dispel the predominant hierarchical interpretation of John's organic metaphor in "The Physiological Significance of the Organic Metaphor in John of Salisbury's *Policraticus*," pp. 213–15.

42. *S*, p. 95; *P* 554d–555a.

43. *S*, p. 257; *P* 626a.

44. *S*, p. 243; *P* 619b.

45. *S*, p. 256; *P* 625b–c.

46. *S*, p. 246; *P* 620d.

47. *S*, p. 244; *P* 619c.

48. *S*, p. 276; *P* 634a.

49. *S*, p. 247; *P* 621c.

50. Throughout the *Policraticus*, *aequitas* is used interchangeably with *iustitia*; where there is a distinction between them, it seems to turn on the legal character of equity in relation to the moral nature of justice. John most clearly articulates this difference at *S*, p. 6; *P* 514c–d.

51. *S*, p. 58; *P* 537c–d. Compare with Cicero, *De officiis*, I.7.3.

52. *S*, p. 58; *P* 538a.

53. *S*, pp. 74–75; *P* 544d–545b. The definition of the virtues in terms of *habitus* was a favorite theme in John's work; see Nederman and Brückmann, "Aristotelianism in John of Salisbury's *Policraticus*," pp. 216–23; and Cary J. Nederman, "Aristotelian Ethics and John of Salisbury's Letters," *Viator* 18 (1987): 162–66.

54. It should be noted, however, that John was hardly alone among twelfth-century thinkers in adopting this position; see Cary J. Nederman, "Nature, Ethics and the Doctrine of *Habitus*: Aristotelian Moral Psychology in the Twelfth Century," *Traditio* (forthcoming).

55. The royal function as legislator is attributed at *S*, p. 7; *P* 515c–d.

56. *S*, p. 86; *P* 550c–d.

57. *S*, p. 126; *P* 569a.
58. *S*, p. 112; *P* 562b–d.
59. *S*, p. 123; *P* 567c.
60. *S*, p. 166; *P* 588a.
61. *S*, p. 173; *P* 589a–b.
62. *S*, pp. 199–200; *P* 600d–601a.
63. *S*, p. 244; *P* 609c.
64. For further discussion of the emphasis placed on the royal will in medieval political theory, see Cary J. Nederman, "The Royal Will and the Baronial Bridle: The Place of the *Addicio de Cartis* in Bractonian Political Thought," *History of Political Thought* (forthcoming).
65. *S*, p. 356; *P* 788d.
66. Rouse and Rouse, "John of Salisbury and the Doctrine of Tyrannicide," pp. 703–704, 709.
67. *S*, pp. 375–77; *P* 797a–798b.
68. *S*, p. 375; *P* 797b.
69. See *S*, p. 373; *P* 796c–d.
70. This doubt has been explicitly raised by van Laarhoven, "Thou Shall *Not* Slay a Tyrant!", pp. 328–29.
71. I have discussed John's notion of liberty at length in "The Aristotelian Doctrine of the Mean and John of Salisbury's Concept of Liberty," *Vivarium* 24 (November 1986): 128–42.
72. *S*, p. 47; *P* 533a.
73. *S*, p. 335; *P* 777c–d.
74. *S*, p. 339; *P* 779c–d.
75. This doctrine is entailed by John's supposition of a unity between head and members, such that the character and moral status of each is ordinarily reflected in the other. See *S*, pp. 258–59, 264; *P* 626b–d, 629a–b.
76. *S*, p. 403; *P* 811b.
77. John stresses the king's moderating influence at *S*, pp. 367–78; *P* 793c–d. The theme of moderation is an extremely significant one in the *Policraticus* and throughout John's other works. See Nederman and Brückmann, "Aristotelianism in John of Salisbury's *Policraticus*," pp. 210–16; Nederman, "The Aristotelian Doctrine of the Mean and John of Salisbury's Concept of Liberty," pp. 128–42; Nederman, "Aristotelian Ethics and John of Salisbury's Letters," pp. 166–72; and Cary J. Nederman, "Knowledge, Virtue and the Path to Wisdom: The Unexamined Aristotelianism of John of Salisbury's *Metalogicon*," *Mediaeval Studies* (forthcoming 1989).
78. *S*, p. 376; *P* 797a.
79. *S*, p. 368; *P* 794a.
80. Plato argues at *Republic* 571a–577e that the tyrant necessarily arises out of the society in which men are least just and most self-interested, namely, democracy.
81. *S*, p. 368; *P* 794a.
82. *S*, p. 369; *P* 794a–b.
83. Among the scholars who have emphasized this are Ullmann, "The Influence of John of Salisbury on Medieval Italian Jurists," p. 388; and Rouse and Rouse, "John of Salisbury and the Doctrine of Tyrannicide," pp. 698–99.
84. *S*, p. 373; *P* 796c.
85. *S*, p. 373; *P* 796d.
86. John's general conception of human knowledge lays stress on its fallible character; see *P* 446a–b and *Metalogicon* 935b.
87. John uses the term "publicum hostem" recurrently throughout the *Policraticus*, as at *F*, p. 212; *S*, pp. 371, 393; *P* 512d, 795d, 807a.

88. *S*, p. 395; *P* 808a.
89. *S*, p. 364; *P* 792c.
90. *S*, p. 265; *P* 629b.
91. *S*, p. 43; *P* 531d.
92. This is consistent with what scholars have asserted about John's use of examples more generally in the *Policraticus*. See Liebeschütz, *Mediaeval Humanism in the Life and Writings of John of Salisbury*, pp. 67–73; and Peter von Moos, "The Use of *Exempla* in the *Policraticus* of John of Salisbury," in Wilks, *The World of John of Salisbury*, pp. 207–61.
93. A judgment widely held by scholars: compare the remarks of Clement C. J. Webb, "John of Salisbury," *Proceedings of the Aristotelian Society*, 2, no. 2, ii (1894): 96; Sidney Painter, "John of Salisbury and the Renaissance of the Twelfth Century," in *The Greek Tradition*, ed. G. Boas (Baltimore: Johns Hopkins University Press, 1939), p. 87; Ronald E. Pepin, "John of Salisbury: An American Tribute," *Hatcher Review* 9 (1980): 17.
94. The recent work of Janet Martin, establishing the precise manuscript sources of John's references, in no way diminishes his reputation, but only demonstrates that some classical works thought to be directly accessible in the mid-twelfth century were actually known only through intermediates; see Martin, "John of Salisbury's Manuscripts of Frontinus and Gellius," *Journal of the Warburg and Courtauld Institutes* 40 (1977): 1–26; "Uses of Tradition: Gellius, Petronius and John of Salisbury," *Viator* 10 (1979): 57–76; and "John of Salisbury as Classical Scholar," in Wilks, *The World of John of Salisbury*, pp. 179–201. On the other hand, it seems clear that John was one of the very first to know and use the full text of Aristotle's *Topics*; see Nederman and Brückmann, "Aristotelianism in John of Salisbury's *Policraticus*," p. 204.
95. The suggestion that John himself created the *Institutio Traiani* as a pseudo-authoritative source was first proposed by Liebeschütz in a 1943 article and has been actively debated ever since. For a brief review of the debate including a full bibliography, see Max Kerner, "Randbemerkungen zur Institutio Traiani," in Wilks, *The World of John of Salisbury*, pp. 203–206.
96. *S*, pp. 256–57; *P* 788d (italics supplied).
97. *S*, p. 367; *P* 793c (italics supplied).
98. *S*, pp. 372–73; *P* 798b.
99. This follows from John's more general discussion of feudal bonds at *S*, p. 261; *P* 627d–628a.
100. *S*, p. 373; *P* 796b–c.
101. *S*, p. 359; *P* 789d.
102. *S*, p. 373; *P* 796c.
103. For example, the suggestion of Roger II of Sicily by Helene Wieruszowski, "Roger II of Sicily, *Rex-Tyrannus*, in Twelfth-Century Political Thought," *Speculum* 38 (January 1963): 68–70; Frederick Barbarossa by Spörl, "Gedanken zum Widerstandsrecht und Tyrannenmord im Mittelalter," p. 21; of King Stephen by Liebeschütz, *Mediaeval Humanism in the Life and Writings of John of Salisbury*, p. 52; and (perhaps) of Henry II by Rouse and Rouse, "John of Salisbury and the Doctrine of Tyrannicide," pp. 704–709.
104. *S*, pp. 392–93; *P* 806d–807b. For an interesting discussion of this passage, see von Sivers, "John of Salisbury," pp. 70–71.
105. Thus, Clement Webb, *John of Salisbury* (London: Methuen, 1932), p. 66, remarks that John's treatment of tyrannicide "was a natural development of the republican rhetoric which he found in classical writers; and we have no reason to think that he was ever disposed to make a practical application of it." Similarly Rouse and Rouse, "John of Salisbury and the Doctrine of Tyrannicide," p. 709,

conclude that "the doctrine of tyrannicide is purely theoretical, in the sense that John was not proposing it as a plan of action."

106. On John's conception of philosophy as "practical," and his consequent reservations about its academic aspects, see Nederman, "Aristotelian Ethics and John of Salisbury's Letters," pp. 172–73 and "Knowledge, Virtue and the Path to Wisdom."

107. An earlier version of this paper was read at the University of California, Log Angeles. Thanks are due to Professors Richard Rouse and Robert Benson, and Dr. Mary Rouse, for their insightful and challenging criticisms and suggestions. The author is also grateful to the anonymous reader for the present journal for numerous helpful comments.

VIII

The Aristotelian Doctrine of the Mean
and John of Salisbury's Concept of Liberty

One tenet of conventional wisdom among historians of medieval moral and political philosophy holds that the dawn of the thirteenth century marked the beginning of a new direction in the trajectory of social ideas. An intellectual reorientation is said to have been necessitated by the reintroduction into the West of the body of Aristotle's writings on ethics and politics. It is thus commonplace for scholars to declare that Western social theory underwent a "conceptual revolution" during the period from 1200 (when fragments of the *Nicomachean Ethics* came into circulation) until 1250 (by which date the whole *Politics* seems to have been translated). These five decades are taken to be a watershed in the development of European philosophy.[1] In turn, two conclusions are ordinarily drawn from the postulate of an Aristotelian revolution in the early thirteenth century: first, after about 1200, and certainly by 1250, the foundations of ethical and political thinking in Latin Christendom were wholly and irredeemably Aristotelian; and second, it is senseless to look for the influence of Aristotle's ideas on moral and social treatises composed prior to 1200.

Although these canons of interpretation have become paradigmatic, they are by no means engraved in stone. On the one hand, it may be demonstrated that even the most Aristotelian of thirteenth and fourteenth century authors were often less indebted to Aristotle than to other classical and medieval sources. Aristotle, once recovered, in no way supplanted, but instead supplemented, the other authorities upon which the Middle Ages depended.[2] On the other hand, Aristotle's social ideas were not entirely unknown to, and uninfluential with,

---

[1] It would, of course, be a massive undertaking to document all of the authors who have adopted this view. For a representative sampling, see: Walter Ullman, *Medieval Political Thought*, Harmondsworth, Middlesex 1975, p. 159; Quentin Skinner, *The Foundations of Modern Political Thought*, 2 vols., Cambridge 1978, I, pp. 50-1; and Brian R. Nelson, *Western Political Thought*, Englewood Cliffs, NJ 1982, p. 89.

[2] I intend to establish this in a forthcoming series of investigations into the influence of Aristotle on medieval political theory after 1250.

Latin philosophers prior to the thirteenth century. Indeed, earlier research has already shown that one of the most prominent twelfth century treatises on moral and political matters, John of Salisbury's *Policraticus*, is unmistakably imbued with Aristotelian doctrines.[3] John's access to these doctrines indicates the existence of an "underground" tradition of Aristotelian thought about man in society running throughout the Middle Ages prior to the recovery and transmission of Aristotle's *Ethics* and *Politics*.[4] Admittedly, knowledge of the structure of the Aristotelian argument was fragmentary until the thirteenth century. But Aristotle *did* exert a philosophically interesting influence over earlier moral and political concepts in the medieval West.

The mere presence of Aristotelian terminology and ideas in texts completed before 1200 does not, it is true, prove their importance to medieval philosophizing. Rather, what is required is an analysis of how Aristotelian principles were assimilated and integrated into significant aspects of medieval philosophical discourse. With this broader issue in mind, the present paper will argue that a key element of Aristotle's moral thought, his definition of virtue as a mean, was not only known to and used by John of Salisbury in the *Policraticus*, but also was the indispensible basis for the doctrine of individual and political liberty espoused by John.[5] Defense of this claim necessitates the investigation of three matters: first, the range of sources from which John may have drawn the idea of virtue as a mean; second, John's application of the concept of the mean within the *Policraticus*; and third, the conclusions about liberty reached in the *Policraticus* as a result of John's notion of the mean. By focussing our attention on John of Salisbury, we shall discover how, in at least one instance, the

---

[3] Cary J. Nederman and J. Brückmann, *Aristotelianism in John of Salisbury's* Policraticus, in: Journal of the History of Philosphy, 21 (1983), pp. 203-29.
[4] For a similar argument about the work of Henry Bracton, see Cary J. Nederman, *Bracton on Kingship Revisited*, in: History of Political Thought, 5 (1984), pp. 61-77.
[5] For the sake of a broader, non-specialist audience, references to the *Policraticus* will be drawn from the existing translations (with occasional modifications). The "political" sections of the *Policraticus* have been translated by John Dickinson under the title *The Statesman's Book* (New York 1927); the "courtly" chapters have been rendered into English by J. B. Pike as *Frivolities of Courtiers and Footprints of Philosophers* (Minneapolis 1938). Both translations are based on the excellent 1909 critical edition of the *Policraticus* (lately reprinted) produced by C. C. J. Webb (Frankfurt a.M., Unveränderter Nachdruck, 1965), 2 vols.; citations will also be given to the marginal numbers in Webb's edition. In future references, the critical edition will be abbreviated as *P*, *The Statesman's Book* as *S*, and the *Frivolities of Courtiers* as *F*.

"underground Aristotle" provided the foundations for an innovative contribution to the moral and political philosophy of the Middle Ages.

I

It would be a difficult and perhaps futile task to identify all of the documents from which John of Salisbury could have extracted the equation of virtue with a mean between excess and deficiency. Elements of this doctrine pervaded the Roman and Christian traditions, and were often expressed by poets and theologians as well as philosophers.[6] But while moderation or the mean as a general principle was commonly advocated by pre-medieval authors, John would have known comparatively few works which provided a thorough articulation of the concept. In particular, there appear to be two possible sources for a more detailed Aristotelian account of virtue: first, Aristotle himself, some of whose treatises on logic and language survived in Latin to the mid-twelfth century; and second, the writings of Cicero, who occasionally reported and even accepted Aristotle's moral ideas. It may be that other potential authorities (such as Boethius) have been overlooked. But it is sufficient for the present argument to demonstrate that *some* texts familiar to John contained the substance of Aristotle's doctrine of the mean.

In preparation for an examination of the sources to which John had direct access, however, we ought first to survey the salient features of Aristotle's classic and complete definition of virtue in the *Nicomachean Ethics*. Aristotle claims that the virtuous soul is possessed only by the person who has learnt all the virtues *in their proper measure*. Goodness in human action is thus defined as hitting the mark (or mean) between excess and deficiency; evil occurs when the agent's behaviour is either "too much" to "too little". For instance, it is equally bad to be foolhardy as to be timid when the virtue sought is courage. Aristotle teaches that "whereas the vices either fall short of or exceed what is right in feelings and actions, virtue ascertains and adopts the mean."[7] This suggests that we ought not simply to contrast good and evil, virtue and vice. Instead, the good and the virtuous must be juxtaposed to

---

[6] For example, John himself cites Terence and Horace on moderation at *P* 398a-b (*F*, p. 25); and we find even St. Augustine advocating a moderate lifestyle in *De libero arbitro*, Book 3, sec. 48.

[7] Aristotle, *Nicomachean Ethics* II.vi.16, 1107a; H. Rackham translation, 2nd ed., Cambridge, Mass 1934.

two forms of vice, excess and deficiency, both of which are in turn contrary to one another.[8] It is noteworthy that, on this account, to hit the
mean is to be *moderate* in one's moral conduct, but that moderation (as
opposed to temperence or self-control) has no standing separate from
the specific virtues. Good or virtuous action consists in following a
middle path between opposite wrongs. Therefore, moderation or the
mean is characteristic of all the virtues without ever being construed as
a virtue in itself.

Various logical and linguistic complexities arise from the structure
of ethical propositions. Consequently, Aristotle's works on language
and syllogistic logic often address moral ascriptions and, by extention,
concepts. Some of these writings, known collectively under the label of
the *Organon*, were available during the Middle Ages even prior to the
massive influx of Aristotelian texts that commenced at the end of the
twelfth century. For example, the *Categories* had been translated into
Latin by Boethius and was read widely by early medieval men, including John of Salisbury; similarly, the *Topics*, the transmissional
history of which is a bit more confused,[9] was known already to John
when he composed the *Metalogicon* in the late 1150s.[10] In each of these
works, Aristotle had expressly referred to the doctrine of the mean
both as one way of understanding the term "good" and as an important exception to general rules about the use of contraries. As a result,
the *Topics* and *Categories* contain several passages which present the notion of the mean in a manner parallel to the *Nicomachean Ethics*. The
Topics declares, for instance, that the word "good" is applicable to
"that which is moderate; for that which is moderate is also called
good."[11] Aristotle later expands on this remark with the explanation
that "defect and excess are in the same genus—for both are in the
genus of evil—whereas what is moderate, which is intermediate between them, is not in the genus of evil, but that of good."[12] Essentially
the same argument is also found in the *Categories*: "What is contrary to
a bad thing is sometimes good but sometimes bad. For excess, which is
itself bad, is contrary to deficiency, which is bad; yet the mean is con-

---

[8] See ibid., II.viii.1, 1108b.

[9] This is dealt with, at least in part, by Eleonore Stump, *Boethius's De topicis differentis*, Ithaca, NY 1978, pp. 159-236.

[10] As John himself tells us at *Metalogicon* Book 3, Chapter 5 (trans. D. D. McGarry
(Berkeley 1955), p. 172).

[11] Aristotle, *Topics* I.15,107a11-13; E. S. Forster translation (Cambridge, Mass.
1960).

[12] Ibid., IV.3, 123b27-30.

trary to both and it is good."[13] According to both the *Topics* and *Categories*, then, moral goodness may be found in moderation understood as a mean between excess and deficiency. Attaining to virtue consists in measured action, and by extension vice may equally well arise out of either an absence or a surplus of virtue.

There is no doubt that classical authors in the centuries after Aristotle both knew and recounted the doctrine of the mean. The most prominent of these thinkers writing in the Latin language was Cicero, many of whose works were retained and disseminated by the intelligensia of both late Roman and medieval Christendom. Cicero's application of Aristotle's notion of the mean was not, it must be admitted, thorough-going or consistent. In his mature moral thought, represented by *De officiis*, Cicero generally adopts the tenets of the Stoic ethical system. Nevertheless, he does on occasion refer to "the doctrine of the mean... approved by the Peripatetics, namely, that "happy mean which lies between excess and defect."[14] Moreover, *De officiis* teaches that in dress and in generousity "the rule of the golden mean is best."[15] This view accords with Cicero's claim that "moderation in all things" is embraced by the concept of *decorum*, that is, the quality which pertains to every act of moral rectitude.[16] But the very essence of *decorum*, *De officiis* declares, is the Cardinal Virtue of Temperence.[17] In other words, moderation really forms a part of substantive virtue in *De officiis* rather than a structural characteristic of all the virtues. Cicero is truer to Aristotle's doctrine of the mean in a youthful essay on rhetoric, *De inventione*, which was, like *De officiis*, widely read throughout the Middle Ages. In *De inventione*, as in the *Organon*, the concern is not with ethics *per se*, but with the linguistic nature of moral ascriptions. Specifically, Cicero objects to the conventional paring of one virtue with its opposite vice, e.g., courage with cowardice. Instead, Cicero maintains that the standard virtues (justice, courage and the rest) are contrary both to their customary opposites (injustice, cowardice, etc.) and to another set of qualities which are composed of virtue taken to excess. *De inventione* insists that "each virtue will be found to have a vice bordering upon it, either one to which a definite name has become attached, as temerity which borders

---

[13] Aristotle, *Categories* 11, 14a2-6; J. L. Ackrill translation (Oxford 1963).
[14] Cicero, *De officiis*, I.89; W. Miller translation (Cambridge, Mass. 1913).
[15] Ibid., II.59; cf. I.130 and II.66.
[16] Ibid., I.93-4.
[17] Ibid., I.100.

on courage ... or one without any definite name. All of these as well as the opposites of good qualities will be classed among things to be avoided."[18] Cicero's analysis thus captures what was crucial to Aristotle's original account of the mean: that it is no better to display a surplus of virtue than a surfeit. Missing the mark in either the direction of defect or of excess is bound to lead the individual into vice.

II

We can now see that John of Salisbury possessed an ample number of authorities on which to base an Aristotelian conception of the virtues as a mean between excess and deficiency. We should not be surprised, then, to discover reverberations of this doctrine throughout the text of the *Policraticus*. John certainly had a good historical reason for including Aristotle's doctrine of the mean. The *Policraticus* was composed, after all, as a critique of many of the practices associated with the courtly conduct of the twelfth century feudal aristocracy in England and on the Continent. John's primary concern is to illuminate the vices of noblemen and rulers in order to instruct them in the forms of behaviour becoming men of status and power.[19] To impose upon such magnates a monastic or ascetic regimen would be, however, unrealistic and ultimately self-defeating. The feudal aristocracy, as John knew well, was properly composed of war-like men of action who would never heed seriously the bookish virtues normally advocated by contemplative churchmen. Since the *Policraticus* is intended to be a practical guidebook, John is willing to allow that "if moderation is displayed, I do not judge it unbecoming... to dwell at times upon the pleasures of the senses; as has often been said, nothing is unseemly except that which is beyond measure... Modestly pursued for purposes of recreation, they are excused under the license of leisure."[20] In this way, John orients the values he upholds towards the actual conditions under which knights and princes lived. The *Policraticus* seeks to temper the behaviour of warriors, not to suppress all the amusements of court.

---

[18] Cicero, *De inventione*, II.65; H. M. Hubbell translation (Cambridge, Mass. 1949).
[19] The range of John's courtly concerns is addressed by Cary J. Nederman and N. Elaine Lawson, *The Frivolities of Courtiers Follow the Footprints of Women: Misogyny and the Crisis of Virility in John of Salisbury's* Policraticus, in: C. Levin et al., eds., *Medieval and Renaissance Women*, Detroit (Forthcoming).
[20] *F*, p. 373; *P* 761b-c, 761d.

The audience to which John addresses himself thereby helps to determine his conception of virtue. For throughout the *Policraticus*, John maintains that if any action "exceeds the mean, it is a fault. Every virtue is marked by its own boundaries, and consists in the mean. If one exceed this, one is off the road, not on it."[21] It is a characteristic of genuine moral goodness, John teaches, to be neither excessive nor deficient, but rather to follow a middle course between opposite evils. Bad men, accordingly, "withdraw from the mean between vices, which is the field of virtue."[22] Employing the metaphor of the left and right hands, the *Policraticus* observes that "to incline to the right signifies to insist too enthusiastically upon the virtues themselves. To incline to the right is to exceed the bounds of moderation in the works of virtue, the essence to which is moderation. For truly all enthusiasm is the foe of salvation and all excess is a fault: nothing is worse than the immoderate practice of good works."[23] While this view may seem strange for an orthodox twelfth-century churchman, it reveals the extent to which John's concerns about the condition of the feudal nobility result in his presentation of a fundamentally Aristotelian account of virtue. It is in the nature of all virtues, John says, that they may be attained only when pursued within definite limits. Moderation or the mean indicates the manner in which the boundaries defining virtuous action are to be constructed. John seeks particularly to establish the harm which may result from the zealous exercise of virtue. For instance, the individual who, in the name of justice, shows mercy to someone whose actions warrant punishment has committed as grave an injustice as if punishment had been meted out unfairly. Perhaps referring directly to Aristotle,[24] John comments that "the philosopher warns us to avoid excess; for if a man depart from this caution and moderation, he will in his lack of caution foresake the path of virtue itself... What can then be of any profit if justice herself, the queen of the virtues, is hurtful in excess?"[25] Overstepping the bounds of goodness in the name of goodness itself will be as repugnant as the utter absence of moral propriety. Moderation pertains to the essential structure of virtue, in the sense that any

---

[21] *F*, p. 157; *P* 480d.
[22] *F*, p. 374; *P* 762c.
[23] *S*, p. 43; *P* 731c-d.
[24] Nederman and Brückmann, *Aristotelianism in John of Salisbury's* Policraticus, pp. 215-6.
[25] *S*, p. 43; *P* 731d.

action is virtuous if and only if it participates in and is guided by the measure or mean.

But how can one know what the virtuous mean is in any specific case requiring a moral decision? In the *Nicomachean Ethics*, Aristotle had held that the mean is always *relative* to the agent.[26] So far as can be discovered, however, this position is not reproduced anywhere in the *Organon* or in the Aristotelian-influenced thinkers available to John. Nevertheless, the solution proposed in the *Policraticus* does not differ greatly from Aristotle's own. "Discretion with regard to time, place, amount, person and cause," John states, "readily draws the proper distinction" between virtuous and vicious action; indeed, circumstantial discretion "is the origin and source of moderation in its widest sense without which no duty is properly performed."[27] In deciding how to conduct himself, each individual must determine all relevant circumstantial considerations and choose the course of action which is appropriately moderate within its context. According to John, most actions cannot be judged apart from their circumstances. To cite but one case, it is clearly vicious to take a human life; yet as a form of punishment, or as the outcome of a justly fought battle, it may be vicious *not* to take a life. In John's view, there would seem to be a few moral absolutes in the realm of human conduct. His circumstantialist doctrine leads to a form of individualism,[28] although not, of course, to complete relativism, insofar as one is still subject to the ultimate assessment of divine judgement.

Another consequence of the claim that all virtue is characteristically governed by moderation is that various actions which John first appears to condemn as morally reprehensible he eventually allows to be morally acceptable in the proper measure. After a lengthy and scathing critique of hunting—a favourite pastime of the Anglo-Norman aristocracy—John ostensively reverses himself: "The activity, however, is laudable when moderation is shown and hunting is pursued with judgement and, when possible, with profit."[29] The seeming contradiction between John's obvious distaste for hunting and his later acceptance of it may be explained precisely by his view

---

[26] See Aristotle, *Nicomachean Ethics*, II.viii, 1109a.

[27] *F*, p. 373; *P* 761d-762a.

[28] A view which has been proposed by Kate Langdon Forhan, *The Individual in the Body Politic: The Political Thought of John of Salisbury*, presented to the 1984 annual meeting of the American Political Science Association, Washington, D.C.

[29] *F*, p. 25; *P* 398a.

that the virtuous mean arises out of circumstantial determinations. In this instance, the relaxation afforded by hunting to the warrior aristocracy may render it a proper form of behaviour at times. The *Policraticus* analyzes courtly music in an analogous fashion. Although John recognized that the morals of courtiers and knights are threatened by contemporary musical lyrics and styles, he stops short of the condemnation of music altogether. While objecting to those lavacious and wanton tones which "exceed the mean," the *Policraticus* also declares that if singing "be kept within moderate limits, it frees the mind from care, banishes worry about things temporal, and by imparting joy and peace and by inspiring a deep love for God draws souls to association with the angels."[30] As the examples of hunting and music illustrate, John's central goal is to promote that "moderation without which a good life is impossible."[31] Such moderation requires that virtue and vice be judged on the basis of the individual agent's chosen action in a particular set of circumstances. What may at one place and time be correct for one person may at another place and time be improper for another person (or even for the same person). The overarching moral lesson of the *Policraticus* is that virtue stems from performing the right act in the right situation, which constitutes the very essence of moderation.

If the *Policraticus* is addressed generally towards the medieval court aristocracy, then its more definite target is the prince and his immediate circle of advisors. We should not be surprised, then, that John applies this conclusions about virtue as a mean to the specific conditions and problems confronting feudal rulers (primarily kings, but also, by extension, other independent magnates). Fundamental to John's approach is the claim that the political qualities of the community are inextricably linked to the moral qualities of its royal head. Hence, the prince of virtuous moral character assures the stability and cohesion of the polity; a vicious prince will destroy the body politic. But insofar as virtue has already been defined as a mean between excess and deficiency, John must maintain that the actions of the good prince will themselves be moderate. Indeed, the *Policraticus* advocates exactly the view that the moderate ruler engenders peace and security among his people: "With how much care should the prince moderate his acts, now with the strictness of justice, and now with the leniency

---

[30] *F*, p. 32 (translation altered); *P* 402d-403a.
[31] *F*, p. 161; *P* 482c.

of mercy, to the end that he may make his subjects all be of one mind in one house, and thus as it were out of discordant dispositions bring to pass one great perfect harmony in the service and in the works of charity.''[32] We ought not to infer, however, that the ruler is to be the absolute arbiter of the morals of his subjects. Rather, the prince should instruct mainly by his own example, adopting that ''tranquil moderation of mind'' so valued in the magistrates of antiquity.[33] While never overlooking or encouraging moral error on the part of subjects, John's monarch would not actively punish those evils within the polity which do not endanger public order or religious orthodoxy. On the one hand, John insists that ''the measure of the affection with which [t]he [prince] should embrace his subjects like brethren in the arms of charity must be kept in the bounds of moderation,''[34] lest he commit the vice implied by excessive kindness. Still, on the other hand, the *Policraticus* protests against the ruler ''who is too ready to fault his subjects, and take revenge on them for their faults.''[35] Both routes are of great harm to the body politic, John says, although he would prefer to err on the side of royal tolerance.[36] While the king should rapidly suppress those ''flagrant outrages'' which ''it is not permissable to tolerate or which cannot be tolerated in good conscience,'' he should also show patience towards whatever faults of subjects ''which can honorably be tolerated.''[37] Special princely virtue, the art of statesmanship, consists in the moderate use of divinely granted authority. The virtuous prince will aim for a mean between two contrary uses of political power: excessive charity and intolerance. By conceiving of the moral character of the monarch within the terms of virtue defined as a mean, John has built his political theory upon essentially Aristotelian foundations. In the case of the prince, as for all other men, whosoever follows the moderate course, by carefully determining the circumstances in which action is to be performed, may properly be admired for his virtue.

III

Our analysis of John of Salisbury's application of the Aristotelian doctrine of the mean has so far demonstrated that virtuous moderation

[32] *S*, p. 39; *P* 530b.
[33] *S*, pp. 40, 41; *P* 530d.
[34] *S*, p. 37; *P* 529a.
[35] *S*, p. 43; *P* 531d.
[36] *S*, p. 44; *P* 532a.
[37] *S*, p. 265; *P* 629b.

must be counted among the key themes of the *Policraticus*. But John, having established that moral goodness consists in the mean, additionally infers from this precept a set of corollary principles. Specifically, John's acceptance of the doctrine of the mean leads him to adopt two claims about liberty—one of a moral character, the other political:

1) Each individual agent must be at liberty to make his own circumstantial determinations regarding the mean in a particular contexto and

2) The prince has a responsibility to ensure each subject's liberty by steering a political course between license and slavery, so that a virtuous community entails the continued liberty of the virtuous individuals within that community.

Both of these principles of liberty are dependent upon John's account of virtue as moderation. For John acknowledges an intrinsic connection between virtue and liberty: "Virtue cannot be fully attained without liberty, and the absence of liberty proves that virtue in its full perfection is wanting. Therefore a man is free in proportion to the measure of his virtues."[38] Liberty and virtue are in principle inseparable. He who is most virtuous is most free and the freest man enjoys the greatest virtue.

But why does John posit this intimate and inexorable connection between liberty and virtue? The answer, it seems, is that John understands liberty to be the ability to make circumstantial determinations regarding the proper course of conduct (the mean) in any situation. Hence, liberty is required for the individual to discover the moderate, and therefore virtuous, route and to act in accordance with it. "Liberty to do as one pleases is justified if moderation controls the act," the *Policraticus* says, "The circumstances that regulate all freedom from restraint are dependent upon a preceeding consideration of place, time, individual and cause."[39] Liberty consists in the formation of sound, rational judgements by the individual agent about the most appropriate route to virtue: "Liberty means judging everything freely in accordance with one's individual judgement."[40] Virtue is a set of general postulates which through liberty are translated into specific precepts of action applicable as circumstances warrant. Liberty is not, however, quite co-extensive with right reason, insofar as John questions the value "of liberty if it is not permitted those who

---

[38] *S*, p. 323; *P* 705d.
[39] *F*, p. 28; *P* 400a.
[40] *S*, p. 323; *P* 705c.

desire to ruin themselves by luxury.''[41] If liberty is necessary for virtue, then there must remain the possibility that it will be used wrongly, for vice. Indeed, the occasional use of liberty for vicious acts does not constitute for John sufficient grounds for the denial of liberty altogether. Without a measure of liberty, we have no hope of achieving virtue; for this reason, vice must sometimes be tolerated. Full and true liberty demands that the individual serve virtue and perform its duties.[42] But the suppression of liberty in the name of eradicating vice will only result in the simultaneous eradication of virtue.

Consequently, the conception of liberty in the *Policraticus* itself resembles nothing so much as a mean between the excess of license and the defect of slavery. By license is meant unlimited freedom which does not concern itself with circumstantial determinations; by slavery, the inability to make any circumstantial determinations whatsoever. Both license and slavery lead to vice, in John's view, because both constitute denials of that liberty which is a requisite of virtuous action. The man who acts on the basis of license stands opposed to true liberty, since he ''aspires to a kind of fictitious liberty, vainly imagining that he can live without fear and do with impunity whatsoever pleases him; and somehow be straightaway like unto God, not, however, that he desires to imitate the divine goodness, but rather seeks to incline God to favour his wickedness by granting him immunity from punishment for his evil deeds.''[43] License is a sort of self-deification by which man confuses the pursuit of arbitrary desires with his divinely granted freedom. The man of license seeks to make God's will conform with his own, thereby rendering virtuous whatever has been chosen. John is adamant in his condemnation of such license: ''When under the pretext of liberty rashness unleashes the violence of its spirit, it properly incurs reproach, although, as a thing more pleasing in the ears of the vulgar than convincing to the mind of the wise man, it often finds in the indulgence of others the safety which it does not owe to its own prudence.''[44] But if license by its excessive character can lead only to vice, then no better end can be achieved by the utter abolition of liberty through the introduction of slavery. John alternately describes slavery as ''the image of death''[45] and as ''the yoke of vice.''[46] Virtue

[41] *F*, p. 342; *P* 741c.
[42] *F*, p. 365; *P* 756c.
[43] *S*, p. 282; *P* 675c.
[44] *S*, p. 324; *P* 706c.
[45] *S*, p. 282; *P* 675c.
[46] *F*, p. 365; *P* 765c.

can only be voluntary, the result of choice in accordance with right; any action which is involuntary, slavish, can therefore by definition never be virtuous. Indeed, the *Policraticus* suggests more than once that because virtue can never be achieved without liberty, men of good character should be willing to give all they have, even their own lives, in order to "strike off the heavy and hateful yoke of slavery."[47] Even if the slave behaves in all external ways correctly, he can never attain virtue, for he has not exercised the power of his will, that is, the liberty of making one's own circumstantial judgements. On John's account, then, those "things which are done or spoken freely" constitute a mean between "the fault of timidity on the one hand and of rashness on the other,"[48] between the moral attitudes arising out of slavery and out of license. The slavish and the licentious men are equally lacking in liberty, although for quite opposite reasons: from license, no rational, moderate and thus valid choice can be made; under slavery there exists no choice at all.

It is precisely because of the precarious balance required for liberty that John is so fearful of the prince who seeks to enforce morals coercively over his subjects. John acknowledges that "in order to preserve liberty and out of regard for it, it has always been permissible for a free man to speak to persons concerning their vices."[49] Patient correction is the duty of the good man. But correspondingly, the liberty of others must be respected in word and in deed, at least so long as another's freedom does "not involve the casting away of virtue. For since each virtue shines by its own proper light, the merit of tolerance is resplendant with a very special glory."[50] It pertains especially to the prince to ensure the liberty of those over whom he reigns. Indeed, John's famous distinction between the prince and the tyrant turns on his doctrine of liberty. By definition, "the prince fights for the laws and the liberty of the people: the tyrant thinks nothing done unless he brings the laws to nought and reduces the people to slavery."[51] Since John elsewhere tells us that "good laws were introduced for the sake of liberty,"[52] we may surmise that the true king's efforts are directed entirely towards the preservation of each subject's individual freedom.

[47] *S*, p. 323; *P* 705c. A similar opinion is expressed at *S*, p. 282; *P* 765c.
[48] *S*, p. 324; *P* 706b.
[49] *S*, p. 331; *P* 710b.
[50] *S*, p. 324; *P* 706b.
[51] *S*, p. 335; *P* 777d.
[52] *S*, p. 323; *P* 705d.

Nor does John leave any doubt about what the protection of liberty involves: "So long as they have peace and practice justice and abstain from falsehood and perjury," members of the body politic "enjoy liberty and peace in such fullness that there is nought that can in the least degree disturb their repose."[53] The intimacy which obtains between a body politic and its royal head depends upon the maintenance of a proper moral and political order. This order is the special responsibility of the prince and his government. The right ordering of society secures liberty and liberty procures the virtue of individuals and of the whole community. Disorder, by contrast, stems from immoderate government and results in the loss of liberty in one of two manners: through rule based on license and through tyranny. Any monarch corrupted by license will invariably succomb to evil, since his government "does not know its own just measure, nor will it repress its intemperence before it has fallen into the last extremity of baseness through overindulgence in license."[54] Simultaneously, those subjected to such licentious rule either will become corrupt themselves from lack of moral guidance and example or will rebel against public immorality.[55] In both cases, the consequence is an absence of peace and justice within the community, hence the denial of liberty. Yet the tyrant fares no better, for he too disturbs political order by demanding slavish obedience from his subjects. Those over whom a tyrant rules should never make a virtue out of their situation; to do so is to confuse "the semblance of liberty" with "real and pure liberty."[56] In response to their enslavement, rather, men should seek to correct the tyrant, they should pray to God for his removal, and they may even act as God's representative in such removal.[57] Tyranny destroys liberty and thus virtue just as surely as does licentious government. Only in moderation is the authority of the prince used rightly and legitimately. In effect, the prince is not free (if he is to retain the name of prince) to force his subjects to surrender their liberty—even in the name of virtue. The distinguishing mark of any vicious government will be a populace deprived of its own appropriate liberty and led instead into either licence or slavery.

[53] S, p. 54; P 536b-c.
[54] S, p. 222; P 610b.
[55] S, pp. 222-3; P 610b-d.
[56] F, p. 184; P 496d.
[57] John's views about tyranny have been thoroughly treated by Richard Rouse and Mary Rouse, *John of Salisbury and the Doctrine of Tyrannicide*, in: Speculum, 42 (1967), pp. 693-709.

In a sense, the indispensible political lesson of the *Policraticus* is that individual liberty provides the limiting condition defining good and valid government. The virtuous prince knows when to suppress the flagrant vices of his subjects without denying to them the liberty to make their own moral determinations. That John comes to this conclusion of the basis of a concept of liberty informed by the doctrine of virtue as a mean indicates the philosophical importance of Aristotelian ideas in the *Policraticus*. It is true that John, in constructing a political analysis directly relevant to the problems of twelfth century feudal society, has added a new dimension to the Western conception of liberty. Unlike the ancient Greeks, John teaches that liberty can be maintained without necessarily devolving into license.[58] In contrast to the Church Fathers, John claims that liberty is not merely the submission of one's own will to God, but implies a process of genuine individual judgement and choice.[59] John thereby creates a notion of liberty which points the way towards modern principles of freedom.[60] Yet, all the same, the idea of liberty proposed in the *Policraticus* has at its root the Aristotelian doctrine of the mean: the qualitites John attributes to liberty depend upon his logically prior definition of virtue in terms of moderation. Although John laboured without direct knowledge of either the *Ethics* or the *Politics*, the moral and political concepts of the *Policraticus* owe a profound debt to Aristotle. This and similar debts must be not only acknowledged but analyzed if we are to assess the full extent of the "underground" tradition of Aristotelian philosophy present during the Middle Ages.[61]

---

[58] This may be contrasted, for example, with Plato's objections to liberty in *Republic*, VIII, 561b-563e and *Laws*, III, 699a-701e.

[59] Cf. St. Augustine, *De libero arbitrio*, Book II, sec. 37.

[60] This is not to reject the observation of Hans Liebeschütz, *Medieval Humanism in the Life and Writings of John of Salisbury* (London 1950) that John's notion "of liberty is a medieval one, and that liberty for him means that each distinct sphere should be allowed to enjoy its special rights undisturbed" (p. 54). It is by no means absurd to say that the peculiarly medieval conception of liberty, arising from the privatized jurisdiction typical of feudal society, was a necessary condition for the emergence of the modern notion of liberty. In many ways, John's Aristotelian conception of liberty is compatible with the historical idea of feudal liberty.

[61] This essay was composed with the support of the Mactaggart Research Fellowship programme at the University of Alberta. An abbreviated version of the present paper was presented to the Medieval and Renaissance Guild of the same University.

KNOWLEDGE, VIRTUE AND THE PATH TO WISDOM: THE UNEXAMINED ARISTOTELIANISM OF JOHN OF SALISBURY'S *METALOGICON*

A LTHOUGH he could never be construed as a scholastic, there was probably no philosopher of the Middle Ages more devoted to Aristotle and his teachings than the mid-twelfth century churchman John of Salisbury. Admittedly, John knew far less of the Aristotelian corpus than would St. Thomas Aquinas a century later. But the elements of Aristotle's thought with which John was familiar, culled from those treatises available to him (*Categories, De interpretatione, Topics* and *Posterior* and *Prior Analytics*), and gleaned from intermediaries like Cicero and Boethius, made a singular impression upon him.[1] Certainly, Aristotle exercised an important, albeit subtle, influence in John's *Policraticus* and his letters.[2] But it is in the *Metalogicon*, a survey of assorted issues in educational theory and speculative philosophy, that John gives freest reign to his sentiments about Aristotle.[3] We are repeatedly told that Aristotle so 'excelled practically all other philosophers in nearly every regard' that he 'established his right to the common name of "philoso-

---

[1] For the Aristotelian tradition as it emerged in later classical times and was transmitted to the Middle Ages, see two studies by R. McKeon, 'Aristotelianism in Western Christianity' in *Environmental Factors in Christian History*, ed. J. T. NcNeill, M. Spinka and H. R. Willoughby (Chicago, 1939), pp. 206-231; and 'The Hellenistic and Roman Foundations of the Tradition of Aristotle in the West', *Review of Metaphysics* 32 (1979) 677-715.

[2] The present author has sought to establish this claim in a series of recent articles: 'Aristotelianism in John of Salisbury's *Policraticus*' (with J. Brückmann), *Journal of the History of Philosophy* 21 (1983) 203-229; 'The Aristotelian Doctrine of the Mean and John of Salisbury's Concept of Liberty', *Vivarium* 24 (1986) 128-42; and 'Aristotelian Ethics and John of Salisbury's Letters', *Viator* 18 (1987) 161-73.

[3] Quotes in English from the *Metalogicon* are taken, with occasional revision, from the standard translation by D. D. McGarry (*The Metalogicon of John of Salisbury. A Twelfth-Century Defense of the Verbal and Logical Arts of the Trivium* [Berkeley, 1955]). The quotes in Latin in the notes are taken from the edition by C. C. J. Webb (*Iohannis Saresberiensis episcopi Carnotensis Metalogicon. Libri IIII* [Oxford, 1929]) and are indicated by page references from that edition followed by column numbers and letters from PL 199. In cases where only the English version is given, references to Webb's edition and the PL are also included in the notes.

Reprinted from *Mediaeval Studies* Vol. 51 (1989), pp. 268–286, by permission of the publisher. Copyright © 1989 by the Pontifical Institute of Mediaeval Studies, Toronto.

pher", as in a way his own special prerogative'.[4] John depicts Aristotle's teaching as pervasive and inescapable: ideas propounded by the Christian Fathers, no less than by the philosophers of pagan antiquity, are 'traceable to Aristotle, from whom, as from a fountain, all have drunk'.[5] Nor is John himself shy about partaking of the Aristotelian fount; Aristotle is the most widely cited author in the *Metalogicon* by a margin of more than two-to-one against his nearest competitor, St. Augustine. (Boethius, Cicero and Quintilian together are not cited as often as Aristotle).[6] As a consequence, the *Metalogicon* is a virtual compendium of Aristotelian learning as it had advanced to the middle of the twelfth century. Indeed, John's exceptionally vast knowledge of Aristotle placed him on the cutting edge of contemporary scholarship.[7]

In view of the prominence of Aristotle in the text of the *Metalogicon*, we would expect close adherence to Aristotle's thinking with regard to logic, language and the other subjects covered by the various treatises which comprise the *Organon*. In fact, much of the modern literature on the *Metalogicon* has already demonstrated how John's use of Aristotelian sources (both the *Organon* and intermediaries like Boethius) contributed to the pedagogical method recommended by him.[8] But there are two aspects of the *Metalogicon*, at least, which have not previously been examined for an Aristotelian influence: John's account of the acquisition of knowledge and his conception of the moral implications of educa-

---

[4] *Metalogicon*, p. 213; '...Aristotiles, qui alios fere omnes et fere in omnibus philosophos superabat, hinc commune nomen sibi quodam proprietatis iure uendicaret' (p. 171 [920A]). See also *Metalogicon*, p. 110: 'Sed cum singuli suis meritis splendeant, omnes se Aristotilis adorare uestigia gloriantur; adeo quidem, ut commune omnium philosophorum nomen preminentia quadam sibi proprium fecerit. Nam et antonomastice, id est, excellenter, "Philosophus" apellatur' (p. 90 [873C-D]).

[5] *Metalogicon*, p. 175; '...tractum quidem ab Aristotile, quoniam de fonte isto hauserunt omnes...' (p. 142 [904A]).

[6] Further evidence for John's dedication to Aristotle is suggested by his *Entheticus de dogmate philosophorum* (or longer *Entheticus*), where he discusses Aristotle and the Peripatetics at far greater length than any other authors from Greek and Latin antiquity. See the count provided by Phyllis Barzillay in 'The *Entheticus de dogmate philosophorum* of John of Salisbury', *Medievalia et humanistica* 16 (1964) 15 n. 34. Also see the new edition of the text by J. van Laarhoven, *Entheticus Maior and Minor* (Leiden, 1987).

[7] For precise evaluations of John's place in, and contributions to, the Aristotelian revival of the twelfth century, see C. C. J. Webb, 'John of Salisbury', *Proceedings of the Aristotelian Society* 2.2 (1893) 102; L. Minio-Paluello, 'Iacobus Venetius Grecus: Canonist and Translator of Aristotle', *Traditio* 8 (1952) 291-95; E. Türk, *Nugae curialium. Le règne d'Henri Plantagenêt (1145-1189) et l'éthique politique* (Geneva/Paris, 1977), p. 86; and É. Jeauneau, 'Jean de Salisbury et la lecture des philòsophes' in *The World of John of Salisbury*, ed. M. Wilks (Oxford, 1983), p. 103.

[8] See D. D. McGarry, 'Educational Theory in the *Metalogicon* of John of Salisbury', *Speculum* 23 (1948) 659-75; B. P. Hendley, *Wisdom and Eloquence: A New Interpretation of the Metalogicon of John of Salisbury* (Ph.D. diss., Yale, 1967) and 'John of Salisbury and the Problem of Universals', *Journal of the History of Philosophy* 8 (1970) 289-302. To judge from the contributions to *The World of John of Salisbury*, interest in the *Metalogicon* as a work of philosophy, rather than as documentation of twelfth-century intellectual history, is currently waning.

tion. Of course, there appears to be excellent reason for excluding in advance any detectable Aristotelian origin for John's reflections on these two matters. Composing in the late 1150s, John could not after all have been exposed to the contents of Aristotle's works on psychology (*De anima*) and ethics (the *Nicomachean* and *Eudemian Ethics* and the *Magna moralia*) which constituted the primary documentation of the Aristotelian positions on the acquisition of knowledge and moral conduct. There is no evidence that any of these treatises was available to the Latin West in even abbreviated form much before 1200, and certainly not as early as the date of John's writing.

Yet the *prima facie* facts of transmission do not put an end to the matter. For in the *Organon* itself, Aristotle did (however tangentially) address the topics of knowledge and virtue in terms essentially consistent with his remarks in other works. Furthermore, it is possible to detect intermediary Latin sources which facilitated transmission of some elements of Aristotle's thought which were not directly available by means of the *Organon*. Thus, it seems plausible to ask: are there Aristotelian features of the *Metalogicon*, along the lines just mentioned, which have so far escaped identification and investigation? The answer, I would assert, is in the affirmative; the *Metalogicon* draws more broadly on Aristotelian doctrines than has heretofore been suspected. Specifically, John incorporates into the central argument of his treatise two previously unattributed claims which are of demonstrable Aristotelian provenance: first, knowledge is only really possessed once the knower has formed a firm and stable disposition, which is acquired through regular and rigorous practice; and second, no lesson is rightly learned which is not in accordance with the virtuous mean between excess and deficiency. Readers familiar with the Aristotelianism of John's *Policraticus* and letters will not be surprised by his reliance upon these particular doctrines in the *Metalogicon*. But the fashion in which John applies his Aristotelian views to the main issues of the *Metalogicon* is both provocative and profound. For from this Aristotelian foundation is constructed the core of John's account of how a suitably designed liberal education will lead to the attainment of a wisdom which is both unshakable in its knowledge and humble in the awareness of its limitations. To achieve wisdom, according to the *Metalogicon*, is to follow principles derived from the Aristotelian doctrines which John so greatly admired.

I

There is no single one of Aristotle's works which is primarily or essentially devoted to his philosophy of knowledge. The most complete statement of the Aristotelian position on that topic is contained within his treatise on the soul, *De anima*. One of Aristotle's main insights in the *De anima* is that knowledge has several connotations which must be distinguished in order to provide an adequate account.[9] In the first place, an individual knows in the sense that his soul possesses by nature a general capacity to acquire particular elements of knowledge. In another sense, knowledge denotes the factual act of knowing, as when one exercises or applies one's knowledge of grammar or mathematics. Finally, there is an intermediate concept of knowledge as a fully formed and stable disposition of the mind from which proceeds the actual exercise of knowledge. In this last sense, the knowledge said to be possessed by the knower is both actual and potential: actual, because the knower has thoroughly internalised the precepts of the knowledge in question; potential, because the presence of the knowledge need not be coextensive with its employment or display. It is in virtue of this epistemic notion that one may attribute knowledge to a sleeping person, for instance, even though he demonstrates no immediate signs of knowing. Thus, knowledge of an intermediate sort is conceptually distinct from both the capacity for and the actualisation of knowledge.

But how is it possible that knowledge may still be predicated of a knower when it is unactualised at a given moment? The Aristotelian solution to this question is to identify the genus of knowledge as *hexis*,[10] a word variously rendered into English as 'habit', 'condition', 'state', and 'disposition'. Aristotle conceives of *hexis* as a kind of quality; it is a way of attributing a qualitative ascription to a subject or substance. In general terms, a *hexis* is the ingrained inclination of a subject or substance to behave according to a definite principle of action.[11] *Hexis* is often contrasted to *diathesis* ('condition' or 'disposition' in a transitory sense, such as when a basically healthy individual catches a cold). In comparison with *diathesis*, a *hexis* is not susceptible to rapid, radical change. Instead, *hexis* indicates a sort of quality which has become so firmly rooted in that which it qualifies as to form virtually a 'second nature', rendering it almost impossible to alter.[12] Hence, in associating knowledge with *hexis*, Aristotle is assuring us that what is known has become an entrenched feature of the soul.

But if the soul by first nature has only the indifferent capacity to know or be ignorant (knowledge in its most general sense), how is it that a specific *hexis* is inculcated? Aristotle hints at the answer in *De anima* when he remarks that the

---

[9] For the following, see *De an.* 2.5 (417a21-b15). The translations from the works of Aristotle used in the body of the article are taken from the Loeb editions with occasional revisions by the present author.

[10] *Top.* 4.2 (121b37-39).

[11] See *Metaph.* 5.20 (1022b3-14) for another general discussion of *hexis*.

[12] As Aristotle makes clear in the *Nicomachean Ethics* 3.3-4 (1105a35-b1) and 3.5 (1114a18-21). It is for precisely this reason that *hexis* as an ethical category has proved so problematic for students of Aristotle's philosophy; see W. Bondeson, 'Aristotle on Responsibility for One's Character and the Possibility of Character Change', *Phronesis* 19 (1974) 59-65.

hexis towards a definite type of knowledge (such as mathematics or grammar) develops 'through learning, and after frequent changes'.[13] In other words, instruction of a repeated sort will lead to the acquisition of a particular *hexis* or to the replacement of one *hexis* (say, ignorance) by another (knowledge). This view is confirmed by Aristotle's much more complete account of the formation of *hexeis* presented in the *Nicomachean Ethics*. The virtues, like the fields of knowledge, arise from *hexeis*, Aristotle argues, insofar as man is born with merely a natural capacity for virtue.[14] Thus, moral qualities can be acquired solely by 'having actually practiced them... We become just by the practice of just acts, self-controlled by exercising self-control, courageous by doing courageous acts'.[15] The inculcation of a propensity towards virtue occurs by way of a steady repetition of a course of action so as to render that conduct habitual. Indeed, Aristotle expands this claim about the acquisition of moral characteristics to encompass *hexis* in general: '*Hexeis* develop from corresponding activities. Hence we must see that our activities are of a certain kind, since the quality of our *hexeis* depends upon what we do'.[16] In the case of knowledge, the natural capacity of the knower is transformed into a *hexis* by way of the rigorous exercise of particular mental acts. The formation of a *hexis* of mathematical knowledge, for instance, requires the repeated use of arithmetic formulae and axioms until the knower is thoroughly and unfailingly disposed to apply his learning to the solution of mathematical problems. While in one sense the potentiality (natural capacity) precedes the actuality (*hexis*), in another sense the actuality (practice) proceeds the potentiality (*hexis*). According to the Aristotelian scheme, the effective internalisation of knowledge depends vitally upon the consistency and constancy with which the knower has exercised his intellectual faculties. Proper application yields a well-formed *hexis* (a knowledgeable soul) and that *hexis* in turn assures that the knower will be in firm possession of the knowledge he has acquired.

What is significant for present purposes is that Aristotle generates essentially the same account of knowledge as a *hexis* fixed by practice in the *Organon*. We hear often in the *Topics* of the connection between knowledge and *hexis*, if only because of Aristotle's concern to demonstrate how the process of dialectical reasoning occurs. In particular, the *Topics* seeks to explain the relational nature of knowledge. All knowledge has an object, Aristotle teaches, in the sense that 'knowledge is knowledge of something'.[17] Aristotle maintains that it is by means of *hexis* that this relationship between knowledge and its object is mediated: 'That which

---

[13] *De an.* 2.5 (417a33).
[14] *EN* 2.1 (1103a16-25) and 2.5 (1106a7-13).
[15] ibid., 2.1 (1103a31-33) and 2.1 (1103b1-3).
[16] ibid., 2.1 (1103a22-24).
[17] See, for example, *Top.* 4.4 (124b39-125a2).

belongs to the state (*hexis*) will belong also to that which is described in terms of the state (*hexis*) and that which is described in terms of the state will belong also to the state'.[18] In other words, *hexis* allows one subject or substance to acquire a quality in imitation, as it were, of another subject or substance. Consequently, whatever is true of the latter will also be true of the former. In the case of knowledge, whatever properties are characteristic of the object of knowledge are transferred through the formation of a *hexis* to an individual's soul. If the object of knowledge is grammar, then the soul itself becomes endowed with the qualities necessary for the possession of grammatical abilities. 'Knowledge is said to be of the knowable, but it is a *hexis*', Aristotle insists, 'not of the knowable but of the psyche'.[19] The genus of knowledge in all its forms must be *hexis*, insofar as *hexis* permits the knower to transfer and incorporate into himself on a fixed basis the crucial features of the object of knowledge.

As often as one encounters the connection between *hexis* and knowledge in the *Topics*, however, Aristotle never examines its broader implications in that work. Not so in the *Categories*, where he presents a treatment of *hexis* in general, and the *hexis* of knowledge in particular, which is more extensive than any other in his corpus. *Hexis* ought not to be confused with *diathesis*, Aristotle maintains, for '*hexis* differs from *diathesis* in being more lasting and more stable'.[20] Aristotle cites knowledge as a prime example of *hexis*: 'Knowledge, even when acquired in only moderate degree, is, it is agreed, abiding in its character and difficult to displace, unless some great emotional upheaval takes place, through disease or a like cause.'[21] Consequently, a form of knowledge should, strictly speaking, never be attributed to anyone who is not in ordinary and established possession of it. 'Those who lack retention of knowledge, and are volatile, are not said to possess a particular *hexis* as regards knowledge', Aristotle remarks.[22] However, it may be that the volatile individual, who has at best a *diathesis*, ultimately becomes more settled in his knowledge. Once, 'through lapse of time', knowledge is rendered 'inveterate and almost impossible to sway... we should perhaps call it a *hexis*'.[23] Otherwise, the person remains possessed of an ephemeral *diathesis*; he is easily changed and completely unpredictable in his actual knowledge.[24] Aristotle even addresses in the *Categories* how a *hexis* is acquired by means of steady practice over a long period of time. To develop a well constituted *hexis*, one must be 'brought into a better way

---

[18] *Top.* 5.4 (133a25-28).
[19] *Top.* 4.4 (124b33-34).
[20] *Cat.* 8 (8b27-28).
[21] ibid., (8b29-32).
[22] ibid., (9a5-6).
[23] ibid., (9a2-4).
[24] ibid., (9a7-8).

of life and thought'.[25] Gradually, through slight improvements, he will displace his previous qualities with whatever new behaviour he has learnt to perform, until, 'as this process goes on, it will change him totally and establish him in the contrary *hexis*, provided he is not prevented by lack of time'.[26] The *Categories* conveys the lesson that steady and rigorous application is the sole method for the acquisition of *hexis*; the most one can hope for otherwise is an unstable and variable *diathesis* which requires further practice in order to be transformed into a *hexis*.

That John of Salisbury understood the nature of *hexis* (or its Latin rendering, *habitus*) is clear. Besides Aristotle's writings, he was familiar with the discussions of *habitus* contained in Cicero's *De inventione* and Boethius' *De topicis differentiis*.[27] Moreover, John employed *habitus* in its technical, Aristotelian sense in both his letters and *Policraticus*; the latter, indeed, explicitly describes knowledge as a *habitus* of the soul.[28] But it is in the *Metalogicon* that the significance of Aristotle's definition of *episteme* in terms of *hexis* is most thoroughly explored. We might say, in fact, that the entire project of the *Metalogicon* is impossible except insofar as John works from Aristotelian premises. The *Metalogicon*'s main purpose, John emphasises, is to oppose the views of the pseudonymous 'Cornificius' and his followers.[29] John never expressly identifies this 'Cornificius', a fact which has led modern commentators to perceive him as a composite of certain intellectual tendencies rampant in the twelfth century or, alternatively, to associate him with an actual scholar of the age with whom John had contact.[30] In spite of John's reluctance to reveal the true identity of 'Cornificius', however, he has no such qualms about specifying the reason he finds the Cornifician philosophy so repugnant. The Cornificians reject the value of the study of the art of rhetoric on the grounds that 'eloquence...is a gift that is either conceded or denied to each individual by nature'.[31] For those to whom nature has granted facility with speech,

---

[25] *Cat.* 10 (13a23-24).

[26] ibid., (13a29-31).

[27] This is explored at greater length by Nederman in 'Aristotelian Ethics and John of Salisbury's Letters', 163.

[28] John of Salisbury, *Policraticus*, ed. C. C. J. Webb, 2 vols. (Oxford, 1909; rpt. Frankfurt-am-Main, 1965), 2.21: '...cum anima primo affectionis motu in ualescens disponatur ad cognitionem rerum, eaque si radicata fuerit, ut aut omnino aut sine iniuria naturae conuelli non possit, habitu suo informat animam facitque scientem. Hic ergo habitus rectissime scientia appellatur, licet et res subiectae interdum scientiae nomine censeantur. Vnde et uicissim nominibus mutuatis quod unius est transit ad alterum. Sic utique et scientia dicitur multa, cum tamen multitudo rerum potius quam scientiae sit' (p. 117 [446a-b]).

[29] *Metalogicon*, pp. 12-20 (pp. 7-20 [827d-833c]).

[30] For differing perspectives on this issue, see H. Liebeschütz, *Mediaeval Humanism in the Life and Writings of John of Salisbury* (London, 1950), p. 118; McGarry, 'Educational Theory in the *Metalogicon* of John of Salisbury', 660; and R. B. Tobin, 'The Cornifician Motif in John of Salisbury's *Metalogicon*', *History of Education* 13 (1984) 1-6.

[31] *Metalogicon*, p. 24; 'eloquentie; quoniam eam cunctis natura ministrat aut negat' (p. 20 [833c]).

IX

practice is redundant and wasteful; those lacking original endowment can hardly expect to alter through education what nature has denied them, according to 'Cornificius'.[32]

John condemns this aspect of Cornifician teaching as particularly pernicious and invidious. In the first place, to say that none can improve his linguistic abilities regardless of effort or training is empirically absurd. It is true, as any careful observer realises, that people 'learn how to talk in their nurses' arms before they receive instruction from doctors who occupy official chairs. The way one talks in manhood often smacks of the manner of speech of one's nurse. Sometimes the strenuous efforts of teachers cannot extricate one from habits imbibed at a tender age'.[33] But this proves only that one must pay special attention to early education, not (as the Cornificians think) that nature is insusceptible to alteration or improvement. After all, John points out, 'natural ability easily deteriorates when neglected', and 'is strengthened by cultivation and care.... Nothing is so strong and robust that it cannot be enfeebled by neglect, nothing so well constructed that it cannot be razed. On the other hand, diligent application can build up and preserve the lowest degree of natural talent'.[34] In opposition to the Cornificians, then, the *Metalogicon* maintains that nature must be supplemented first by instruction and then by regular practice if eloquence is to flourish and prosper. Consequently, the blessings of eloquence[35] accrue properly and fully to those who studiously devote themselves to internalising and applying the rules of rhetoric. The Cornifician appeal to nature as the sole determinant of the eloquent man is bogus and deceptive, entailing a theologically unwarranted and empirically unsubstantiated presumption that 'first nature' is perfect and complete in itself.[36] In contrast to such erroneous opinions, John affirms the progress (perhaps even the perfectibility) of man's rhetorical capacities through the appropriate combination of nature, grace, instruction and application.

It is in this regard that the measure of John's commitment to an Aristotelian concept of knowledge becomes apparent. The *Metalogicon's* opposition to Cornifician naturalism shares with Aristotle the general view that nature's role in human intellect is limited to the endowment of a capacity of the soul to acquire knowledge

---

[32] *Metalogicon*, p. 28 (pp. 23-24 [835B-D]).

[33] *Metalogicon*, p. 25; '...commercium uerbi ante a nutricum sinu quam a cathedra doctorum excipiunt. Nutricis linguam plerumque redolet etas uirilis; nec potest interdum ab eo quod tenerior etas ebiberat doctorum diligentia erudiri. Quam recte loquuntur, quam expedite, singule gentes in linguis quas eis decreti diuini constitutio assignauit!' (p. 21 [833D-834D]).

[34] *Metalogicon*, pp. 30-31; '...tamen, sicut facile corrumpitur a negligentia, sic a cultura et a cura sepissime mansuescit...Nichil enim est tam ualidum, tam robustum, quod diligentia non eneruet, nichil tam erectum, quod non deiciat; sicut e contra quamlibet humilem gradum cura diligens erigit et conseruat' (pp. 25-26 [836C-D]).

[35] These are enumerated by John at *Metalogicon*, pp. 26-27 (pp. 21-23 [834B-835B]).

[36] *Metalogicon*, pp. 28-29 (pp. 23-24 [835B-D]).

(*scientia*).[37] As a consequence, John teaches that the eloquent man becomes so by means of regular practice until he has firmly and forever internalised the principles of rhetoric. In sum, John reiterates the essential features and terminology of Aristotle's notion of *habitus* – and does so in a manner which sometimes closely resembles the parallel texts of the *Organon*, especially the *Categories*. Thus, while John's ideas of eloquence and education may owe a substantial debt to Latin authors like Cicero and Quintilian,[38] it is to Aristotle that the *Metalogicon* turns for its fundamental insights into those subjects.

The essence of John's Aristotelian outlook is that the capacities ceded to man by 'first nature' need to be completed by the formation of a second, acquired nature. Specifically, John teaches that what we know depends upon what we do: 'Assiduous application... smooths the way for understanding'.[39] The ignorant man has been accustomed to false or incorrect precepts because his actions were not of a proper kind. Likewise, the knowledgeable individual has repeatedly practiced the behaviour which accords with true knowledge of a discipline or skill. 'And the art, which becomes firmly established by use and practice, yields a faculty of accomplishing those things that are proper to it'.[40] The argument is particularly compelling in the case of eloquence. To propound abstract and obscure rules without concern for application (as John accuses the schoolmen of doing) provides no true instruction at all.[41] 'Rules alone are useless', the *Metalogicon* proclaims,[42] since whoever learns the theoretical principles associated with rhetoric is by no means eloquent. Rather, eloquence in speech is assured only to those who practice it carefully and regularly for a long period of time. In a passage which echoes *Categories* (13a23-31), John remarks that 'what is difficult when we first try it, becomes easier after assiduous practice, and once the rules for doing it are mastered, very easy, unless languor creeps in, through lapse of use or carelessness, and impedes our efficiency'.[43] Eloquence, like other sorts of knowledge, is not readily acquired or retained; the successful rhetorician must take care to monitor all his behaviour during his formative stage, or must be closely watched by an

---

[37] *Metalogicon*, p. 34 (pp. 28-29 [838B-C]).

[38] As has been emphasised by Liebeschütz, *Mediaeval Humanism*, pp. 87-90; and B. Munk-Olsen, 'L'humanisme de Jean de Salisbury, un cicéronian au 12ᵉ siècle' in *Entretiens sur la Renaissance du 12ᵉ siècle*, ed. M. de Gandillac and É. Jeauneau (Paris, 1968), pp. 53-83.

[39] *Metalogicon*, p. 64; '...operis scilicet assiduitas...uias tamen parat intelligentie' (p. 52 [853A]).

[40] *Metalogicon*, pp. 215-16; 'Porro ab arte, que usu et exercitatione firmata est, prouenit facultas exequendi ea que ex arte gerenda sunt' (p. 174 [921B]).

[41] *Metalogicon*, pp. 206-207 (pp. 218-19 [946B]).

[42] *Metalogicon*, p. 245; 'inutilis est opera preceptorum' (p. 195 [932C]).

[43] *Metalogicon*, p. 34; '...ut quod difficile fuerat in prima agitatione, ab assiduitate usus reddatur facilius; et cum regulas hoc faciendi deprehenderit, fiat, nisi desuetudinis et negligentie torpor obsistat, facillimum' (p. 29 [838C]).

experienced tutor. Usage assures that *scientia* will be deeply rooted rather than facile.

But how does practice achieve this profound implantation of knowledge within the individual? John answers this query in characteristically Aristotelian fashion by explaining that usage is the sole determinant of *habitus*, and that no knowledge is truly grasped which does not involve the acquisition of a *habitus*. Mastery of the principles of any branch of knowledge can only be ascribed once 'the *habitus* of employing them is firmly fixed by practice and exercise'.[44] This means that *habitus* becomes the very criterion for the possession of knowledge in the *Metalogicon*. When a particular object of knowledge has become so characteristically a part of an individual that it is virtually insusceptible to change or alteration, then we may speak of that person as knowledgeable in the discipline. Otherwise, he must continue to work at acquiring the knowledge by steady and continuous application. The man who has totally mastered the art of rhetoric, for instance, will be eloquent without constantly engaging in the use of eloquent speech: rhetorical skills inhere in him so completely that his eloquence can always be counted on.

Nor does John allow this idea to stand without further explanation or defence. On the contrary, he explicitly introduces into the *Metalogicon* the Aristotelian distinction, drawn from *Categories* 8b-9a, between *diathesis* (*dispositio*) and *hexis* (*habitus*): 'Theoretical principles must be consolidated by practice and assiduous exercise, except perhaps where a disposition has already been transformed into a habit [*habitus*]'.[45] The end of all instruction ought to be the full formation of a 'second nature' which complements and completes the capacities granted by 'first nature'. We may say that such a 'second nature' is present only when a *habitus* has been engendered, that is, when the *dispositio* towards a form of knowledge is so thoroughly a part of the individual that it becomes a more or less permanent quality of him. In this fashion, at least, 'second nature' resembles 'first nature'; just as the former can never be eradicated or altered utterly, so the latter can safely be counted as a fixed feature of a person once its formation is complete. Thus, John can forestall a potential response to his criticism of Cornifician naturalism, namely, that by denying nature as the crucial determinant of knowledge, one removes the stability and endurance that is commonly associated with *scientia*. By conceiving of the goal of education in Aristotelian terms, as the creation of a *habitus* of knowledge, the *Metalogicon* identifies an acceptable alternative foundation for the persistence and permanency which seem to be characteristic of knowledge.

[44] *Metalogicon*, p. 171; '...his enim perfecte cognitis, et habitu eorum per usum et exercitium roboratis' (p. 139 [902B]).
[45] *Metalogicon*, p. 245; '...si non usu et exercitio assiduo roboretur; nisi forte cum in habitum transierit dispositio' (p. 195 [932C]). Oddly, despite the fact that this passage is almost identical to the one in the *Categories*, McGarry's edition cites Quintilian as John's source (note 318 on page 245).

John's Aristotelian connection of *habitus* with *scientia* conveys another connotation which ought not to be missed. The *Metalogicon* defends John's general belief that philosophy, so far from being an abstruse and purely contemplative discipline, properly belongs in a more concrete setting as a guide for human thought and conduct.[46] Surely, John's own career provides the model: trained in the best schools of France, in association with the greatest minds of the twelfth century, he nonetheless saw his education as preparation for a life of administration and public affairs.[47] 'Pure' philosophy, the dry speculative stuff of the schoolmen, would seem to offend against the very nature of that wisdom which philosophers claim to love, in John's judgement. For the wisdom which men seek by means of abstract contemplation is nonetheless rooted in sense perception, that is, in the realm of *scientia* which is the product of human action.[48] Thus, none can be wise except through learning based on practical experience. 'By experience one acquires knowledge, which relates to action', the *Metalogicon* declares, so that man 'derives the various rivulets of the sciences and wisdom from the fountainhead of sense perception'.[49] This empirical foundation suggests, in effect, that the path to wisdom begins with the practice of particular acts, leading to the creation of a definite *habitus* of knowledge. And once the individual is firmly in possession of knowledge (the prerequisite of wisdom), the powers of reason and understanding lead him towards the fruits of wisdom. Philosophy which neglects this practical route to wisdom is not deserving of the name.[50] In sum, the pedagogical theory of the *Metalogicon* prefers the man of affairs and experience to the schoolman on the grounds that training by way of diligent application accomplishes what scholastic instruction cannot: it points the way which the wise man must follow. But John's ability to justify fully such a presumption rests squarely on his commitment to an Aristotelian interpretation of *scientia* as a *habitus* formed by exercise and use. It is from this Aristotelian premise that John provides a philosophical foundation for the claim that action and wisdom, so far from being incommensurable, are

---

[46] *Metalogicon*, p. 94 (p. 76 [866B-C]). This is also a recurring theme in John's correspondence, where he attempts to introduce philosophical principles into the conduct and analysis of public affairs; see Nederman, 'Aristotelian Ethics and John of Salisbury's Letters'.

[47] The relationship between John's philosophical training and his later career is examined by Klaus Guth in *Johannes von Salisbury (1115/20-1180). Studien zur Kirchen-, Kultur- und Sozialgeschichte Westeuropas im 12. Jahrhundert* (St. Ottilien, 1978), pp. 23-81; K. L. Forhan, 'A Twelfth-Century "Bureaucrat" and the Life of the Mind: The Political Thought of John of Salisbury', presented at the Tenth International Conference on Patristic, Medieval and Renaissance Studies at Villanova University in 1985 and published in *Proceedings of the PMR Conference*, 10 (1985) 65-74; and Beryl Smalley, *The Becket Conflict and the Schools. A Study of Intellectuals in Politics* (Totawa, N.J., 1973), pp. 11-12.

[48] *Metalogicon*, p. 231 (pp. 184-85 [927A-C]).

[49] *Metalogicon*, pp. 231, 232; '...per experientiam obsequii scientiam assecutus est; hec enim actionis est...de fonte sensuum...elicit uarios riuulos scientiarum et sapientie' (p. 185 [927B, 927C]).

[50] *Metalogicon*, p. 93 (p. 76 [866B-C]).

necessarily intertwined and indeed inseparable elements in the growth of human intellect.

II

One of the central features of Aristotle's moral philosophy is his claim that the absolutely virtuous soul is characterised by the inculcation of the virtues in their proper measure. Thus, much of the text of the *Nicomachean Ethics* (not to mention the remainder of Aristotle's ethical corpus) describes the various specific forms of moral goodness as mean points between excess and deficiency. To be good is to locate a middle way which is neither 'too much' nor 'too little'; divergence from the mean in either direction entails the performance of vicious acts.[51] 'Whereas the vices either fall short of or exceed what is right in feelings and actions, virtue ascertains and adopts the mean'.[52] This position yields several additional conclusions. First, the mean or moderate course is not to be confused with temperance or self-control. The latter is a specific virtue concerned with the soul's relation to pleasure and pain: temperance is the virtue pertaining to the sensuous aspect of human existence.[53] Moderation, on the other hand, is characteristic of all the virtues without ever being construed as a virtue in itself. To follow the mean in one's conduct is a precept which applies across the board, regardless of which particular virtue is under consideration. A second corollary of Aristotle's emphasis on the mean is that the ordinary language opposition between good and evil is deceptive. It is true that good and evil are, in absolute terms, contraries. But in particular cases, that which is good must be juxtaposed to two sorts of evil, both of which are in turn contrary to one another.[54] Hence, moral discourse is considerably more complex than is commonly conceived, for in many instances the possession of 'too much' of a virtue is as dangerous (if not more so) than the possession of 'too little'. In this way, Aristotle cautions his reader to exercise care lest fanatical virtuosity lapse into the commission of clearly vicious acts.

It is the potential for logical and linguistic confusion, engendered by the moderate nature of the virtues, that leads Aristotle to turn to the theme of the mean in some of the works of the *Organon*. In the first place, Aristotle is concerned that the mean be understood as one manner in which goodness may be ascribed to a subject. 'Often too the word "good" is applied to...that which is moderate (*tou metrion*); for that which is moderate, too, is called good'.[55] Thus, to speak of a man

---

[51] *EN* 2.7 (1107a32-b21).
[52] *EN* 2.6 (1107a4-6).
[53] *EN* 3.10-3.12 (1117b24-1119b19).
[54] *EN* 2.8 (1108b11-35).
[55] *Top.* 1.15 (107a11-13).

as good may signify that he adopts the virtuous mean, rather than that he is skilled, or useful, or whatever. But Aristotle's primary reason for addressing the mean in the *Organon* is to explain an important exception to many of the rules governing the correct usage of contraries. Generally speaking, Aristotle asserts, good and evil are contrasting terms, neither of which admits of degree. A tailor, for instance, cannot be 'too good'. In matters of virtue, however, the situation is not so simple. As Aristotle observes in the *Categories*, 'What is contrary to badness is sometimes good but sometimes bad. For excess, which is itself bad, is contrary to deficiency, which is bad; yet the mean (*mesotes*) is contrary to both and is good'.[56] The attribution of goodness in the sense of virtue is thereby logically peculiar: it requires that we designate as good a middle term which is opposed to two forms of extremes even as each of the extremes are also opposed to each other. This implies that calling someone 'bad' (in the moral connotation of that word) is inadequate; we must further specify whether the evil involved is one of excess or of defect. Yet, by the same token, both forms of moral extreme are more or less equally vicious, insofar as Aristotle emphasises that 'defect and excess are in the same genus — for both are in the genus of evil — whereas what is moderate (*to de metrion*), which is intermediate between them, is not in the genus of evil but of good'.[57] No one can escape culpability by claiming that either excess or defect is 'less evil' in some instance: both fall into the classification of badness and are thus also absolutely contrary to whatever is good. Consequently, the *Organon* allows us to differentiate between the forms of vice without ever denying that all vice remains utterly opposed to the moderate course of virtue.

For all of its complexities, the Aristotelian doctrine of the mean enjoyed considerable popularity among authors of Latin antiquity. In Horace, for example, we find a clear (if brief) presentation of the mean as essential to virtue: 'There is a mean in things, there are certain definite limits, / right consisting of what is neither beyond nor short'.[58] Nor were poets alone in propounding the moderate path to virtue. Cicero's writings contain many references to the mean in basically Aristotelian terms. As early as his youthful essay on rhetoric, *De inventione*, Cicero demonstrates a thorough appreciation of the intricacies of Aristotle's moral theory. In particular, Cicero questions the convention of associating every virtue with a single opposing vice, such as courage with cowardice or liberality with cheapness. Instead, in *De inventione*, he points out, '...each virtue will be found to have a vice bordering upon it, either one to which a definite name has become attached, as rashness which borders on courage...or one without any definite name. All of these as well as the opposites of good qualities will be classed among things to be

---

[56] *Cat.* 11 (14a2-6).
[57] *Top.* 4.3 (123b27-30).
[58] Horace, *Die Satiren*, ed. K. Büchner (Bologna, 1970), 1.1, lines 106-107.

avoided'.[59] Cicero returns to the same theme of moderate conduct as the key to virtue in his mature treatise on moral instruction, *De officiis*. To the man who wishes to behave in accordance with ethical rectitude, Cicero repeatedly counsels that 'the rule of the golden mean is best'.[60] *De officiis* furthermore explains that this 'happy mean which lies between excess and defect' has a very definite origin: it is 'the doctrine of the mean...approved by the Peripatetics'.[61] Thus, Cicero's work not only captures the crucial facets of Aristotle's account of the mean, but also attributes the doctrine explicitly to an Aristotelian source.[62]

It hardly seems possible that such a well-read and careful twelfth-century scholar as John of Salisbury could have remained ignorant of the doctrine of the mean or of its Aristotelian provenance. Indeed, considerable evidence culled from the *Policraticus* and the correspondence exists to indicate that John's persistent appeals to the moderate character of virtue reflected a familiarity (whether directly or indirectly) with Aristotle's ethical concepts.[63] But what place could the Aristotelian definition of virtue in terms of a mean between excess and defect possibly have in the *Metalogicon*, a tract on education? The answer rests upon an admission which John makes in his prefatory remarks to the *Metalogicon*. 'I have purposely incorporated into this treatise some observations concerning morals', John confides to his reader, 'since I am convinced that all good things read or written are useless except insofar as they have a good influence on one's manner of life. Any pretext of philosophy that does not bear fruit in the cultivation of virtue and the guidance of one's conduct is futile and false.'[64] Even in a treatise which purports to discuss topics of a more speculative and abstract nature, John cannot resist his practical impulse. Making men virtuous is not an enterprise distinct from making them intelligent or knowledgeable; it is of no value to be well educated if one is unable to put this learning to the service of moral rectitude. Moreover, the very techniques one employs in the acquisition of knowledge are subject to ethical evaluation and judgement. Proper learning is not defined merely by the quantity

[59] Cicero, *De inventione. De optimo genere oratorum. Topica*, trans. H. M. Hubbell (Cambridge, Mass., 1949), 2.165, p. 333.

[60] Cicero, *De officiis*, trans. W. Miller (Cambridge, Mass., 1913), 2.59 (pp. 230-33); cf. 1.130 (pp. 130-33) and 2.66 (pp. 240-41).

[61] *De officiis*, 2.89 (pp. 264-67).

[62] This is glossed over by scholars who interpret John of Salisbury as a Ciceronian on the basis of his views on moderation (see Munk-Olsen, 'L'humanisme de Jean de Salisbury,' 65-66).

[63] The evidence for this claim has been presented in Nederman and Brückmann, 'Aristotelianism in John of Salisbury's *Policraticus*', 213-16; and Nederman, 'The Aristotelian Doctrine of the Mean and John of Salisbury's Concept of Liberty', 130-33 and 'Aristotelian Ethics and John of Salisbury's Letters', 166-67.

[64] *Metalogicon*, p. 6; 'De moribus uero nonnulla scienter inserui; ratus omnia que leguntur aut scribuntur inutilia esse, nisi quatenus afferunt aliquod adminiculum uite. Est enim quelibet professio philosophandi inutilis et falsa, que se ipsam in cultu uirtutis et uitae exhibitione non aperit' (p. 4 [825B]).

of knowledge inculcated, but also by the quality of the educational experience. Specifically, John believes that the Aristotelian doctrine of the mean is essential to any pedagogy which takes seriously its duty to mold morals as well as intellects.

The theme of moderation appears most prominently in the *Metalogicon's* discussion of the correct attitude which the student ought to adopt towards his subject matter.[65] In general, John advocates the principle that men must find a middle ground between an absence of intellectual curiosity and an overzealous pursuit of all topics. Intellectual discipline, John feels, arises out of adherence to a mean course between excess and defect: 'However, once we go beyond the proper limits, everything works in reverse, and excessive subtlety devours utility'.[66] One should strive always in one's studies to exercise a vigilance which 'tempers them lest anything become excessive'.[67] What this means in large measure is that the intellect ought not to wander into those regions which are inappropriate to it. On the one hand, the mind must discriminate among its potential subjects of study in order to eliminate those which are unsuitable, namely, matters that pertain to God alone and also 'whatever is noxious, such as images that encourage melancholy, anger, and lust, or their daughters, envy, hate, calumny, carnal wantonness (*luxuria*), and vanity'. Yet, on the other hand, excessive caution yields an intellect which resists inquiry into new or foreign territory at all. Should the mind be inclined to be 'overly cautious, it risks becoming timid, whereas if it grows too uncautious, it is in peril of becoming foolhardy'.[68] John thus maintains that proper philosophical investigation demands careful reflection upon the boundaries of one's intelligence, so as not to thrust oneself 'temerariously and rashly into questions which exceed comprehension'.[69] There are some topics with which the human mind is unprepared to deal, and to inquire after these is to court danger in the present world and in the afterlife. Nonetheless, John does not wish to discourage man from the correct application of his powers of reason. It is just as wrong to waste those capacities which God has granted to man as to presume that intellectual prowess gives him carte blanche to seek after any subject at all.

---

[65] Daniel D. McGarry observes that, 'consistent with his view that the main objective of general education is the development of facility in reasoning and verbal expression, John's pedagogical method is "student centered"' ('Educational Theory in the *Metalogicon* of John of Salisbury', 672).

[66] *Metalogicon*, p. 90; 'Si autem moderatio desit, omnia hec in contrarium cedunt; subtrahitur namque subtilitati utilitas' (p. 74 [865B]).

[67] *Metalogicon*, p. 229 (translation altered); '...uigilans diligentia, que exercitium temperat, ne quid nimis' (p. 183 [926C]).

[68] *Metalogicon*, pp. 219-20; '...que nociua declinet; ut sunt ex quibus dolor, ira, cupiditas, et sequele istorum, puta invidia, odium, detractio, luxuria, uanitas. Dum uero nimis cauet, ad formidinem; dum parum, ad temeritatem accedit' (p. 176 [922D]).

[69] *Metalogicon*, p. 270 (translation altered); '...ut ausu temerario in ea que inscrutabilia sunt non irrumpat' (p. 214 [943D]).

It is well enough to say that moderation should be the guide in planning and pursuing one's intellectual instruction. But how has this precept any applicability to pedagogical practice? It is fortunate that John filled the *Metalogicon* with relevant examples of the usefulness of moderation in education. In the first place, John believes that a moderate attitude towards study is manifested in the very extent of the materials one consults. The *Metalogicon* warns that 'to study everything that everyone, no matter how insignificant, has ever said, is either to be excessively humble and cautious, or overly vain and ostentatious'.[70] The well-trained scholar will survey those authorities who are deserving of respect, but ignore works that do not merit effort and attention. Another consequence of the principle of moderation as used by John is that learning ought not to be an all-consuming and exclusive way of life; those scholars who are unable to turn their minds to other pursuits manifest the weakness of their educations by exceeding the mean. How much better it is that 'study should be moderated by recreation, so that while one's natural ability waxes strong with the former, it may be refreshed by the latter...While innate ability proceeds from nature, it is fostered by use and sharpened by moderate exercise, but it is dulled by excessive work'.[71] Constant study is a hindrance, rather than a boon, to the intellect; the overzealous scholar, no less than the too enthusiastic prince or prelate,[72] courts counterproductive conduct if not the peril of his soul.

Even in the classroom, the doctrine in the mean has an appropriate role. As we have already discovered in examining John's Aristotelian account of knowledge, a thorough education rests largely on accustoming 'one's students to practice the art they are studying'. Such practice, however, can be taken to excess; the exercise of the learner's faculties, especially when done publicly in the presence of other students, should be pursued only 'provided that charity regulates enthusiasm'.[73] The patience of the instructor will bear fruit if he does not expect too great an improvement from his students too rapidly. Practice must be steady and slow as well as regular and extensive.

The *Metalogicon*'s reliance on the Aristotelian doctrine of the mean furthermore suggests an additional component of John's conception of wisdom. For if knowledge is necessary to wisdom, as John believes, and if likewise the acquisition of

---

[70] *Metalogicon*, p. 70; '...persequi quid quis unquam uel contemptissimorum hominum dixerit, aut nimie miserie, aut inanis iactantie est, et detinet atque obruit ingenia, melius aliis uacatura' (pp. 56-57 [855c]).

[71] *Metalogicon*, pp. 35-36; 'Sedulo igitur ingenium tam studii quam remissionis moderatione excolendum est, ut ab altero conualescat, ab altero confortetur...Ingenium a natura proficiscitur, usu iuuatur, immoderato labore retonditur, et temperato acuitur exercitio' (p. 30 [839B]).

[72] A point John makes in both the *Policraticus* and in his correspondence; see Nederman, 'The Aristotelian Doctrine of the Mean and John of Salisbury's Concept of Liberty', 140-41 and 'Aristotelian Ethics and John of Salisbury's Letters', 170-72.

[73] *Metalogicon*, p. 70; 'sedulitatem regit caritas' (p. 57 [856A]).

knowledge has a fundamentally moral component, then the person whose learning exceeds the mean will lack wisdom just as surely as he who remains forever ignorant. In particular, excessiveness in education leads to a mind which refuses to be humble in the face of its own inadequacies and to recognise the need for grace.[74] The price of immoderation in learning is intellectual arrogance, which renders wisdom impossible to attain because it entails an affront to God who is the fount of all wisdom. The wise man, by contrast, will study that which is accessible to him, shun that which is beneath him, and accept on faith those mysteries of a divine nature which are beyond his rational comprehension.[75]

The notion that wisdom entails a moderate cast of mind appears to form the basis for John's criticism of pedagogical techniques current in the schools of his own day. 'Anyone who makes an effort to be moderate in word and action', the *Metalogicon* complains, 'is judged to have hidden motives'.[76] In this regard, John feels that the classroom is no different from the royal court; the temper of the times discourages observation of the mean.[77] Thus, instructors prompt students to all manner of intellectual excess. Disputations are conducted 'at all times, in all places, and on all topics',[78] in spite of the fact that 'the excesses of those who think dialectical discussion consists in unbridled loquacity should have been restrained by Aristotle'. It is thereby in a self-consciously Aristotelian vein that John objects to the unrestrained use of the verbal duel: 'The tongue of man...throws our life into confusion, and, unless it is checked by the reins of moderation, it hurls our entire person into the abyss'.[79] Nor does John make this criticism as an outsider, a cleric with limited experience of the methods of the schools. Rather, John devoted more than a decade to study under the great Parisian masters, and he observed how their dedication to a narrow pattern of logical discourse stunted their mental growth.[80]

[74] *Metalogicon*, pp. 64-65 (p. 23 [835B-C]).

[75] *Metalogicon*, p. 270 (p. 214 [943C-D]).

[76] *Metalogicon*, p. 4 (I have amended McGarry's translation according to a suggestion made to me by Ms. Allison Holcroft); 'Qui modestiam sequitur sermonis et operis, censetur factiosus' (p. 1 [823B]).

[77] John's criticism of the wantonness of courtly life has been surveyed by C. J. Nederman and N. E. Lawson, 'The Frivolities of Courtiers Follow the Footprints of Women: Public Women and the Crisis of Virility in John of Salisbury' in *Ambiguous Realities. Women in the Middle Ages and the Renaissance*, ed. C. Levin and J. Watson (Detroit, 1987), pp. 82-96.

[78] *Metalogicon*, p. 93; '... semper, ubique, et de omnibus eque disputant' (p. 76 [866B]).

[79] *Metalogicon*, p. 92; 'Debuerat Aristotiles hanc compescuisse intemperiem eorum qui indiscretam loquacitatem dialectice exercitium putant.' 'Lingue...conturbat uitam, et totum hominem, nisi moderationis uinculo refrenetur, agit in preceps' (p. 75 [866A, 865D-866A]).

[80] John describes his education in one of the classic examples of medieval intellectual autobiography at *Metalogicon*, pp. 95-100 (pp. 77-83 [867D-869B]). This passage provides much of the source material for the famous controversy about the existence of a major school of philosophy at Chartres during the twelfth century. See Liebeschütz, *Mediaeval Humanism*, pp. 111-13; and R. W. Southern, 'Humanism and the School of Chartres' in *Medieval Humanism and Other Studies* (Oxford, 1970), pp. 61-85.

Given the opportunity to visit with his old associates from school days, and to gauge the progress of their thought, John reports that he came away sorely disappointed. Over the years, these compatriots had acquired no greater wisdom and had benefitted not at all from the potential fruits of philosophy. Indeed, 'they had changed in but one regard: they had unlearned moderation; they no longer knew restraint'.[81] Precisely on this ground, the *Metalogicon* condemns the contemporary practice of philosophical studies. When logic and dialectic are employed without any regard for the pursuit of wisdom, when their practice moves beyond the mean, they will be sterile and pointless. The path to wisdom, which philosophy purports to chart, demands that philosophers recognise the limitations of their own techniques and methods. When philosophy becomes immoderately fond of its own image, the goal of wisdom ceases to be paramount.

*
* *

The identification of Aristotelian epistemic and ethical ideas as components of John of Salisbury's theory of education, while previously unexamined, might have been expected, given the unabashed admiration he showed for Aristotle in the Metalogicon. But this discovery does have some far-reaching implications for the categories of analysis commonly employed by the historian of medieval philosophical trends. First, it provides a clear illustration of what I have elsewhere described as the dual character of the Aristotelian tradition in the Middle Ages.[82] On the one hand, in the twelfth century, the technical doctrines of the *Organon* were widely employed and incorporated into medieval modes of thought, preparing the ground for the massive influx of Aristotle's psychology, metaphysics, science, ethics and politics into thirteenth-century Europe. But, on the other hand, the Aristotelian treatises on logic and language (in conjunction with such intermediate transmitters as Cicero and Boethius) also provided to twelfth-century authors a wealth of substantive doctrines in the areas of moral and speculative philosophy, the extent and influence of which is only now coming to be realised. Thus, the customary interpretation of medieval philosophy, which posits a sort of epistemological break around the year 1200 generated by the transmission of the bulk of Aristotle's texts, must be reexamined and subjected to scrutiny.[83] Indeed, it seems likely that the Aristotelian tradition exercised a broader and more intricate

---

[81] *Metalogicon*, p. 100; '...profecerant in uno dumtaxat, dedicerant modum, modestiam nesciebant' (pp. 82-83 [869B]).

[82] C. J. Nederman, 'Bracton on Kingship Revisited', *History of Political Thought* 5 (1984) 76-77.

[83] For an example of how an allegedly Aristotelian idea was transmitted to the Middle Ages long before the reappearance of the *Politics*, see G. Post in *Studies in Medieval Legal Thought. Public Law and State, 1100-1322* (Princeton, 1964), pp. 494-561.

influence upon the earlier medieval mind than has previously been credited. This is not to dispute the significance of the full recovery of the Aristotelian corpus, but instead to provide a partial explanation for its rapid acceptance and dissemination by medieval Christians in spite of the various sanctions intended to halt the spread of certain of Aristotle's ideas.

Furthermore, the location of demonstrably Aristotelian doctrines at the core of John of Salisbury's educational philosophy also explodes an alleged basis for the dichotomy between scholasticism and medieval humanism. The scholastics are generally regarded to have been whole-heartedly devotees of Aristotle's thought at the expense of previously entrenched Latin and Patristic modes of study.[84] The humanistic school, by contrast, is said to have abhorred Aristotle for engendering a narrow and technical approach to education. While admitting a limited value to Aristotelian teachings, the core of humanism supposedly owed its primary debt to Cicero, Quintilian, St. Augustine and a host of other Roman figures.[85] But surely this dichotomy is wrong with regard to that archetypical medieval humanist, John of Salisbury. Might it also be mistaken when attributed to others of the humanist persuasion? Only a great deal of additional research will allow us to reach a definite conclusion. In the case of John, what we appear to confront is one version of Aristotle interpretation, emphasising the substance of Aristotle's moral and epistemic doctrines, opposing another group of Aristotelians more concerned with the purely technical and formal aspect of his philosophy. Thus, the debate between humanism and scholasticism might plausibly be represented as a controversy between two schools of essentially Aristotelian thinkers, each concentrating on a different side of the philosopher's teachings. It is in precisely this sense that the two Aristotles of the Middle Ages, one above the surface, the other 'underground', not only coexisted but sometimes entered into direct conflict.

---

[84] See G. Paré, A. Brunet and P. Tremblay, *La Renaissance du XIIe siècle. Les écoles et l'enseignement* (Paris and Ottawa, 1933), pp. 142-43; D. Knowles, 'The Humanism of the Twelfth Century', *Studies* 30 (1941) 57-58; and R. R. Bolgar, *The Classical Heritage and Its Beneficiaries* (Cambridge, 1954), pp. 161-62.

[85] This is essentially the view of John of Salisbury's humanism one finds in Liebeschütz, *Mediaeval Humanism*, pp. 63-67 and passim; Munk-Olsen, 'L'humanisme de Jean de Salisbury', 53-83; and K. Guth, 'Hochmittelalterlicher Humanismus als Lebensform: Ein Beitrag zum Standesethos des westeuropäischen Weltklerus nach Johannes von Salisbury' in *The World of John of Salisbury*, pp. 63-76.

ARISTOTELIAN ETHICS AND JOHN OF SALISBURY'S LETTERS

To philosophers and political theorists, John of Salisbury represents the pinnacle of twelfth-century learning, his *Policraticus* and *Metalogicon* reflecting the breadth and depth of medieval intellectual accomplishment.[1] To political and ecclesiastical historians, John is primarily valuable for the observations about great events and important men reported in his extant correspondence and chronicles.[2] Of course, this somewhat schizophrenic image of John's work is overshadowed by his more general reputation as the Latin humanist and man of letters preeminent in his age—equally comfortable as administrator, secretary, legal advisor, politician, and schoolman.[3] But it is nevertheless the case that little effort has been made among recent scholars to explore in detail John's multicompetent mind by examining the connections between his abstract philosophical speculations, on the one hand, and his more documentary activities as correspondent and chronicler, on the other. In particular, we seldom hear asked (let alone answered) the question of how (or whether) John's theoretical insights are brought to bear on his analyses of contemporary political occurrences and personalities.

One potentially fruitful line of approach in this regard may be the examination of the relation between the moral categories which John developed in his philosophical works and the character profiles on which he based the political recommendations of his correspondence. Much of John's ethical thought, as expounded in the *Policraticus*, benefits from an "underground" tradition of Aristotelian moral theory running throughout the Middle Ages.[4] Thus, although John enjoyed no direct access to the moral and social writings of Aristotle,[5] he extracted from various sources many of the

[1] For example, Ewart Lewis, *Medieval Political Ideas* (London 1954) 169 describes the *Policraticus* as "the outstanding treatise on political theory before the work of Aquinas: a rich storehouse of the opinions which were current in the minds of scholarly churchmen before the discovery of the *Politics* of Aristotle." Similarly, Frederick Copleston, *A History of Philosophy: Medieval Philosophy* pt. 1 (Garden City, N.Y. 1962) 190 regards John as "the most gifted of the humanist philosophers . . . . He represents what was best in twelfth-century philosophic humanism."

[2] To cite but two cases, consider the use made of John's work by D. C. Douglas, *The Norman Fate, 1100–1154* (Berkeley 1976) and Robert Somerville, *Pope Alexander and the Council of Tours* (Berkeley 1977).

[3] The classic treatment of John's humanist strain is that of Hans Liebeschütz, *Mediaeval Humanism in the Life and Writings of John of Salisbury* (London 1950).

[4] This thesis has been developed in somewhat greater detail in C. J. Nederman and J. Brückmann, "Aristotelianism in John of Salisbury's *Policraticus*," *Journal of the History of Philosophy* 21 (1983) 227–229, and C. J. Nederman, "Bracton on Kingship Revisited," *History of Political Thought* 5 (1984) 76–77. For some pre-medieval sources of this "underground tradition," see Richard McKeon, "The Hellenistic and Roman Foundations of the Tradition of Aristotle in the West," *Review of Metaphysics* 32 (1979) 677–715.

[5] Unless one is willing to accept Michael Wilks's dubious speculation that "John has access (presumably in France or Italy rather than in Canterbury Cathedral library) to some sort of rudimentary version, or perhaps

important terms and concepts of Aristotelian ethics. Since this linguistic and intellectual apparatus originated uniquely with Aristotle, John's reliance on it is relatively easy to identify. Is it possible, however, that John applied the same doctrines to his more concrete work as secretary, advisor, and correspondent? Careful examination reveals that two aspects of Aristotelian thought employed in the *Policraticus* can be isolated in John's letters as well: first, virtue arises from a fixed disposition to act which is acquired through regular practice; and second, all the virtues consist in following the moderate or mean course between extremes. In both cases, John's use of these ideas, far from being ancillary, is central to his purposes as a correspondent. We shall proceed by first establishing the Aristotelian provenance and transmission of each precept, and its place in the *Policraticus*, as a prelude to the investigation of the influence of Aristotle's philosophy within John's letters. Ultimately, we shall begin to see the consistency with which John employed certain philosophical principles, regardless of whether he was composing a speculative treatise or an epistle on current events.

I

One of the cornerstones of Aristotle's moral psychology is the notion of *hexis* (commonly mistranslated as "habit," but more properly rendered as "disposition" or "state"). As a general concept within the Aristotelian system, *hexis* refers to a type of quality, that is, the ascription of a qualitative property to a subject or substance. In particular, *hexis* denotes those qualities which become so firmly rooted in what they qualify as to form a "second nature." Such qualities, accordingly, are difficult or even impossible to change. In the realm of moral philosophy, Aristotle claims that "*hexis* is the genus of virtue" and that "the virtues are *hexeis*."[6] By addressing virtue in terms of *hexis*, Aristotle posits the relative permanence and stability of the virtue of the good man without the need to specify that moral qualities are inborn or natural. Aristotle maintains that virtuous *hexeis* are acquired by exposure to and practice of virtuous actions. The repeated performance of virtuous deeds, through which a course of conduct is rendered habitual, constitutes the Aristotelian recommendation for moral education.[7] To develop the correct moral habits is to mold one's *hexeis* aright, since "*hexeis* arise from corresponding activities" and the "quality of our *hexeis* depends on what we do."[8] At its core, Aristotle's definition of virtue by reference to *hexis* assures that moral action will spring "from a firm and unchangeable character."[9] For whoever possesses a *hexis* which disposes him towards good conduct will without fail or deviation do what

epitome, of Aristotle's *Politics*"; see M. Wilks, "John of Salisbury and the Tyranny of Nonsense," in *The World of John of Salisbury*, ed. Wilks (Oxford 1984) 280. Wilks multiplies sources beyond necessity (and beyond evidence), insofar as he does not survey the similarities in doctrine between Aristotle and Cicero, which would account for many of the Aristotelian political views he identifies in the *Policraticus*. I hope to offer a corrective to Wilks's interpretation in a forthcoming essay, "The Ciceronian Tradition and the 'Aristotelian Revolution' in Late Medieval Political Thought."

   [6]Aristotle, *Nicomachean Ethics*, ed. H. Rackham (Cambridge, Mass. 1934), 1106a14 and 1143b24–25. All translations from Greek into English are my own.
   [7]Ibid. 1103a31–33 and 1103b1–3.
   [8]Ibid. 1103b22–24.
   [9]Ibid. 1105a35–b1.

X

is virtuous; the mature *hexis* prevents the individual from committing uncharacteristically immoral acts. (Aristotle's doctrine is, however, symmetrical; it is likewise true that a vicious disposition, once acquired, is equally difficult to alter or improve.[10]) In sum, Aristotle assigns to the concept of *hexis* the function of guaranteeing the stability and fixity of one's moral attributes.

The classical and Christian Latins normally translated *hexis* as *habitus*, facilitating transmission of the term and its conceptual implications to the twelfth century. John of Salisbury was intimately familiar with at least three distinct Latin sources in which the Aristotelian doctrine of *habitus* was articulated. First, Cicero's *De inventione* defines virtue generally, and justice more specifically, in terms of *habitus*, while explaining that "we call *habitus* a constant and absolute feature of the soul or body in some particular, such as the acquisition of virtue or an art or some special knowledge or again some bodily capacity not give by nature."[11] Similarly, Boethius remarks in *De topicis differentiis* that virtue may be defined as "habitus mentis bene constitutae," a definition which he infers from the claim that all species of virtue are themselves dispositional qualities of a well-ordered mind.[12] Finally, the most thorough source for the notion of *habitus* in the twelfth century was Aristotle himself, whose *Categories* and *Topics* were available in Latin translation during John's time.[13] In both works, virtue and its species are defined with reference to *habitus*.[14] In addition, Aristotle clearly explains that *habitus* entails a quality which is "stable and long lasting," so that "through length of time [it] ultimately becomes a part of man's nature and as such immovable or exceedingly difficult to change—this one would call *habitudo*."[15] Thus, not only did John of Salisbury have access to an ample number of intermediary texts which reported the Aristotelian idea of *habitus*, but he was exposed directly to Aristotle's own statements on the matter.[16]

It is hardly surprising, then, that we find *habitus* accorded a role by John in the *Policraticus*. One of the central lessons of the *Policraticus* is that a good or well-formed moral character (*mos* or *mores*) is indispensable to the proper performance of the public functions of the warrior, the courtier, and the king. Consequently, John holds that an

---

[10]Ibid. 1114a18–21.

[11]Cicero, *De inventione*, ed. H. M. Hubbell (Cambridge, Mass. 1961) 1.25, 36: "Habitum autem appellamus animi aut corporis constantem et absolutam aliqua in re perfectionem, ut virtutis aut artis alicuius perceptionem aut quamvis scientiam et item corporis aliquam commoditatem non natura datam." This and all other translations from Latin are my own. Also see 2.9, 30 and 2.50, 159–160.

[12]Boethius, *De topicis differentiis*, PL 64.1188c–d.

[13]A recent evaluation of John's knowledge of the *Organon* is provided by Edouard Jeauneau, "Jean de Salisbury et la lecture des philosophes," in *World of John* (n. 5 above) 103.

[14]See Aristotle, *Categories*, 8b29 and 8b33–35; *Topics*, 121b27–39, 144a16 and 144a17–18. Latin citations will follow the Boethius translations of the *Categories* (in L. Minio-Paluello, ed., *Aristoteles latinus* 1.1–5 [Bruges 1961]) and the *Topics* (in L. Minio-Paluello, ed., *Aristoteles latinus* 5.1–3 [Leiden 1969]).

[15]Aristotle, *Categories*, 8b28 and 9a2–4: "Permanentior et diuturnior . . . Per temporis longitudinem in naturam cuiusque translata et insanabilis vel difficile mobilis, quam iam quilibet habitudinem vocet."

[16]Professor Brückmann and I (n. 4 above) 206 argue for the likelihood that John's use of Aristotelian doctrines derived directly from the *Organon* rather than from intermediary sources. This hypothesis may, at least with regard to *habitus*, be confirmed by the fact that in the midst of a summary of the *Categories* in his *Historia pontificalis*, John comments, "In ethicus proprium dicitur esse virtutis, ut habitum bene componat" (ed. M. Chibnall [London 1956] 34). Strangely, Chibnall attributes the phrase to Boethius and Cicero despite the fact, as we have just seen, that *habitus* is repeatedly discussed in the *Categories*.

164

unstable body politic is directly attributable to the vicious qualities of those who guide it, especially its royal head. Similarly, a stable and well-governed polity reflects the incorruptible virtue of its leaders and great men.[17] Thus, the essential prerequisite for good government is the correct moral education of those who rule. But how does such education occur? John's explanation of the process through which moral character is acquired is redolent of the Aristotelian conception of *hexis/habitus*.

> *Mos* is a *mentis habitus* from which proceeds assiduously particular acts. If [an act] is done once or more often, it does not immediately become part of *mores*, unless by assiduous practice it passes into usage . . . When anyone is said to acquire reverence because of *mores*, it is meant that he has virtues which deserve honor. Who ought not to revere and respect him who is wise, brave, temperate, and just?[18]

The *Policraticus* thereby defines moral character in terms of *habitus*, and stipulates that the possession of such a disposition occurs only after repeated practice of certain sorts of actions. This disposition toward virtue assures constancy and permanency of conduct, at least once the acquisition process is completed. These typically Aristotelian elements of moral psychology seem to support John's insistence elsewhere in the *Policraticus* that habits (*consuetudines*) inculcated through steady repetition are rendered quasi-natural: "Usage . . . is hard to unlearn, and habit becomes second nature."[19] In the formation of such nature-like habitual behavior, *habitus* performs a kind of regulative function. The development of a *habitus* requires regular practice or usage (*usus*), out of which emerges those qualities of moral character whose stability and fixity are guaranteed by the mature *mentis habitus* itself. On two counts, then, John's presentation of *habitus* parallels the Aristotelian idea: first, the formation of moral disposition occurs through the repetition of particular actions; and second, the disposition, once fixed, is relatively constant in the sense that the agent's conduct will consistently reflect an ingrained disposition of mind.

In John of Salisbury's letters, likewise, the Aristotelian principle of *habitus* as a necessary constituent of moral character finds a place. Throughout the period of his most intense correspondence (1154–1170), John was ambassador for and advisor to two active and influential archbishops of Canterbury, Theobald and Becket, and confidant to many other prominent men besides.[20] In this capacity, John was expected to report his evaluations of the personalities and behavior of the great laymen and clerics of mid-

---

[17]See John of Salisbury, *Policraticus*, ed. C. C. J. Webb (1919; repr. Frankfurt a.M. 1965) 538c–d, 626b–d, and 633d–634b.

[18]Ibid 544a–545a: "Mos autem est mentis habitus ex quo singulorum operum assiduitas manat. Non enim si quid fit semel aut amplius, statim moribus aggregatur nisi assiduitate faciendi vertatur in usam . . . . Cum itaque a moribus quis reverentiam contrahere dicitur, ei virtutes, quibus honor exhibendus est, inesse significatur. Quis, enim non veneretur et vereatur illum quem prudentem fortem temperantem credit et iustam?"

[19]Ibid. 489b: "Usus enim . . . egre dediscitur, et consuetudo alteri naturae assistit."

[20]Far and away the best study of John's career, mapped against the background of his network of personal and political connections, is by Klaus Guth, *Johannes von Salisbury (1115/20–1180): Studien zur Kirchen-, Kultur- und Sozialgeschichte Westeuropas im 12. Jahrhundert* (St. Ottilien 1978). This book, along with Guth's contribution to *World of John* (n. 5 above) 63–76 ("Hochmittelalterlicher Humanismus als Lebensform: Ein Beitrag zum Standethos des Westeuropäischen Weltklerus nach Johannes von Salisbury"), represents a notable exception to the scholarly tendency of separating John's topical writings from his philosophical works. Even Guth, however, makes little attempt to demonstrate how John's philosophy was brought to bear on his judgments in the realm of practical politics.

twelfth-century Europe. Even in his more private correspondence, John often dissected the qualities of particular individuals, especially with regard to their moral character. Thus, we receive quite honest appraisals not only of John's political and personal enemies—Henry II, Frederick Barbarossa, John of Oxford, Gilbert Foliot, and their ilk—but also of his friends and allies—Becket, successive popes (in particular Alexander III), the French king Louis VII, and so forth. Perhaps as significant, we gain insight into John's own character and intellect. At their core, John's sketches of and remarks about his contemporaries return to two themes: first, those who have by previous word and deed shown themselves to be opponents of right and justice are not to be trusted in future dealings despite the appearance of contrition; and second, constancy of *moral* commitment, even in the face of physical adversity, is to be admired as the preeminent token of well-formed character. The first theme arises in the context of John's recommendations to his archiepiscopal masters regarding the moral and political reliability of those who had once oppressed the church or who had not opposed such oppression; the second emerges from John's sustained praise for men (like himself) who steadfastly endured empoverishment, exile, and outlawry in the name of ecclesiastical liberty and moral rectitude. Common to both themes, however, is the assumption that human conduct remains fundamentally consistent over time because of the ingrained features of a mature character.

We could hardly expect that John's letters, which are after all mainly nonspeculative in nature, would contain any articulation or explication of the premises from which his character studies proceed. But on occasion John does let slip in his correspondence the otherwise implicit principles of his moral psychology; and these passages parallel closely the Aristotelian views expressed in the *Policraticus*. In a particularly reflective letter to William of Diceia, dating from about 1168, John noted that, while it is relatively easy to comprehend the "intellectual principles" ("praecepta intellectu") of a skill, the acquisition of the skill in "usus" is a considerably greater challenge. This applies most especially to the realm of morals. For a man to possess true virtue, John asserts, he must practice it from an early age ("huic ab ineunte operam dedi"). John offers as an example (drawn from personal experience) the acquisition of a charitable and amenable disposition: "assiduousness in friendship has conferred on me an *usus*, and use rendered into *habitus* compels me to be friendly even to the unfriendly."[21] Through long usage arises a *habitus*, John tells his correspondent, and once that *habitus* is fixed the acts flowing therefrom cannot be varied. The individual who has evolved through practice a firm moral characteristic such as charity will continue to behave charitably even towards those who show no charity in return. John thus employs the Aristotelian doctrine of *habitus* in order to explain how men are able, even in the face of extreme adversity, to follow a particular course of moral action—it is because they can do no other.

This view is confirmed by an earlier letter from John to Bishop Bartholomew of Exeter, written in July 1166, which distinguishes between mankind's "primitiva natura" and the quasi-natural elements of "mos." Our "primitiva natura" springs from God's grace, whereas "mos" is the result of human effort for good or ill unaided by direct

---

[21]John of Salisbury, *Letters* 2, ed. W. J. Millor and C. N. L. Brooke (Oxford 1979) 512: "Assiduitas ergo amandi et obsequendi contulit usum, et ille versus in habitum me semper amare compellit etiam non amantes."

divine intervention. But because it rests on practice, "mos" can appear to have virtually the same permanence as nature. "Use is second nature," John observes (citing Cicero as authority), "from which escape is very difficult."[22] Although character is not the work of God acting through nature, we should not expect to encounter vast inconsistencies in the moral behavior of a given individual. Because of its acquisition through repeated practice, character becomes second nature. The essentially Aristotelian doctrines of moral character, *habitus* and *usus*, incorporated into the *Policraticus* have thus been included in John's correspondence as well, where they would seem to provide the underlying assumptions of the moral psychology on the basis of which he advised his friends and masters. The presence of this Aristotelian account of the acquisition of moral character can hardly be dismissed as extraneous to the understanding of John's correspondence. On the contrary, the realization of John's purpose in composing many of his letters—to deduce from the previous behavior of individuals what could be expected of them in the future—depended on his adherence to the Aristotelian principles we have surveyed. Therefore, John could not abide any separation between the abstract philosophical precepts of the *Policraticus* and the more practical aim of his letters. Instead, the Aristotelian evaluation of moral character in terms of *habitus* explicated by his correspondence illustrates a consistency and continuity in John's thought regardless of audience or tool of expression.

II

A similar yet even more striking example of continuity within John of Salisbury's *corpus* is afforded by the definition of virtue as a mean between excess and deficiency. Of course, this conception of virtue also has its source in Aristotle's philosophy. In the *Nicomachean Ethics*, Aristotle argues that acquisition of the truly virtuous soul requires learning all the virtues *in their proper measure*. Goodness in human action is thus defined as achieving the mean between extremes; evil results from an agent whose behavior is either "too much" or "too little." For example, one ought to be neither timid nor temerarious when the virtue sought is courage. "Whereas the vices either fall short of or exceed what is right in feelings or actions," Aristotle insists, "virtue ascertains and adopts the mean."[23] Thus, in Aristotle's account moderation—as distinct from temperance or self-control—is meaningless separate from the specific virtues. If good or virtuous action consists in following the middle path between opposite vices,[24] then the mean can never be construed as a virtue in its own right. Rather, moderation or the mean is a structural property of each of the virtues, an indispensable feature of any form of moral rectitude.

While the general precept of "moderation in all things" pervaded classical and Christian thinking, comparatively few sources known to the twelfth century provided a thorough articulation of the specifically Aristotelian equation of virtue with a mean between excess and deficiency. In particular, John of Salisbury would likely have had access to only two authors (although there may be others I have failed to identify) in

---

[22]Ibid. 144: "Usus altera natura est . . . a quo difficillium est avelli." For the appropriate passages from Cicero, see ibid. 145 n. 18.

[23]Aristotle, *Nicomachean Ethics* 1107a2–6.

[24]See ibid. 1108b11–35.

whose work Aristotle's conception of moderation was incorporated. First, Cicero sometimes followed Aristotle regarding the doctrine of the mean, as in *De officiis* where he praises "moderation . . . which is between defect and excess,"[25] and in a lengthy passage of *De inventione* which shows how the virtues are contrary both to their customary opposites and to another set of qualities representing virtue taken to excess.[26] Second, in Aristotle's *Organon* we once again can detect significant traces of his moral teachings, this time with regard to moderation. The *Topics* explains that "defect and excess are in the same genus—for both are in the genus of evil—whereas what is moderate, which is intermediate between them, is not in the genus of evil, but that of good."[27] Likewise, in the *Categories* Aristotle observes that "what is contrary to a bad thing is sometimes good, sometimes bad (for excess, which is bad, is contrary to deficiency, yet the mean is contrary to both and is good)."[28] Both writings reiterate the view of the *Nicomachean Ethics* that virtue consists in measured conduct, in charting a moderate course between excess and deficiency. A well-read twelfth-century thinker like John of Salisbury could hardly have avoided the doctrine of the mean or overlooked its Aristotelian provenance.[29]

Indeed, the *Policraticus* shows considerable evidence of the benefits which its author accrued from his familiarity with the Aristotelian conception of each of the virtues as a mean between excess and deficiency. Throughout the *Policraticus*, we encounter reliance on the position that "what exceeds the mean verges on fault. Every virtue is marked by its limits and consists in the mean; if excessive, one is off the road, not on it."[30] A characteristic of genuine moral goodness, in John's eyes, is that it follows a middle path between opposing evils. Bad men, accordingly, "recede from the mean between vices, which is the ruler of virtue."[31] Nor does John seek to avoid the logical implication of this doctrine, namely, that it is just as evil to be overzealous in the pursuit of virtue as to be negligent. To illustrate this point, John employs the spatial metaphor of inclining towards the left or the right.

> To incline to the right is to insist too vehemently upon the virtues themselves. To incline to the right is to exceed the mean in works of virtue, which consists in the mean. Truly all vehemence is inimical to salvation, and all excess is a fault; nothing is worse than the excessive practice of good works . . . The Philosopher says: beware what is excessive; because, if one departs from caution and moderation, he will recede in his incaution from the path of virtue itself.[32]

[25]Cicero, *De officiis*, ed. W. Miller (Cambridge, Mass. 1913) 1.89: "mediocritatem . . . quae est inter nimium et parum."

[26]Cicero, *De inventione* 2.65.

[27]Aristotle, *Topics* 123b27–30: "Instantia quoniam egestas quidem et superhabundantia in eodem genere (in malo enim ambo), mediocre autem cum sit medium horum non in malo sed in bono est." See also 107a11–13 and 113a3–7.

[28]Aristotle, *Categories* 14a2–6: "Malo vero aliquotiens bonum contrarium est, aliquotiens malum (diminutioni enim, quae mala est, superfluitas quae et ipse mala est contrarium est)."

[29]Thus, it is insufficient to argue, as B. Munk Olsen has suggested, that John's infatuation with moderation is due primarily to his affection for Cicero's thought; see his "L'humanisme de Jean de Salisbury, un cicéronien au 12e siècle," in M. de Gandillac and E. Jeauneau, eds., *Entretiens sur la Renaissance du 12e siècle* (Paris 1968) 53–83.

[30]John of Salisbury, *Policraticus* 480d: "Qui si modum excesserit, vergit ad culpam. Omnis enim virtus suis finibus limitatur et in modo consistit; si excesseris, in invio est et non in via."

[31]Ibid. 762c: "recedentes a medio vitiorum, quae regio virtutis est."

[32]Ibid. 531c–d: "Ad dextram declinare est virtutibus ipsis vehementer insistere. Ad dextram declinare

The reference to "philosophus" suggests John's awareness of the Aristotelian origins of this doctrine. But in any case, John has captured the essential elements of Aristotle's notion of the mean. For John as for Aristotle, any and all of the virtues may be attained solely when pursued with definite limits. Overstepping the bounds of goodness in the name of goodness itself is necessarily as repugnant as the complete absence of moral propriety. Moderation pertains to the inherent structure of virtue, since an act is virtuous if and only if it remains within the boundary fixed by the measure or mean. Thus, the agent must take special care in the selection of a correct course of action by affording particular attention to the conditions under which the act(s) shall occur: "Discretion with regard to place, time, amount, person, and cause readily distinguishes what is excellent . . . . This is the fount and origin of all moderation, without which no duty is rightly performed."[33] In deciding how to conduct oneself, one must determine all relevant circumstantial considerations and choose the course of action which is appropriately moderate in its context. According to John, most actions cannot be judged apart from their circumstances because the mean path between vices can only be ascertained once all relevant variables are identified. John thereby recognizes that the necessary corollary to the Aristotelian doctrine of the mean is the principle of measuring one's acts so as to fit the particulars of the situation.[34]

Even in the *Policraticus*, John's Aristotelian emphasis on the virtuous mean does not remain an abstract moral teaching. Rather, John translates moderation into a practical precept applicable to the behavior of the princes, courtiers, and knights whom he is discussing. This means that many activities (such as hunting and musical performance) which John personally abhors he nevertheless allows to be practiced "if true moderation forms the limit."[35] John's counsel is always guided by the rule: "Nothing decorous is without the mean."[36] The same impulse to recommend the moderate course in practical affairs extends to John's letters, regardless of the person or issue in question. For instance, in reference to the schism provoked by Emperor Frederick I which had commenced in 1159,[37] John remarks, "I do not believe that the thing is to be approached contentiously, but is to be completed by a happy moderation, especially when the wise man recalls that the moderation of wisdom disposes all things according to their proper place."[38] The man of virtuous wisdom will no more seek to impose his knowledge by force than to embrace ignorance; instead, he will pursue a

---

est in virtutis operibus, quae in modo consistit, modum excedere. Omnis vero vehementia salutis inimica est, et excessus omnis in culpa; bonarumque rerum consuetudo nimia pessima est . . . . Et philosophus: Cave quod est nimium; quia, sic haec ipsa cautela modestiam deserit, eo ipso a tramite virtutis incaute recedit."

[33]Ibid. 671d–762a: "Haec autem facillime distinguit loci temporis modi personae et causae superius memorata discretio . . . . Haec est enim fons et origo totius modestiae, sine qua nichil recte in officiis exercetur."

[34]Aristotle, *Nicomachean Ethics* 1106a expresses essentially the same position by insisting that the mean course is always relative to the agent.

[35]John of Salisbury, *Policraticus* 402d: "si vero moderationis formula limitantur."

[36]Ibid. 761b: "Nichil decorum est sine modo." This remark is reminiscent of Cicero, *De officiis* 1.93.

[37]On John's interest in German affairs, see Timothy Reuter, "John of Salisbury and the Germans," in *World of John* (n. 5 above) 415–425.

[38]John of Salisbury, *Letters* (n. 21 above) 2.70: "Nec credo rem istam adeundam iurgiis, sed felici moderatione complendam, praesertim a sapiente qui meminit quia modestia sapientiae a fine suaviter usque ad finem universa disponit."

middle path towards truth. John applies this principle to himself no less than to the behavior of others. In a letter to Ralph of Lisieux, he suggests that it may not be proper to quote excessively from Scripture: "I prefer to employ the bridle of moderation, keeping my pen still rather than collecting articles of divine law which, even rightly quoted, nevertheless lead to the harm of listeners."[39] In sum, even zeal for the citation of God's word must be held in check by the moderating reins of virtue. Just as the *Policraticus* objects to those who insist to excess upon virtue, so John in his letters denounces conduct which strays from the bounds of moderation in the name of truth or religion.[40]

John's use of an Aristotelian doctrine of the mean in his correspondence was not, however, limited to a few isolated references. On the contrary, moderation forms a central theme in the decade-long running commentary on the Becket conflict which the bulk of his letters compose. John emphasizes moderation in his analysis of the three primary contestants in the dispute—Henry II, the English bishops, and Becket himself —and criticizes each at various points for adopting immoderate views and acting altogether excessively. The condemnation of Henry on these grounds is probably the most expected, given John's affiliations.[41] A missive addressed to John of Canterbury, bishop of Poitiers, observes that Henry would enjoy universal praise and acclaim "if only he would defer more to the Church of God, and act more moderately with those who reason with him, and inhibit his language and spirit from outbreaks of anger and other reprehensible emotions, according to a measure of royal dignity."[42] It is for precisely this reason, John tells Gerard Pucelle, that Henry so desperately needs to reconcile himself with Becket: "The archbishop of Canterbury will inspire the soul of the lord king to employ moderately his divinely given license."[43] John perceives Becket as a counterbalance to Henry, as a defender of the liberty of the church whose exile has allowed the king to give full play to his tyrannical tendencies. John's letters regularly style Henry "tyrannus,"[44] a term which in the usage of the *Policraticus* means an individual of authority who has employed his power in order to suppress the personal liberty of those subject to him.[45] The true king rules within the bounds of moderation, tolerating faults when possible, punishing only when necessary—but always according a proper measure of freedom to those over whom he reigns.[46] The danger, both

---

[39]Ibid 298: "Malo enim moderationis habena calamum cohibere quam divinae legis articulos congerere qui, etsi recte prolati fuerint, interdum non nisi ad subversionem proficiunt auditorum."

[40]It is surely for this reason that John, in an early letter authored on behalf of Theobald, urges the pope to temper his commands with "moderatio" so as not to cause undue friction between the church and lay magnates; *Letters* 1, ed. W. J. Millor, H. E. Butler, and C. N. L. Brooke (London 1955) 41.

[41]For John's attitude toward Henry II, see Guth, *Johannes* (n. 20 above) 207–213.

[42]John of Salisbury, *Letters* (n. 21 above) 2.634: "Si ecclesiae Dei ut oportet deferret magis, et cum his modestius ageret qui cum eo contrahunt aliqua ratione, et impertu irae vel alterius reprimendi affectus ad mensuram regiae gravitatis linguam cohiberet et animum."

[43]Ibid. 686: "Cantuariensis . . . inspirabit animo regis ut divinitis indultam sibi licentiam moderetur."

[44]For instance, see ibid. 237, 429, and 455–456. A careful accounting of the various uses of the word "tyrannus" in John's letters and elsewhere has been prepared by Jan van Laarhoven, "Thou Shall *Not* Slay a Tyrant! The So-Called Theory of John of Salisbury," in *World of John* (n. 5 above) 333–341.

[45]For a more thorough articulation of this notion of tyranny, see Nederman and Brückmann (n. 4 above) 224, and C. J. Nederman, "The Aristotelian Doctrine of the Mean and John of Salisbury's Concept of Liberty," *Vivarium* (1987), forthcoming.

[46]John of Salisbury, *Policraticus* 529a, 530b, and 531d–532b.

to the king's soul and to his realm, occurs when he departs from the moderate course. Such a ruler, John asserts in a letter of 1168 to Baldwin, archdeacon of Totnes, is Henry of England, who shows no moderate inclination towards his subjects: "It is the man's nature to make light of all the merits of one who for whatever reason breaks or postpones obedience to a single mandate, no matter what it is. The 'moderation' of his requests . . . is such that it is sometimes necessary to disobey."[47] John's lesson is not to be missed: it is incumbent upon the subjects of immoderate rulers like Henry to resist those commands which disturb and disrupt the liberty of individuals and communities. By crossing the appropriate bounds fixed by the proprietous mean in his treatment of Becket and the English church generally, Henry's eternal soul and quite possibly his kingdom are imperiled.[48] Henry's propensity towards excessive behavior renders him morally unfit to govern the English realm and to serve the English church.

John cites similar grounds for condemning those bishops of England who actively sided with Henry in the Becket dispute or who chose the route of neutrality. John believed that the behavior of such men represented a fundamental threat to ecclesiastical liberty in England. He could only explain their actions by imputing to them an immoderate desire to preserve or enhance their lives and fortunes at the expense of the church. Thus, in one letter John remarks that God knows of and will surely judge harshly the lack of "modestia" exercised by the bishops;[49] to another correspondent John complains about the conduct of the bishop of Worcester, whose antipathy towards Becket was reportedly "more than manly moderation dictates" ("plus quam tante modestiae virum deceat").[50] That these observations ought to be read as more than passing jibes is clear from a lengthy letter to his brother, Richard, dating from mid-1166. The topic of the letter is the collective behavior of the English bishops, who had just filed a joint appeal against Becket to Rome;[51] its main theme is moderation. John initially expresses concern about Richard's own master, the bishop of Exeter, whose sympathies seem to have been uncertain: "In this conflict of power and right he should behave with such moderation, with law guiding, grace leading, and reason supporting, that he ought not to seem temerarious in opposing the power which God ordains, nor consent to iniquity to the detriment of the church for fear of power or love of transitory goods."[52] John's counsel of moderation, then, is specifically intended as a warning against the vice of temerity (an excess of courage) in episcopal dealings with the archbishop, Becket. While John acknowledges that it is difficult for anyone to remain faithful in practice to the "golden mean" ("aurea mediocritas"), he nevertheless insists that whoever truly wishes to serve his church and his God must approximate the virtuous mean insofar as possible. This has been a failing of other of the English bishops, whose conspiratorial behavior against Thomas could only occur because they

---

[47]John of Salisbury, *Letters* (n. 21 above) 2.468: "Ea enim est natura hominis, ut apud eum iacturam faciat omnium meritorum qui quacumque ratione praeterierit aut distulerit unum, qualecumque sit, adimplere mandatum. Ea autem est moderatio precum . . . ut ei quandoque necesse sit obviari."

[48]See ibid. 454, 456.

[49]Ibid. 242.

[50]Ibid. 464.

[51]This is explained in ibid. #171.

[52]Ibid. 128: "In hoc conflictu potestatis et iuris ea moderatione incedat, praevia lege, duce gratia, iuvante ratione, ut nec temeritatis videri debeat adversus potestatem quam Deus ordinavit, nec metu potestatis aut amore bonorum evanecentium iniquitati consentiat in depressionem ecclesiae."

X

are "worried and timorous, and this beyond the mean."[53] Instead of aiding and abetting the royal attack on the liberties of the English church, John encourages the bishops "to imitate the good deeds we read about, such as Hushai the Archite, who strove to dissipate the evil counsel of Achitophel by moderation."[54] In effect, the contents of the letter represent an impassioned plea for the bishops to subordinate their private interests and personal safety to the pressing need of the church. John accomplishes this task by arguing that the bishops lack the moral courage (the mean virtue between temerity and timorousness) to stand up to the demands and threats of Henry II. Thus, John's repeated references to moderation have a strict Aristotelian connotation: the bishops stand accused of departing from that path of moderate conduct whose source can only be the soul which has acquired the virtues in their proper measure.

Henry II and the English bishops are, of course, obvious targets for John's accusations of immoderation, since they were responsible for the exile of Becket and his supporters. It may be somewhat surprising, however, to discover that the greater number of John's discussions of virtuous moderation came in letters to or about his friend and master, Archbishop Thomas.[55] The eccentricities and peculiarities of Becket's personality, and their impact on his conflict with Henry, are commonly acknowledged in contemporary scholarship.[56] But John, too, was well aware of the defects of his master's character, which he largely attributed to Becket's compulsive tendency to exceed all moderate bounds in his behavior. In the early years of John's exile, when he was desperately seeking to reconcile himself with Henry II, he repeatedly admitted this fault in Becket's personality. To Humphrey Bos, John bluntly states, "I have kept the faith owed to the church and archbishop of Canterbury, and I have stood faithfully by him in England and on the Continent when justice and moderation seemed to be his. If ever he seemed to detour from justice or exceed the mean, I stood up to him to his face."[57] John's message is clear: he will not follow Becket blindly. When the archbishop adheres to a moderate course in his behavior, John is obliged to keep faith with him; but whenever Thomas strays from the mean, John will oppose him strenuously. The difficulty is that Becket shows little sense or discretion witth regard to judgments of circumstance. John tells Bartholomew, bishop of Exeter, that "He who inspects our hearts and judges our words and acts knows that I—more than any other mortal— have upbraided the lord archbishop on the grounds that he has from the beginning inadvisedly provoked the resentment of the king and court by his zeal, since many provisions should have been made for place and time and persons."[58] This passage echoes

[53]Ibid. 130: "turbari et timere, et utrumque supra modum."

[54]Ibid. 130, 132: "imitetur quod bonos fecisse legimus, ut Cusai Arachitem, qui consilium et malitiam Achitophel moderatione adhibita studuit dissipare."

[55]For recent evaluations of the relationship between Becket and John of Salisbury, based on the letters and other evidence, see Guth, *Johannes* (n. 20 above) 239–251, and Anne Duggan, "John of Salisbury and Thomas Becket," in *World of John* (n. 5 above) 427–438.

[56]The literature on Becket is far too enormous to summarize effectively here. An especially balanced appraisal of Becket's character and behavior may be found in C. N. L. Brooke, "Thomas Becket," in *Medieval Church and Society* (London 1971) 121–138.

[57]John of Salisbury, *Letters* (n. 21 above) 2.20, 22: "Ecclesiae et archiepiscopo Cantuariensi debitam servari fidem et ei, ubi iustitia et modestia videbantur adesse, et in Anglia et in partibus cismarinis fideliter astiti. Sicubi vero aut exorbitare a iustitia aut modum excedere videbatur, restiti ei in faciem."

[58]Ibid. 48: "Novit enim cordium inspector et verborum iudex et operum quod saepius et asperius quam aliquis mortalium corripuerim dominum archepiscopum de his, in quibus ab initio dominum regem et suos

two of the key moral teachings of the *Policraticus*: first, that overzealous pursuit of virtue is just as vicious as a lack of enthusiasm, if not more so; and second, that identifying the moderate course requires careful consideration of the conditions under which action is to occur. John believes that Becket has learned neither lesson very well (despite the fact that the *Policraticus* was addressed to him). As for John's contention to Humphrey and Bartholomew that he has condemned his master's immoderation to his face, we find confirmation in two letters of counsel to Becket dating from mid-1166. In one missive, John advises Becket on an appropriate response to the latest machinations of his disobedient English inferiors. Clearly fearing Becket's propensity toward rash behavior, John exhorts the archbishop to seek reconciliation with, rather than further alienation of, his church by approaching his opponents with virtuous moderation. "It is especially expedient that your moderation be known to all," John recommends. "With moderation write and state the conditions, since it seems to be certain that the souls of the enemies of God's church are so hardened that they will admit no condition at all."[59] With regard to the oft-heard accusation that Becket's actions are not motivated by considerations of virtue, but by pride and hatred, "this opinion should be answered by exhibiting moderation, in deeds and words, in conduct and dress, which is not very profitable in God's eyes unless it is the product of our deepest conscience."[60] A few lines later, John is again extolling the moderate path. Becket is encouraged to exercise "modestia" in framing his response; he should imitate "modestissimus David," so that "you can moderately reply" to "those who reprove, indeed severely deride you."[61] Generally speaking, this counsel is repeated in the second letter directed to Becket. There as before, John suggests to the archbishop that "in all things behave such that your moderation may be known to all." But John specifies that such moderation can only be achieved by reference to present circumstances: "Attend to the state of the times, the condition of the Roman church, the needs of the English realm."[62] Consideration of such factors is an indispensable prerequisite for judging which actions approximate the virtuous mean. In his observations about Becket's moral character, then, John comes closest to a complete restatement of the Aristotelian doctrine of the mean articulated in the *Policraticus*. Yet in the background of *all* his remarks about moderation—whether they pertain to Becket, the bishops of England, or Henry—remains John's conviction that the virtuous path in every matter of religion and politics lies between the twin evils of excess and deficiency.

* * *

It should by now be quite clear that Aristotelian language and concepts permeate the ethical components of John of Salisbury's correspondence. What may temper in some

---

zelo quodam inconsultius visus est ad amaritudinem provocasse, cum pro loco et tempore et personis multa fuerint dispensanda.''

[59]Ibid. 168: "Modestia vestra, quod plurimum expedit, omnibus innotescat . . . eoque modestius scribendum et condiciones conseo exigendas, quo michi certior esse videor animos adversantium ecclesiae Dei sic induratos esse ut nullam omnino conditionem admittant.''

[60]Ibid. 170: "Huic opinioni occurrendum est exhibitione moderationis, tam in factis et dictis quam in gestu et habitu; quam tamen apud Deum non multum prodest, nisi de archano conscientiae prodeat.''

[61]Ibid. 172: "Poteritis modeste respondere . . . istis increpatoribus, immo detractoribus vestris.''

[62]Ibid. 190: "Ita per omnia incedatis ut modestia vestra omnibus innotescat . . . Attendanda enim est instantia temporis, condicio ecclesiae Romanae, necessitas regni Angliae.''

measure our initial surprise at this conclusion is our awareness that John, without direct knowledge of Aristotle's ethical writings, still had access to a wide range of sources through which he could familiarize himself with the Philosopher's moral teachings. From the roots of this "underground tradition" of Aristotelian thought grows a trunk with many branches, most of which have yet to be explored. But just as important, tracing Aristotelian argumentation from the *Policraticus* into the letters illustrates an essential unity in John's intellectual perspective. John did not discriminate radically between his speculative and his practical work. On the contrary, he seems to have been quite prepared to incorporate philosophical precepts into his analysis of contemporary events and persons, as the examples of *habitus* and moderation demonstrate. Surely, this represents one of the cornerstones of John's much vaunted humanism: the attempt to impart to current affairs a distinctly philosophical cast intrigued John as much as it would his successors in the Renaissance. Indeed, John's composition of the *Policraticus* appears to have crystallized the views on moral character and its political significance which he espouses in his correspondence. The *Policraticus* was completed in 1159; it is only in the letters written after this date that the language of moderation and the dispositional evaluation of personal qualities become regular elements of his correspondence. Where John's earlier letters are the work of a sound legal intellect, his later missives reflect philosophical principles which he had already developed and defended in the *Policraticus*.[63] Thus, reading John's correspondence as an extension of the *Policraticus* can be a fruitful enterprise. As the case of the doctrines derived from Aristotelian moral thought demonstrates, John of Salisbury believed that philosophy was not to be left at the schoolhouse steps.[64] Rather, philosophical discourse had a place in the world at large: its task was to aid in discerning the good from the evil, the right from the merely expedient, the true from the false, and so to illuminate the path of rectitude in matters of politics and personal conduct. This devotion to the practical implications of abstract thought is all the encouragement that should be required for philosophers and political theorists to examine John's correspondence and for political and ecclesiastical historians to pay closer attention to his philosophical teachings.

---

[63] I discuss a similar case of John's use in a letter of a doctrine originating with the *Policraticus* in a forthcoming essay entitled "The Physiological Significance of the Organic Metaphor in John of Salisbury's *Policraticus*."

[64] This partially accounts for the various antischolastic jibes that John includes in his letters, such as the remark that "scolaris exercitatio interdum scientiam auget ad tumorem" (*Letters* [n. 21 above] 2.34).

NATURE, SIN AND THE ORIGINS OF SOCIETY:
THE CICERONIAN TRADITION IN MEDIEVAL POLITICAL
THOUGHT

The idea that man is by nature a social and political creature enjoyed a long and rich career during the Latin Middle Ages.[1] Indeed, it is perhaps not too implausible to say that the naturalness of human association was one of the few doctrines to which virtually all medieval political thinkers would subscribe, in one or another version. A primary reason for this widespread agreement was an analogous near-unanimity on the part of the philosophical and theological sources available to the Middle Ages. At one time it was supposed that social and political naturalism was strictly an inheritai ce from the transmission of Aristotle to the West in the thirteenth century.[2] Despite occasional relapses,[3] however, this view has been discredited on the grounds that most of the influential classical and Christian authorities accessible throughout the whole of the Middle Ages articulated essentially the same concept.[4] Cicero, Seneca, the Latin poets, St. Augustine, Lactantius—these figures (and others besides) all reinforced the notion that man was meant by nature to live in community with his fellows. Thus the rediscovery of Aristotle's *Politics* by the West merely confirmed the naturalism that had almost universally permeated medieval political, philosophical, legal, and theological treatises. The predominance of naturalistic conceptions of human association in political thought from at least the twelfth century onwards was more a function

[1] The formulation "social and political" or "civil and social" was generally preferred throughout the Middle Ages, even after the dissemination of Aristotle's doctrine of the *zoon politikon*. This may be an inheritance from Seneca (*De beneficiis* 7.1.7), Macrobius (*Commentatiorum in Somnium Scipionis* 1.8), Lactantius (*Divinae institutiones* 4.10), or a host of other Latins.

[2] Although this view was espoused almost universally during the middle of the twentieth century, it is perhaps best summarized by Walter Ullmann, *Principles of Government and Politics in the Middle Ages* (London, 1961), 248: "Earlier conceptions of nature ... did not lend themselves to an application in the field of human social relations. But the Aristotelian naturalist premises in fact encouraged its application to the problem of human government, since it was primarily of a human—as distinct from a divine—provenance."

[3] For example, D. E. Luscombe, "The State of Nature and the Origin of the State," in N. Kretzmann, A. Kenny, and J. Pinborg (eds.). *The Cambridge History of Later Medieval Philosophy* (Cambridge, 1982), 759-60; R. W. Southern, *Medieval Humanism and Other Studies* (Oxford, 1970), 56; and Michael Haren, *Medieval Thought* (Houndsmill, Basingstoke, 1985), 28-29.

[4] The largest share of responsibility for this development should be accorded to Gaines Post, especially "The Naturalness of Society and the State" in his *Studies in Medieval Legal Thought: Public Law and the State, 1100-1322* (Princeton, 1964), 494-561.

4

of basic harmony among numerous sources than the product of the intellectual force of any single authority.

Yet social and political naturalism presented some very real philosophical difficulties to medieval thinkers. There was, for instance, the context of Christian theology to consider. Christianity taught that some of the original nature of man had been sacrificed in the aftermath of the Fall. Post-lapsian "nature" was regarded to be a perversion of its source, since mankind was created good and immortal but chose to be evil and mortal.[5] In particular the range of sins deplored by the Western tradition of Christianity—pride, covetousness, lust, and the like—tended to be profoundly anti-social. Since in their sinful condition human beings were essentially egoistic, it was hard to see how they could continue to manifest any "natural" disposition to associate. As St. Augustine expressed the matter, "There is nothing so social by nature, so unsocial by its corruption, as this [human] race."[6] A central problem with which medieval political authors had to cope, then, was the implied dichotomy between natural sociability and human sin. To what extent was it possible for men to recapture in the present life that associative nature with which they had been created but which they had lost through the commission of evil? By what means could man's sinful tendencies be overcome sufficiently to give new vitality to the social element of man's relinquished nature? Was it within man's power to restore some semblance of God's original concession of sociability to human beings? No political thinker of the Middle Ages could afford to ignore such questions, though their responses varied according to specific intellectual and historical circumstances.

In general scholars have identified two medieval lines of approach to the problem of man's social nature.[7] The first model is essentially Augustinian, maintaining that at least within the limits of the *civitas terrena*, man's perverted nature renders him susceptible to discord and strife. It is necessary, therefore, for men to introduce political institutions in order to enforce peace and earthly justice, compelling submission to a coercive power capable of suppressing behavior which arises from wrongly ordered passions. In this sense organized human relations can hardly be regarded as an extension of man's natural propensities; they are artificial and purely conventional institutions designed (albeit at the behest of divine inspi-

[5] See Ullmann, *Principles of Government and Politics in the Middle Ages*, 239-43.
[6] St. Augustine, *The City of God*, tr. M. Dods (New York, 1950), 410 (Book 12, Chapter 27).
[7] The following juxtaposition of Augustinian and Aristotelian models is derived from recent accounts by Quentin Skinner, *The Foundations of Modern Political Thought* (2 vols; Cambridge, 1978), I, 50; Brian Tierney, *Religion, Law, and the Growth of Constitutional Thought, 1150-1650* (Cambridge, 1982) 38-39; Bernard Guenée, *States and Rulers in Later Medieval Europe*, tr. J. Vale (Oxford, 1985), 37-43; and Arthur P. Monahan, *Consent, Coercion and Limit* (Kingston, 1987), 29-42.

ration) to bridle those people who, as residents of the earthly city only, are unable to control the consequences of fallen human nature. On the Augustinian account, man's natural desire to be sociable does not extend into the post-lapsarian world of coercive politics.

By contrast the second version of human nature ordinarily attributed to the Middle Ages (of an Aristotelian provenance) proposed that no factor could preempt man's impulse to associate, since society in general and political society in particular represented the fulfillment of the range of man's physical and spiritual needs. Each primary form of human community—from the family to the political body—has its own specific *telos* or purpose within the natural scheme: the household exists for economic security, the village for defense and exchange, the *polis* (which the medievals extended to encompass cities, provinces, and kingdoms) for the intellectual and moral improvement of citizens. In other words it is only in the context of a fully articulated social and political system that the complete and self-sufficient life of human happiness ordained by God is to be found. The fact that men often behave unjustly and anti-socially does nothing to diminish their fundamental and inalterable nature. Within each human creature rests a principle of motion which impels him to join together with his fellows in spite of all apparent impediments.[8]

Certainly, we encounter each sort of view during the Middle Ages: Augustine found medieval counterparts in such authors as Augustinus Triumphus and Wyclif,[9] while Aristotle was quite closely followed by St. Thomas Aquinas, among others.[10] But it is far from clear whether the choice was entirely between Augustinian and Aristotelian ideas when it came to medieval attempts to explain how temporal political and social relations arose among post-lapsarian men. A third, clearly delineated tradition of thought, taking its substance from the writings of Cicero and connecting it with the doctrine of original sin, held that while men always retained their natural inclination to congregate—even after the Fall— the recognition of this nature and its implications for their lives needed to be awakened in and drawn out of them by means of reason and persuasion. Men will only unite, in other words, when they become expressly aware that it is natural (not to mention beneficial) for them

---

[8] This reflects the doctrine of the *Physics* 192b9-193b21 that the difference between "nature" and "artifice" is concerned with the location of the principle of change within a subject or object. That which is natural has within itself its own source of motion, whereas the cause of alteration in artificial things is characteristically external.

[9] On Augustinus Triumphus see Michael Wilks, *The Problem of Sovereignty in the Later Middle Ages* (Cambridge, 1963), 58-60 and 269-70; on Wyclif see L. J. Daly, *The Political Theory of John Wyclif* (Chicago, 1962), 74-80; and on medieval adherents to the Augustinian conception of political society, Otto Gierke, *Political Theories of the Middle Ages*, tr. F. W. Maitland (Cambridge, 1900), 108-10, n. 16.

[10] Wilks, *The Problem of Sovereignty*, 122-25.

to do so. Thus this account, unlike Aristotle's, makes it impossible to say that man's associative nature is sufficient to inspire and incite the creation of a community. The Ciceronian position is a conventionalist one in the sense that it does not maintain the natural necessity of human society, but it is simultaneously naturalistic insofar as it holds that endemic to mankind is an inclination (if not quite a compulsion) to gather together. Consequently, the doctrine of the medieval Ciceronians represents a sort of *via media* between the extremes of the Augustinian and the Aristotelian viewpoints: it accords sin a central place by asserting that men behave anti-socially because they do not recognize the consequences of their common nature; yet it also admits that the natural human propensity to associate continues to be efficacious even in the post-lapsarian state of iniquity.

It has perhaps been too seldom appreciated in recent scholarship that Cicero was the only political thinker of pagan antiquity whose writings continued to be accessible to the Christian West following the collapse of Roman domination.[11] Cicero's two major political treatises, *De res publica* and *De legibus*, were not directly circulated during the Middle Ages,[12] but these sources were widely cited through intermediary patristic sources like St. Augustine and Lactantius.[13] More importantly, Ciceronian tracts on moral matters (*De officiis*) and rhetorical technique (*De inventione*) contained many passages that were extremely germane to political speculation. We can be sure that Cicero's ideas on the subjects of politics and society were broadly disseminated because *De officiis* and *De inventione* were among the most widely read and revered texts in the medieval West.[14] Significantly, both *De officiis* and *De inventione* present natur-

---

[11] For documentation of Cicero's impact on early Christian authors, see Otto Schilling, *Naturrecht und Staat nach der Lehre der Alten Kirche* (Paderborn, 1914); Baziel Maes, *La Loi Naturelle selon Ambroise de Milan* (Rome, 1967); Manfred Wacht, "Privateigentum bei Cicero und Ambrosius," *Jahrbuch für Antike und Christentum*, 25 (1982), 28-64; and Marcia L. Colish, *The Stoic Tradition from Antiquity to the Early Middle Ages* (2 vols; Leiden, 1985), II. The classic evaluation of Cicero's reception by the Middle Ages is by Hans Baron, "Cicero and the Roman Civil Spirit in the Middle Ages and Early Renaissance," *Bulletin of the John Rylands Library*, 22 (1938), 72-97.

[12] On the transmissional history see Georges de Plinval, "Autour du *De legibus*," *Revue des Études Latines*, 47 (1969), 296-97; Peter L. Schmidt, *Die Überlieferung von Cicero's Schrift "De Legibus" im Mittelalter und Renaissance* (Munich, 1974), 201-79; Pierre Boyancé, *Etudes sur l'Humanisme Cicéronien* (Brussels, 1970), 180-82; and Peter L. Schmidt, "Cicero 'De re publica': Die Forschung der letzten fünf Dezennien," in H. Temporini (ed.), *Aufstieg und Niedergang der Romanische Welt*, I, *Von den Anfängen Roms bis zum Ausgang der Republik* (Berlin, 1973), iv, 276-79.

[13] As established by de Plinval, "Autour du *De legibus*," 296, and Schmidt, "Cicero 'De re publica,' " 271-73.

[14] The medieval reception of these two treatises has been examined by Richard McKeon, "Rhetoric in the Middle Ages," *Speculum*, 17 (1942), 1-19; Mary Dickey, "Some Commentaries on the *De inventione* and *Ad Herennium* of the Eleventh and Early Twelfth Centuries," *Medieval and Renaissance Studies*, 6 (1968), 1-41; Karin M. Fred-

alistic accounts of society and government derived from the modified Stoic ideas expressed in *De res publica* and other of Cicero's explicitly political works.[15] Thus, by way of a variety of sources, Cicero's version of the origins of human community would have stood out as a separate and coherent theory to its medieval inheritors.

The central claim of the Ciceronian conception of human society is that men join together because of their natural powers of reason and speech. Reason induces in human beings the desire to live in civil unity, while speech offers the method by which association may be achieved. The same basic principle is retained throughout Cicero's corpus. In *De inventione*, one of the earliest of his treatises to survive, Cicero postulates men in a primordial condition where they lead a scattered, brutish existence devoid of rationality, religion, family and law.[16] But these primitive men also harbor the powers of reason and speech which give them a natural impulse towards sociability. Speech in particular is crucial to human association insofar as "it does not seem possible that a mute and voiceless wisdom could have turned men suddenly from their habits and introduced them to different patterns of life."[17] The realization of men's social sentiments required the guidance of a wise and eloquent man through whose persuasion other men exchanged their solitary existence for a social one. They learned useful and honorable occupations, assembled into cities, obeyed voluntarily the commands of others, observed laws, and in general were "transformed ... from wild savages into a gentle and kind folk."[18] All of these developments Cicero attributes to the natural ability of speech coupled with reason: not merely does rational discourse separate man from lesser animals, but it renders possible the mutual understanding through which the sacrifices and burdens of human association may be explained and justified. In the absence of reason combined with eloquence none of the blessings of the social and political community may be acquired. Still, it is not strictly for the sake of these blessings but because of the natural sociability arising out of language itself that men are first moved to join with their fellows, according to *De inventione*.

Cicero maintains the essential features of *De inventione*'s account of

---

borg, "The Commentary of Thierry of Chartres on Cicero's *De inventione*," *Cahiers de l'Institut de Moyen Age Grec et Latin* (Copenhagen, 1970), 1-36; John O. Ward, "From Antiquity to the Renaissance: Glosses and Commentaries on Cicero's Rhetorica," in J. J. Murphy (ed.), *Medieval Eloquence* (Berkeley, 1978), 25-67; N. E. Nelson, "Cicero's *De officiis* in Christian Thought: 300-1300," *Michigan University Publications: Language and Literature*, No. 10 (1933), 59-160; and Maurice Testard, Introduction to *Cicéron, Les Devoirs*, I (Paris, 1965), 67-70.

[15] Cf. Cicero, *De republica*, ed. C. W. Keyes (Cambridge, Mass., 1928), I.25.
[16] *De inventione* I.1-3.
[17] *Ibid.*, I.3.
[18] *Ibid.*, I.2.

the natural growth of society in *De officiis*, his last completed work, although in the latter work, he explores the same themes in greater detail. *De officiis* argues that the primary cause of all forms of human community—from the family to the state—is the natural gregariousness of mankind which is manifested in the common faculties of reason and speech.[19] The primacy accorded to reason and speech reflects the fact that it is in virtue of these powers that "the processes of teaching and learning, of communicating, discussing and reasoning associate men together and unite them into a sort of natural fraternity."[20] In Cicero's view intellect and language may be regarded as nature's method of endowing the human species with the capacity it needs to survive.[21] Insofar as reasoning and speaking lead men to associate, their society is itself a work of nature, the disturbance of which may be considered "unnatural." On these grounds Cicero denies that self-interest or material gain can be counted among the motives underlying the formation of human society. A wholly economic explanation of the origination of the community fails to capture the depth of the social instinct,[22] for it implies that if men were (or became) physically self-sufficient they would have no need of association.[23] Nor can the desire to protect one's property be the basis of human social ability, since Cicero is adamant that private ownership does not arise out of nature.[24]

Yet once men have joined together by means of their natural impulse to associate, they profit both collectively and individually from their communal, civilized life. For from social contact emerged the full range of political and economic relationships: "Without the association of men, cities could not have been built or peopled. In consequence of city life, laws and customs were established, and then came the equitable distribution of private rights and a definite social system. Upon these institutions followed a more humane spirit and consideration for others, with the result that life was better supplied with all it requires, and by giving and receiving, by mutual exchange of commodities and conveniences, we succeed in meeting all our wants."[25] In effect, the result of the natural sociability of man is the preservation and protection of his material interests. Man's natural powers of reason and speech alone render possible all the advantages of political and economic association. If, as *De officiis* claims, it is human reason and speech which provide the immediate natural impetus for society, then the various political and economic byproducts of human association come to possess the stamp of nature

[19] *De officiis* I.11-12, 107, 156.
[20] *Ibid.*, I.50.
[21] *Ibid.*, I.11.
[22] *Ibid.*, I.159.
[23] *Ibid.*, I.158.
[24] *Ibid.*, I.21, 51.
[25] *Ibid.*, I.15.

by virtue of their compatibility with the gregarious impulse; and whatever tends towards the disturbance of political and economic order stands opposed to man's naturally social inclination. Consequently, the highest calling to which the state can aspire is the reinforcement of the full range of civil and private rights which men have acquired through social intercourse.[26]

The Ciceronian description of the natural foundations of human society hence embraces several unique features. As previously suggested, Cicero asserts that men are not necessarily (in an Aristotelian sense) drawn towards the actual formation of communities even though they are by nature sociable beings. Cicero's conception of nature is not of an active or driving force in man's life but of a more passive and implicit feature of human experience, on the order of a proclivity requiring an external stimulus to awaken and invigorate it. In turn this explains the Ciceronian emphasis upon the faculties of speech and reason as the twin natural bases of association. Unlike a teleological conception of nature, which involves an inexorable pull towards the completion or realization of a purpose, Cicero's concentration on natural faculties implies a propensity which may or may not be employed according to circumstance. It is this factor which lends to the Ciceronian presentation of the origins of society its "conventional" quality, while still functioning within a naturalistic context.

Two other conclusions may also be deduced from Cicero's account of the transformation of primordial into civilized and social man. The first is that entry into human society is at the same time renunciation of the primacy of one's private and individual interests. Thereafter the common welfare and benefit take precedence over the needs and desires of particular members of the community. This is the sacrifice which must be made in order to acquire all of the advantages which an ordered and harmonious social life affords. A second consequence of the Ciceronian version of the community's genesis is that the process of congregation is totally consensual. Cicero held that social and political arrangements were the product of explicit common agreement among primitive men arrived at through non-coercive means, viz., through the application of reason and persuasion. While not a social "compact" in the sense that a formal contract amongst a people c᾽ with a government was approved, the primordial consensus postulated by Cicero demonstrated that human association could originate as something other than the creation of blind nature or sheer force. A naturalistic explanation of the early development

[26] This argument is examined in greater detail by Neal Wood, "The Economic Dimension of Cicero's Political Thought: Property and the State," *Canadian Journal of Political Science*, 16 (1983), 742-44, 749-50, and in his forthcoming book, *An Introduction to Cicero's Social and Political Thought* (Berkeley, 1987), a draft of which I was fortunate enough to read in manuscript.

of social and political institutions was not therefore incompatible with the doctrine that individual choice alone determined the existence of legitimate authority.[27]

That Cicero's account of the natural origins of society enjoyed wide currency throughout the Latin Middle Ages is beyond dispute. Beginning already in the eleventh century, glosses on *De inventione* referred to the idea that association enjoyed a basis in the natural faculties of speech and reason.[28] Likewise, medieval moralists were demonstrably imbued with the naturalistic description of social organization contained in *De officiis*.[29] But this is not to suggest that medieval authors merely parroted Cicero's doctrine of the genesis of society and politics without comprehending its significance. Rather they employed his notion to explain how men who are social yet sinful can be joined together into a permanent and harmonious bond without the exercise of coercion and hence in a manner strictly consistent with their own nature. Of course various authors tailored their use of Cicero to fit a broad spectrum of philosophical and political concerns: John of Salisbury sought to reveal the foundations of a liberal education, John of Paris to defend the necessity of monarchy, and Marsiglio of Padua to prove the illegitimacy of arbitrary modes of authority.

Yet it remains possible to identify a core of Ciceronian thought which imparts to all the theorists mentioned a similar view of the origins of human society. The essence of this core idea—which distinguishes it from both Augustinian and Aristotelian perspectives—is that human nature, while imperfect and imperfectable without God's grace, is still endowed with a cognitive and verbal capacity which, when stimulated, will generate a united community even in the face of sin. Of course Cicero influenced medieval political theory in many other significant ways,[30] and his concept of social genesis was widely influential beyond the authors already mentioned.[31] But our present goal is merely to illuminate a coherent medieval tradition of Ciceronian thought regarding the natural origins of man's

[27] The observation of Bernard Guenée, *States and Rulers in Later Medieval Europe*, 42, that "the natural state weighed heavily on the individual," only pertains to the Aristotelian polity.

[28] Dickey, "Some Commentaries on *De inventione* and *Ad Herennium* in the Eleventh and Early Twelfth Centuries," 11, 22, 25-26.

[29] Nelson, "Cicero's *De officiis* in Christian Thought," 76-155.

[30] See the generally favorable judgment of E. K. Rand, *Cicero in the Courtroom of St. Thomas Aquinas* (Milwaukee, 1946).

[31] A thorough discussion of Cicero's impact on the Middle Ages would include *Moralium Dogma Philosophorum*, ed. J. Holmberg (Uppsala, 1929); Brunetto Latini, *Li Livres dou Tresor*, ed. F. J. Carmody (Berkeley, 1948); John O. Ward, *Artificiosa Eloquentia in the Middle Ages* (Unpubl. diss., University of Toronto, 1972), 31-33, citing Petrarch; and Aeneas Silvius Piccolomini, *De ortu et auctoritate Imperii Romani*, in R. Wolkam (ed.), *Der Briefwechsel des Eneas Silvius Piccolomini*, in *Fonte Rerum Austriacarum*, 67 (1912), 6-24.

social and political relations, a tradition which, among authors who otherwise shared little in common, is significant for recognizing and seeking to resolve the apparent contradiction between the Christian teaching about fallen man and the doctrine of man's natural inclination to associate. In evaluating the role of the Ciceronian tradition, we must consider not just the sheer number of thinkers who contributed to it, but also the diversity of their interests and aims.

As the leading exponent of twelfth-century Latin humanism, John of Salisbury was intimately familiar with the extant portions of the Ciceronian corpus.[32] John is regarded as one of the most astute and "humanistic" moral and political philosophers of his age,[33] and it is not surprising that his political ideas should in many instances be tinged with a distinctly Ciceronian flavor.[34] In particular there is some evidence that John's famed organic metaphor for the commonwealth, sketched in his *Policraticus*, was partially rooted in Cicero's thought.[35] But for all its naturalistic imagery—including a clear statement that art imitates nature[36]—the *Policraticus* does not actually defend the position that social and political arrangements result from a natural propensity on the part of man. This is to be found, rather, in his *Metalogicon*, a treatise, composed at roughly the same time as the *Policraticus*, in which he propounds his educational philosophy and metaphysics. The location of this discussion is not as odd as first glance might indicate. Because John adopted, as we shall see, an essentially Ciceronian approach to the origins of society, he regarded the transformation of primordial into civil man as a consequence of human capacities of reason and language—abilities which properly fall within the province of the theory of education, instead of political philosophy.

It is important that we grasp the context within which John appealed to a Ciceronian conception of the natural foundations of society. Large sections of the *Metalogicon* were addressed to the doctrine, ascribed to the possibly mythical Cornificius and his followers, that the qualities and powers with which men are born constitute the limit of their knowledge

---

[32] A. C. Krey, "John of Salisbury's Knowledge of the Classics," *Transactions of the Wisconsin Academy of Sciences and Letters*, 14 (1909/1910), 948-87.

[33] See Hans Liebeschütz, *Mediaeval Humanism in the Life and Writings of John of Salisbury* (London, 1950).

[34] B. Munk-Olsen, "L'Humanisme de Jean de Salisbury, un Cicéronien au 12e Siècle," in M. Gandillac and E. Jeauneau (eds.), *Entretiens sur la Renaissance du 12e siècle* (Paris, 1968), 53-83.

[35] See my "The Physiological Significance of the Organic Metaphor in John of Salisbury's *Policraticus*," *History of Political Thought*, 8 (1987) 211-24.

[36] John of Salisbury, *Policraticus*, ed. C. C. J. Webb (Oxford, 1909), 619c-d. On this naturalistic doctrine, see Tilman Struve, "Vita civilis naturam imitetur ... Der Gedanke der Nachahmung der Natur als Grundlage der Organologische Staatskonzeption der Johannes von Salisbury," *Historisches Jahrbuch*, 101 (1981), 341-61.

and faculties.[37] This implies that human beings, endowed with weak natures, ought not to seek to improve their lot or condition on earth, ought not to develop their minds and skills. Instead, they may only find redemption directly in the grace of God, shunning the material world and their own natures completely.[38] Is it any wonder, inquires John, that so many of the Cornifician bent have removed themselves altogether from the world and entered the cloister?[39] In opposition to Cornificius, John argues that the mundane and sinful character of human nature does not end the debate. For God through nature has granted to mankind the capacity to improve its lot on earth by diligent application of the native faculties of reason and speech. This is not to say that John considers man's nature (in Aristotelian terms) to be wholly perfectable; grace is still required to complete what nature has begun. Yet men may accomplish much by nature alone, and indeed the path to beatitude is blocked, according to the *Metalogicon*, by the Cornifician teaching that no attempt can (or perhaps should) be made to develop the characteristics associated with man in his post-lapsarian state.[40]

The major testimony in John's case against the lessons of Cornificius is an adapted version of Cicero's depiction of the primitive development of human association. John deploys his Ciceronian source in order to demonstrate that social interaction among men is an important wellspring of true (albeit partial, because merely mortal) happiness (*beatitudo*). The *Metalogicon* regards nature (in Stoic fashion) as imprinted with a divine plan, "the most loving parent and best disposer of all that is."[41] Thus, if nature has granted to man alone the powers of speech and reason, this is so he above all other creatures may "obtain true happiness."[42] Such a plan is evident in the first place from the observation and investigation by reason of the structure of the universe. God has "disposed the parts of the universe so that each needs the aid of the others, and they mutually compensate for their respective deficiencies. . . . All things are lacking when isolated, and are perfected by union, since they support one another mutually."[43] This theme of reciprocity runs throughout John's corpus; it is employed in his correspondence and forms the basis for his organic metaphor for the polity.[44] But in the *Metalogicon*

[37] See Rosemary B. Tobin, "The Cornifician Motif in John of Salisbury's *Metalogicon*," *History of Education*, 3 (1984), 1-6.

[38] *Metalogicon*, 825c-832a. Translations from this and other Latin texts are mine, unless otherwise indicated.

[39] *Ibid.*, 730b-c.

[40] *Ibid.*, 826d.

[41] *Ibid.*, 825c.

[42] *Ibid.*, 825d.

[43] *Ibid.*, 826c-d.

[44] Nederman, "The Physiological Significance of the Organic Metaphor in John of Salisbury's *Policraticus*."

the model of the mutual intercommunication of members is seen to indicate the natural course which ought to guide human behavior. "One cannot imagine how any kind of happiness could exist entirely apart from mutual association and divorced from human society," John declares, for reason's knowledge of the world dictates that this is the essence of nature as designed by the divine will. Therefore, whosoever wishes to achieve supreme happiness is well advised to seek earthly happiness in accordance with nature, that is, in association with his fellow human beings. Such communal congregation constitutes "the sole and unique fraternity among the children of nature."[45] To imperil society by assailing man's capacity to improve his rational powers—an accusation which John levels against Cornificius—is thus to cut man off from the happiness which God has allotted to him in the present life, as well as to exclude the possibility of fulfilling the terms of divinely bestowed grace.

John's view in effect is that human nature demands of man a level of sociability unparalleled in the rest of nature. In true Ciceronian fashion, however, the *Metalogicon* argues that reason's discovery of the naturalness of association is *per se* insufficient. For the rational faculty is individual and personal in its impact, so that left to itself it could never actually generate the community which it knows to be natural to and beneficial for human existence. Rather, reason must be made manifest by speech (and eloquent speech at that) if the sociability implicit within human nature is to be widely awakened and invigorated.[46] Enlightened eloquence "has borne so many outstanding cities, has made friends and allies of so many kingdoms, and has unified and bonded through love so many people."[47] For speech is the mechanism by which mute wisdom translates its insights into public proclamations and persuades men to follow their natural inclination by surrendering their private interests in favor of the common good. Should human beings be deprived of this faculty of discourse, even if they retained their rational abilities, they "would degenerate to the condition of brute animals, and cities would seem like corrals for livestock, rather than communities composed of human beings united by a common bond in order to live in society, serve one another and cooperate as friends."[48] John's vision of society is thus comparable to Cicero's in its quasi-contractual quality: human association is not simply a matter of several persons living in close geographic proximity; it is an agreement to share a common life in faith, morals, economic transactions, and all the other features which compose a community. Speech alone renders such an explicit agreement possible, and it must be an eloquent use of language indeed which can convince basically selfish men that by

[45] *Metalogicon*, 826c.
[46] *Ibid.*, 827a-b.
[47] *Ibid.*, 827b.
[48] *Ibid.*, 827c.

nature they prefer the common good to personal welfare. In this regard John's reliance on Cicero is most pronounced: the *Metalogicon* presumes that the bond of association among men, while natural, is simultaneously a product of their active cooperation. Properly speaking, therefore, civil institutions are not necessary because they are contingent upon the acknowledgment and approval of all persons subject to them.

By means of these Ciceronian arguments John believes that he has exposed the real significance of the Cornifician position. It is evident to him that Cornificius is an opponent of "all cities and political life,"[49] since the claim that men should not develop their capacities for reason and speech denies any opportunity for man to associate. While the price paid by man for original sin was high, it did not include the eradication of any communal proclivity in his nature. Indeed, for human beings to be rendered utterly incapable of association it would have been necessary to silence them and strip them of their reason, and this never occurred as a result of the Fall. The Cornifician error is to interpret the weakness of post-lapsarian human nature as a permanent condition and thus to deny the original formation of society. Yet John recognizes that conscious effort is required on the part of men if they are to join together in a communal life. Human nature is incapable of impelling them to congregate apart from diligent application of rational inquiry combined with eloquent persuasion. Without this activity on behalf of social unity, the sinful and egotistic side of man will prevail, and no common civil relations and institutions can emerge. Human association consequently seems to be conceived by John as a process of man refining and improving his own abilities in order to aid the cause of nature. The *Metalogicon*'s understanding of the genesis of society is profoundly indebted to Cicero's notion that nature's endowment is only a point of departure which men must develop and shape if they are truly to live in accordance with their own natural inclinations.

From such a renowned medieval devotee of Cicero as John of Salisbury we might reasonably expect a Ciceronian account of the origins of social organization, but hardly from authors whose intellectual loyalties lay elsewhere. In particular, given the presence after about 1250 of Aristotle's *Politics*, with its doctrine that man is a naturally associative and political creature, it might be supposed that the need for reference to Cicero would rapidly recede. Yet, as Brian Tierney has observed, "the combination of Aristotelian naturalism with Stoic conventionalism was common enough from 1300 onward."[50] What neither Tierney nor other scholars have really explained, however, was why some later medieval authors found it necessary to go beyond Aristotle and into the work of Cicero in order

---

[49] *Ibid.*, 827d.
[50] Tierney, *Religion, Law, and the Growth of Constitutional Thought*, 35.

to supplement their presentations of man's transformation into a civilized creature. The answer to this question, already suggested here, seems to be that Cicero assisted medieval Aristotelians in making a place for the Christian notion of human sinfulness while retaining the basic insight of the *Politics* that social and political relations are natural to man.

We may test this hypothesis in the first instance against John of Paris's tract *De potestate regia et papali* (1302-3). A pupil of St. Thomas Aquinas and a prominent exponent of medieval Aristotelianism, John succeeded his master in the Arts Faculty at the University of Paris, the undisputed center of Western Aristotelian studies.[51] Among historians of scholastic philosophy John is known for his treatises and *quaestiones* on matters of speculative inquiry,[52] as well as for his contributions to contemporary political debate.[53] Not surprisingly, then, like Aquinas and a host of other Parisian Aristotelians,[54] John defends the superiority of kingship over other forms of rule and he asserts that "man is by nature a political and civil animal. . . . Man only must necessarily live in a multitude and in such a multitude as is sufficient for all the necessities of life."[55] But immediately after espousing this orthodox Aristotelian doctrine, John raises an issue which was decidedly beyond the scope of Aristotle's concerns, namely, the relationship between the good of the individual and the welfare of the community. It is fair to say that for Aristotle the individual as individual could claim no special standing precisely on the grounds that nature fulfills itself only within the civic totality.[56]

The individual poses far greater difficulty for John of Paris. In spite of reference to the *Politics*, *De potestate* seems to regard man in traditional Christian terms as a self-seeking and egotistic being whose primary concern is personal welfare. John does not think that the individual's fixation upon his own private advantage can be eliminated even in a perfect and self-sufficient community. Indeed, it is as a bridle upon the self-interested aspect of human individuality—a factor which corresponds to the sinfulness of post-lapsarian men residing in the earthly city—that government is instituted. Since men as individuals cannot look after the common good, a guardian of the public utility must be appointed. John foresees

[51] On John's career and associations, see Marc F. Griesbach, "John of Paris as a Representative of Thomistic Political Philosophy," in C. J. O'Neill (ed.), *An Etienne Gilson Tribute* (Milwaukee, 1959), 33-35 and notes.

[52] Ambrose J. Heiman, "Two Questions Concerning the *Esse* of Creatures in the Doctrine of Jean Quidort," in *An Etienne Gilson Tribute*, 51 and passim.

[53] See Paul Saenger, "John of Paris, Principal Author of the *Quaestio de potestate papae (Rex pacificus)*," *Speculum*, 56 (1981), 41-55.

[54] See Thomas Renna, "Aristotle and the French Monarchy, 1260-1303," *Viator*, 9 (1978), 309-24.

[55] John of Paris, *De potestate regia et papali*, ed. F. Bleienstein (Stuttgart, 1969), 75-76.

[56] *Politics*, 1253a.

that "a society in which everyone seeks only his own advantage will disperse and disintegrate divisively unless it is ordered to the good of all by some one ruler who has charge of the common good."[57] As with so many French thinkers after him, John treats the king as the embodiment of a public welfare, performing from a lofty office the communal tasks which individuals are incapable of doing for themselves.[58] No invisible hand may be invoked to conjure the common good out of the many forms of egoistic behavior, nor will the introduction of royal rule alter the selfish impulses of individuals. While the common good enforced by the king is obviously superior to any private benefit, individuals cannot be expected to respect the public welfare of their own accord. Hence, the monarch, if he is to impose the common utility over the community, must be endowed with a coercive capacity.

In this regard John's position differs little from that of St. Augustine, who deemed coercion necessary in order for rulers to keep in check the volatile side of those who inhabit the *civitas terrena*. The argument of *De potestate* is rooted in the conviction that there exists an unbridgeable chasm between individual advantage and common welfare. "What is particular is not the same as what is common. For it differs as to what is particular whereas what is common joins together," John observes, "so it is necessary that there should be provision made for the promotion of the common good in addition to that moving each individual to seek his own good."[59] Men who are oriented towards their own advantage cannot at the same time rule themselves and others according to a principle of public benefit. For this reason it is necessary to distinguish sharply between that person whose duty it is to supervise the common utility and the great mass of individuals for whom self-interest constitutes the primary goal.

John's claims about the relationship between individual and community would consequently seem to be at odds with his earlier statement that humans are by nature social and political creatures. Is it possible to reconcile these two sides of his thought? In *De potestate* John seeks to resolve this dilemma in Ciceronian fashion by asserting that however much men are naturally suited by physical need, linguistic facility, and gregarious instinct for communal life, their actual assembly is not a foregone conclusion. Human beings require active prompting in order to be transformed according to the associative inclinations endemic to their nature. In the absence of such stimulation men will adopt a style of life appropriate to their sinful and depraved (hence, unnatural) status. John

---

[57] *De potestate*, 76.

[58] On the development of this theme in later French political thought see Nannerl O. Keohane, *Philosophy and the State in France* (Princeton, 1980), and Ellen M. Wood. "The State and Popular Sovereignty in French Political Thought: A Genealogy of Rousseau's 'General Will.'" *History of Political Thought*, 4 (1983), 281-315.

[59] *De potestate*, 76.

reports that "before the time of . . . the first persons to exercise rulership, men lived against nature without rule, not living as men but in the manner of beasts."[60] As evidence for this bit of anthropological speculation, John cites Cicero's *De inventione*, as well as Orosius and (somewhat less accurately) Aristotle.

John postulates that such primordial men "live a solitary life," saved only from assimilation to the lesser animals by the fact that they are able to employ reason instead of relying merely on "natural instinct."[61] This isolated situation is clearly regarded by John as typical of mankind after the Fall, when humans renounced the fraternity of paradise and turned to an existence for their own benefit alone. In such circumstances, John observes, it is not sufficient that the primitive asocial beings retained their inclination to congregate with their fellow creatures. For so bound were they to the promotion of their individual advantage that "these men could not by the use of the speech common to all men bring themselves to live the common life natural to them and to abandon a state more fitting for beasts than man."[62] Thus, in John's view, nature does not impart its own inherent principle of motion. There is no assurance that post-lapsarian men will always and necessarily assemble together just because it is a feature of their nature to do so. Rather, perhaps because human nature has been rendered defective by the Fall, men only enter into communities when "others, moved by the situation of these men in their error, and using their reason to better effect, tried to bring them by more persuasive arguments to an ordered life in common under one ruler, as Cicero says."[63] *De potestate*'s adaptation of Cicero is of considerable significance. It allows John to demonstrate that man, while weakened by sin and thus less benevolently disposed towards his fellow creatures, nevertheless retains the capacity to constrain voluntarily the unlimited pursuit of his individual aims through the authorization of a guardian of the common good. The activation of this capacity for acknowledging the need for rulership depends, however, upon the cogent presentation of the rationale for and benefits of allegiance to the principle of public utility and to its royal embodiment. In no way, then, may the institution of government be regarded as the imposition of coercion over an unwilling populace. The rule of kings is only legitimate (viz., in accordance with nature) when established by a consensual process in which men agree on the basis of rational persuasion to be governed within the confines of the precept of the common good. Individuals are not bound to submit to the public welfare represented by monarchy if they have not first assented to subject themselves to it.

[60] *Ibid.*, 77.
[61] *Ibid.*, 75.
[62] *Ibid.*, 77.
[63] *Ibid.*, 77-78.

John returns to Ciceronian themes later in *De potestate* in order to elaborate upon and apply them to his major arguments regarding the structure of church and secular government.[64] His fidelity to Cicero's view is particularly well reflected in the presentation of his famous distinction between *dominium* (lordship) and jurisdiction.[65] It is John's contention that the lordship which a private lay person enjoys over his goods is a purely individual concern: property "is acquired by individual people through their own skill, labor and diligence and individuals qua individuals have right, power and valid lordship over it."[66] Such *dominium* is both logically and historically prior to all modes of jurisdiction, that is, the determination of what is just and unjust with regard to the uses of private goods.[67] John stipulates that "goods are not mutually ordered or interconnected nor do they have any common head who might order or administer them, since each person arranges what is his according to his will."[68] By contrast jurisdiction arises in order to redress grievances and provide for common needs (such as territorial defense) which would otherwise be overlooked when each person pursues his private goals in isolation from other *domini*. The "ruler has been appointed by the people to take charge in such situations" as require a neutral arbitrator whose primary aim is to promote the good of the whole community.[69] Jurisdiction, in other words, derives *ex post facto* from the solitary circumstances of *dominium* and enforces a public welfare which is distinct from the amalgamation of individual utilities.

The Ciceronian argument which John had articulated in his explanation of the origins and nature of society forms the obvious background for the differentiation of *dominium* from jurisdiction. John indicates that lordship is pre-civil, originating in those particular interests which characterized man prior to the awakening of his social and political nature. For all the efforts of recent scholars to compare John's concept of lordship favorably with the Lockean theory of property,[70] one important difference stands out. *De potestate* never refers to the condition of man prior to government as "natural" or "according to natural instinct." On the

[64] For example, John maintains that men join together "from natural instinct which is from God that they may live civilly and in community. . . . One supreme monarchy on earth for everyone is commanded neither by natural inclination nor by divine law" (*ibid.*, 82).

[65] See Janet Coleman, "Medieval Discussions of Property: *Ratio* and *Dominium* According to John of Paris and Marsiglio of Padua," *History of Political Thought*, 4 (1983), 209-28.

[66] *De potestate*, 96.

[67] *Ibid.*, 98.

[68] *Ibid.*, 96-97.

[69] *Ibid.*, 97.

[70] Most recently by Janet Coleman, "*Dominium* in Thirteenth and Fourteenth Century Political Thought and its Seventeenth Century Heirs: John of Paris and Locke," *Political Studies*, 33 (1985), 73-100.

contrary it would appear that this primordial world of unbridled individual appropriation and consumption corresponds precisely to that state which John previously described as "against nature." What conforms with nature, rather, is a system in which individuals relinquish a large measure of their autonomy in order to live in a peaceable and law-abiding community under the direction and governance of a ruler assigned to protect the common good. But the same passage also stipulates that the actual formation of a monarchy or similar government cannot be left to blind natural instinct. As is clear from De potestate's emphasis upon the elective element of kingship,[71] legitimate rulership can only be established where it has been explicitly established by the conscious choice of the individuals who are to submit to it. The jurisdiction of the king is ultimately validated by the fact that it was originally imposed by individuals upon themselves for the benefit of all.

In sum, John's reliance upon Cicero's account of the origins of human association permits him to steer a via media—one of De potestate's favorite concepts[72]—between a polity founded completely on coercion and one whose unity depends upon untutored natural disposition. Entry into the community is for John an affirmation of the citizen's natural inclination to assemble. Yet at the same time, political society cannot offer any ultimate remedy for human sin and must therefore be vigilant lest man's iniquity incapacitate his sociability. What makes it possible to coerce the individual in the name of the common good within the context of a belief in the natural human propensity to associate is the fact that each member of the community has confirmed his nature by originally choosing to unite with his fellows.

Scholars have recognized John of Paris's reliance upon Cicero's social and political naturalism (even if they have not taken care to investigate its implications thoroughly),[73] but the same cannot be said for their treatment of Marsiglio of Padua. Indeed, although references to Cicero pervade Marsiglio's major treatise, the Defensor pacis,[74] completed in 1324, modern readers are in no way encouraged to see any important Ciceronian influence in its doctrine of the genesis of society. For example, Jeanine Quillet's survey of Marsiglio's political thought makes only a single passing reference to Cicero.[75] More overtly, Alan Gewirth remarks

[71] In one passage John explicitly states "ad bene vivendum in communi rectores eligant" (De potestate, 82), while elsewhere he claims that "est a Deo et a populo regem eligente" (ibid., 113; cf. 158, 173).

[72] Ibid., 69, 72.

[73] See Ewart Lewis, Medieval Political Ideas (2 vols.; London, 1954), I, 158; and Tierney, Religion, Law, and the Growth of Constitutional Thought, 35.

[74] See Defensor pacis, ed. C. W. Previté-Orton (Cambridge, 1928): I.1.4, I.4.2, I.16.7, I.16.21, I.19.13, II.12.7, II.15.7, II.26.13.

[75] Jeanine Quillet, La Philosophie politique de Marsile de Padoue (Paris, 1970), 134.

that "it is significant that while Marsiglio quotes from Cicero (*De officiis* I.viii.22) the Stoic dictum 'homines hominum causa generatos esse' . . ., he applies it only to his own practical enterprise and not to his doctrine of man and the State as such."[76] Instead, Marsiglio is depicted as a sort of biological Aristotelian, or as a naturalistic Augustinian, or as a combination of the two.[77] If only because the *Defensor*'s version of man's transformation into a communal creature resists most of the standard categories attributed to medieval thought, however, we would be well advised to reconsider its connection to the Ciceronian tradition.

Once we turn to the text of the *Defensor*, we can readily appreciate the confusion which Marsiglio's conception of the development of human communities has engendered. On the one hand he presents a carefully elaborated but faithful recapitulation of the Aristotelian evolution of the political body out of the household and village.[78] The complete and self-sufficient life of human beings "necessitates all the things which exist in the city and are done by the association of men in it."[79] Citing the teaching of Aristotle's *Politics* that men are impelled by nature to associate, Marsiglio declares that man's earthly good and happiness entails "the necessity of the civil community, without which this sufficient life cannot be obtained."[80] But Marsiglio halts short of proclaiming the Aristotelian precept that man is by nature social or political.[81] He instead casts his naturalism in a purely physiological mold. Thus, the process of social and political progress is interpreted as the increasing differentiation and perfection of the arts and skills necessary for the organic subsistence and comfort of human beings.[82] It is because men are physically weak, born unsheltered against the elements, and hence always susceptible to extinction, that they band together into groups and share the fruits of their individual talents. Humans hope that in society their own harm might be avoided and that they may share in the enjoyment of the various arts.[83] Marsiglio's naturalism consequently appears to amount to little more than the view that man's biological infirmities drive him into the arms of his fellows for the sake of survival.

[76] Alan Gewirth, *Marsilius of Padua and Medieval Political Philosophy* (New York, 1951), 91, n. 31.

[77] See *ibid.*, 88-91; Tilman Struve, *Die Entwicklung der Organologische Staatsauffassung im Mittelalter* (Stuttgart, 1978), 257-88; and Georges de Lagarde, "Une Adaptation de la Politique d'Aristote au XIVe siècle," *Revue historique de droit français et étranger*, 2 (1932), 233-38.

[78] *Defensor pacis*, I.3.3-5.

[79] *Ibid.*, I.4.2.

[80] *Ibid.*, I.4.3.

[81] The closest he comes, in *ibid.*, I.2.3, is to say that "civitatem esse velut animatum seu animalem naturam," which provides the basis for his version of the organic metaphor of the political body; see I.15.5-6, I.17.8.

[82] *Ibid.*, I.3.5.

[83] *Ibid.*, I.4.3.; cf. I.5.5-9.

Beneath the surface of Marsiglio's physiological understanding of human nature would seem to rest a commitment to an Augustinian theology. Marsiglio attributes the defects of man's biology to the "transgression of the first parents," as a result of which "the whole posterity of mankind was weakened in soul and was born weak, whereas previously it had been created in a state of perfect healthy, innocence and grace."[84] The dissipation of human nature involves ominous consequences for the relationship between man and his fellows. Had Adam not sinned, "the establishment or differentiation of civil offices would not have been necessary for him or his posterity, because nature would have produced for him the advantages and pleasures of the sufficiency of this life in the earthly or pleasurable paradise, without any punishment or suffering on his part."[85] The "punishment or suffering" in question was God's withdrawal of eternal happiness from mankind, symbolized by human mortality and vulnerability. When men are viewed in this fashion as above all children of the Fall and therefore basically sinful and self-aggrandizing creatures, it is little wonder that Marsiglio expects them to engage in "disputes and quarrels which, if not regulated by a norm of justice, would cause men to fight and separate and thus would bring about the destruction of the city."[86] Marsiglio shows all the signs of dedicated adherence to Augustinian political theory, firm as he is in his conviction that the prime social good is peace and tranquility, yet fearful that without the exercise of coercive authority the harmony of the community could never be achieved.[87] Such a polity can be considered "natural" only in the superficial sense that it enforces a level of concord adequate to the fulfillment of man's physical needs.

If Marsiglio were no more than a thoroughgoing Augustinian, however, he would be relatively unconcerned about the institutional apparatus employed to impose the public peace. But the *Defensor* is widely acclaimed for its emphatic insistence that only those rulers who govern strictly in accordance with the consent of their citizen-subjects are legitimate and deserving of obedience. How does Marsiglio reconcile this doctrine of consent with an Augustinian interpretation of society's foundations? It is precisely in order to deal with this problem that the *Defensor* invokes the Ciceronian version of the generation of the human community. According to Marsiglio, "when men at first convened in order to ordain the civil community and law," their unity was premised upon an agreement about those matters necessary for the "sufficiency of life." This seems to be what Marsiglio meant by his earlier emphasis upon the biological bases of ʰuman association. But it is not strictly biological

[84] *Ibid.*, I.6.2.
[85] *Ibid.*, I.6.1.
[86] *Ibid.*, I.4.4.
[87] *Ibid.*, I.1.1.

need which is the efficient cause of assembly. The original men "were summoned not by the coercive authority of one or many persons, but rather by the persuasion or exhortation of prudent and able men. The latter, exceptionally endowed by nature with an inclination for this task, later through their own efforts made progress in their various pursuits and guided others either successively or simultaneously to the formation of a perfected community, to which men are naturally inclined so that they readily complied with this persuasion."[88] Although Marsiglio cites Aristotle's *Politics* as his source for this doctrine, its provenance is obviously Ciceronian, a fact which the *Defensor*'s editors and commentators have consistently missed.[89]

Nor is it often recognized that this passage solves much of the confusion surrounding Marsiglio's conception of society's origins. In the first place it is clear that man does indeed possess a natural inclination to join together that transcends the merely physiological explanation ordinarily attributed to the *Defensor*. But Marsiglio well realizes that this inclination differs from the Aristotelian notion of internally regulated motion towards an end, from which arises his refusal to state in the *Defensor* that man is a political animal. The natural inclination to associate is instead constituted as an implicit feature of human nature, requiring reasoned persuasion in order to stimulate and direct it towards realization. Like John of Paris, Marsiglio believes that the success or failure of this process of socialization is largely dependent upon the presence of one or a few men who are particularly well endowed with the rational and rhetorical faculties necessary to convince the mass of men to assemble as a community. It ought to be noted in this regard that nature is not co-extensive with necessity; while men can only enjoy a full and happy temporal life when they are within a communal context, their fallen and sinful condition makes this unification continually problematic. Men may be persuaded to assemble in a civil life—they are after all naturally inclined to do so—but it is by no means assured that they will in fact assent or that they will persist in upholding their agreement.

It should consequently be evident that despite his predilection for Augustinian theology, Marsiglio cannot accept the related view that any

---

[88] *Ibid.*, II.22.15.

[89] So, for instance, Quillet, *La Philosophie politique de Marsile de Padoue*, 80, quotes this passage in its entirety and discusses its significance without once observing that it does not correspond at all to Aristotle's own views. Mario Grignaschi, "Le Rôle de l'Aristotélisme dans le *Defensor Pacis* de Marsile de Padoue," *Revue d'histoire et de philosophie religieuses*, 35 (1955), 307, (referring to II.22.15), argues that Marsiglio constructs out of Aristotle a highly original "synthesis" of naturalism and social contract theory—indeed, that this constitutes the major achievement of Dictio I—while apparently oblivious to the Ciceronian origins of the passage and indeed the doctrine he attributes to the *Defensor pacis*. Grignaschi (339-40) believes his interpretation to be vindicated, at least in part, by analogous remarks by Gewirth, *Marsilius of Padua*, 89.

government which maintains public peace is *eo ipso* legitimate. The Ciceronian aspect of his argument precludes submission to any application of power which has not acquired the prior approval of the citizen body over which it is wielded. It is in these terms that we may best understand the *Defensor*'s unwavering commitment to the consent of the populace as the prerequisite for duly constituted rulers, laws, and all other manner of government activity.[90] Indeed, Marsiglio is so insistent upon the necessity of consent that in one passage he even argues that social utility must be subordinated to the agreement of each and every individual in the authorization of law.[91]

The political and ideological significance of Marsiglio's consent theory is complex, but its philosophical substance is rooted firmly in Cicero's idea of man's transformation into a civilized creature.[92] Unlike Aristotle, for whom the origins of society are essentially beyond human volition or control, Marsiglio maintains that from the start the community and its government must be guided by the whole citizen body. The individual thereby possesses and retains a discretionary autonomy which acts as a check upon the use of political power in an arbitrary manner, that is, in a way inconsistent with consent. Yet unlike St. Augustine, the *Defensor* holds that man's fall from grace does not erase completely that element of his nature that leads him to seek the company of his fellows. Marsiglio's conception is rather more dualistic: the sinful aspect of man renders it difficult for him to live peacefully with other human beings, yet his earthly happiness and comfort make it imperative that he enter into a civil community. Therefore, political authority needs to be adequate to coerce those citizens who are incapable of controlling their temptation to behave iniquitously; yet the ruling part must still not interfere with the free choice to associate (in accordance with natural inclination), which forms the basis of all communal institutions, by enforcing obedience unilaterally. What renders this position consistent and coherent is Marsiglio's presumption, along Ciceronian lines, that the inclinations which nature imparts to man are only the beginning of social and political development. Nature's gift must thereafter be discovered and put to use by each individual through the application of reason and the dissemination of its determinations by means of language. Neither can such natural associative tendencies be forced, nor will they manifest themselves without active human cooperation. For Marsiglio, as for Cicero, the only valid path to a properly fashioned community is man's collaboration with nature in the fulfillment of those gregarious propensities inherent within him.

[90] *Defensor pacis*, I.9.5-6, I.12.5-9, and I.16.11-20; similar considerations undergird the ecclesiology he propounds in Dictio II.

[91] *Ibid.*, I.12.6.

[92] I pursue this in a recently completed monograph entitled *Marsiglio of Padua and the Feudal Polity*.

24

Scholars have largely withdrawn from the traditional claim that Aristotle was solely responsible for introducing a naturalistic component into the political thought of the Middle Ages. Yet there remains a pronounced tendency to treat the mid-thirteenth century as a significant dividing point in the development of social philosophy, an intellectual watershed generated by the transmission of the *Ethics* and *Politics*.[93] The presence and persistence of the Ciceronian account of the natural origins of society during the Middle Ages suggests, however, a fundamental flaw in this perspective. In part this flaw is the function of the erroneous assumption that medieval authors prior to about 1200 knew nothing of Aristotle's social doctrines.[94] More significantly, the literature has uncritically presumed that slavish devotion to Aristotle's moral and political philosophy characterized the attitude of Western authors in the period after 1250. The existence of Cicero's thought as a viable theoretical alternative to Aristotle is but one counterexample to the alleged intellectual uniformity of political theory in the late Middle Ages.[95] What the evidence suggests, then, is that we must sustain George Sabine's fifty-year-old judgment that "the recovery of Aristotle did not at once change the main lines of political philosophy."[96] The failure of Cicero's influence to wane following the return of the Philosopher's texts to circulation is indicative of the need to lay permanently to rest the thesis of an "Aristotelian revolution" in the language and concepts of political philosophy dating to the mid-thirteenth century. Accuracy demands a more evolutionary approach to the reception and integration of Aristotelian thought over the whole course of the Latin Middle Ages.

Similarly, we must reconsider the claim, so evident in the work of some recent historians of political thought, that medieval interest in the origins of society presaged early modern theories of the social contract.[97]

---

[93] Skinner, *The Foundations of Modern Political Thought*, I, 48-53; Tierney, *Religion, Law and the Growth of Constitutional Thought*, 29-30 and 39; and Henry A. Myers, *Medieval Kingship* (Chicago, 1982), 269.

[94] In several recent papers, I have argued for the existence of an "underground tradition" of Aristotelian learning about social matters filtered through a variety of direct and indirect sources and applied to a wide range of medieval concerns. See Cary J. Nederman and J. Brückmann, "Aristotelianism in John of Salisbury's *Policraticus*," *Journal of the History of Philosophy*, 21 (1983), 203-29; Cary J. Nederman, "Bracton on Kingship Revisited," *History of Political Thought*, 5 (Spring 1984), 61-77; Cary J. Nederman, "The Aristotelian Doctrine of the Mean and John of Salisbury's Concept of Liberty," *Vivarium*, 24 (1986), 128-42.

[95] For other examples of significant divergences from strict fidelity to Aristotle's social and political philosophy, see Antony Black, *Guilds and Civil Society in European Political Thought from the Twelfth Century to the Present* (Ithaca, 1984), 91-92 and Cary J. Nederman, "Aristotle as Authority: Alternative Aristotelian Sources of Late Medieval Political Theory," *History of European Ideas*, 8 (1977), 31-44.

[96] George H. Sabine, *A History of Political Theory*, first ed. (London, 1937), 246.

[97] See Tierney, *Religion, Law, and the Growth of Constitutional Thought*, 33-34, 36, and passim; and for a summary of earlier literature which embraced this theme, Francis

Such an observation has limited validity for understanding the historical significance of those authors—like John of Salisbury, John of Paris, and Marsiglio of Padua—who subscribed to an essentially Ciceronian conception of the development of human association. Unlike their modern counterparts, medieval theorists of a Ciceronian bent saw the problem of social genesis as a direct consequence of broader theological concerns. To the Middle Ages the central question was: in man's post-lapsarian state of sinfulness, how is it possible for him to assemble with his fellows and to maintain this association more or less permanently? To respond to such a query, medieval followers of Cicero maintained that it was manifestly unnatural for men, even in their fallen condition, to live isolated and solitary lives. In contrast to later social contractarians, man's presocial and prepolitical existence was not a "state of nature" but the very antithesis of what nature directed. Men did not, therefore, have to create a wholly artificial contract in order to enter into a durable community with other human beings. They merely followed their inherent inclination to be sociable, even though it required the prompting of eloquent men in order to convince them to act upon their natural impulse and thereby to renounce (however temporarily) the anti-social practice of iniquity. By entering into a communal arrangement, man recaptures a small measure of the temporal happiness which his forebears had known in pre-lapsarian times; but at the same time, because sin continues to plague human society, coercion must also be introduced by means of the full range of political institutions, including law and government. These manifestations of authority exist in order to make men conform to their natural inclinations by suppressing and punishing the varieties of sin which threaten to separate them from their fellows and to demolish social bonds. Conventional, coercive politics simply reinforces man's associative propensities instead of enforcing an alien social system in the absence of or in opposition to nature.

The evidence contained within the present study also suggests the need to examine afresh the importance of Cicero's influence among political authors throughout the Middle Ages. The subsistence of the Ciceronian tradition we have identified was neither an aberration nor a departure from the mainstream of medieval political thought. On the contrary the figures who have been selected to represent the Ciceronian tradition were themselves major contributors to the theoretical framework that arose out of the Latin Middle Ages. And although Augustinian and Aristotelian approaches to the genesis of society certainly enjoyed their special advocates, one wonders whether it might not be possible to regard the middle route charted by Cicero as the predominant medieval model

---

Oakley, "Legitimation by Consent: The Question of Medieval Roots," *Viator*, 14 (1983), 303-5.

of the origins of human association.[98] This hypothesis would merely reaffirm another judgment that was taken as received wisdom earlier in the present century: that "there was substantially no difference of opinion about [Cicero's general principles of government] on the part of anyone in the whole course of the Middle Ages; they became a part of the common heritage of political ideas."[99] As the reputation of Cicero in general has eroded, so has cognizance of his significance for the understanding of medieval political philosophy. Perhaps the time has arrived for a reversal in current scholarly attitudes about Cicero's contributions to the political ideas of the Middle Ages.[100]

[98] Besides the texts and authors mentioned in note 31 above, it may be possible to detect Ciceronian echoes in numerous other medieval accounts of social and political genesis, including William of Ockham, *Breviloquium de Potestate Papae*, ed. L. Baudry (Paris, 1937), 85-87; Jean Gerson, *De Potestate Ecclesiastica* in P. Glorieux, ed., *Oeuvres Complètes*, VI (Paris, 1965), 246-47; and John Major, *In Quartum Sententiarum Quaestiones Utilissimae* cited in Skinner, *The Foundations of Modern Political Thought*, II, 118.

[99] Sabine, *A History of Political Theory*, 167. It is also no coincidence that the Carlyles began their monumental history of medieval political thought with a chapter on the political theory of Cicero; see *A History of Mediaeval Political Theory in the West*, I (London, 1962), 1-18.

[100] Previous versions of this essay were presented at the University of Alberta and to the 1985 Northeastern Political Science Association conference in Philadelphia. The author wishes especially to credit the criticism and suggestions for improvement offered by Marcia Colish, Francis Oakley, Brian Tierney, and Jeremy Paltiel.

XII

The union of wisdom and eloquence before the Renaissance: The Ciceronian orator in medieval thought*

It is widely supposed among students of Renaissance humanism that one of the unique contributions of the humanists was their 'rediscovery' of the classical, essentially·Ciceronian, ideal of the orator as the man who employs both reason and eloquence in order to serve the common good. In turn, this conception of oratory in Cicero's thought is closely aligned with his teaching that human association arises from the awakening of an implicit human gregariousness by means of the eloquence and wisdom of a primitive orator. This paper demonstrates that the Ciceronian idea of oration was a recurrent feature of scholastic thought from the twelfth to the early fourteenth century rather than an innovation of the Renaissance. In support of this claim, a wide range of writings, including the work of Thierry of Chartres, Brunetto Latini, John of Paris and Marsiglio of Padua, is considered. It is shown how these authors all derive from Cicero the lesson that the foundation and maintenance of communal bonds requires the presence of a wise and eloquent orator who will place the public interest above his own ends. In the Ciceronian ideal of oration, such medieval authors found a model for their conception of community and a framework for the determination of the responsibilities of rulers and citizens.

*   An earlier version of this essay was presented at the 1991 meeting of the American Political Science Association in Washington, DC. The author wishes to acknowledge the aid of Professor Walter Nicgorski in sharpening the arguments of the paper in its published form.

It would be difficult to overestimate the influence exercised by the writings of the Roman statesman and philosopher Marcus Tullius Cicero upon Western thought during the fifteen centuries following his death.[1] During late antiquity, he found an audience among pagans and Christians alike for his rhetorical teachings as well as for his summation of the teachings of the main schools of classical philosophy.[2] Cicero's work on rhetoric attained textbook status during the Latin Middle Ages and was the object of numerous commentaries, while his social and moral thought shaped the principles and also practical conduct of medieval churchmen.[3] And, of course, Renaissance humanists revered Cicero for his erudition no less than for his exemplary public career.[4] Few educated individuals in the West between the end of the Roman Republic and the beginning of the *cinquecento*, regardless of intellectual orientation or spiritual commitment, escaped the impact of the Ciceronian tradition.

Yet there has been much dispute about the way in which the reception of Cicero's texts changed and evolved during the course of these fifteen hundred years. For example, one commonly encounters some version of the claim that, until the dawn of the Renaissance, the full significance of Cicero's work was not, and perhaps could not be, adequately appreciated. A central achievement of the Renaissance, by contrast, is said to be the 'recovery' of an 'authentic' or 'genuine' comprehension of Cicero, which amounted to a complete reorientation away from medieval intellectual patterns. Virtually every important recent student of Renaissance thought adheres to the position that humanism viewed Cicero from a new, and more historically accurate or 'truly classical', perspective. For example, Hans Baron documents "how the aspect of Cicero the Roman citizen and thinker was . . . seized upon in the Quattrocento by humanists as an essential aid in their efforts to break away from many of the assumptions held during the Middle Ages".[5] Paul Kristeller notes that

[1] P. MacKendrick, *The philosophical books of Cicero*. (London, 1989), 258–60.
[2] M.L. Colish, *The Stoic tradition from antiquity to the early Middle Ages*, 2 vols (London, 1985).
[3] Among the more recent studies of Cicero's impact upon medieval thought are M. Dickey, 'Some commentaries on the *De inventione* and *Ad Herennium* of the eleventh and early twelfth centuries,' *Medieval and Renaissance Studies*, 6 (1968) 1–41. J.O. Ward, 'From antiquity to the Renaissance: glosses and commentaries on Cicero's rhetorica,' in: *Medieval eloquence*, ed. J.J. Murphy (Berkeley, 1978). J.O. Ward, *Artificiosa eloquentia in the Middle Ages*. Unpublished thesis (Toronto, 1972). N.E. Nelson, 'Cicero's *De officiis* in Christian thought: 300–1300,' *University of Michigan publications: language and literature*, 10 (1933) 59–160. R.H. Rouse and M. Rouse, 'The medieval circulation of Cicero's "Posterior analytics" and the *De finibus bonorum et malorum*', in: *Medieval scribes, manuscripts and libraries: essays presented to N.R. Ker*, ed. M.B. Parker and A.G. Watson (London, 1978). C.J. Nederman, 'Nature, sin and the origins of society: the Ciceronian tradition in medieval political thought', *Journal of the History of Ideas*, 49 (1988) 3–26.
[4] H. Baron, *The crisis of the early Italian Renaissance*. Second edition (Princeton, 1966).
[5] H. Baron, *In search of Florentine civic humanism. Essays on the transition from medieval to modern thought* (Princeton, 1988), vol. 1, 197.

the humanists were keenly aware of the great difference that separated medieval and especially scholastic Latin from that of the ancient Roman writers, above all Cicero.... They attempted with some success to imitate and restore classical Latin as a living language and to bring about a kind of linguistic and literary revolution that discredited and gradually abolished many, if not all, features of medieval Latin.[6]

And Jerrold Seigel proclaims, "To the humanists of the fourteenth and early fifteenth centuries, Cicero was the central figure of classical culture, the inspiration and guide for those who sought to return to the classical world".[7] These scholars, who otherwise arrive at quite disparate conclusions about the nature of Renaissance humanism, are united in their vision of a 'revival' of the 'real' Cicero as an animating principle of the humanist project (a view echoed by Skinner,[8] Rubinstein[9] and Tuck[10]).

An obvious question about the alleged Renaissance recovery of an authentic Ciceronianism is: what element(s) of Ciceronian thought unavailable to the Middle Ages had been recaptured by humanism? What makes the humanist reading of Cicero more valid than its predecessors? Although this problem has stimulated a wide variety of responses, ranging from Baron's so-called 'civic humanist' thesis to Seigel's argument about the 'relation between philosophy and rhetoric',[11] at least one area of broad agreement may be identified within the scholarship. For it is widely asserted that Cicero's ideal of the orator as the man who employs reasoned eloquence in order to speak publicly about matters touching upon the common good was unappreciated during the Middle Ages but formed a central tenet of the Renaissance humanist outlook.

Seigel perhaps presses this case most forcefully.[12] While not denying the importance of rhetorical training to medieval authors, he identifies "the disappearance of the classical orator" as a defining intellectual mark of the Latin Middle Ages.[13] Seigel claims that in Cicero's writings, and again during the Renaissance, oratory was recognized as a distinct discipline,[14] and indeed as "the doorway to general education and political life.... Cicero's orator had derived his identity from

---

[6]   P.O. Kristeller, 'Humanism,' in: *The Cambridge history of Renaissance philosophy*, ed. C.B. Schmitt and Q. Skinner (Cambridge, 1988), 122–3.
[7]   J. Seigel, *Rhetoric and philosophy in Renaissance humanism. The union of wisdom and eloquence, Petrarch to Valla* (Princeton, 1968), 3.
[8]   Q. Skinner, *The foundations of modern political thought* (Cambridge, 1978), vol. 1, 87–8.
[9]   N. Rubinstein, 'Political theories in the Renaissance,' in: *The Renaissance. Essays in interpretation* (London, 1982), 154.
[10]   R. Tuck, 'Humanism and political thought,' in: *The impact of humanism on Western Europe*, ed. A. Goodman and A. Mackay (London, 1990), 50–1.
[11]   A. Rabil, Jr., 'The significance of "civic humanism" in the interpretation of the Italian Renaissance,' in: *Renaissance humanism: foundations, forms and legacy* (Philadelphia, 1988), vol. 1, 141–171.
[12]   It is interesting that Seigel does not seem to have drawn such a strict distinction between medieval and Renaissance intellectual patterns in his earlier work. See J. Seigel, '"Civic humanism" or Ciceronian rhetoric? the culture of Petrarch and Bruni,' *Past and Present*, 34 (1966), 3–48.
[13]   Seigel, *Rhetoric and philosophy*, 178.
[14]   Seigel, *Rhetoric and philosophy*, 259–60.

his practice of rhetoric and thus had tended to regard many other aspects of life and thought from the viewpoint of oratory".[15] By contrast, for medieval thinkers, rhetorical teaching was 'mere ornament', a practical technique useful for the composition of letters (*ars dictaminis*) and the preaching of sermons (*ars praedicandi*) but having no purpose or identity in its own right.[16] Thus, the medieval rhetorician "was not an orator in the classical sense: he could not claim to fill the many-sided role of the classical orator . . . . Medieval practitioners of rhetoric had some other primary identity and hence regarded rhetoric as an adjunct to some other task".[17] With the dawn of the Renaissance, the Ciceronian conception of oratory emerged as a unique, and to some extent superior, field of study.

Seigel's basic approach accords with positions adopted by other scholars with whom he shares little else in common. His arch-opponent Baron declares that Cicero "was a leader in efforts to transform rhetorical training into a general program of studies stressing the indivisibility of thought and expression in all intellectual pursuits... [rather than] technical training for orators or for those practising the art of writing".[18] At the center of this program, according to Baron, was the congruence of a primary duty to engage in political activity with a dedication to the pursuit of wisdom and philosophical learning.[19] In a similar vein, Quentin Skinner posits a "revolution engineered by the humanists in the study of ancient rhetoric and philosophy" which rejects "all attempts to fit Cicero's writings into the pre-established [medieval] tradition of rhetorical instruction" and which instead subscribes to Cicero's own idea "that, by uniting wisdom with eloquence, [the art of oratory] enables a knowledge of the truth to be effectively communicated, and so allows the most salutary doctrines of the philosophers to exercise their proper influence on the conduct of public affairs".[20] Likewise, Benjamin Kohl and Ronald Witt have claimed that "humanism in the fourteenth century revived the traditional view of the rhetorician as a moral philosopher, teacher, and champion of virtue", supplanting formalized medieval rhetoric with a Ciceronian belief that "through his words [the orator] was responsible for moving the hearts and wills of his listeners toward good".[21] The scholarly literature, then, lends considerable weight to Seigel's assertion that a central feature of Renaissance humanism was its recognition of the special qualities and role of the Ciceronian orator.

The aim of the present paper, however, is to dispute the contention that the

---

[15]   Seigel, *Rhetoric and philosophy*, 178.
[16]   Seigel, *Rhetoric and philosophy*, 179, 176.
[17]   Seigel, *Rhetoric and philosophy*, 178.
[18]   Baron, *Florentine civic humanism*, 95.
[19]   Baron, *Florentine civic humanism*, 122–3.
[20]   Skinner, *Foundations*, 86–7.
[21]   *The earthly republic. Italian humanists on society and government*, ed. B. Kohl and R. Witt (Manchester, 1978), 7, 3.

classical, essentially Ciceronian, image of the orator only re-entered the European cultural milieu with the rise of humanist learning after the middle of the fourteenth century. Rather, in line with a recent trend in scholarship towards emphasizing the continuity of medieval and Renaissance understandings of Cicero[22], I shall argue that the Ciceronian conceptions of oratory and the orator were a commonplace of scholastic thought between the twelfth and the early fourteenth centuries. This claim will be defended in two ways. First, I shall consider a range of scholastic authors for whom the figure of the orator, conceived as the especially wise and eloquent man, constituted a necessary ingredient in the foundation and perpetuation of human social relations. Thus, the function of the orator was explicitly connected throughout the history of medieval philosophy with public activity on behalf of the common good. Second, I shall consider in greater detail an especially illustrative case of the role of oratory in scholastic political theory, afforded by the writings of Marsiglio of Padua. While he is commonly viewed as a paragon of late medieval scholasticism, Marsiglio not only considers the orator to be the founder of human association but proposes a conception of community rooted in the principles of oratory as eloquent speech in which truth is communicated for the good of all. In sum, there is compelling evidence to suggest that scholastic political thought had already embraced the ideal of oratory advanced by Cicero well before the advent of humanism with Petrarch in the mid-fourteenth century.

The Ciceronian order

The attempt to document the diffusion of the Ciceronian image of the orator in scholastic writings, however, must be preceded by an outline of some of the key elements of Cicero's own teachings, at least insofar as they were available to the Latin Middle Ages.[23] The characterization of oratory in his writings depends upon his conception of human nature. For Cicero, human beings are both rational and linguistic creatures, simultaneously capable of reasoning and speaking. Neither faculty is sufficient or primary; the full realization of one's human nature requires both the inquiry into truth and the eloquent statement of one's knowledge. When cultivated in isolation, each is barren. As Cicero says in a famous passage from the opening paragraph of his youthful *De inventione*, "Wisdom without eloquence leads to very little of value for civic bodies (*civitatibus*), while eloquence

---

[22]   For instance, Q. Skinner, 'Ambrogio Lorenzetti: the artist as political philosopher, *Proceedings of the British Academy*, 72 (1986), 1–56; and Q. Skinner, 'Machiavelli's *Discorsi* and the pre-humanist origins of republican ideas,' in: *Machiavelli and republicanism*, ed. G. Bok, Q. Skinner and M. Viroli (Cambridge, 1990).

[23]   For what follows, I am indebted to the account of N. Wood, *Cicero's social and political thought. An introduction* (Berkeley, 1988), 70–104 and to an unpublished essay by Walter Nicgorski, 'Nationalism and transnationalism in Cicero,' which was presented to the Second Conference of the International Society for the Study of European Ideas, Leuven, Belgium, September 1990.

without wisdom for the most part performs in an excessive fashion and leads to nothing".[24] This theme is still prevalent in his thought roughly three decades later. His mature treatise on rhetoric, *De oratore*,[25] repeatedly insists upon the union of wisdom and eloquence: "eloquence... could never have been attained except by a knowledge of all matters";[26] "excellent speaking cannot exist unless those matters which are spoken about are understood by those who speak of them";[27] "no one could flourish or be at all prominent in eloquence not only without learning in speech but also without wisdom in all matters".[28] Even in works where Cicero devotes greater attention to the rational aspects of human nature, such as *De officiis*, he accords to speech a primary role. It is not reason alone, but rather "the bonds of reason and speech", which together form the essential quality of human nature: "In no other way are we farther removed from the nature of beasts, about which we perhaps say that they have courage (as in the case of horses or lions) but about which we do not say that they have justice, equity or goodness; for they are devoid of reason and speech".[29] Regardless of where we look in the Ciceronian corpus, we encounter basically the same claim about human nature: the linguistic and rational capacities unique to mankind are inextricably interlinked and mutually reinforcing.

Cicero's unification of speech and reason, of eloquence and wisdom, leads him to posit a close relation between the two fields of study through which those subjects are taught: rhetoric and philosophy. In contrast with the preceding Greek tradition upon which he drew, Cicero refused to favour either discipline to the exclusion of the other. He saw little to be gained by promoting or joining in the so-called 'quarrel of philosophy and rhetoric'.[30] On the contrary, it was the establishment of an indissoluble bond between philosophical and rhetorical modes of learning that motivated Cicero, a tie that realized as fully as possible the potentialities implicit within the rational and linguistic aspects of human nature. The individual who most completely embodied the unity of philosophy and rhetoric, of wise reason and eloquent speech, was the orator.

Cicero recognized, of course, that this characterization of the orator and his art was open to challenge on grounds of the conceptual incongruity of philosophy

---

[24] M.T. Cicero, *De inventione* (Cambridge, MA, 1949) I.1.1.

[25] It should be noted that *De oratore* was intended by Cicero to replace *De inventione*, which he regarded as an *inchoata ac rudia* product of his adolescence: Cicero, *De oratore* (Cambridge, MA, 1942) I.2.5.

[26] Cicero, *De oratore*, II.2.6.

[27] Cicero, *De oratore*, II.11.48.

[28] Cicero, *De oratore*, II.1.5.

[29] M.T. Cicero, *De officiis* (Cambridge, MA, 1913) I.16.50.

[30] On this theme in Cicero's work, and its place in the history of ancient thought generally, see A. Michel, *Rhétorique et philosophie chez Cicéron* (Paris, 1960); Seigel, *Rhetoric and philosophy*, 3–30; N. Struever, *The language of humanism in the Renaissance. Rhetorical and historical consciousness in Florentine humanism* (Princeton, 1970), 5–39; MacKendrick, *Cicero*, 13–16, 31–5.

and rhetoric. The philosopher seeks to discover truths which were necessarily esoteric or inaccessible to the untutored masses; philosophy requires strict adherence to the principles of logic and rational argumentation. By contrast, because rhetoric teaches effectiveness in appealing to public opinion and commonly held belief, it might seem to be regulated by standards other than those of pure truth-seeking. As Seigel has documented,[31] precisely this tension accounts for much of Cicero's ambivalence regarding the philosophy of the Stoics. Yet Cicero regards the alleged dichotomy between philosophy and rhetoric to be largely a falsification, the result of an historical process in which both rhetoricians and philosophers acquired too great a measure of disciplinary autonomy. In *De inventione*, Cicero narrates the story of how in early times, a distinction existed between those who, possessing wisdom and eloquence, occupied themselves with public affairs and those who, in the absence of philosophical and rhetorical instruction, acquired the external trappings of eloquence by honing the skills of advocacy in the sphere of private litigation. But this differentiation became increasingly blurred once wise and eloquent men were compelled to enter the arena of law suits in order to protect their intimates: for since, in the prosecution of such private cases, "one who had obtained eloquence alone while disregarding the study of wisdom was often viewed as equal, indeed even superior, in speaking, it happened that it seemed both to his own judgement and to that of the multitude that he might deservedly rule the republic".[32] Cicero describes two consequences of this development. First, eloquence in the public realm was left in the hands of *stultorum et improborum* who shunned virtue because their skills of persuasion were without foundation in philosophy. Second, wise men in the future disdained to involve themselves in political affairs, abandoning the study of eloquence altogether; in the end, philosophy was pursued in seclusion and without reference to its public expression and application.[33] It is clear, both in *De inventione* and elsewhere, that the abdication of eloquence by men of wisdom is as deserving of reproval and derision as the usurpation of rhetoric by persons untutored in philosophy. In *De oratore*, for instance, Cicero decries how "persons too generously supplied with leisure" have invaded the study of wisdom and "ridicule the orator like Socrates in Plato's *Gorgias*".[34] In Cicero's mind, the division between philosophical inquiry and rhetorical practice was primarily the product of a dereliction of duty on the part of certain wise men.

Cicero's evidence for the illusory character of the breach between rhetoric and philosophy, and hence his defense of oratory as a practical goal as well as an ideal, relies heavily upon his account of the origins of human association. In both

---

[31] Seigel, *Rhetoric and philosophy*, 22–5.
[32] Cicero, *De inventione*, I.3.4.
[33] Cicero, *De inventione*, I.3.4–5.
[34] Cicero, *De oratore*, III.31.122.

De inventione and *De oratore*, Cicero argues that the very realization of social intercourse requires the activity of an orator.[121] While he contends that all human beings possess a potential for sociability implicit in their common rational and linguistic nature, their primordial existence was a scattered and brutish one, devoid of cities, laws and the fruits of civil community. They would have been destined to remain permanently in this condition, Cicero believes, without the "existence of one from among the infinite multitude of mankind who, either alone or with a few others, could induce what is given to everyone by nature".[122] Such a person was the first orator, by whose application of reason and eloquence communities came to be established, cities founded, and laws and rights instituted. As Cicero explains,

> At a certain time, a great and wise (*sapiens*) man discovered that there was a natural property contained within the souls of human beings for the largest field of opportunity, if one could draw it out and render it better through education.... He transformed them from wild beasts and savages into tame and gentle creatures on account of heeding speech and reason more diligently. It does not seem to me, at least, that a wisdom either silent or lacking speech (*inops dicendi*) could have accomplished the sudden conversion of men from their habits and the conveyance of them into different modes of life.... This seems to be the first birth and lengthy progression of eloquence, and likewise afterwards in matters of peace and war it came to be of the greatest utility amongst human beings.[123]

The origins of human association and of oratory are thus identical. Society itself could not have arisen without the primitive orator, who was both a persuasive speaker and a man of special insight and wisdom, capable of recognizing that latent power which existed within all men. At the moment of its first triumph in the distant past, oratory was already the embodiment of the Ciceronian union of rhetoric and philosophy, eloquence and wisdom.

Cicero in turn charges the latter-day orator to imitate the heroism of his archetype, by not only discovering what is truly good for his fellow creatures (in the manner of the philosopher) but also communicating it to them in the most forceful and convincing manner so that they may put it to use. His writings consistently ascribe to the successors of the primeval orator a special duty towards the maintenance and defense of the principles of communal life. In *De inventione*, he declares that "eloquence is to be studied. . . all the more vigorously, lest evil men are the most powerful to the detriment of good men and the common disaster of everyone. . . . For this [eloquence] attains the greatest advantage for the republic if wisdom, the director (*moderatrix*) of all matters, is present".[124] Likewise, *De oratore* proclaims: "The guidance (*moderatione*) and wisdom of the perfect orator preserves not only his own dignity, but also the well-being of most individuals and of the

---

35   Cicero, *De oratore*, I.8.33 and *De inventione*, I.1–2.2.
36   Cicero, *De oratore*, I.8.31.
37   Cicero, *De inventione*, I.2.2–34.
38   Cicero. *De inventione*, I.4.5.

whole republic".[125] It would seem to be precisely the combination of eloquence and wisdom characteristic of the orator which assures that he will speak on behalf of the interests of the entire community. By contrast, the philosopher may know the good, but lacks the skill or training to convey it to the multitude; indeed, at times Cicero states[126] that the realm of so-called 'practical philosophy' (philosophy touching on *vitam atque mores*) falls more properly within the domain of the orator than of the philosopher. Inherent in the subject- matter of oratory, then, is a regard for one's fellow human beings and, especially, fellow citizens which imposes upon the orator an overarching duty to disseminate the dictates of reason in the service of public welfare.

The scholastic reception

Cicero's association with the *studia humanitatis,* in conjunction with the prevalence of the (perhaps overdrawn) dichotomy between 'humanistic' and 'scholastic' learning (whether in the Middle Ages or the Renaissance), has often blinded scholars to his popularity as a source for the ideas of medieval schoolmen.[127] Yet Cicero's wide reputation as a teacher of rhetorical skills and rules did not emerge in isolation from knowledge about his political doctrines and values. Indeed, the Ciceronian ideal of the orator, at least as articulated in *De inventione* (*De oratore* was only available during the Middle Ages in an imperfect version which was not widely read), found a strikingly congenial home within the writings of many authors between the twelfth and the mid-fourteenth centuries.

Not surprisingly, the earliest medieval appreciation of Cicero's concept of the orator may be located in commentaries on *De inventione*, the composition of which was widespread during the late eleventh and twelfth centuries.[128] The influential commentary composed by Thierry of Chartres in the 1130s, for example, devotes a disproportionate amount of attention to the 'prologue' of *De inventione* in which Cicero introduces the orator and his role.[129] Thierry demonstrates an excellent understanding of the background to the Ciceronian argument, rapidly confronting

---

39   Cicero, *De oratore*, I.8.34.
40   Cicero, *De oratore*, I.15.68–9.
41   There are, however, a very few exceptions to this generalization, for example, E.K. Rand, *Cicero in the courtroom of St. Thomas Aquinas* (Milwaukee, 1946); Nederman, 'Nature, sin,' 3–26 and C.J. Nederman, 'Nature, justice and duty in the *Defensor pacis*: Marsiglio of Padua's Ciceronian impulse,' *Political Theory*, 18 (1990), 615–32.
42   See Ward, *Artificiosa eloquentia*.
43   By my rough estimation, nearly 10 percent of Thierry's commentary addresses the prologue to *De inventione*, whereas it occupies only 3.5 percent of Cicero's total text. On the background to Thierry's commentary, see K.M. Fredborg, *The commentary of Thierry of Chartres on Cicero's De inventione* (Cahiers de l'Institut de moyen age Grec et Latin, Copenhagen, 1971); and J.O. Ward 'The date of the commentary on Cicero's "De inventione" by Thierry of Chartres (ca 1095–1160?) and the Cornifician attack on the liberal arts, *Viator*, 3 (1972), 219–73.

the potential problem implicit in the relationship between wisdom and eloquence. He carefully analyzes the terms of Cicero's statement at the beginning of *De inventione* about the dangers posed by either wisdom or eloquence when not associated with one another. Thierry also locates Cicero in his intellectual milieu: he emphasizes how the Roman sought to refute Plato and, especially, Aristotle, for whom the art of persuasion "opposed in many ways the truth, because it supplanted truth with falsity in human opinion".[44] In this regard, Thierry highlights Cicero's concern with demonstrating that the worthiness of the study of rhetoric depends upon 'utilitarian' considerations; it is not 'good' or 'evil' in itself, but should be judged according to its usefulness for human beings.[45]

Thierry seems to recognize that the appeal to utility raises two further questions. First, to whom should rhetoric be useful? Second, how does one ensure that it will be useful? The answers to these queries are connected. Thierry contends that when eloquence is joined with wisdom, the orator will necessarily serve the welfare of the *res publica*, a term which he construes to mean both the private good of individuals *and* that of the civic body.[46] In order to achieve this goal, the orator must study all the departments of speculative and practical wisdom, "which we call philosophy", as well as rhetoric: "by means of the conjunction of wisdom with eloquence, one is fit to defend one's country".[47] In a later passage, Thierry even cites *De oratore* – the sole reference to that work in his commentary – in support of the assertion that the orator must enjoy a broad basis of learning just in order to perform his functions adequately.[48]

The civic orientation of Cicero's conception of the union of wisdom and eloquence is reaffirmed by Thierry in his gloss on the Ciceronian account of the origins of human society. As reconstructed by Thierry, Cicero is taken to say:

> There was a certain time at the start of the world, during which men were in their original state and lived according to the character of wild animals and not one of them engaged in the study of wisdom, but only exercised the strength of the body without any reason; at this time, some man of wisdom and eloquence – since these properties would seem to be included in man's divine and rational soul, for which reason it would be known that he was suited to be capable of being persuaded – then and on account of this impulse wisely started using eloquence and suppressed the original state and gathered men together to live according to laws and taught the correct laws to the congregated persons. In this manner, he shows both the unformed state of the exercise of eloquence and the cause for which eloquence began to be exercised, and the occurrence of an order which was most advantageous and was useful.[49]

This general summary by Thierry, which precedes a more detailed examination of the passage, elaborates upon Cicero's text in certain interesting ways. Most

---

[44]   *The Latin rhetorical commentaries of Thierry of Chartres*, ed. K.M. Fredborg (Toronto, 1988), 56.
[45]   Thierry of Chartres, 56–7.
[46]   Thierry of Chartres, 57.
[47]   Thierry of Chartres, 59.
[48]   Thierry of Chartres, 72.
[49]   Thierry of Chartres, 60–1.

significantly, he describes the primitive orator as *sapiens et eloquens*, whereas Cicero merely calls him *vir magnus et sapiens*, a variation which suggests directly that the duties of modern oratory are prefigured by the founding of the earliest societies. And he stresses that the need for the orator to persuade human beings to assemble establishes the "usefulness" (and hence goodness) of the "learning of the art of rhetoric".[50] Thierry's commentary hence demonstrates an appreciation of the broader significance of Cicero's presentation of the emergence of human association.

In connection with the civil bearing of rhetoric, Thierry also attempts to explain why the study of philosophy, and hence the acquisition of wisdom, constitutes an assurance of the public utility of eloquence. For what distinguishes the orator from the man who merely "speaks well" is virtue. Thierry describes the "greatness" and "wisdom" of the primitive orator as a manifestation of his "virtue" and "discretion".[51] Furthermore, he distinguishes formally between wisdom and "cleverness" (*calliditatis*): real eloquence manifests a philosophical education, replete with the study of *ethica*,[52] whereas empty persuasion relies on skills which have no basis in philosophy. Hence, Thierry declares, "A distinction is to be noted between wisdom and cleverness, for no one is wise without virtue, yet cleverness is obtained by many people lacking virtue".[53] He arrives at this conclusion on the basis of very slender evidence in Cicero's text itself: *De inventione* remarks only that the speaker of "talent dependent upon malice" exercised "a depraved imitation of virtue" which destroyed men and their communal association.[54] By contrast, Thierry goes on to ascribe virtue to the orator as a direct result of his combination of eloquence with wisdom. This seems to be the ultimate reason why for Thierry "eloquence in conjunction with wisdom is highly advantageous for cities", whereas "eloquence without wisdom is of little advantage for the arrangement and rule of cities".[55] The orator's virtue, imbedded in his wisdom, impels him to serve the good of the civic body, while the lack of wisdom attributable to the clever speaker means that he will pursue his own aims without regard for the welfare of his fellow creatures.

Medieval commentators on *De inventione* such as Thierry of Chartres were in large measure responsible for drawing attention to and promoting the Ciceronian vision of the orator among educated clerics and schoolmen. Throughout the twelfth and early thirteenth centuries, however, Cicero's teachings were primarily confined to the province of rhetorical studies. After the middle of the thirteenth

---

[50]   Thierry of Chartres, 60.
[51]   Thierry of Chartres, 62.
[52]   Thierry of Chartres, 59.
[53]   Thierry of Chartres, 64.
[54]   Cicero, *De inventione*, I.2.3.
[55]   Thierry of Chartres, 62–3.

century, by contrast, one encounters a new trend: authors familiar with *De inventione* begin to employ its idea of oratory in the context of more general discussions of politics and practical philosophy. An early benchmark in the diffusion of Ciceronian thought in a less specialized manner is Brunetto Latini's *Li livres dou tresor*, a philosophical encyclopedia compiled between 1260 and 1266.[56] Latini, a Florentine who was trained as a professional rhetorician, was not a scholastic in a narrow sense, but his education and career afforded him knowledge of the current Aristotelian learning. *Li livres dou tresor* relies heavily, for instance, upon Robert Grosseteste's recently completed Latin version of the *Nicomachean Ethics*, although it shows no direct awareness of Aristotle's *Politics*, which William of Moerbeke had translated around 1260. The work is divided into three sections: the first treats the fields of theology, history, geography and natural philosophy; the second examines ethics; and the third surveys *de bone parleure*, under which heading Latini includes rhetoric and politics.

Latini's rationale for associating rhetoric and politics in this fashion is expressly Ciceronian. With *De inventione* I.5.6 apparently in mind, he claims, "Tully says that the highest science of governing the city is rhetoric, that is to say, the science of speaking; for without speaking, there were not and would not have been either cities or the institution of justice or human companionship".[57] Although the chapters immediately following this statement read like a brief commentary on *De inventione*, Latini's purpose is quite different from that of the medieval commentators. Brunetto seeks to introduce the study of rhetoric as a subject which the prospective ruler of a city must master. For after examining the elements of rhetoric, he immediately moves on to discuss the duties connected with civic government. And among the primary requirements elucidated by Latini for appointment to public office is that he be "a very good speaker",[58] as well as be knowledgeable in "everything concerning matters of truth".[59] These attributes indicate that a necessary precondition for competence as a governor is attainment of qualifications as an orator.

Li livres dou tresor signals its recognition of the issues connected with the Ciceronian conception of oratory early in its treatment of *bone parleure*. Like Thierry, Latini addresses the Aristotelian charge that the science of *bien parler* ('speaking well', which seems to be his translation of *eloquentia*) is "evil, because by means of speech men have done more harm than good".[60] The problem, Brunetto admits, has much to do with the relation of speech to wisdom. Adopting a more purely Stoic line than Cicero, he remarks that "just as it is the case that

---

[56]   See Skinner, *Foundations*, 35–48 and 'Ambrogio Lorenzetti,' 16–31.
[57]   *Brunetto Latini. Li livres dou tresor*, ed. F.J. Carmody (Berkeley, 1948), III.1.2.
[58]   Brunetto Latini, III.75.8.
[59]   Brunetto Latini, III.75.5.
[60]   Brunetto Latini, III.1.4.

speech is given to all men, Cato says that wisdom (*sapience*) is given to a few".[61] Latini then enumerates four different types of relationship which are possible between eloquence and wisdom: when reason and good speech are present together, "it is the flower of the world"; when neither are present, it is a "great disaster"; when one speaks well but lacks reason, there is "very great peril"; and when one possesses reason, yet eloquence is absent, instruction and aid are required.[62] Brunetto says nothing more about the second and fourth categories. Instead, he concentrates upon promoting the union of wisdom and eloquence, and hence upon averting the disaster that arises from their disjunction. He even observes that, in one sense, the Aristotelian and Ciceronian viewpoints on rhetoric concur:

And in another way, Tully accords well with what Aristotle says about speech, namely, that it is an evil art; but this is speech without wisdom; when a man has the appearance of good language and he has not given any counsel at all, this speech is extremely perilous to the city and to friends.[63].

Latini acknowledges here both the centrality of the conjunction of wisdom and eloquence and the potential danger to the community which arises when persuasive speech is not accompanied by a well formed intellect.

But *Li livres dou tresor* does not embrace the Aristotelian conclusion that rhetoric is in all cases evil. Rather, Latini adopts the Ciceronian position that oratory as the union of wisdom and eloquence is of the greatest benefit to the whole community: "And when wisdom is joined to speech, who will say that it cannot give rise to goodness"?[64] His evidence for the usefulness of oratory rests, in turn, on Cicero's claim that society itself would be impossible in the absence of an orator:

Tully says that, in the beginning, men lived according to the law of beasts, without their own houses and without knowledge of God, in the forests and in rural retreats, without regard for marriage or cognizance of parents or children. Then there appeared a wise and well spoken man, who counselled the others and pointed out the greatness of the soul and the dignity of reason and of discretion, so that he recalled them from their savagery and urged them to come together as one and to protect reason and justice. And by the use of good speech which was accompanied by reason, this man was almost like a second God, who created the world for the sake of the arrangement of human companionship.[65]

Latini's appreciation of the contribution of the primitive orator, and especially his comparison of the activity of the wise and eloquent speaker to the creative power of God, is striking in its force. The orator is placed by *Li livres dou tresor* at the very center of the communal affairs of his city: his words are the fount of civic life.

That Latini views this oratorical role as a continuing feature of the community

[61]   Brunetto Latini, III.1.2.
[62]   Brunetto Latini, III.1.2.
[63]   Brunetto Latini, III.1.9.
[64]   Brunetto Latini, III.1.6.
[65]   Brunetto Latini, III.1.7.

is made clear by the idea of 'counsel' which runs throughout the third part of *Li livres dou tresor*. At times, he seems to mean by 'counsel' or 'giving counsel' simply one of the three technical divisions of rhetoric (namely, *deliberativo)* enumerated by Cicero (following Aristotle's classification) in *De inventione*.[66] But in the suggestion that the primitive orator 'counselled', and that the man who merely speaks well does not 'give counsel', there is an indication that the discipline of oratory teaches counsel in a normative sense. 'Counsel' seems to connote wise speech for the purpose of achieving public welfare or rectitude. This impression is reinforced by Latini when he turns directly to the governance of the city: citizens should ᵣᵉek 'wise counsel' when deciding whom to appoint as their ruler;[67] they are charged with giving their governor "counsel and aid for maintaining his office";[68] and one of the primary duties of rulers is to assemble the chief and wise men of the city in order to request and consider their 'counsel' regarding important matters, such as the conduct of diplomatic affairs.[69] Oratory appears to form the basis for such counseling functions: the properly trained orator may be taken to speak on behalf of the interests of the community because his eloquence is coupled with the wisdom to recognize the public good. Not only the ruler, but the body of the citizens (or at least its leading segments), ought to be trained in the field of oratory.

One might suppose that interest in Cicero's political ideas, and hence his conception of the orator, would have waned in the years immediately after Latini's composition of *Li livres dou tresor*, as the Latin translation of Aristotle's *Politics* gained wide circulation in the West. But Cicero continued to be an important source for medieval political authors, even among those scholastics whose dedication to Aristotelian learning is generally undisputed. Consequently, we find reliance on Cicero's teachings about oratory in some of the classic works of later medieval scholastic political thought, such as *De potestate regia et papali*, composed by Parisian Master of Arts John Quidort (often known as John of Paris) in 1302-1303.[70] John's most explicit use of Cicero occurs in the midst of his account of the nature and origins of royal government. In Chapter 1 of *De potestate*, he catalogues the commonplace medieval arguments (derived from scriptural as well as pagan sources) favoring the "rule of one man according to virtue",[71] while also presenting the main elements of the Aristotelian doctrine of man as a "social and political

---

[66] Cicero, *De inventione*, I.5.7; compare with Brunetto Latini, III.2.20 and III.52.11.
[67] Brunetto Latini, III.75.1.
[68] Brunetto Latini, III.74.4. This echoes, of course, the terms of the traditional feudal oath in which the vassal promises to provide *consilium et auxilium* to his lord or king.
[69] Brunetto Latini, III.87–9 and 95.
[70] M.F. Greisbach, 'John of Paris as representative of Thomistic political philosophy,' in: *An Etienne Gilson tribute*, ed. C.J. O'Neill (Milwaukee, 1959).
[71] *John of Paris. De potestate regia et papali*, ed. F. Bleienstein (Stuttgart, 1969) 76.

animal".[72] Although John concludes that nature as well as divine decree support the superiority and utility of monarchical government, he still needs to demonstrate how such a regime is consistent with Aristotelian naturalism, which by ascribing a political nature to all human beings (or at least adult males) might seem to undercut the foundations of kingship.

John establishes this compatibility by subtly recasting Aristotle's philosophical anthropology in Ciceronian terms. He refers to a primordial era, "before the time of Belus and Ninus, who were the first to exercise government", when human beings lived contrary to their natures as untamed and ungoverned animals.[73] Orosius and Cicero's *De inventione* are cited in support of this claim, as is Aristotle's *Politics* inasmuch as "the Philosopher speaks of those who live like gods or beasts but not like men".[74] But John misconstrues Aristotle, who actually says that those who do not live within a political community *are* either wild animals or deities; the *Politics*, unlike *De inventione*, contains no sustained image of a primitive existence without any form of stable or permanent human association. (Even if the family and village are chronologically prior to the *polis*, these constitute social groupings which Cicero does not deem possible in his primeval world.) Consequently, Ciceronian and Aristotelian teachings are artificially merged into a single version of the origins of civil society.

John's conflation of Cicero with Aristotle is neither innocent nor accidental. For he then proceeds to attribute the development of monarchy to the infirmities of this primitive condition.

Since men could not use the speech shared by all human beings to live the common life natural to them, and to abandon a state more fitting for beasts than for men, others, animated by the errors of their fellows, using their reason to better effect, attempted to draw them by more persuasive reasoning to an ordered life in common under one ruler, as Cicero says. Thus united, they were bound by definite laws to live communally.[75]

John subscribes to the position that nature in itself is insufficient to stimulate communal association.[76] His argument resembles that offered by Latini: While all human creatures share in the faculty of speech, the powers of reason (or at any rate, of eloquent reason) are less broadly distributed. It requires an orator (whom Cicero in *De oratore* regards as the rarest of people because of the many fields of learning he must master)[77] to awaken the multitude to the advantages of political life. The orator, in whom persuasive speech has been joined with wisdom, achieves what nature left to its own devices cannot: he leads scattered human beings to recognize their own natural propensities and to accept the rule

---

[72]   John of Paris, 75–6.
[73]   John of Paris, 77.
[74]   John of Paris, 77.
[75]   John of Paris, 77–8.
[76]   See Nederman, 'Nature, sin,' 18–19.
[77]   Cicero, *De oratore*, I.3.11.

of a king. Civil society itself is regarded by John as an impossibility without the intervention of the primordial orator. Oratory, still understood as the harmonious application of wisdom and eloquence towards the end of realizing the common good, hence occupies a critical role in the political theory sketched in *De potestate*.

Marsiglio of Padua

It might nevertheless be argued that, even if a schoolman like John of Paris could find a place for oratory in the process through which society was formed in the distant past, he still envisioned no part for the orator in the ordinary conduct of public affairs. This may indeed be true for some of the scholastics who were especially devoted to monarchy, although it in no way vitiates the significance of their reliance on the Ciceronian image of the orator. But other authors whose scholastic credentials were equally excellent found in Cicero's thought not merely an explanation of the origins of human association, but a model for the practice of politics on a day-to-day basis. The political writings of the early fourteenth-century Parisian Master Marsiglio of Padua afford us a particularly compelling instance of such a full application of the Ciceronian doctrine of oratory during the late Middle Ages.

It has only recently come to be recognized that the account of the origins of human society presented by Marsiglio in his *Defensor pacis* (completed in 1324) relies heavily on Cicero.[78] Scholars have noted with some consternation Marsiglio's failure to adopt the Aristotelian definition of man as a political creature, an anomaly which they have explained by reference to the presence of Augustinian or Averroistic propensities within the *Defensor pacis*.[79] But Marsiglio's understanding of the emergence of society is in fact couched in terms of the stimulation of man's inherently associative tendencies by means of wise oration. Marsiglio reports that the human faculties of reason and speech were stirred and energized,

by the persuasion and exhortation of prudent and able men. The latter, exceptionally endowed by nature with an inclination for this task, later through their own efforts made progress in their various pursuits and guided others either successively or simultaneously to the formation of a perfected community, to which men are naturally inclined so that they readily complied with this persuasion.[80]

The natural disposition to associate is constituted as an implicit feature of human nature, requiring reasoned persuasion to stimulate and direct it towards realization. Marsiglio believes that the success or failure of this process of socialization

---

[78]   Nederman, 'Nature, sin,' 20–2 and 'Nature, justice,' 621–4.
[79]   A. Gewirth, *Marsilius of Padua and medieval political philosophy* (New York, 1952), 54–6, 88–91; J. Quillet, *La philosophie politique de Marsile de Padoue* (Paris, 1970), 64–6; P. di Vona, *I principi del Defensor pacis* (Napoli, 1974), 379–80.
[80]   *Marsilius of Padua. Defensor pacis*, ed. C.W. Previté-Orton (Cambridge, 1928), II.22.25.

is largely dependent upon the presence of one or a few men who are particularly well endowed with the rational and rhetorical faculties necessary to convince the mass of human beings to assemble as a community. As with Latini and John of Paris, Marsiglio regards the orator as an exceptional being who, by appealing to the basic human properties of speech and reason, guides his fellow creatures towards the common good.

What distinguishes Marsiglio from preceding theorists, however, is his clear insistence that oratory plays a continuing role in the conduct of public affairs. It has been observed that the procedures according to which legislation in Marsiglio's fully formed civic body is to be promulgated constitute a kind of recapitulation of the original process through which the community was founded.[81] He stipulates that draft statutes are to be framed by *prudentes* who, by virtue of their leisure and superior experience, are best qualified to discover just and useful laws.[82] Yet the *Defensor pacis* also stresses that the wisdom of the few does not entitle them to enact legislation on behalf of the general mass of citizens.[83] Rather,

Although the multitude cannot by itself discover true and useful matters, still it can discern and judge what is discovered and proposed to it by others, as to whether there should be additions or subtractions or complete changes or rejection. For many things which a man could not initiate or discover by himself can be comprehended and completed after they have been explained to him by someone else.[84]

Thus, the whole body of citizens (which Marsiglio terms the *legislator humanus*) must consent to draft statutes in order to give them the status of "coercive commands", that is, laws which the community is obligated to obey.[85]

The *Defensor pacis* ascribes to oratory two pivotal functions in this process of a 'bill becoming a law'. First, it is assigned to the *prudentes*, when they present their legislative proposals to the citizen body, to "explain" publicly the measures they have recommended; and their fellow citizens are likewise bound to "listen attentively" to the arguments given.[86] The *prudentes* in effect play the role created by the primordial orator: they must attempt to persuade the assembly of citizens that the draft statutes are consistent with justice ("true cognitions of the just")[87] and contribute to the common good, while it is left to the multitude, whose powers of reason are less well developed, to reflect upon the justifications presented to them and to approve (or withhold approval from) laws. Second, Marsiglio views

[81]   C.J. Nederman, 'Knowledge, consent and the critique of political representation in Marsiglio of Padua's *Defensor pacis*,' *Political Studies*, 39 (1991), 19–35, especially 32.
[82]   Marsilius of Padua, I.12.2.
[83]   Marsilius of Padua, I.13.4.
[84]   Marsilius of Padua, I.13.7.
[85]   Marsilius of Padua, I.12.7.
[86]   Marsilius of Padua, I.13.7.
[87]   Marsilius of Padua, I.10.5.

the occurrence of legislative authorization as an occasion for general public discussion and debate amongst the members of the civic body. He insists that "if any citizen thinks that something should be added, subtracted, adjusted or completely rejected, he can say (*dicere*) so. . . In the general assembly of citizens, those citizens will have been heard who have wished to make some reasonable statements with regard to them".[88] Like Latini, Marsiglio regards oratory as a field of learning which can benefit not just public officials but the rest of the citizens as well. But Marsiglio goes much further than his predecessor by insisting that the whole citizen population must have an opportunity to speak about the matters of communal concern placed before it and that the words of the populace are ultimately binding. Where in *Li livres dou tresor*, the process of public oratory took the form of 'counsel' offered by the leaders of the community, in the *Defensor pacis* political discourse is open to all citizens and represents the final authority in every case.

Marsiglio also cites another, and in some ways more significant, circumstance in which the talents of the orator are demanded. One of the most influential features of the *Defensor pacis* was its advocacy of a conciliar theory of the church according to which the ultimate power within the community of believers rests with a general council composed of delegates from throughout Christendom. Marsiglio viewed conciliarism as a primary tool in the struggle against papal despotism, a position which he upheld in his later writings as well. Although the *Defensor pacis* provides us with very little insight into how he envisaged the actual operation of the general council, he offers some interesting observations regarding this matter in his *Defensor minor*, a summary restatement and defense of his earlier work which he composed about 1340.[89]

In the *Defensor pacis*, Marsiglio had identified the purpose of the general council as the canonical interpretation of Holy Scripture and determination of the articles of the Christian faith.[90] While its members are elected by the church as a whole, Marsiglio does not construe the council as a representative body in a modern, political sense.[91] Rather, since the truths of Scripture are fixed for all time, the council's duty is solely to discover and articulate such truths with reference to the Holy Spirit instead of a historical constituency. In this sense, the general council is infallible in a way that individual priests or prelates, or various groupings thereof, cannot be; the council alone has access to eternal truth. During the 1330s, William of Ockham had launched a stinging attack on this doctrine of conciliar infallibility

---

[88]   Marsilius of Padua, I.13.8.
[89]   For the circumstances surrounding the composition of the *Defensor minor*, see my editor's introduction to *Marsiglio of Padua: Writings on the Empire*, forthcoming from Cambridge University Press.
[90]   Marsilius of Padua, II.18.8.
[91]   Nederman, 'Knowledge,' 21–3.

by claiming that since individual members of the council were not capable of unerring insight into God's wisdom, neither could the council as a whole know unequivocally what is true.[178]

Marsiglio's response to Ockham's challenge, framed in the twelfth chapter of the *Defensor minor*, represents a sort of return to the emphasis on reasoned public debate which characterized his conception of the secular civic assembly in the *Defensor pacis*. He declares,

A multitude of the faithful is joined together in a council; for by each one listening to the others, their minds are reciprocally stimulated to the consideration of that truth at which none of them would arrive if he existed apart or separately from the others.[179]

Marsiglio then proceeds to describe the procedures according to which the early church settled disputes and addressed doubtful matters: the elders assembled the whole church and all deliberated jointly about issues of common concern. He answers Ockham by insisting that what cannot be accomplished by one person may often be achieved by the cooperation of many. 'Cooperation' in the case of a general council denotes the public presentation of speeches for the edification of the members of the council, by means of which a consensus about the truth is eventually attained. Here we have the highest calling of the Christian orator: he employs his wisdom and eloquence towards the end of discovering and disseminating the common welfare and salvation of the whole body of the faithful. Yet even transposed into the Christian context of the general council, this Marsiglian concept of oration does not lose any of the essential components of the Ciceronian ideal: the orator must still use his learning and skill for good purposes which he shares in common with other members of his community. Whether addressing the civic body or the general council, the genuine orator is trained to speak what he knows to be the truth in such fashion as to convince his audience to follow the correct and beneficial path in all matters.

The medieval heritage

Paul Kristeller points out that scholars often leave their readers with the false impression that medieval rhetoric was wholly concentrated upon two functions: letter- writing and preaching.[180] In fact, as Kristeller has persuasively argued,[181] there exists a substantial body of literature within the medieval rhetorical tradition which addresses the central oratorical activity of public speaking (*ars arengendi*), the "very existence" of which "is sufficient to prove the rise and relative importance

[92] See B. Tierney, *The origins of papal infallibility* (Leiden, 1974).
[93] *Marsile de Padoue. Oeuvres minueres*, ed. J. Quillet and C. Jeudy (Paris, 1979), 260.
[94] P.O. Kristeller, *Renaissance philosophy and its sources* (New York, 1979), 94.
[95] Kristeller, *Renaissance philosophy*, 114.

of secular oratory as a historical phenomenon which until very recently had been overlooked by most students of medieval rhetoric". Yet even among scholars who acknowledge a growing interest (especially among the Italians) during the late Middle Ages in oratory as a feature of public life, there is a pronounced skepticism about whether such practices reflected any awareness of the classical conception of the orator as the wise and eloquent man. Kohl and Witt observe that "with rare exceptions rhetoricians [of thirteenth-century Italy], usually laymen, wished to achieve eloquence in order to win favor for a person or a policy or accomplish the opposite result. Theirs was in effect an eloquence without a conscience".[96] In other words, the public speakers of the Middle Ages stand accused of lacking an appropriate theoretical self-understanding, of merely 'speaking well' without comprehending the real nature of oratory as defined by Cicero.

Any claim about the inability of medieval orators to appreciate the full (classical) dimensions of their art is rendered considerably less plausible when viewed in light of the evidence presented here. Indeed, judging from the recognition of the predicament of the orator exhibited as early as Thierry of Chartres, one might even conclude that the theoretical awareness of the Ciceronian image of oratory was far more advanced than medieval practice. Could the scholastic retention and perpetuation of the ideal of the orator have been a factor in the actual reemergence of public speaking as a feature of political life? Any answer to this question must be purely speculative at present, given our ignorance about the nature and extent of the penetration of school learning into the communal affairs of twelfth and early thirteenth century Western Europe. But it seems at least defensible to claim that scholastic interest in oratory as a distinct field of learning and activity reinforced and generated an intellectual framework for the rise of the *ars arengendi* in Italy during the 1200s.

The present study also lends support to the contention (often associated with the work of Paul Kristeller[97]) that an essential continuity exists between medieval and Renaissance approaches to rhetoric, although the current evidence changes in some ways the character of this conclusion. Kristeller has argued that "the eloquence of the humanists was the continuation of the medieval *ars arengendi* just as their epistolography continued the tradition of the *ars dictaminis*"[98]. He means this as a claim about the art of public speaking as a practical affair. Yet, as the present study reveals, the Ciceronian ideal of oratory itself was available to and embraced by medieval thinkers starting in the early twelfth century, if not before. Thus, both humanism's praise of wise eloquence, and its connection of oratory with a concern for and devotion to public affairs, may be taken as continuations

---

96   *The earthly republic*, 5.
97   By, for instance, Skinner, *Foundations*, vol. I, 102–5.
98   Kristeller, *Renaissance philosophy*, 94.

of medieval theoretical frameworks as well as actual practices. Even scholasticism, which is so often denigrated as the implacable enemy of humanism, could grasp these 'authentic' features of Cicero's thought. Careful examination of medieval texts indeed reveals how too firm a distinction between the Middle Ages and the Renaissance, or between the scholastic and humanist outlooks, may become an obstacle to the appreciation of the more subtle contours of these intellectual traditions. Oratory was just as much admired by medieval thinkers, and regarded by them as crucial to the orderly conduct of public affairs, as by their humanist successors in the *quattrocento*. Nothing in Cicero's ideal of the wise and eloquent orator was precluded by or incompatible with the most cherished presumptions of medieval rhetorical and political authors. On the contrary, Cicero's conception of oratory revealed to the Middle Ages an important dimension of public life – one which was largely ignored or even rejected by other classical sources – and thereby perhaps stimulated continuing interest in speech as a necessary feature of political experience even when the opportunities for its full expression were absent.

XIII

BRACTON ON KINGSHIP REVISITED†

It is a testimony to the seminal and authoritative status of Henry de Bracton's thirteenth-century legal manual, the *De legibus et consuetudinibus angliae*, that so many prominent historians of medieval political thought, law and institutions have contributed to the body of literature on it. During the middle of the present century, in particular, controversies raged about the accurate reconstruction of Bracton's text,[1] about the intellectual and historical sources of his ideas,[2] and more broadly, about his theoretical insights into the nature of kingship and government.[3] But after flourishing as a vital

---

† This paper could not have been composed without the intellectual guidance and personal encouragement of the late John Brückmann, to whose memory it is dedicated. A portion of this essay was presented to the 19th International Congress on Medieval Studies, Western Michigan University, Kalamazoo.

[1] See Hermann Kantorowicz, *Bractonian Problems* (Glasgow, 1941); Gailliard Lapsley, 'Bracton and the Authorship of the "*Addicio de Cartis*" ', *English Historical Review*, 62 (1947), pp. 1–19; Charles H. McIlwain, 'The Present Status of the Problem of the Bracton Text', *Harvard Law Review*, 57 (1943–1944), pp. 220–40; Charles M. Radding, 'The Origins of Bracton's *Addicio de Cartis*', *Speculum*, 44 (1969), pp. 239–46; H.G. Richardson, *Bracton: The Problem of His Text* (London, 1965); and Fritz Schulz, 'Critical Studies on Bracton's Treatise', *Law Quarterly Review*, 59 (1943), pp. 172–90.

[2] J.L. Barton, 'Bracton as a Civilian', *Tulane Law Review*, 42 (April 1968), pp. 555–83; Mitchell Franklin, 'Bracton, Para-Bracton(s) and the Vicarage of the Roman Law', *Tulane Law Review*, 42 (April 1968), pp. 455–518; Gaines Post, 'A Romano-Canonical Maxim, "Quod omnes tangit," in Bracton', *Traditio*, 4 (1946), pp. 197–251; H.G. Richardson, 'Azo, Drogheda and Bracton', *English Historical Review*, 59 (1944), pp. 22–47; H.G. Richardson, 'Tancred, Raymond and Bracton', *English Historical Review*, 59 (1944), pp. 376–84; H.G. Richardson, 'Studies in Bracton', *Traditio*, 6 (1948), pp. 61–104; and Fritz Schulz, 'Bracton on Kingship', *English Historical Review*, 60 (1945), pp. 136–76.

[3] Wiebke Fesefeldt, *Englische Staatstheories des 13. Jahrhunderts: Henry de Bracton und sein Werk* (Gottingen, 1962); Donald Hanson, *From Kingdom to Commonwealth* (Cambridge, Mass., 1970), pp. 97–133 and *passim*; Ernst H. Kantorowicz, *The King's Two Bodies* (Princeton, 1957), pp. 143–92; Ewart Lewis, 'King Above Law? "Quod principi placuit" in Bracton', *Speculum*, 39 (1964), pp. 240–69; Charles H. McIlwain, *Constitutionalism: Ancient and Modern* (Ithaca, NY, 1958), pp. 67–92; S.J.T. Miller, 'The Position of the King in Bracton and Beaumanoir', *Speculum*, 31 (1956), pp. 263–96; Gaines Post, 'Bracton on Kingship', *Tulane Law Review*, 42 (April 1968), pp. 519–54; Brian Tierney, 'Bracton on Government', *Speculum*, 38 (1963), pp. 295–317; and Walter Ullmann, *Principles of Government and Politics in the Middle Ages* (London, 1961), pp. 176–8 and *passim*.

and active field of inquiry among medieval scholars, Bracton studies have experienced something of a decline in recent years. In due course, most of the research problems posed by the *De legibus* found increasingly detailed and thorough solutions: substantial consensus was achieved on an authentic text; the Romanist, canonistic, scriptural and common law materials which influenced Bracton's doctrines were established; and the character of the political theory of the *De legibus* was elucidated in clearer and more coherent terms. As Gaines Post remarked in 1968, 'So much has been written about Bracton . . . that surely it is difficult to add anything of significance'.[4] Even the publication of S.E. Thorne's revised critical edition and translation of the *De legibus* between 1968 and 1977,[5] so far from producing the 'outburst of scholarly activity' expected by A.A. Schiller,[6] has failed to stimulate fresh insights into Bracton's thought.

The aim of the present paper, however, is not simply to recount the state of scholarship on Bracton.[7] Instead, one ought not to infer from the current silence among commentators that the interpretive book on the *De legibus* may now be declared entirely closed. For in reviewing the Bracton literature of the past few decades, one may still identify live and unresolved issues which cut straight to the heart of the arguments of the *De legibus*. An illustration of the puzzles about Bracton's work which lack a final solution is afforded by his conception of the king's relationship to law. On initial inspection, the *De legibus* appears to propose a paradoxical set of claims. On the one hand, Bracton ostensibly upholds the validity of the famous Roman law maxim that *quod principi placuit legis habet vigorem*. Yet, at the same time, he clearly maintains that the monarch's duty lies in obedience to the law, so that the royal will is forever subject to, or under, the *leges et consuetudines* of the realm.[8] Despite attempts to argue that this 'paradox' was a real one, imbedded in the contradictory circumstances of the medieval English

---

[4] Post, 'Bracton on Kingship', p. 519.

[5] Bracton, *De legibus et consuetudinibus angliae*, ed. G.E. Woodbine, rev. and trans. S.E. Thorne, 4 vols. (Cambridge, Mass., 1968–1977). (Hereafter cited as *De legibus*, followed by volume and page numbers.)

[6] As Schiller remarks in his review of the first and second volumes of Thorne's edition, in *Speculum*, 45 (July 1970), p. 498.

[7] This task has been admirably performed by Jason Myers, 'The Historical Interpretation of Political Theory: Some Medieval Paradoxes', presented to the Canadian Political Science Association, Ottawa, Ontario, June 1982.

[8] The relevant passages are to be found in *De legibus*, II, 305–6.

monarchy,[9] the historical practices of the feudal polity of thirteenth-century England do not seem to raise any such dilemma.[10] Moreover, careful analysis of the text and sources of the *De legibus* reveals that no logical self-contradiction is implied by Bracton's statements. It is rather the case that Bracton took the king to be *non sub homine, sed sub deo et sub lege*. The monarch, in other words, was expected to obey the law and the lawful statutes of his kingdom, although no man or group of men could 'bridle' him by imposing these requirements upon him.[11] The Bractonian king was a God-fearing and law-abiding man whose unique and characteristic powers rendered him nevertheless insusceptible to correction by his earthly inferiors (or even, at least in temporal matters, by the spiritual authority of the ecclesiastical hierarchy).[12]

Yet this account remains incomplete. For given Bracton's stipulation that the king *should* obey the law, what is to ensure that he will in fact do so when he is not subject to the enforcing power of any human agency? Insofar as the ruler is not *sub homine*, that is, how can there be any effective guarantee that

---

[9] This view has been defended, in particular, by McIlwain, *Constitutionalism*, pp. 77–90; Ullmann, *Principles of Government and Politics in the Middle Ages*, p. 176; and Hanson, *From Kingdom to Commonwealth*, pp. 119–34.

[10] For the relevant historical conditions of the medieval English state, see Cary J. Nederman, *State and Political Theory in France and England, 1250–1350: Marsiglio of Padua, William of Ockham and the Emergence of 'National' Traditions of Discourse in the Late Middle Ages* (Toronto: Unpublished doctoral dissertation, York University, 1983), pp. 125–87. Bracton's views were in fact widely accepted among other English authors of the thirteenth and fourteenth centuries, as I have established in *ibid.*, pp. 245–312. For an instance from earlier in the medieval English tradition of a similar view, compare Bracton with John of Salisbury, *Policraticus*, ed. C.C.J. Webb (Frankfurt, 1965), 515a: 'Princeps tamen legis nexibus dicitur absolutus, non quia ei iniqua liceant, sed quia is esse debet, qui non timore penae sed amore iustitiae aequitatem colat, rei publicae procuret utilitatem, et in omnibus aliorum commoda privatae praeferat voluntati. Sed quis in negotiis publicis loquetur de principis voluntate, cum in eis nil sibi velle liceat, nisi quod lex aut aequitas persuadet aut ratio communis utilitatis inducit?'

[11] The textual evidence for such a position is provided by Lewis, 'King Above Law?', pp. 261–8; Tierney, 'Bracton on Government', p. 303; and Post, 'Bracton on Kingship', pp. 519–25. The only substantial evidence which does not favour this interpretation is to be found in the so-called *addicio de cartis*, in which is stated: 'Rex habet superiorem, . . . curiam suam, videlicet comites et barones, quia comites dicuntur quasi socii regis, et qui socium habet, habet magistrum. Et ideo si rex fuerit sine fraeno, id est sine lege, debent ei fraenum apponere' (*De legibus*, II, 110). For our purposes, it matters not whether this passage is the work of another author, or represents a later addition by Bracton himself, since there is no doubt that it was not meant to be consistent with Bracton's other remarks about kingship which are clearly genuine. Hence, for the present paper, we may legitimately set aside questions regarding the authenticity or authorship of the *addicio de cartis*.

[12] *De legibus*, II, 304 and IV, 281.

he will actually behave and judge in accordance with the law of the land (which has been declared with the assent of the lords of the realm)?[13] The existing scholarship is either entirely silent or uncomfortably evasive with regard to such questions. For instance, Ewart Lewis vaguely acknowledges the 'practical dilemma' implied by 'the king's voluntary acceptance of the bridle that cannot be forced upon him',[14] while Brian Tierney apparently does not think it at all problematic that the monarch's 'observance of the law could be ensured only by his good will, not by judicial coercion'.[15] In the recent literature, only Gaines Post has educed any concern about how, if Bracton's king is *non sub homine, sed sub deo et sub lege*, he might reasonably be expected to impose the laws of the realm upon himself. Post's account is promising. Following the lead of Fritz Schulz,[16] he argues that Bracton supposed the ruler to be *morally* bound to obey the statutes of the realm.[17] This moral compulsion is manifested by the *De legibus* in two ways, Post says. First, it is echoed in Bracton's statement that the king who refuses to follow legal precepts and give justice will be sufficiently reprimanded by God the Avenger,[18] who imposes upon unjust men the ultimate punishment of eternal damnation.[19] Second, the moral dimension of the royal will (*voluntas*) is expressed by the obligations which the monarch undertakes in his coronation oath, whereby he voluntarily swears observance of the laws and customs of the kingdom.[20] In short, Bracton's king, as understood by Post, consciously chooses and announces his intention to obey the law (by means of the coronation oath) in full recognition that the flagrant violation of this duty will result in divine retribution and the imperilling of his soul. The combination of

---

[13] On the element of consent to law, see *De legibus*, II, 19 and 305.

[14] Lewis, 'King Above Law?', p. 263.

[15] Tierney, 'Bracton on Government', p. 303. We need not dwell on Ernst Kantorowicz's convoluted and circular argument that since royal power in the *De legibus* is conferred by the *lex regia*, the king is obligated to obey the law which made him (Kantorowicz, *The King's Two Bodies*, pp. 150–1). Not only is textual evidence lacking for this interpretation, but it assumes a logical connection between the *lex regia* (a specific piece of legislation) and the body of law as a whole which cannot be substantiated.

[16] Schulz, 'Bracton on Kingship', p. 161.

[17] Post, 'Bracton on Kingship', p. 538, note 13.

[18] *De legibus*, II, 33 and III, 43.

[19] Post, 'Bracton on Kingship', pp. 525–35. The punishments meted out by the Avenging God are detailed at some length by Bracton in *De legibus*, II, 21–2.

[20] Post, 'Bracton on Kingship', pp. 535–44.

a freely conceded earthly agreement with the fear of other-wordly punishment, Post believes, would be adequate to convince any medieval ruler to
submit himself strictly to law.

While surely correct in emphasizing that the royal decision to observe
human legislation derives from the moral condition of the king, Post's
interpretation is not entirely convincing. True,· the king who commands
through arbitrary, rather than lawful, action faces the truly frightening prospect of a hellish afterlifė, according to the *De legibus*.[21] Yet an Avenging God
is not a strictly *moral* consideration, insofar as the threat of damnation still
involves a coercive component external to the royal will itself. Furthermore,
as even Post admits,[22] Bracton was at best peripherally interested in the
acceptance of the terms of the coronation oath as a statement of royal
responsibility for the maintenance of law. Indeed, Bracton's formulation of
the oath does not include the customary promise to observe the *leges et
cõnsuetudines* of the realm.[23] Allowing Post the 'probability' that the coronation oath was nevertheless in Bracton's mind,[24] its presence forms no very
explicit part of the argument in the *De legibus* that the king will uphold law
without the imposition of a bridle upon him through the judgment and
restraint of his inferiors. While it perhaps would have been far simpler for
Bracton to place the monarch *sub homine*, as the anonymous authors of the
Carmen de Bello Lewensi and the *Speculum Justiciariorum* were to do somewhat later,[25] the fact that Bracton consistently resisted this option (except in
the possibly spurious *addicio de cartis*)[26] should indicate to us some very
compelling basis for his supposition that rulers would ordinarily prefer law to
their personal *voluntas*. It is crucial to an understanding of kingship in the *De
legibus*, then, that we ask: What grounds does the treatise offer for the
vindication of Bracton's clear conviction that the king will routinely accept
and live under the *moral* obligation to confine his actions to those in accordance with law in the absence of all human constraint? The answer, ultimately, must have less to do with extrinsic factors like oaths and divine

---

[21] See *De legibus*, II, 33 and 305.

[22] Post, 'Bracton on Kingship', p. 535.

[23] *De legibus*, II, 304.

[24] Post, 'Bracton on Kingship', p. 553.

[25] See *Carmen de Bello Lewensi*, ed. C.L. Kingsford (Oxford, 1890), ll. 921–30, and *Speculum Justiciariorum*, ed. W.J. Whittaker (London, 1895), p. 7.

[26] On the matter of the *addicio de cartis*, see note 10 above.

retribution than with the intrinsic nature of the royal will, as even Post realizes in his passing remark that the king's *voluntas* 'must be guided by reason and justice'.[27] Post apparently did not think he could elaborate upon this comment within the limits of Bracton's text. In this regard, he was quite mistaken.

There can be no doubt about the presence of a moral component in the *De legibus*. Bracton classified his work as a whole under the category of 'ethicae' or 'morali scientiae quia tractat de moribus',[28] although he none the less also distinguished between jurisprudence (that is, law and judgment) and justice (morals narrowly conceived and virtue). Jurisprudence deals with matters of decision and judgment, with the rendering of equity (*aequitas*); justice is an attribute or quality of the individual who pronounces judgment on the basis of the law.[29] Bracton's primary intention in the *De legibus*, of course, is the education of judges and magistrates in the techniques of jurisprudence.[30] It is no wonder, then, that he has relatively little to say about justice; he no doubt believed that making men just fell in the province of philosophers and theologians. But Bracton also clearly supposed that even if a judge—and the first and greatest judge of the realm is always the king himself[31]—has acquired facility in jurisprudence, he has no business ascending to the judgment seat unless he has also learnt to be just and what justice is.[32] Therefore, early in the *De legibus*, Bracton undertakes to demonstrate the nature of justice, if only to indicate the *moral* preconditions he thinks are requisite for the competent judge. In line with customary Roman legal usage, Bracton defines *iustitia* as 'constans et perpetua voluntas ius suum cuique tribuens'.[33] Justice thus conceived is an orientation of the *voluntas*,[34] which is to be found

---

[27] Post, 'Bracton on Kingship', p. 553.

[28] *De legibus*, II, 20.

[29] *Ibid.*, 25.

[30] *Ibid.*, 20.

[31] *Ibid.*, 33 and 304.

[32] *Ibid*, 21, 25, 306 and 307.

[33] *Ibid.*, 23; Bracton follows precisely at this point Azo's *Summa Institutionum*, which itself draws from the *Digest*.

[34] *De legibus*, II, 26.

'in mentibus iustorum',[35] existing as a virtue 'in anima'.[36] In short, it is Bracton's view that justice is a moral quality which inheres within those who are just, rather than some external standard or constraint imposed from without.

Bracton further identifies two sorts of justice: justice in the Creator and justice in the created.[37] Justice in the Creator, that is, God, we may wish to describe as justice in an absolute sense, since it is ultimately the case that 'auctor iustitiae est deus'.[38] Specifically, Bracton declares that divine

> iustitia sit dei dispositio, quae in omnibus rebus recte constituit et iuste disponit. Ipse enim deus tribuit unicuique secundum opera sua. Ipse non est variabilis neque temporalis in dispositionibus et voluntatibus suis, immo eius voluntas est constans et perpetua. Ipse enim non habuit principium, nec habet nec habebit finem.[39]

The justice contained within the divine will, Bracton maintains, is fixed and does not admit of variation. What God's *voluntas* determines to be just is eternally and immutably so, since his will cannot by its essence be other than a purely good will. It is this characteristic justice of the Creator, for instance, which allows him to judge the actions of men and to assign to them their appropriate deserts and punishments. In effect, the absolute justice of the divine will is the necessary attribute of God the Avenger, whose judgment is to be feared by all men, irrespective of rank, because He is a respecter of no man with regard to his earthly condition.[40] For those who escape their rightful judgment in this world, whether by virtue of position (like the king) or chance, will still have to confront the unfailingly just *voluntas* of God, who is utterly disposed to grant each his due in the afterlife.

Justice in created beings is of a similar quality, Bracton says, though not so absolutely or completely. Just men imitate the justice of the divine will; but because of human fallibility and vulnerability, they can never attain the singularly and permanently good *voluntas* which characterizes God's judgments. It is precisely because human justice 'imitates' (albeit imperfectly) the key features of divine justice that Bracton is able to speak recurrently of the king, and indeed of inferior magistrates, in terms of 'dei minister et vicarius',[41]

---

[35] *Ibid.*, 25.

[36] *Ibid.*, 27.

[37] *Ibid.*, 23.

[38] *Ibid.*, 22.

[39] *Ibid.*, 23.

[40] *Ibid.*, 32.

[41] *Ibid.*, 166 and 305.

as Jesus Christ's 'vices gerit in terris',[42] sitting 'in throno dei',[43] so that 'cor regis bene regentis dicitur esse in manu dei'.[44] While such phrases connecting the earthly monarch with the Eternal King appear frequently enough in patristic sources and medieval tracts,[45] Bracton's use of them conveys in particular the notion that the similitude of divine and royal wills is based on a common or shared principle of justice. It is in this sense that Bracton remarks,

> Ad hoc autem creatus est rex et electus, ut iustitiam faciat universis, et ipsum ut in eo dominus sedeat, et per ipsum sua judicia discernat . . . Potestas itaque sua iuris est non iniuria . . . Exercere igitur debet rex potestatem iuris sicut dei vicarius et minister in terra, quia illa potestas solius dei est, potestas autem iniuriae diaboli et non dei, et cuius horum opera fecerit rex eius minister erit cuius opera fecerit. Igitur dum facit iustitiam vicarius est regis aeterni, minister autem diaboli dum declinit ad iniuriam.[46]

By doing and giving justice, the temporal ruler conforms himself to and partakes of the justice which composes God's very existence. Precisely as the essence of the divine will is justice, in other words, so the mind and will of the king must be firmly fixed upon what is just if he is to be properly called a king at all. The salient feature of kingship on Bracton's account is the granting of justice to all subjects who may require it.[47] Hence, among men, the true king's *voluntas* must imitate and resemble most completely the absolutely good will of God himself.

But insofar as divine justice is a quasi-metaphysical attribute of God's being, while it is by no means 'natural' or essential to the souls of human beings *per se*, we are still left with the question of *how* the just man can be said to imitate the will of God. Bracton resolves this problem with the specification that in the human world,

> Dicitur iustitia *constans* secundum definitionem, prout iustitia est in creatura, ut per hoc quod dicit *voluntas* intellegatur mens, et per hoc

---

[42] *Ibid.*, 33.

[43] *Ibid.*, 20.

[44] *Ibid.*, 20 and 305.

[45] These uses are reviewed by Schulz, 'Bracton on Kingship', pp. 147–9.

[46] *De legibus*, II, 305.

[47] As Bracton insists in *De legibus*, II, 33, 304 and 305.

quod dicit *constans* intellegatur bonum. Constantia enim semper accipitur in bonum . . . Constantia enim non admittit variationem. Per hoc autem quod dicit *perpetua* intellegatur habitus, quia iustitia est habitus mentis bonus, vel mentis bene constitutae.[48]

Bracton reformulates here the elements of the general definition 'Iustitia est constans et perpetua voluntas ius suum cuique tribuens' into a description of the justice which specifically pertains to men as 'habitus mentis bonus'. But what is the significance of Bracton's introduction of the latter phrase? While not immediately apparent, the notion of 'habitus mentis bonus' has behind it a long and important tradition which has been insufficiently appreciated in the scholarship on Bracton. Indeed, if properly understood, Bracton's inclusion of the statement 'Iustitia est habitus mentis bonus' in the *De legibus* provides the foundations for the moral obligation placed upon the king to observe the law. We ought thus to turn briefly to a reconstruction of the tradition on which this expression rested.

The Latin term *habitus* (often rendered, erroneously, into English as 'habit') represents a translation of the Greek word *hexis*, which is commonly reproduced in English as 'habit', 'condition', 'characteristic', and more accurately, as 'state' or 'disposition'. *Hexis* formed a key part of the conceptual and linguistic apparatus of Aristotle's philosophy, and especially his moral thought. As a general precept, Aristotle conceives of *hexis* as a type of quality, that is, as a way of ascribing a qualitative property to a subject or substance. Specifically, *hexis* is the term employed by Aristotle to denote those qualities which become so firmly rooted in that which they qualify that they form virtually a 'second nature', and are accordingly difficult (if not impossible) to change. In the *Nicomachean Ethics*, Aristotle maintains that '*hexis* is the genus of virtue' and that 'the virtues are *hexeis*', that is, fixed dispositions for action acquired by habituation.[49] Aristotle's appeal to *hexis* with regard to his ethical theory arises in response to a problem stemming from his denial that one is born with anything more than a natural *capacity* for virtue.[50] For if such is the case, how is it that moral goodness persists among men? In other words, how is it that the truly good man becomes and always remains virtuous in his conduct and sentiment despite external changes of fortune and circumstance? By addressing virtue in terms of *hexis*, Aristotle is

---

[48] *Ibid.*, 23.

[49] Aristotle, *Nicomachean Ethics*, 1106a14 and 1143b24–25. Translations into English from the Greek will be mine unless otherwise noted, and will be based on the Loeb edition of the Aristotelian corpus.

[50] Aristotle, *Nicomachean Ethics*, 1106a7–13 and Aristotle, *Topics*, 126a30–b3.

able to construct the foundations for the relative permanence and stability of the virtue of the good man without resorting to arguments about nature. This is so because the virtues are acquired by exposure to and practise of virtuous conduct; performing virtuous acts so as to render a course of action habitual constitutes the basis for a proper moral education.[51] In turn, evolving the right moral habits, and becoming good thereby, is a matter of moulding one's *hexeis*, since '*hexeis* develop from corresponding activities' and 'the quality of our *hexeis* depends on what we do'.[52] It is as a result of this connection between moral action and *hexis*, then, that virtue is said to spring 'from a firm and unchangeable character'.[53] For a man whose *hexeis* have disposed him towards good conduct will always and forever do what is virtuous; the *hexeis* he has developed will in effect prohibit him from committing uncharacteristic (*viz.* immoral) acts. This leads us to the underlying import of Aristotle's definition of virtue as a settled *hexis*.[54] The genuinely good man, Aristotle says, 'judges everything correctly; what things truly are, that they seem to him to be, in every department . . . What chiefly distinguishes the good man is that he sees the truth in each kind, being himself the standard and measure.'[55] The sovereignty of such a morally good man depends crucially for Aristotle upon the fact that moral character itself is 'something permanent and not easily subject to change'.[56] Otherwise, the good man might be able to alter his characteristic conduct and act in a fashion inconsistent with virtue, in which case Aristotle could never treat him as the 'standard and measure' of virtuousness. The function of guaranteeing the stability and fixity of the moral attributes of the good man, in short, Aristotle assigns to the concept of *hexis*.

The Aristotelian notion of *hexis* was transmitted to the Latin Middle Ages prior to the recovery and translation of the *Nicomachean Ethics*, and was associated specifically with the idea of justice, by the agency of at least two distinct sources. The first was Aristotle himself, who spoke about the ethical dimensions of *hexis* in both the *Categories* and the *Topics*, Latin versions of which were widely accessible to authors during the High Middle Ages. Not

---

[51] Aristotle, *Nicomachean Ethics*, 1103a31–33 and 1103b1–3.

[52] *Ibid.*, 103b22–24.

[53] *Ibid.*, 1105a35–b1.

[54] *Ibid.*, 1106b36.

[55] Aristotle, *Nicomachean Ethics*, trans. H. Rackham (Cambridge, Mass., 2nd edn., 1934), slightly revised, 1113a30–34.

[56] *Ibid.*, 1102b.

only did these translated works expressly and repeatedly define virtue in terms of *habitus*,[57] and more particularly refer to *iustitia* as *habitus*,[58] but they further explained that *habitus* itself entailed a quality which was 'permanentior et diunturnitor'.[59] Commenting on the unique features which delineate *habitus* from other sorts of attributes, Aristotle states in the *Categories*, 'Similiter autem et in aliis, nisi forte in his quoque contingit per temporis longitudinem in naturam cuiusque translata et insanabilis vel difficile mobilis, quam iam quilibet habitudinem vocet.'[60] Thus, Aristotle clearly conveys that what is essential to any quality described as a *habitus* is its relative permanence and fixity over time, rendering it resistent to flux or alteration.

The other classical author who contributed to the transmission of this idea of *habitus* as a moral construct was Cicero. Although the principle of *habitus* does not appear in Cicero's mature ethical thought, a youthful essay on rhetoric, the *De inventione*, which was commonly read and cited in the Middle Ages, employed the term in an overtly Aristotelian sense. Cicero declares there that 'nam virtus est animi habitus naturae modo atque rationi consentaneus'.[61] Earlier in the same text, he had proposed that 'habitum autem appellamus animi aut corporis constantem et absolutam aliqua in re perfectionem, ut virtutis aut artis alicuius perceptionem aut quamvis scientiam et item corporis aliquam commoditatem non natura datam.'[62] Cicero, indeed, emphasizes the relation of *habitus* thus understood to the particular cardinal virtue of justice: 'Iustitia est habitus animi.'[63] In effect, the *De inventione* reproduces the essential features of Aristotle's account of *hexis* as an ethical doctrine. *Habitus* for Cicero expresses the constant, even quasi-natural, orientation of the soul towards virtue and especially justice.

There is no evidence, of course, that Bracton ever read either Aristotle or Cicero. But among the acknowledged sources of the *De legibus* are several

[57] See Aristotle, *Categories*, 8b29; and Aristotle, *Topics*, 121b27–39, 144a16 and 144a17–18.

[58] As in Aristotle, *Categories*, 8b33–35.

[59] *Ibid.*, 8b28; the Latin translation is that of Boethius, which was available throughout the Middle Ages, and which is printed in *Aristoteles Latinus*, ed. L. Minio-Paluello (Bruges-Paris, 1961), Vol. 1, parts 1–5.

[60] Aristotle, *Categories*, 9a2–4; Boethius trans.

[61] Cicero, *De inventione*, II, 50, 159; references are to the Loeb edition of H.M. Hubbell (Cambridge, Mass., 1961).

[62] *Ibid.*, I, 25, 36; a similar claim is asserted at II, 9, 30.

[63] *Ibid.*, II, 50, 160.

which drew directly upon either the *Organon* or the *De inventione* in their use of *habitus*. Medieval glossators, for instance, regularly referred to *habitus* in their discussions of *iustitia*, citing for their authority Cicero.[64] In the *Glossa Ordinaria*, we find *iustitia* described in terms of 'quasi habitus mentis bonus. Sed Tullius sic definit: "Iustitia est habitus animi".' Similarly, Azo in his *Summa Institutionum*, which provided the prototype for Bracton in the *De legibus*, declared that 'iustitia est habitus mentis bonus vel bene constitutae'. And the *Quaestiones de iuris subtilitatibus*, probably composed in the late twelfth century by Placentius,[65] commented, 'Michi visa est ineffabili dignitatis habitu Iustitia.' Through the transitional figure of Cicero, then, the glossators disseminated the Aristotelian principle of *hexis/habitus* to medieval Europe, and thence to Bracton.

But what assurance have we that Bracton, so far from parroting the words of his Roman Law masters, actually understood the Aristotelian significance of the association of *iustitia* with *habitus mentis bonus*? Beyond the internal evidence of the *De legibus*, where Bracton explicitly equates *habitus mentis bonus* with 'perpetua voluntas', there is a further source for his awareness of the full meaning of *habitus*. In the mid-twelfth century moral and political advice-book to princes, known as the *Policraticus*, John of Salisbury had asserted that

> Mos autem est mentis habitus ex quo singulorum operum assiduitas manat. Non enim si quid fit semel aut amplius, statim moribus aggregatur, nisi assiduitate faciendi veratur in usam . . . Cum itaque a moribus quis reverentiam contrahere dicitur, ei virtutes, quibus honor exihendus est, inesse significatur. Quid enim non veneretur et vereatur illum quem prudentem fortem temperantem credit et iustum.[66]

John thus possessed a clear insight into the Aristotelian conception of *habitus*: each manner of virtue (including justice) is a *habitus* from which flows a constancy and permanency of conduct, acquired by repeated practise of certain sorts of actions. It seems quite probable that John of Salisbury's use of *habitus*, among other Aristotelian ideas, reflected his immediate familiarity with the Latin translations of Aristotle's *Categories* and *Topics*, rather than his reading of an intermediary source.[67] But more to the point at present,

---

[64] The sources for the following passages from the glossators are to be found in Kantorowicz, *The King's Two Bodies*, p. 108, note 59.

[65] The arguments for Placentius' authorship of this tract are presented by *ibid.*, p. 107, note 57.

[66] John of Salisbury, *Policraticus*, 544d–545a.

[67] This is the argument of Cary J. Nederman and J. Brückmann, 'Aristotelianism in John of Salisbury's *Policraticus*', *Journal of the History of Philosophy*, 21 (April 1983), pp. 203–29.

commentators have definitively identified the influence of the *Policraticus* in the *De legibus*; so many of Bracton's views (such as the distinction between king and tyrant)[68] have their origins in passages of the *Policraticus* that no doubt remains about his direct exposure to that work.[69] Hence, we may be assured that when Bracton employed the definition of *iustitia* as a *habitus mentis bonus*, the significance he would have attached to *habitus* bore a striking resemblance to Aristotle's original concept of *hexis*.

It should be evident, then, that Bracton's equation of the good will of the just man with 'habitus mentis bonus, vel mentis bene constitutae' contains far-reaching implications for his notion of human justice. The just man on Bracton's account is he who has justice so firmly implanted in his mind (or soul) that his will is perpetually disposed towards the performance of just deeds. Justice in this way forms an inhering quality of the mind which is not readily lost or suppressed. Consequently, the Bractonian appeal to *habitus* established decisively that the truly good and just *voluntas* is not fickle, subject to drastic fluctuations and alterations, but instead is characterized by a certain predictability and consistency of orientation and action. When applied specifically to the condition of the royal will, this principle eliminates many of the difficulties surrounding the basis of the moral obligation incumbent upon the king. For if *voluntas* is understood by reference to *habitus mentis*, then the ruler can be expected, in the absence of external constraint, to bridle himself and resist injustice by a self-imposed and purely internal moral disposition. The will, in other words, is never the source of wholly arbitrary action; the king's conduct always involves, rather, the disclosure or manifestation of the justice and virtuousness which is an abiding attribute of his soul. Hence, Bracton's supposition that the monarch could ordinarily be counted on to correct *iniuria* through the exercise of his *voluntas* in a just cause[70] does not appear so unreasonable as it might on first reckoning. The king's good will, conceived as a *habitus mentis bonus*, becomes such a fixed and nearly intransigent quality of his soul that the performance of just actions is like second nature to him.

Yet this solution is still incomplete. For part of our initial problem has not been addressed: how does the ruler's resolute moral disposition towards justice specifically inform his obligation to observe the law of the realm? Like

---

[68] This distinction is to be found in *De legibus*, II, 305.

[69] See Schulz, 'Bracton on Kingship', pp. 153, 164–5; Lewis, 'King Above Law?', p. 260, note 57; and Fesefeldt, *Englische Staatstheories de 13. Jahrhunderts*, pp. 45–50.

[70] Which is clearly stated in *De legibus*, II, 33, 109–10 and III, 43.

most of his medieval counterparts, and in sharp contradistinction to modern 'positivist' notions of law, Bracton posited an intimate relationship between legislation and justice. Since it is Bracton's view that 'ius ergo derivatur a iustitia',[71] and in addition that 'ius et lex idem significant',[72] a soundly constructed bridge links what is just with what is lawful. This close connection between law and justice indeed recurs throughout the *De legibus*. 'Si autem leges [defecerint], sic exterminabitur iustitia',[73] Bracton remarks in his opening paragraph; without law and custom, 'non poterit quis esse iustus, ut faciat iustitiam et iustum iudicium.'[74] Bracton's argument is *not* that justice is an attribute of law *per se*; he stipulates, as we have already seen, that justice pertains to the mind or soul of the just man. Rather, the *De legibus* maintains that no law may truly be so called which is not in accordance with the dictates of justice: 'lex . . . specialiter significat sanctionem iustam, iubentem honesta, prohibentem contraria'.[75] It is precisely this conformity of law with the principle of justice that would lead the king, upon whom no bridle may be imposed, to follow carefully the legal precepts ordained in his kingdom. For because his will is construed as a *habitus mentis* to act justly, and the law is designed on the pattern of justice, hence the monarch is morally disposed towards obedience to law. The element of compulsion derives from the essential character of the just man, whose possession of a *habitus mentis bonus* orients him constitutionally towards goodness. Such a characteristically good man cannot, on the Aristotelian account of *hexis/habitus* adopted by Bracton, do other than virtuous and just deeds, which are the very sort of deeds commanded by law. The king may be expected to submit to the law without external constraint, then, because the justice embodied therein is congruent with the fixed and unshakable quality of justice inscribed upon his soul.

The details surrounding the acquisition of this royal trait of justice constitute a matter for which Bracton shows little concern, beyond passing references to such wisdom as may be learnt or divinely granted.[76] It is no doubt significant that Bracton's brief description of the wisdom which leads to justice closely parallels the account of John of Salisbury's *Policraticus*.[77] For Bracton, while repeatedly objecting to the ascension of those 'minus sapiens et indoctus' to the judgment seat,[78] feels competent only to instruct in the

---

[71] *Ibid.*, II, 23.

[72] *Ibid.*, 22.

[73] *Ibid.*, 19.

[74] *Ibid.*, 23.

[75] *Ibid.*, 22.

[76] *Ibid.*, 306; also see 21.

[77] *Ibid.*, 306–7.

[78] *Ibid.*, 19, 21 and 307.

technique of *iuris prudentia*, which is 'iusti atque iniusti scientia'.[79] Education in virtues like justice, on the other hand, he implicitly leaves to whichever wise and faithful men (and perhaps also books) may tutor and counsel the prince. Quite regardless of how the king acquires his characteristic orientation towards justice, however, Bracton's point stands that there is no need to compel the obedience of the monarch. Rather, the prince complies out of a deeply rooted and firmly implanted disposition to do justice, which will always be congruent with the 'sanctionem iustam' of law. It is unnecessary to place 'external' controls on an individual who is so 'internally' in control of himself.

In this way, moreover, we arrive at a comprehensive interpretation of Bracton's claim that the king's power extends only to what is in accordance with the law. Bracton declares in one passage that 'non est enim rex ubi dominatur voluntas et non lex'.[80] Elsewhere the *De legibus* asserts that 'nihil enim aliud potest rex . . . nisi ad solum quod de iure potest', such that he 'temperet igitur potentiam suam per legem quae frenum est potentiae, quod secundum leges vivat.'[81] Bracton is not merely maintaining here that because the king's power is derived from law, he must subject himself to it, as Ernst Kantorowicz supposed;[82] nor is Bracton saying that the king is only king legitimately and definitionally when he observes the law. On the contrary, the justice inhering in the soul of the monarch, which disposes him to the performance of just deeds and lawful judgment, is completely ingrained in him to the extent that he is incapable of action not in conformity with justice and law. The force of the law, as an expression of justice, is moral, instead of legal-coercive, for the king; but the moral stricture is utterly compelling and irresistible. The king's powerlessness to do what is unlawful or injurious is purely a function of the *moral* resolve stemming from his *mentis habitus bonus*. Recall that to be in possession of a *habitus* is to be so thoroughly oriented towards certain sorts of action that it is effectively impossible to behave uncharacteristically (at least within the realm of intentional conduct).[83] In the case of the king specifically, who is king insofar as he imitates the justice of the divine will, it is beyond the power arising from his moral state

---

[79] *Ibid.*, 25.

[80] *Ibid.*, 33.

[81] *Ibid.*, 305.

[82] Kantorowicz, *The King's Two Bodies*, p. 151.

[83] Bracton himself recognizes the corollary to *voluntas* (and hence, *mentis habitus*) is intention: 'Affectio quidem tua nomen imponit operi tuo' (*De legibus*, II, 23).

to perform unjust deeds. And since violation of legal statute constitutes exactly such an unjust deed, it is not within the power of the royal *voluntas* to disobey the law. Hence, the 'internal' fixity of a *habitus* is more constraining than even 'external' considerations like sworn oaths or fear of a vengeful God; even if the latter elements were not present, the just king would always conduct himself according to the justice contained within his soul. The ruler does what the law commands because the orientation of his characteristically good will, understood as a *habitus mentis bonus*, dictates that he cannot do otherwise.

Bracton's reliance on an essentially Aristotelian principle of moral psychology, even though he was not a philosopher and enjoyed no direct access to Aristotle's writings, should not surprise us. For the Aristotelian influence during the Middle Ages was considerably more pervasive and subtle than is ordinarily credited. In matter of fact, for all the talk of the dramatic 'recovery' and 'revival' of Aristotle's thought between roughly 1150 and 1250,[84] there had survived throughout medieval times an 'underground' tradition of Aristotelian learning, transmitted through the few translated works of the *Organon* and those classical and early Christian authors (like Cicero and Boethius) who drew upon his concepts and vocabulary.[85] In much the same way as the glossators and John of Salisbury, Bracton was heir to this 'underground' tradition which by his own day had become an ingrained feature of the intellectual world of the West. It may not be an exaggeration to say that the Middle Ages knew two Aristotles: one was present throughout medieval times, if only in dim awareness; the other was disseminated rapidly beginning in the twelfth century and forced medieval thinkers to re-evaluate their cherished orthodoxies. It is ultimately crucial to the comprehension of the intellectual contours of medieval Europe, as well as of the place of particular authors such as Bracton, that we establish how these 'two Aristotles' complemented and perhaps contradicted each other. While this

[84] Typical of this attitude is Walter Ullmann, *Medieval Political Thought* (Harmondsworth, 1975), p. 159: 'The influence of Aristotle from the second half of the thirteenth century onwards wrought a transmutation in thought that amounts to a conceptual revolution. In fact and in theory the Aristotelian avalanche in the thirteenth century marks the watershed between the Middle Ages and the modern period.' Similar remarks may be found, for example, in Steven Ozment, *The Age of Reform, 1250–1550* (New Haven, 1980), p. 7, and Frederick Copleston, *A History of Philosophy: Late Medieval and Renaissance Philosophy*, Part II (Garden City, NY, 1963), p. 238.

[85] A slightly enlarged defense of this position is undertaken in Nederman and Brückmann, 'Aristotelianism in John of Salisbury's *Policraticus*', pp. 237–9 and notes 96–99. What is in fact required, of course, is a magisterial study of the impact of the 'underground' Aristotle in the Middle Ages, with particular emphasis on the ethical and political concepts of Aristotelian provenance which were conveyed through this 'tradition' to medieval thinkers.

project falls outside the narrow confines of the present paper, the appearance and importance of an Aristotelian component in Bracton's *De legibus et consuetudinibus angliae* illustrates the need for a more accurate and thorough study of Aristotle's influence during the Christian Middle Ages as a whole.

Kings, Peers, and Parliament: Virtue and Corulership in Walter Burley's *Commentarius in VIII Libros Politicorum Aristotelis*[*]

Although he was one of the most eminent philosophers of the early fourteenth century,[1] Walter Burley has seldom attracted much attention for his contributions to political theory.[2] To some extent, this neglect may be blamed on the unfortunate history of the dissemination of Burley's major political work, the *Commentarius in VIII Libros Politicorum Aristotelis* (composed between 1338 and 1343).[3] While widely circulated during the later Middle Ages, a fact indicated

[*]This essay was composed in honor of the retirement of Neal Wood as Professor of Political Science at York University. An earlier version was presented at the 1991 meeting of the Canadian Political Science Association in Kingston, Ontario and benefitted from the comments of Professors Bob Fenn and James Moore. Thanks are also due to the anonymous readers for *Albion* for their helpful suggestions.

[1]For an outline of Burley's life and career as we know it, see Conor Martin, "Walter Burley," *Oxford Studies Presented to Daniel Callus* (Oxford, 1964), pp. 194-230. The best general examination of Burley's philosophical contributions is Agustin Uña Juarez, *Aristotles en siglo XIV: La Tecnica Comentaristica de Walter Burley al "Corpus Aristotelicum"* (Madrid, 1978).

[2]Within the "classic" histories of Western political thought in the Middle Ages, Burley is unnamed, as documented by S. Harrison Thomson, "Walter Burley's Commentary on the *Politics* of Aristotle," *Melanges Auguste Pelzer* (Louvain, 1947), p. 562. Among more recent works of scholarship, a similar lack of attention is apparent. There is no mention of Burley in such survey works as: Walter Ullmann, *Principles of Government and Politics in the Middle Ages* (London, 1961); John B. Morrall, *Political Thought in Medieval Times* (New York, 1962); and, more recently, Arthur P. Monahan, *Consent, Coercion and Limit: The Medieval Origins of Parliamentary Democracy* (Kingston and Montréal, 1987). In the massive *Cambridge History of Medieval Political Thought*, ed. J. H. Burns (Cambridge, 1988), Burley merits only a single brief mention (pp. 485-86).

[3]This dating of the *Commentarius* is offered by Lowrie J. Daly, "The Conclusions of Walter Burley's Commentary on the *Politics*, Books I to IV," *Manuscripta* 12 (1968): 80. Burley also addresses some issues related to political theory in his own *Expositio super decem libros Ethicorum Aristotelis* (Venice, 1498). Moreover, in the *Commentarius* Burley refers to a "tractatus de regno" (see below note 17), which Thomson, "Walter Burley's Commentary," takes to refer to "some work he planned to write," but that "it seems safe to assume...remained only a plan and a hope" (p. 577). This has been disputed, however, by Lowrie J. Daly, "Walter Burley and John Wyclif on Some Aspects of Kingship," *Melanges Eugénes Tisserant*, 4 vols. (The Vatican, 1964), 4: 169 n17, who wonders "if Burley could simply have meant his 'tractatus tertius' of the third book of the *Politics* that he describes as a 'tractatus specialiter de regno.'" While Daly's interpretation remains implausible—since the context for the reference is Burley's discussion of the king's calling of Parliament, which is never addressed in the commentary on Book Three—the real meaning of the citation will probably never be known short of the discovery of a "de regno" (or mirror of rulers) treatise that can be safely ascribed to Burley's hand.

by the large number of extant manuscripts,[4] the *Commentarius* did not follow Burley's other commentaries on Aristotle's writings into print during the late fifteenth and early sixteenth centuries.[5] To my knowledge, no satisfactory explanation has ever been adduced for this lacuna, but it has not been rectified to the present day; a printed edition of the *Commentarius*, based either on a single manuscript or a critical examination of all the manuscripts, has yet to appear. This absence of a printed version of the text is especially inexplicable in view of the rarity of commentaries on the *Politics* prior to the end of the fourteenth century.[6]

Another reason that the name of Walter Burley remains unfamiliar to all but a few specialists on medieval political thought might be the very nature of the conventions within which he was writing. It is true generally speaking that the commentary genre was not conducive to highly innovative thought; the commentator was too closely bound by the text that he was glossing.[7] In the case of Burley's *Commentarius*, this tendency away from independent philosophical inquiry may have been exacerbated by several factors. First, his text draws heavily upon the thirteenth-century commentary on the *Politics* begun by Thomas Aquinas and completed by Peter of Auvergne, and indeed it seems sometimes to be as much a summary of the views of Thomas/Peter as a direct examination of Aristotle.[8] Second, Burley's work is characterized by greater brevity than other, comparable commentaries of the period, so that it demonstrates less inclination to criticize or expand upon specific Aristotelian

[4]A manuscript census was attempted by Thomson, "Walter Burley's Commentary," p. 564, which he admits is not complete (pp. 564-65 n30). It was supplemented by Anneliese Maier, "Zu Walter Burley's Politik-Kommentar," *Recherches de Theologie ancienne et medievale* 14 (1947): 332-36 and by Jean-Philippe Genet, "The Dissemination of Manuscripts Relating to English Political Thought in the Fourteenth Century," in *England and her Neighbours*, ed. M. Jones and M. Vale (London, 1989), pp. 218-19, 232. There may be as many as 40 extant manuscripts of the *Commentarius*. In the present essay, I shall be citing (with corrections) from the version in MS. Balliol 95, ff. 161^r-232^r.

[5]Thomson, "Walter Burley's Commentary," pp. 560-61.

[6]For the development of the commentary tradition on the *Politics*, see: Martin Grabmann, *Die mittelalterlichen Kommentare zur Politik des Aristoteles* (Munich, 1941); F. Edward Cranz, "Aristotelianism in Medieval Political Theory: A Study of the Reception of the Politics" (Ph.D. diss., Harvard University, 1940); Conor Martin, "The Commentaries on the Politics of Aristotle in the Late Thirteenth and Early Fourteenth Centuries" (Ph.D. diss., University of Oxford, 1949); Martin, "Some Medieval Commentaries on Aristotle's *Politics*," *History* 36 (February & June 1951): 29-44; Jean Dunbabin, "Aristotle in the Schools," in *Trends in Medieval Political Thought*, ed. B. Smalley (Oxford, 1965), pp. 65-85; and Dunbabin, "The Reception and Interpretation of Aristotle's *Politics*," in *The Cambridge History of Later Medieval Philosophy* ed. N. Kretzmann, A. Kenny and J. Pinborg (Cambridge, 1982), pp. 723-37.

[7]Martin, "Some Medieval Commentaries," pp. 34-35.

[8]This influence is documented by Daly, "Walter Burley and John Wyclif," pp. 179-83.

doctrines. Finally, Burley apparently designed his commentary more as a piece of pedagogical exegesis than as a work of advanced scholarship. The manner in which it is organized, and especially its reliance upon lists of *quaestiones principales, propositiones notabiliores* and *conclusiones,*[9] suggest that it was primarily intended as an instructional aid for Masters of Arts candidates who were grappling with basic comprehension of the *Politics*. Thus, while helpful in giving us "a good insight into what the medieval professor thought was important for the student of Aristotle's *Politics* to know and understand,"[10] the *Commentarius* might easily be construed as simply a textbook, concerned with clear and concise exposition of its topic instead of novel argumentation.

When Burley's *Commentarius* has been singled out, then, the reasons have been other than because of its theoretical substance. In particular, the work has attracted attention for its relatively developed awareness of current events. Burley is regularly cited as an important exception to the lament of historians of political thought that scholastic political writing is wholly bereft of explicit political content or reference to contemporary issues.[11] Robert Eccleshall concludes that "it is not too fanciful to interpret this statement of Aristotelianism as the philosophical justification of what was in practice occurring."[12] And Jean Dunbabin observes that its direct appeal to English circumstances renders Burley's *Commentarius* "original" in spite of its otherwise heavy reliance upon the Thomas/Peter version.[13] It might be argued that reference to historical conditions simply underscores the instructional origins of the work: Walter incorporated concrete examples into his own lectures in order to make the ideas of the *Politics* seem more relevant to his students. This would certainly be in line with his general attitude towards historical illustrations. Near the close of his commentary on Book Four, for instance, he states that he has deleted all of Aristotle's historical examples because they were unfamiliar to him: "Yet since examples from the deeds of the Greeks and other remote nations are not known to us, and since we employ examples on account of gaining knowledge, I have not bothered to employ those of his examples from which we would not be

---

[9]The method of the *Commentarius* is described by Thomson, "Walter Burley's Commentary," pp. 567-69 and Lowrie J. Daly, "Some Notes on Walter Burley's Commentary on the Politics," in *Essays in Medieval History Presented to Bertie Wilkinson*, ed. T. A. Sandquist and M. R. Powicke (Toronto, 1969), pp. 276-79.

[10]Ibid., p. 281.

[11]Thomson, "Walter Burley's Commentary," p. 574; Martin, "Some Medieval Commentaries," p. 39; and Lowrie J. Daly, "The Conclusions of Walter Burley's *Commentary* on the *Politics*, Books V and VI," *Manuscripta* 13 (1969), p. 144.

[12]Robert Eccleshall, *Order and Reason in Politics* (Oxford, 1978), p. 71.

[13]Dunbabin, "The Reception and Interpretation of Aristotle's *Politics*," pp. 729-30.

able to gain a better understanding."[14] The pedagogical value of concrete case studies, Burley apparently believes, is constrained by the availability of independent knowledge about their historical context.

Unfortunately, while scholars have highlighted Burley's use of examples drawn from contemporary history, they have also consistently treated these references as mere curiosities or aberrations rather than as features of a systematic theoretical framework.[15] The present essay proposes to challenge this approach to Burley's political theory by arguing that the *Commentarius* presents a unique and coherent vision of politics that employs the experiences of fourteenth-century England as a guide to the reinterpretation and reconstruction of Aristotelian doctrines. In particular, I will claim that Walter injects into his presentation of the optimal royal constitution precisely the cooperative spirit of politics as a joint enterprise between the king and the nobility that formed the core of medieval English practices. This cooperative spirit manifests itself in the *Commentarius* as a theory of corulership, by means of which Burley reformulates the very nature of royal virtue itself. Moreover, I will also argue that Burley's thought constitutes an important stage in the general course of the development of the tradition of political theory in medieval England.

I

Two passages of the *Commentarius* have commanded most of the attention and discussion that scholars have directed to the historical dimension of the text. We encounter the first of these in the midst of Burley's analysis of *Politics* 1282b1-13, which addresses the extent to which personal rule is necessary to supplement the "sovereignty of law" because of the "difficulty of framing general rules for all circumstances."[16] There is an apparent contradiction in Aristotle's text, insofar as he has just argued (1282a38-42) that the people should enjoy rights of judgement over their leaders and yet proceeds to claim at 1282b3 that "supremacy" may pertain to either "a single ruler or a body of rulers." Burley attempts to explain this ostensive inconsistency by asserting that even monarchic regimes are not strictly constituted by the rule of a single individual independent of a people:

> It is understood that in just constitutions other than kingdoms a multitude rules and this is many men; and even in a kingdom, a multitude, constituted by the king and nobles and wise men of the kingdom, in certain measure rules. Consequently, such a multitude rules as much or more than the king alone, and on account of this the

---

[14]MS. Balliol 95, f. 198ᵛ: "...tamen quia exempla de factis Grecorum et nationum remotarum non sunt nobis nota, et exempla ponimus propter noticiam habendam non curam ponere exempla sua per quae non poterimus melius cognitionem habere."

[15]For instance, Thomson, "Walter Burley's Commentary," p. 577 terms them "a few interesting details."

[16]In the present essay, I shall follow the Greek edition of the *Politics* by H. Rackham (Cambridge, Mass., 1932); translations will be mine.

king convokes parliament for the expediting of arduous business. This is made clearer in the treatise on kingship.[17]

Burley's reference to Parliament is, to my knowledge, the earliest mention by a scholastic philosopher of that assembly, although the term had long been in use within administrative and legal documents in England and throughout Europe.[18] For this reason if no other it deserves special attention.

Scholars have been frankly perplexed, however, by Burley's remark. Jean Dunbabin, for instance, states that "it is difficult to know what to make of this. It may be that Burley read this whole passage in the *Politics* as an argument for power-sharing and broadly-based government rather than for the participation of the man in the street; but it is also possible that he believed Parliament to be in some way representative of the people, offering them participation, although very indirectly, in the *ordo principatus* that is the life of the state. But Burley's terse style leaves his real meaning a mystery."[19] For Dunbabin, at least, Burley is potentially sympathetic to a genuinely populist conception of government. Yet the text itself seems quite straightforward in this regard: the multitude to which he refers is identical to the king in conjunction with the other members of Parliament, that is, the magnates and similarly qualified persons. His conception of Parliament is not, admittedly, very advanced in relation to mid-fourteenth-century practices. Where the English Parliament by that time had become a regularized and broad-ranging, as well as widely representative, institution, Burley's assembly is more reminiscent of the baronial *parliamentum* of the thirteenth century. Such early parliaments, composed solely of the great temporal and spiritual lords of the realm, were called (in the words of a 1242 summons) to "treat" with the king "concerning arduous business of ours which especially touch the state of us and of all our realm."[20] But lest Burley's use of the term appear anachronistic, it should be stressed that the composition and functions of parliamentary assemblies were by no means fixed even in Burley's day. The meaning of "Parliament" he chooses to employ would have made perfect sense to his contemporaries and, moreover, fit best as an example in the context of

[17]MS. Balliol 95, f. 182^r: "Intelligendum quod in rectis principatibus aliis a regno principatur multitudo et hoc est plures et adhuc in regno multitudo constitut ex rege et proceribus et saepientibus regni quodammodo principatur. Itaque tantum vel magis principatur huiusmodi multitudo quam rex solus, et propter hoc rex convocat parliamentum pro arduis negociis expediendis. Ista magis patebunt in tractatu de regno."

[18]G. O. Sayles, *The King's Parliament of England* (London, 1975), pp. 21-34 and Antonio Marongiu, *Medieval Parliaments: A Comparative Study*, trans. S. J. Woolf (London, 1968), pp. 48-54.

[19]Dunbabin, "The Reception and Interpretation of Aristotle's *Politics*," p. 730.

[20]Cited in *Constitutional History of Medieval England, 1216–1399*, ed. B. Wilkinson, 3 vols. (London, 1958), 3: 301. On this early meaning of *parliamentum*, see Sayles, *The King's Parliament of England*, pp. 35-47.

his commentary on *Politics* 1282b. For his very point is to illustrate how, even when the law is generally sovereign, there are special circumstances when a statute is necessarily uncertain or imprecise and thus when a personal judgement is required. Whatever other tasks are associated with it, Parliament is the body through which any unforeseeable cases must be addressed and resolved by those in a monarchic regime qualified to judge.

More troublesome is Burley's apparent conviction that monarchy is not strictly speaking the rule of a single person at all, but rather of a king who shares supreme discretionary power (by means of the institution of Parliament) with the important and wise men of his realm. Hence, the king in Parliament enjoys greater authority than the king acting alone. This position, while perhaps fitting uncomfortably with Aristotle's views, is profoundly consonant with the realities of royal government in medieval England. Historians have long ago abandoned the claim that the English Parliament arose in opposition to or as a check upon the king's power. Instead, it seems more accurate to characterize Parliament as an expression of the "partnership" or "cooperative spirit" that infused the relationship between royal household and the English feudal aristocracy.[21] To be sure, the Crown viewed Parliament as an effective means of maintaining the support of its nobility, and the lords for their part regarded Parliament as a conduit for communicating grievances directly to the king. But on both sides, the primary intent of parliamentary conclaves appears to have been the promotion and enhancement of the collective stake which all had in the smooth operation of royal government. Burley gives voice to this typically English belief that the king's governance is a joint enterprise in which all the great men of the kingdom ought to play a role.

On the face of it, Burley's reference to Parliament in his commentary on 1282b stands in stark contrast to his other well-known remark about contemporary English politics, his so-called "eulogy" to King Edward III. At *Politics* 1284b29-34, Aristotle proclaimed that insofar as the man of genuinely pre-eminent goodness should never be subject to the rule of any person of lesser virtue, all others who reside in his polis ought to "pay willing obedience to him" by making him their "king for all time."[22] Aristotle then proceeds to describe the

---

[21]This point is stressed by, for instance, W. M. Ormrod, *The Reign of Edward III: Crown and Political Society in England 1327-1377* (New Haven, 1990), pp. 200-02; Michael Prestwich, *The Three Edwards: War and State in England, 1272-1377* (London, 1980), p. 146; David C. Douglas, *The Norman Achievement, 1050-1100* (Berkeley, 1969), pp. 86, 95 and 113-14; Maurice Keen, *England in the Later Middle Ages* (London, 1973), pp. 12-13; Bertie Wilkinson, "The 'Political Revolution' of the Thirteenth and Fourteenth Centuries in England," *Speculum* 24 (1949): 502-03; and G. L. Harriss, "The Formation of Parliament 1272-1377," in *The English Parliament in the Middle Ages*, ed. R. Davies and J. Denton (Manchester, 1981), pp. 29-60.

[22]For an elaboration of Aristotle's own position on kingship, see W. R. Newell, "Superlative Virtue: The Problem of Monarchy in Aristotle's 'Politics,'" *Western Political Quarterly* 40 (1987): 159-78.

forms of kingship and to analyze the strengths and limitations of the monarchic constitution. Burley, who served on occasion as an envoy for Edward III,[23] takes this opportunity to lavish praise upon the English king:

> For in the best regime each person counts himself as greatly honored on account of such a ruler exceeding others in the goodness of virtue, and each loves his rank and is content; and each individually desires the honor of the king, and it seems to him that he reigns in the king and with the king; and because of the deepest love of citizens for the king, there is the deepest concord amongst the citizens and the kingdom is very strong, as today is evident from the case of the king of the English, on account of whose exceeding virtue there is the greatest concord among the English people because each is content with his rank under the king.[24]

It may be tempting to dismiss this remark as merely another example of the convention of the encomium to which medieval political authors commonly subscribed, especially in light of the conflicts between Edward III and Bishop Stafford that characterized the period during which the *Commentarius* was written. But W. M. Ormrod has recently observed that "the development of a new community of interests between crown and people" during Edward's reign "can be seen as early in the 1340s in the writings of the Oxford philosopher Walter Burley, who argued that every Englishman, according to his own degree, 'ruled in and with the king.'"[25] Beyond considerations of historical verisimilitude, Burley makes an important theoretical point: rather than simply lauding the personal virtue of his monarch, he proposes that direct political consequences flow from the virtuosity of the king. Specifically, a king of excellence unites his people: they love each other because they love him, and therefore the realm is free of strife. Moreover, Burley makes it quite clear that these "citizens" are not all equally inferior to their monarch: they exist in a hierarchical ordering, each according to his particular "rank" (*gradu*); and none seeks to better himself at

---

[23]We know, for instance, that in both 1327 and 1338 Burley served the king in a diplomatic capacity, and that he enjoyed patronage in the form of income from royally-appointed offices. See Daly, "Some Notes on Walter Burley's Commentary," pp. 272-73.

[24]MS. Balliol 95, ff. 184[r]: "In optima enim politia quilibet propter talem principem superexcellentem alios in bono virtutis reputat se multum honoratum, ut quilibet diligit gradum suum et contentus est, et quilibet vult singularem honorem regit et videtur sibi quod in rege and cum rege conregnat, et proper intimam dileccionem civium ad regem est intima inter cives, et est regnum fortissimum sicut hodie patet de rege Anglorum, propter cuius excedentem virtutem est maxima concordia in populo anglicano, quia quilibet est contentus de gradu suo sub rege."

[25]Ormrod, *The Reign of Edward III*, p. 200. Burley's view may be compared with a contemporary encomium of Edward III, couched in highly personalized terms, proposed by William of Ockham in *An princeps* (in his *Opera Politica*, vol. 1, ed. H. S. Offler [2nd ed.; Manchester, 1974], p. 228). In turn, Burley's comments might also fruitfully be contrasted with the more critical remarks about Edward's conduct in the *Speculum Regis Edwardi III* (possibly by William of Pagula); see C. J. Nederman, "Welfare or Warfare? Medieval Contributions," *International Journal of Moral and Social Studies* 1 (Autumn 1986): 224-26. The author of the *Speculum* promises to Edward the "love of the people" in a fashion similar to Burley, but only on condition that the king cease his oppression of the poor and the peasantry.

the expense of his fellows or his ruler. The distinctions of status typical of feudal society are essentially affirmed by Burley.

The theoretical effect of the love engendered by the exceedingly virtuous king is to produce a situation in which each subject "in rege et cum rege coregnat." Jean Dunbabin concludes of this phrase that "rarely was the medieval notion of representation more clearly expressed."[26] In other words, Burley maintains that the king is the very embodiment of the common interest, acquiring honor by doing only what is good for his subjects. Hence, he rules exactly as those beneath him would wish, and so symbolically can "stand in" for everyone within his realm.[27] This reading of Burley is only reinforced by an important variant of the passage in a Vatican manuscript of the *Commentarius*, in which the relevant phrase reads "in rege et cum rege quasi regnat."[28] The virtuous king is a kind of likeness of the real interests of his people; he represents them in a symbolic sense by protecting and serving their welfare.

In comprehending Burley's theoretical point, however, we should not neglect the significance of his historical reference to England. By the time he had begun to write the *Commentarius*, England had weathered over a century of recurrent baronial unrest occasioned by the weakness or incompetence of its rulers. The most recent and perhaps pronounced case of such discontent would have been well known to Burley and his audience: the reign and eventual deposition of Edward II.[29] His son and successor, Edward III, had by contrast proved to be a strong and reliable monarch; at the same time, the English realm itself had been calm, and indeed its aristocracy was beginning to demonstrate that unity of purpose that was to characterize its overseas military adventures in the fourteenth century.[30] Burley seems to have taken note of the coincidence of these two developments, and inferred from it that a superlative king yields a kingdom in which "each is content with his rank under the king." A virtuous monarch inspires cooperation, concord and strength among his subjects by governing as their interests (rather than his own) dictate. Burley concludes that Edward must be such a king, because England during his reign has experienced exactly the effects that virtuous rule generates. Behind his encomium of Edward lies a

---

[26]Jean Dunbabin, "Government," in *The Cambridge History of Medieval Political Thought*, p. 486.

[27]On this concept of representation, see Cary J. Nederman, "Knowledge, Consent and the Critique of Political Representation in Marsiglio of Padua's *Defensor Pacis*," *Political Studies* 39 (March 1991): 19-35.

[28]This divergence is based on the report of MS. Vatican Codex Borghesi 129 given by Daly, "The Conclusions of Walter Burley's Commentary on the *Politics*, Books I to IV," p. 92.

[29]The best recent account of this period is by Natalie Fryde, *The Tyranny and Fall of Edward II, 1321-1326* (Cambridge, 1979).

[30]Perry Anderson, *Lineages of the Absolutist State* (London, 1974), pp. 116-17.

theoretical observation derived from the actual operation of contemporary English government.

III

One might be inclined to agree with Conor Martin that these two discussions of current political affairs in England are "somewhat inconsistent" when set side-by-side.[31] For on the one hand, Burley argues that even in a monarchy it is not the king alone but the king in conjunction with a multitude (the nobles and wise men) who rule (through the institution of Parliament). Yet within two folio pages he has also stated that in the England of Edward III, the king possesses such exceeding virtue that all of his subjects are happy to humble themselves beneath him and to magnify his honor. Can Burley have meant to uphold both of these views simultaneously? Or must we accept the absence of a systematic philosophical framework shaping the course of his commentary? In order to resolve this dilemma, we must turn to yet a third passage of the *Commentarius*, one that has also occasionally attracted the attention of scholars.[32]

Aristotle's appraisal of kingship includes an analysis of several objections to the rule of a single man.[33] One of these is that no individual person is capable of watching over a number of matters at the same time, and therefore any king will have to appoint magistrates to assist him. But this entails that royal officials must share in the virtue characteristic of the king. For in order to be his colleagues (a term that William of Moerbeke translated as *conprinceps*), these officials must be his friends, otherwise they will not be committed to his rule. But in order to be his friends, Aristotle insists, they must be his equals and peers, since according to the doctrine of the *Nicomachean Ethics*, only equals may truly be friends.[34] And, of course, this challenges the very justification of kingship: that it is the rule of the singularly virtuous man over others of lesser goodness who are unequal to him and thereby unqualified to share in government.

Burley produces a comparatively lengthy explication of this text that, however, seems oblivious to the fact that it was intended as a criticism of monarchy:

> Many can inquire and judge what is to be done and what not better than one alone. This is proved by the evidence of examples. Just as it is said to be absurd that one man with two eyes and two ears perceives more and better than many men with many eyes and many ears, and just as it is absurd to say that one man functions better with two hands and two feet than many men with many hands and many feet, so it is absurd to say that one man judges better by his prudence than many. And so we see that rulers appoint for themselves many eyes, many feet and many hands,

[31] Martin, "Some Medieval Commentaries on Aristotle's *Politics*," p. 39.

[32] For instance, Eccleshall, *Order and Reason in Politics*, p. 71.

[33] For the following, see Aristotle, *Politics*, 1287b19-35.

[34] Aristotle, *Nicomachean Ethics*, ed. H. Rackham (Cambridge, Mass., 1926), 1155a33-1155b7; my translation.

since they appoint for themselves many corulers (*comprincipantes*)....And rulers appoint those who are their friends and friends of the government, because if they are a friend of one, namely, the government, but of the other they do not care about the good of the ruler, while if they love the ruler rather than the government they do not care about the good of the government. And because corulers should be friends, and friends must be peers and equals, it is clear that peers and equals by reason of virtue must govern....[35]

Burley's commentary refocuses the direction of the Aristotelian position. He overlooks the inconsistency between the need for monarchs to rely upon a number of like-minded colleagues and the nature of kingship as the sole rule of one supremely virtuous man. Indeed, he concludes from Aristotle's discussion that "it is unnatural for one to be ruler all the time according to his own will over some others who by their virtue are his peers and equals."[36] Burley appears undisturbed that this undermines the very foundation of kingship as conceived by Aristotle.

Instead, Burley concentrates his attention almost wholly upon the nature of the coruling function itself. Aristotle had remarked simply that the "colleagues" of the king must be *both* his friends and friends of his regime. Burley devotes a disproportionate amount of effort to the explication of this statement. Corulership for him entails the association of the ruler with individuals who are simultaneously supporters of monarchic government and peers of the ruler in virtue. Such men will seek to magnify (rather than subvert) the authority of their king while applying the standards of their shared virtue to the conduct of their duties. Burley insists that the "friendship" of the corulers should be construed in a formal rather than literal or personal sense: it is not the private friends of the ruler who are to be included among his entourage but rather those persons who are lovers of his regime and equals to his virtue. As Burley stipulates, "It is to be understood that he who loves the ruler insofar as he is a ruler loves the government, because the cause of the ruler is affirmed by the cause of the government, but not that he who loves the ruler insofar as such a ruler is a man

---

[35]MS. Balliol 95, f. 186^r: "...multi possunt melius inquirere et iudicare quid agendum sit et quid non quam unus solus. Quod probatur probatione exemplari. Sicut inconveniens est dicere quod unus duobus oculis et duabus auribus magis et melius percipiat quam multi multis auribus et multis oculis, et sicut inconveniens est dicere quod unus melius operatur duabus manibus et pedibus quam multi multis manibus et multis pedibus, sic inconveniens est dicere quod unus melius iudicet per suam prudentiam quam multi. Et ideo videmus quod principes faciunt sibi multos oculos et multos pedes et manus, quia faciunt sibi multos comprincipantes....Faciunt autem principes illos qui sunt amici sui et amici principatus, quia si non essent amici utriusque sed alterius ut principatus non curarent de bono principis sed principatus, et si non diligerent principatum sed principem non curarent de bono principatus. Et quia comprincipantes debent esse amici, et amicos oportet esse similes et equales, medium est quod similes quod similes et equales secundum virtutem oportet principari...."

[36]MS. Balliol 95, f. 186^r: "Non est naturale unum semper secundum suam voluntatem principari aliquibus sibi similibus et equalibus secundum virtutem."

loves the government on account of this."[37] An intimate feeling of friendship towards the person of the king is not a precondition for corulership. The joint participants in royal authority are "friends" in the sense that they all seek the same goal of the realization of that virtuous rule which is the purpose of monarchy. Burley introduces here a notion of collective authority and responsibility for the governance of the realm.

The significance of Burley's conception of corulership becomes more transparent when located in the context of the dilemmas and debates that animated medieval English politics. Throughout the thirteenth and fourteenth centuries, one of the most common demands made upon the Crown was for the implementation of a council of nobles or other corporate body that would be charged with the governance of the realm jointly with the king. This proposal was a feature of the initial edition of Magna Carta,[38] although not of its reissues, and it recurred during the time of the Provisions of Oxford.[39] The most pronounced illustration of the application of this principle of shared responsibility for the kingdom emerged out of the events leading up to the proclamation of the Ordinances of 1311. In opposition to Edward II's predilection for favoring his personal friends over the common welfare of the realm (or more properly, its politically important classes), the English magnates asserted their authority to ordain the basic conditions for the conduct of royal government.[40] These nobles viewed themselves expressly as defenders of the interests of the Crown as well as of the kingdom against the personal whims of an incumbent who valued his private relationships above all else. Thus, they proclaimed their purpose to be the promotion of "the honor of God and His Holy Church and the King and his realm,"[41] a statement that echoes the words of the mid-thirteenth-century *Carmen de Bello Lewensi* that the baronial party led by Simon de Montfort "devises nothing against, nor seeks anything contrary to, the honor of the king. Instead, it is zealous to reform and magnify the state of the king (*statem regium*)."[42] In this way, the king's apparent enemies reveal themselves to be

---

[37]MS. Balliol 95, f. 186[r]: "Intelligendum quod qui diligit principem secundum quod rulerps est diligit principatum, quia ratio principis sumitur ex ratione principatus sed non quod qui diligit principem secundum quod talis homo quod propter hoc diligit principatum."

[38]Magna Carta, arts. 52, 55 and 61 in *Sources of English Constitutional History*, ed. C. Stephenson and F. G. Marcham (New York, 1972), pp. 123-26.

[39]Sayles, *The King's Parliament of England*, pp. 48-69.

[40]Bertie Wilkinson, *The Later Middle Ages in England, 1216–1485* (London, 1969), pp. 61, 71-72 and 219-20.

[41]Prologue to the Ordinances of 1311 in *Sources of English Constitutional History*, p. 193.

[42]*Carmen de Bello Lewensi*, ed. C. L. Kingsford (Oxford, 1890), 2: 535-38: "Pars in principio palam protestatur: Quod honori regio nichil machinatur, vel querit contrarium; immo reformare studet statum regium et magnificare."

his true friends: they are devoted to the maintenance of the royal office even when the incumbent damages the powers and prerogatives associated with the Crown.[43]

Burley recasts Aristotle's idea of royal virtue in order to render it congenial to the baronially-inspired ideal of collective responsibility for governance. The virtuous king gathers around himself those who are similar in moral character to him, that is, whose primary concern is directed towards the common good of the whole realm. Indeed, the very mark of royal virtue might, in Burley's view, be construed as a preference for governing with the aid of numerous officials and counsellors because the ruler will be more effective thereby at enforcing law and judging justly. This conception of royal virtue as the foundation of corulership hence knits together the disparate elements of Burley's theory of the best monarchic constitution. On the one hand, it stipulates why the presence of a king of pre-eminent virtue generates concord and love among the people and instills in them a sense of reigning in and with him. For the virtuous ruler gathers around him as corulers all those who share his devotion to the public welfare and so transforms "coreigning" from a symbolic or metaphorical relationship into an effective guideline for governmental practice. Any king of virtue must "naturally" desire to share his authority with persons of similar qualities, because this will extend his own honor and enhance his rule. And Burley's approach quite clearly specifies that "corulers" stand in a relation of friendship with their king *only* because of their similarity in virtue; personal affection, which may cloud judgements about the good of the realm, can have no place in selecting one's corulers. One might even say that the characters of corulers are reflective of the character of the king: they represent *him* in the sense that they are his "peers and equals" in virtue.

Burley's doctrine of corulership also provides the framework for his contention that the 'arduous business' of the realm must be referred to Parliament, which exercises the same or greater power than the king alone. When the virtuous ruler calls upon the many organs and senses of his similarly virtuous corulers, the resulting body is resplendent in virtue. Hence, such an assembly of king and corulers enjoys greater authority in the governing of the realm, inasmuch as the arrayed virtues of its members better qualify it to determine matters related to the common interest. By no means could the king acting jointly with Parliament demonstrate less virtue than the king acting on his own; and in fact, king-in-Parliament is likely to display a greater measure of virtue. Parliament is not therefore conceived by Burley as essentially a populist or even constitutional body at all; it is instead the corporate expression of the virtue

---

[43]On the historical emergence of a distinction between "king" and "Crown" implied here, see J. R. Maddicott, *Thomas of Lancaster, 1307–1322: A Study in the Reign of Edward II* (Oxford, 1970), p. 82, and Keen, *England in the Later Middle Ages*, p. 87.

upon which the coruling function is premised. Parliament is a royal institution to the extent that it is convened by the king in accordance with the dictates of virtue. But its composition cannot be strictly reflective of the will (or private interests) of the king, since it is understood to contain only those who qualify for corulership (the nobles and wise men of the realm). Parliament is the embodiment of the collective interests of the kingdom, a forum where uncertain and difficult issues can be examined and debated carefully and thoroughly by those persons who are especially dedicated to the promotion of the public welfare. Such a non-representative conception of communal institutions was not exceptional in the later Middle Ages; it is apparent, for instance, in the ecclesiology of Marsiglio of Padua.[44] Burley's contribution is to connect it specifically with the idea of *parliamentum* and to root it in the more general principle that royal government is a joint venture among men similarly inclined towards virtue and its realization in the political community.

IV

Burley's analysis of royal government as a cooperative enterprise places him within a venerable tradition of distinctively English political thought stretching from the twelfth to the fifteenth centuries. To appreciate the full significance of Burley's contribution, therefore, we must devote attention to the character of this tradition as it emerged out of the historical pattern that regulated political affairs in medieval England.[45] From the time of the Conquest, the king of England had been viewed as the focal point of political authority within the realm. The royal monopoly on such "banal" powers as taxation, "high" justice, warfare and castle-building, not to mention direct control over such feudal institutions as land tenure, knights service and vassalage, all betokened a king whose powers were far more extensive and advanced than any other contemporary Western European monarch. Yet, at the same time, the growth of centralized royal government in England depended heavily upon the good will and assistance of the feudal aristocracy. By the opening decades of the thirteenth century, the bureaucratic and judicial institutions associated with the English Crown had been transformed into collaborative ventures, in the sense that most offices at all levels were discharged not by a professionalized coterie of royal servants and clerks (as was the case on the continent), but by the lords of the realm themselves. From the greatest earl to the most humble knight of the shire, seigneurs

---

[44]Nederman, "Knowledge, Consent and the Critique of Political Representation in Marsiglio of Padua's *Defensor Pacis*," pp. 21-23.

[45]The following analysis draws from themes most cogently articulated by Philip Corrigan and Derek Sayer, *The Great Arch: English State Formation as Cultural Revolution* (Oxford, 1985), pp. 15-42, and Robert Brenner, "The Agrarian Roots of European Capitalism," in *The Brenner Debate*, ed. T. H. Aston and C. H. E. Philpin (Cambridge, 1985), pp. 254-58. For a more extended historical exposition, see Cary J. Nederman, "State and Political Theory in France and England, 1250-1350" (Ph.D. diss., York University, 1983), pp. 125-87.

were the effective agents of the *potestas* wielded by royal grant and in the king's name. Moreover, the feudal classes were extended a powerful forum for the expression of their interests and concerns in the shape of royal *concilia* and *parliamenta*. Thus, as our examination of Burley's context suggested, the English aristocracy acquired a permanent stake in the formulation of royal "policy," as well as in the implementation of that policy. In effect, the governance of the English kingdom was in most ways as A. H. White once described it: "self-government at the king's command."[46]

However widespread were the practices connected with such royally coordinated self-government, the uniquely English devolution of the Crown's public authority into seigneurial hands posed crucial questions for political theory. The central problem was one of reciprocity: how to maintain a careful balance between the royal dignity and the seigneurial cooperation necessary for the successful governance of the realm. The fact that England had developed a set of collective institutions was the result of no conscious plan, but arose largely because of unacknowledged factors pertaining to the nation's social and economic structure.[47] Thus, political thinkers were confronted with the issue of demonstrating the precise character and bases of cooperation. How did lords acquire their duties and responsibilities towards the governance of the realm? To what extent and in what manner were they to be guided and controlled in discharging their duties? What assurances were there that the public power of the king would not be diminished or dissipated by the delegation of authority? Why must the Crown retain ultimate charge of the government of the kingdom at all? English political treatises of the Middle Ages devoted considerable attention to just these sorts of dilemmas raised by the system of "self-government at the king's command."

Consequently, it is possible for us to arrange many of the works of medieval political theory originating in England around variations on the theme of government as a collaborative venture between the Crown and its subjects in which duly constituted authority is shared rather than concentrated in either king or populace exclusively. The origins of this tradition extend back to John of Salisbury's mid-twelfth-century articulation of a "physiological" conception of the organic metaphor, according to which all the parts of the body politic, from the head to the feet, share responsibility for the performance of justice and the promotion of the common good.[48] The theme of the cooperative spirit was car-

---

[46] A. H. White, *Self-Government at the King's Command* (Minneapolis, 1938).

[47] Some of these have been identified by Brenner, "The Agrarian Roots of European Capitalism," pp. 226–42, 246–53.

[48] On the bodily analogy and its implications for John, see Cary J. Nederman, "The Physiological Significance of the Organic Metaphor in John of Salisbury's *Policraticus*," *History of Political Thought* 8 (Summer 1987): 211–23, and "A Duty to Kill: John of Salisbury's Theory of Tyrannicide," *Review of Politics* 50 (Summer 1988): 365–89.

ried forward into the thirteenth century by the legal and polemical literature associated with the codification of common law and the expression of baronial discontent. The Bractonian *De Legibus et Consuetudinibus Angliae* perhaps best encapsulates the theoretical advances in responding to the dilemmas posed by collaborative government. It argued in internally consistent fashion both for a strong Crown—the king is deemed to be *sub deo et sub lege, sed non sub homine*—and also for a large measure of participation on the part of the noble classes—to the extent that they could "bridle" the king when he committed flagrant injuries.[49] By the dawn of the fourteenth century, attention had shifted to Parliament and the institutionalization of cooperation by means of embryonic king-in-Parliament doctrines: the pseudo-lawbook *Speculum Justiciariorum* may have been the earliest work to propose the quasi-sovereign authority of Parliament,[50] but it was soon joined by the *Modus Tenendi Parliamentum* and a host of other discussions of the role of parliamentary assemblies in the rule of the English realm.[51] Perhaps the culmination of the medieval tradition of thought about the nature and foundations of England's collaborative system is achieved in the work of John Fortescue, who in the late fifteenth century expressly identifies English government as the manifestation of a high degree of cooperation between the Crown and its subjects. Fortescue reaches back to the organic approach to collaboration pioneered by John of Salisbury,[52] while also arguing that in England uniquely the king reigns in accordance with "the permission and judgement of the whole of his realm in parliament."[53] Even political debate during the Tudor and Stuart periods did not easily or entirely surrender medieval concepts and categories.[54]

[49]This is examined by Cary J. Nederman, "The Royal Will and the Baronial Bridle: The Place of the *Addicio de Cartis* in Bractonian Political Thought," *History of Political Thought* 9 (Winter 1988): 415-29. For some of the sources of the Bractonian doctrines, see Charles M. Radding, "The Origins of Bracton's *Addicio de cartis*," *Speculum* 44 (1969): 239-46.

[50]*Speculum Justiciariorum*, ed. W. J. Whittaker (London, 1895), pp. 7-8, 155-56.

[51]For example, the *Modus Tenendi Parliamentum* and other documents in *Parliamentary Texts of the Later Middle Ages*, ed. M. Pronay and J. Taylor (Oxford, 1980) and *Fleta*, ed. H. G. Richardson and G. O. Sayles, 2 vols. (London: Selden Society, 1955), 2: 109.

[52]John Fortescue, *De laudibus legibus Anglie*, ed. S. M. Chrimes (Cambridge, 1949), ch. 13, and *On the Governance of England*, ed. C. Plummer (Oxford, 1885), ch. 2.

[53]Fortescue, *De laudibus legibus Anglie*, ch. 36: "...concessione vel sensu totius regni in parliamento." Fortescue makes similar statements in chs. 18 and 53.

[54]As I have pointed out in "State and Political Theory in France and England," pp. 482-88 and "Bracton on Kingship First Visited: The Idea of Sovereignty and Bractonian Political Thought," *Political Science* 40 (July 1988): 49-66. The theoretical departures occasioned by the rise of the Tudor monarchy are the subject of a forthcoming monograph by Neal Wood, which I have been privileged to consult in typescript.

Walter Burley's significance within this medieval tradition of political theory is assured by several factors. Most obviously, his very attempt to refashion and apply Aristotelian ideas to the examination of contemporary English conditions adds a conceptual and linguistic dimension to the tradition that it had previously lacked. In spite of widespread continental interest in the *Politics*, other English schoolmen of Burley's generation either ignored Aristotle's political theory or made no effort to connect it with current political events.[55] Irrespective of his motives, Burley broke through this barrier and demonstrated how the ideas of the *Politics* could be employed to understand and explore English affairs. He would not be the sole figure in the English tradition to do so: Fortescue, for instance, drew heavily upon Aristotelian doctrines both directly and by way of the Thomas/Peter commentary.[56] But Burley deserves full credit for taking the first step towards the formulation of an Aristotelian interpretation of foundations of English government, thereby opening the window of contemporary politics in England to a scholastic audience.

The *Commentarius* also constitutes a benchmark in the development of the English tradition by virtue of its more explicit recognition of the collaborative ethos. Where earlier authors had largely described the operation of the cooperative relationship between king and subjects without perceiving it to be a unique system of government, Burley introduces the term "corulership" in order to distinguish what occurs in England from other sorts of monarchic constitutions. Indeed, he seems to believe, at least implicitly, that this "coruling" framework yields the best or ideal form of royal regime. In any case, Burley's emphasis upon the theme of corulership indicates an unprecedented level of self-consciousness about the practice of collective authority. The *Commentarius* consequently coalesces much of earlier "operative" political thought, contained within lawbooks and administrative manuals, into a systematic exposition of the conceptual underpinnings of English government.

This conclusion points to the further lesson that it is unwise, when addressing the development of political theory in medieval England, to concentrate our attention wholly upon "operative" documents at the expense of scholastic writings. This position, advocated, for instance, by Donald Hanson in his survey of the emergence of English political ideas during the medieval and early modern periods,[57] falsely assumes that the thought of the schoolmen was impervious to

---

[55]One thinks in this instance especially of William of Ockham, who makes only a single reference to Aristotle (and then to the *Nicomachean Ethics*) in his one treatise on English affairs, the *An princeps*. See Cary J. Nederman, "Royal Taxation and the English Church: The Origins of William of Ockham's *An princeps*," *Journal of Ecclesiastical History* 37 (July 1986): 387.

[56]Given Fortescue's interest in the Thomas/Peter commentary, it would be interesting to know whether he was also familiar with Burley's *Commentarius*. If so, this might help to explain why he was able to bring Aristotle to bear so readily on the conditions of political life in England.

[57]Donald W. Hanson, *From Kingdom to Commonwealth* (Cambridge, Mass., 1970), pp. 12–13.

historical concerns. But the *Commentarius* illustrates that the distance between the classroom and the court or royal chamber was not so great as the anachronistic distinction between academic and public life might lead us to suppose. Burley was not especially exceptional among schoolmen of his day in combining an active involvement in public affairs with a scholarly career.[58] And invariably such experience of politics shapes and molds an author's theoretical insights. In this way, the cross-fertilization of scholasticism and practical politics proved fruitful for generating that Aristotelian dimension within the medieval English tradition of political thought that is represented within Burley's *Commentarius in VIII Libros Politicorum Aristotelis.*

[58]Thomas Aquinas could equally well serve as an example, as has been demonstrated by Jeremy Catto, "Ideas and Experience in the Political Thought of Aquinas," *Past and Present* 71 (May 1976): 3-21.

XV

ARISTOTLE AS AUTHORITY: ALTERNATIVE ARISTOTELIAN SOURCES OF LATE MEDIAEVAL POLITICAL THEORY

The style of political argumentation typical of the Middle Ages, with its heavy emphasis upon authoritative sources instead of rational demonstration, is foreign and disturbing to many modern philosophers and political theorists. Consequently, one hears the complaint that the weight afforded by mediaeval authors to ancient and early Christian authorities results in historically irrelevant and patently unoriginal insights.[1] Admittedly, mediaeval political thinkers seldom dared to assert views for which they could not cite some basis in Scripture, the Fathers or the pagan philosophers. And whenever an authority could not be located, it could always be manufactured.[2] Yet the importance of 'argument from authority' during the Middle Ages should not lead us to infer the slavish devotion of political thinkers to earlier texts at the expense of intellectual independence. It is a mistake to confuse the mediaeval requirement of authoritative citation with the inability of authors to escape from or transcend views culled from the documents which they read and revered. More reasonably, we might assert that political writers adopted from their authorities whatever was useful in addressing problems within mediaeval society, rejected what was deemed irrelevant, and often mispresented or manipulated sources in order to justify truly novel doctrines.

We may test this general hypothesis by reference to Aristotle, whose influence during a great part of the Middle Ages was second only to Scripture. Recent studies of mediaeval political ideas leave the impression that Aristotle's *Politics* (and to a lesser extent *Ethics*) provided the indispensible model for human society to authors working after 1250.[3] In this regard, Aristotle is seen to lay the foundations for a move away from the categories of feudal society, and towards the Renaissance concepts of citizen and state.[4] The reintroduction of Aristotle's *Politics* into Europe is thereby credited with the revitalisation of the Western tradition of political theory. This claim, in turn, rests on the presumption that the major political doctrines defended or articulated after about 1250—at least by authors of an Aristotelian bent—have their primary source in either the *Politics* or the 'political' sections of the *Ethics*. The aim of the present paper, however, is to challenge such an assumption by demonstrating that when mediaeval authors found Aristotle's social and political ideas inappropriate to the problems of feudal society which they confronted, they manifested none of the bookishness so often attributed to them. Careful examination of late mediaeval texts suggests that there was no fear of discussing issues of current concern in secular, feudal society.

Reproduced from Cary J. Nederman, 'Aristotle as authority: alternative Aristotelian sources of late mediaeval political theory', *History of European Ideas* Vol. 8, No. 1 (1987), pp. 31–44, by kind permission from Elsevier Science Ltd., The Boulevard, Langford Lane, Kidlington, Oxford, OX5 1GB, UK.

Yet the requirement of authoritative citation, particularly from Aristotle, could not be neglected altogether. One strategy widely adopted in order to salvage both historical relevance and the appearance of Aristotelian authority was the adaptation of doctrines drawn from Aristotle's writings on speculative and natural topics to meet political problems.[5] Indeed, some of the most significant and novel developments in political writing from 1250 to 1500 were the result of attempts to respond to contemporary political questions through the formulation of ideas derived from Aristotle's non-social treatises. In defence of this general claim, we may refer to three important theoretical contributions originating in late mediaeval texts: (1) the establishment of a principle of limitation upon governmental powers of taxation; (2) the introduction of a unitary order among superior and inferior forms of jurisdiction; and (3) the discovery of comparative techniques for the analysis of nation-states. The first development was pioneered by Pierre d'Auvergne and Pierre Dubois between 1290 and 1310; the second by Marsiglio of Padua during the 1320s; and the third by John Fortescue near the end of the fifteenth century. All of these doctrines, as will be shown, rely for their authority upon Aristotelian texts dealing with metaphysics, nature and language rather than political philosophy. Therefore, exploration of the three cases will illustrate that when the *Politics* failed to generate concepts appropriate to the problems of late mediaeval society, authors did not resist discussion of contemporary events. Instead, they combed the rest of the Aristotelian corpus for the authoritative sources which their technique of argumentation demanded.

I

Direct taxation was a fact of life throughout the Latin Middle Ages. The presence of taxation on a widespread basis may largely be explained by reference to the nature of feudal society itself: taxes were effectively sanctioned by the typically feudal confusion of governmental powers with sources of private income.[6] Indeed, to the extent that rents and other revenues were fixed by custom, whereas seigneurial taxes were generally arbitrary in amount, feudal lords during the Middle Ages increasingly relied for their profits upon their ability to impose the *bannum*. Royal taxes were not, however, so common in early mediaeval Europe. Only with the emergence of centralised, public institutions constructed around the feudal monarchies of the thirteenth century did the king's demand for revenue pose a serious problem. Generally speaking, the Middle Ages distinguished between two forms of royal income: ordinary and extraordinary. The former included whatever revenue could be generated from the king's estates and customary feudal privileges; the latter involved monies received through one or another method of direct taxation. Extraordinary income, as the name implies, was to be sought only on an irregular basis, as 'necessity' required.[7] Such necessity was understood to be of an essentially military nature demanded by the defence of the realm. Thus, direct royal taxes most often took the form of fines in lieu of military service. But as the costs of day-to-day royal administration grew out of all proportion to ordinary income during the thirteenth century, kings began to appeal to necessity more frequently, and to expand by implication the definition of what constituted imminent need.

By the time of Philip the Fair's reign (1285–1314), for example, the French crown was exacting at least one type of direct tax nearly every year.[8] Such regularisation of extraordinary royal revenue enjoyed little support among those subjects whose payment was exacted. Yet because of the *ad hoc* and capricious character of feudal taxes generally, mediaeval men lacked any firm principle on which to base resistance to or restraint of the king's fiscal demands.

Consequently, political authors in the late thirteenth and early fourteenth centuries began to explore various formulas for controlling the flow of extraordinary income into the royal treasury. In spite of the popularity of Aristotle's *Politics*, that work could not provide much assistance in addressing the problem of taxation. The financial mechanisms of the historical Greek polis were not very highly developed,[9] and the *Politics* is virtually bereft of references to matters of public revenue.[10] But Aristotle was not completely without impact; one of the most commonly proposed solutions (in France, at any rate) was derived from the Aristotelian account of causality in the *Physics* and *Metaphysics*. Among Aristotle's primary concerns in each treatise is to distinguish the difference senses of 'cause'.[11] One important Aristotelian distinction is between 'potential' and 'active' causation. The former refers to a formal relationship between a cause and an effect, as when we point to a completed edifice and say that its cause was such-and-such a builder. In this sense, cause and effect exist independently of one another: the builder-cause may die and the building remain; or the building may collapse while the builder yet lives. 'Active' causation, on the other hand, denotes an immediate interaction between cause and effect: the builder is only the cause of the edifice so long as he is in the process of actually constructing it. The completion of the building (the effect) signifies by definition the completion of the cause. According to Aristotle, active 'causes co-exist or cease with their effects (for instance, a particular physician ceases medical treatment whenever a particular patient recovers, and a particular builder ceases building when the course of erection ends)'.[12] Thus, in the case of active causation, the cause and its effect commence and halt simultaneously.

It was Aristotle's doctrine of active causation on which late mediaeval political thinkers sometimes relied when formulating a response to the increasing fiscal demands of kings. The notion of an active cause was encapsulated by the phrase *cessante causa, cessat effectus* ('as the cause ceases, the effect ceases'). A 1298 *quodlibet* by Pierre d'Auvergne was apparently the earliest treatise to employ the doctrine of *cessante causa* in regard to royal taxation. In this document, Pierre argues for the limited nature of a king's powers of taxation.[13] His justification stems from the declaration that 'inasmuch as the cause ceases, the effect should cease. A suitable tax is introduced because of the cause of imminent necessity; when the necessity recedes, therefore, it should cease.' Necessity functions in the manner of an active cause; the effect of taxation, produced by necessity, properly ends at the moment that the need subsides. By thus circumscribing the king's power to tax, Pierre asserts that the continuation of an unnecessary tax is a sin, that subjects can licitly refuse to contribute to such a tax, and that even the offspring of a monarch who taxes unjustly is obliged to reverse his predecessor's command. From the Aristotelian principle of *cessante causa*, Pierre d'Auvergne derives a primitive technique for identifying some limitations on the royal authority to tax.

Pierre Dubois' *De recuperatione terre sancte*, composed about a decade after d'Auvergne's *quodlibet*, expanded considerably on the initial application of *cessante causa*. *De recuperatione* includes a lengthy account of how the king preparing for war ought to staff and finance his army. Dubois insists that the monarch must rely initially upon the traditional feudal array of dukes, counts, barons and others enfeoffed directly of him. But the author of *De recuperatione* possesses a sufficiently realistic outlook to acknowledge that feudal dues of service were occasionally inadequate for the conduct of military campaigns. Thus, whenever the necessity of protecting the realm required it, the king might institute collection of a direct, general tax (such as the *arrière-ban*) from his subjects. This tax was enforcable over all forms of property held by all manner of persons: churches and ecclesiastics, townsmen and free peasants are to be susceptible no less than lay lords when the safety of the kingdom is at stake.[14] Yet Dubois hardly supports royal taxation without qualification, for he immediately stipulates that the king cannot exact the money of his subjects indiscriminately. The specific limitation of the king's discretion in matters of taxation, Dubois explains, arises out of that doctrine which 'all sciences agree on and share: *cessante causa, cessat effectus*. Therefore, when the cause of the confiscation ceases, the lord king may confiscate nothing unless he desires to rob and plunder openly.'[15] Dubois is especially sensitive to the potential for abuse even within cases of legitimate taxation. How are we to regard the prince, Dubois asks, who requires only one hundred thousand marks to meet the necessity but who collects two hundred thousand marks? Dubois responds that 'by the same reasoning' from which *cessante causa* is derived, 'if [t]he [king] requires just one hundred thousand marks of gold and silver, and should confiscate more, he is in that measure robbing and plundering by false word or act, which is the same thing, when, that is, he maintains that the cause for confiscation has not subsided and it has subsided. If the lord king does this with certain knowledge, then he is a liar.'[16] The king who collects taxes in excess of what is determined to be necessary thereby commits a grave and mortal sin which is only remitted once he has returned the surplus to its rightful possessors.

In addition to his concern about the ruler who might attempt to profit illicitly from a military tax, Dubois fears abuses by others within the feudal structure. In particular, kings sometimes pay the costs of knights who, under the feudal oaths by which they are bound, owe unremunerated service to the crown. In other circumstances, knights obligated to provide free service have been known to contract with another magnate who also owes service, thus allowing two warriors to be reprsented by a single body. Because many who owe military service have been released from it or reimbursed for their expenses, 'the lord king has exacted a general tax in cases where it should not have been summoned or exacted. By remitting those services due and exacting service from those who do not owe it, he has most gravely burdened himself spiritually, and them temporally.'[17] Dubois thinks that in the failure to correct such abuses, the king effectively sanctions the collection of taxes which are not strictly necessary to protect the kingdom, in violation of the *cessante causa* doctrine. No less than revenues collected for purely private royal gain, taxes seized because of the government's incompetence or negligence pertain to the moral responsibility of the king. The ruler who does not properly supervise the allocation of personnel and funds, and who hence takes more from his subjects than is needed, is charged before God with restoration of excess taxes to their rightful possessors. Dubois consequently connects the application of *cessante causa* to a plea for the reform and rationalisation of royal administration—a favourite theme of *De recuperatione*. The king must realise that *cessante causa* circumscribes the conduct of his vassals and administrators as well as his personal actions. Only in the situation where a complete and unpaid feudal array proves insufficient to meet the need does Dubois sanction imposition of direct taxes.[18] Otherwise, the principle of *cessante causa* limits the government's access to the resources of the king's subjects. From a maxim of Aristotelian metaphysics, then, Pierre Dubois constructs an elaborate account of the conditions which must be met before a monarch may rightfully use his authority to tax.

II

During the Middle Ages, the decentralised distribution of authority characteristic of feudal society resulted in the persistence of countless jurisdictions, with overlapping rights and relative autonomy of action.[19] At its smallest, such a feudal island might extend no further than the domain of a castellan; at its largest, it might be constituted by a kingdom such as England. But what was typical of all feudal 'fragments' was a pretence to independence in the exercise of powers associated with justice and military affairs. The widespread conduct of private warfare and the localised fashion in which disputes were adjudicated both indicate the disorganised condition of political relations among the greater and lesser lords of the mediaeval West. Given the intertwined duties implied by the structure of feudal institutions—the requirement of lending *auxilium et consilium* to various superiors—there was great confusion regarding the priority of the individual's allegiances, especially once centralised monarchic states began to reappear during the thirteenth century. If service is demanded simultaneously by one's immediate lord and by one's king, whom is one obligated to follow? If one is summoned before the royal court and an honorial court at the same day and time, where ought one to appear? One risked offending or even provoking a superior whose summons was ignored in preference to the will of another superior. Thus, the incoherence of the feudal structure posed a considerable danger to the health and welfare of many a feudal lord.

For late mediaeval political theorists, especially those writing in the shadow of the emerging 'national' states of Europe, the continuation of a wholly decentralised system of feudal power was clearly intolerable. Yet it was effectively impossible—even unthinkable—to eradicate entirely such inferior jurisdictions as counties, duchies, baronies and the like. What was needed was a principle of order that could justify the integration of individual jurisdictions into a coherent unit which would nevertheless maintain the integrity of its constituent elements. The accomplishment of this task could not occur under the terms of Aristotle's social and political theory. For Aristotle shared with the Greek world generally the view that the polis was a singular and indivisible unit, the unique focus of communal life and civic identity, and a self-sustaining entity in a political, social and economic sense.[20] Yet, historically speaking, the particular 'parts' of the feudal puzzle, inferior jurisdictions, *had* proven to be self-sufficient entities. Indeed, during much of the Middle Ages, provinces like

Normandy and Aquitaine had been far more advanced politically and economically than their *de jure* royal master.[21] Hence, the claim of Aristotle's *Politics* that the polis is the *telos* of all other individuals and communities simply did not suit the arrangement of feudal society.[22]

But a potent antedote to the historical limitations of the *Politics* could be adapted from Aristotelian natural philosophy. In his treatise on *The Motion of Animals*, Aristotle addresses the question of how animate bodies are able to move their disparate parts in a co-ordinated fashion without compromising the uniqueness of each part. Aristotle maintains that the principle of order endemic to the body is analagous to that of the universe as a whole: all movement can ultimately be traced to a single prime mover which is itself unmoved. In the body, this prime mover is the soul which directs and guides all the voluntary and involuntary motions of animate creatures.[23] This is because all movement of sentient bodies is purposive and therefore has a definite object of pursuit or avoidance. The object of animalistic action is fixed by intellect, imagination and desire—in short, by functions which pertain to the soul.[24] The soul, by determining the kind of motion, can be called the origin and primary cause of any movement. Thus, it is inaccurate to say that the motion of the shoulder causes the motion of the arm, that the motion of the arm causes the motion of the hand, and so forth. Each appendage is subordinate to the soul precisely insofar as the former performs only a specified function in motion whereas the latter is assigned the generalised task of controlling the whole process. Animals are so constituted that 'each part of them ... is naturally suited to perform its function; so that there is no need of soul in each part, but since it is situated in a central organ of authority over the body, the other parts live by their structural attachment to it and perform their own functions in the course of nature'.[25] The soul singularly directs the harmonious operation of all the specialised parts towards the completion of some end. The soul can therefore be only one in number; multiple 'souls' would produce, at least potentially, conflicting ends and would induce chaotic behaviour. That the parts of the body do move in unison demonstrates to Aristotle that all animals are ordered in relation to a unique soul which fixes the goal for every one of the organism's motions.

The implications of Aristotle's account of animal movement for untangling the web of feudal jurisdictions were explicitly recognised by Marsiglio of Padua in his early-fourteenth-century tract, the *Defensor pacis*. Marsiglio, who as a physician was well acquainted with Aristotelian natural philosophy, devotes the entire seventeenth chapter of the *Defensor's* first discourse to consideration of the numerical unity of the supreme government within any community. Over the course of the chapter Marsiglio strives to justify both the existence of a single central state structure and the maintenance of inferior units of authority. On the one hand, Marsiglio insists that 'the supreme ruler should by necessity be one in number, not many, if the kingdom or city is rightly disposed'.[26] There must be but a single superior government within any civil order, and its superiority must be in principle unchallengable. Yet Marsiglio also argues that the necessity of a single supreme government does not entail the illegitimacy of other inferior political units. He observes that it may be 'expedient' for a kingdom to contain 'a plurality in number or species' of jurisdictions; he requires only that 'between them there be one in number supreme over all, to whom and by whom those remaining would be reduced and regulated, and through whom errors occurring in the lesser would be corrected by the superior'.[27] The suppression of inferior authorities is neither demanded nor advocated by Marsiglio. But no kingdom can long withstand a situation in which several equally powerful governments compete with one another for the primary loyalty of subjects. Without some order among these powers, disputes will invariably arise; should the choice of ultimate obedience to one or another ruler be left to each person, individuals and governments will fight amongst themselves, and men will conclude from the ensuing confusion that 'they are subject to none'.[28] The creation of a unitary, acknowledged superior is Marsiglio's solution to the chaos which results from overlapping and disordered jurisdictions.

Chapter seventeen of the *Defensor's* first discourse is one of only two chapters in Dictio I which contain neither quotation from nor reference to the *Politics* or *Ethics*. (The other instance is Chapter six, which discusses the ends of the priesthood.) Instead, Marsiglio's primary source in the seventeenth chapter is Aristotle's treatise on animal motion. According to Marsiglio, Aristotle teaches that 'in the well-ordered animal the primary principle which commands it and moves it from place to place is one. . . . If there were many of these principles and they gave contrary or different commands at the same time, the animal would either have to be borne in contrary directions or remain completely at rest, and it would have to lack those things, necessary and beneficial to it, which are obtained through motion.' Marsiglio thus accurately reports the Aristotelian emphasis upon a 'central authority' which supervises the bodily parts. But Marsiglio adds that what is true of an animate creature is equally true of a 'well-ordered kingdom'. Drawing on the analogy of the organic body, he concludes that 'just as in the animal a plurality of such principles would be useless and indeed harmful, we must firmly hold that it is the same in the kingdom'.[29] Marsiglio seeks on this basis a political arrangement which has a single government (regardless of constitutional composition) as its focal point. Still, in the unity which he envisages, the particularity and individuality of feudal society are by no means surrendered. The 'parts' of society do not, *formally* speaking, become one unit by submitting to the supremacy of a single ruler; they do not shed their actual separation and distinct identity. Rather, the unity is *relational*, in the sense that each part is interconnected with others to the extent that it is 'ordered and governed' by the same superior ruler.[30] In practical terms, this means that inferior princes and lords can continue to assemble their subjects and exercise their juridical rights.[31] Whenever the powers of various governments come into direct confrontation, however, the ordering principle which places one ruler supreme over others must be invoked. It is the duty of the latter to untangle conflicting commands and to supervise the coherent administration of the realm. With Aristotle's kinesiology, rather than his political philosophy, as a model, Marsiglio of Padua provides a theoretical formula to accommodate the continuing divisions of feudal society with the emergence of more centralised expressions of political unity.

III

Excluding occasional urban forays into 'Republican' rule, the predominant form of government throughout the Middle Ages was monarchy. Even those like

Marsiglio of Padua, who posited a popular rather than divine source of political power, never challenged the pre-eminence enjoyed by monarchic rule.[23] On the contrary, Aristotle's passing assertion in the *Politics* that kingship is under certain conditions the best and most desirable form of government was widely quoted by mediaeval authors.[33] But while in strictly constitutional terms government during the Middle Ages was monotonously uniform, each of the major European crowns evolved a distinctive set of attendant legal, juridical, bureaucratic and political arrangements which resulted in the creation of unique identities among 'national' states. In France and England, particularly, historical developments beginning as early as the thirteenth century led to the recognition of substantial differences in the way in which each kingdom was ruled.[34] The English king enforced a legal code based heavily on precedent, with the aid of a small group of professional administrators and the cooperation of the landholding classes. The French crown was generally in competition with the feudal aristocracy for the exercise of rights and powers, and thus required a large corps of paid functionaries to enforce the civil law. Even if mediaeval European nation-states were not as fully evolved as their early modem successors, much that was essential to their individual structures and configurations had already become apparent by the late fifteenth century.

The emergence of these variations among the political systems of Europe produced an unparalleled opportunity for the comparative study of distinctive 'national' governments. But here as elsewhere, Aristotle's *Politics* did not provide a model suited to the task. While Aristotle and his Greek predecessors were fond of political comparison,[35] their techniques were directed towards the discovery of differences among *politeion*, that is, the constitutional arrangements of poleis. Since a *politeia* was understood to be a consciously enacted set of fundamental laws which defined the essential institutions and bonds of the polis, its application in the less rationalistic political world of the Middle Ages was limited. The comparison of late mediaeval 'national' states could not begin with Aristotle's central assumption that 'the criterion to which we must look in determining the identity of the polis is the criterion of the *politeia*'.[36] Yet, once again, a doctrine drawn from another text within the Aristotelian corpus—this time, the *Rhetoric*—was adapted by mediaeval authors in order to address contemporary circumstances. The central purpose of the *Rhetoric* was to teach the art of persuasion without surrendering the philosophic commitment to the pursuit of wisdom. Thus, Aristotle sought to identify and delineate a style of expression which would succeed in convincing an audience of what was true rather than what was expedient or immediately desirable. One stylistic element which Aristotle especially praises is careful punctuation (the 'periodic' style), which he prefers to more open-ended speaking techniques. The approval of the periodic style reflects Aristotle's concern for simplicity and clarity of argumentation.[37] But each sentence arranged in periodic style must itself have a coherent internal organisation, so that its constituent parts are rhetorically effective. A periodic sentence which has more than one part (clause), Aristotle advises, can be divided either simply or antithetically. A simple division is one where there is conceptual harmony among the elements of the sentence. For example, in the sentence 'I am inspired by herds of cows and flocks of geese', the two parts ('herds of cows' and 'flocks of geese') share a similar element which unites them. On the other hand, the parts of an antithetical sentence involve the paring of opposing terms or ideas, such as 'good' and 'bad' or 'wise' and 'foolish'. In the sentence 'Diamonds are prized by those who possess them as well as by those who lack them', the antithetical or contrasting parts are expressed by 'possession' and 'lacking'. The antithetical division of a sentence thus encompasses comparison by allowing the speaker to set side-by-side conflicting terms and ideas. For Aristotle, this antithetical form of speech is desirable precisely 'because the significance of contraries is most strongly felt when they are juxtaposed'.[38] By careful application of comparisons, a speaker can demonstrate the superiority of his own arguments to those of his opponent.[39] One reason the antithetical style can be so effective is that it has the force of a syllogism: 'by juxtaposing two contrary conclusions, you may prove one of them false'.[40] According to Aristotle, then, the use of antithesis for the formation of comparisons is a valuable instrument of rhetorical method.

To a late mediaeval political author, however, Aristotle's doctrine of antithetical style might have a very different significance. Given the inability of categories drawn from the *Politics* to cope with 'national' state systems, a writer like John Fortescue, who sought to address the evolving structures of government he observed in European countries, appealed to the antithetical style described in the *Rhetoric* as an authoritative source for comparative political analysis. Fortescue's tribute to English political and legal institutions, *De laudibus legum anglie* (finished in 1471), utilises such a comparative technique to accomplish two tasks: first, to establish the differences in political behaviour and organisation which distinguish England from France; and second, to demonstrate the superiority of English arrangements over their French counterparts. Fortescue repeatedly justifies comparison by citing the Aristotelian principle, derived from the *Rhetoric*, that *opposita iuxta se maius apparent* ('opposites juxtaposed are more apparent'). In one instance, Aristotle's account of antithesis is mentioned in defence of the propriety of descriptive comparisons: whenever two rules or ideas 'are set alongside each other, their qualities will stand out more clearly, as the Philosopher says that "Opposites juxtaposed are more apparent"'.[41] In a later chapter of *De laudibus*, Fortescue employs the same principle to a somewhat different effect. He suggests that the function of comparison is to provide information for the discovery of the relative desirability of political systems: 'Instructed by a knowledge of both, you will be able to determine which is preferable to you, as you will recall from above the Philosopher says that "Opposites juxtaposed are more apparent."'[42] Fortescue thereby shifts the thrust of the citation from descriptive contrast to evaluative comparison. Thus, Fortescue attributes to the *Rhetoric* a general principle of analysis that facilitates both of the comparative tasks set forth in *De laudibus*.

As a result, Fortescue compares the political systems of France and England not in terms of formal constitutional structure, but on the basis of the nature of the power vested in the royal head of each respective state. The English monarch, according to Fortescue, 'rules his people with a government not only regal but also political', whereas the authority of the French king is purely legal.[43] This distinction is illustrated concretely by Fortescue with reference to legislation and taxation. In France, the regal monarch may impose law upon his subjects, and may collect 'tallages and other burdens', without consultation among the great men and communities of the realm. The English king, by contrast, may neither determine 'the laws without the assent of his subjects' nor 'burden an unwilling people with strange imposts'.[44] Fortescue insists that, despite appearances, the power wielded by each type of king is of an equal potency. The regal and political ruler can tax and legislate just as surely as the regal monarch; only the procedure distinguishes them.

Fortescue explains the 'cause of this diversity' in purely historical terms.[45] Regal kingship arose where government originated in the domination of a conquerer over a subject people. In such vanquished lands, those ruled eventually came to prefer their masters to the insecurity and uncertainties which would result from the absence of any protection whatsoever. Conquered subjects even tolerated what is the distinguishing mark of regal government, namely, the Roman law maxim that *quod principi placuit habet lex vigorem* ('what pleases the prince has the force of law').[46] Conversely, the development of political and regal rule together Fortescue conceives as a cooperative process, whereby a people already fashioned into a body politic confers authority upon a royal head. The community's sustenance thereby depends upon the mutual agreement of all the bodily parts, rather than merely upon the will of the ruler.[47] The tasks and functions pertaining to the two types of kingship do not vary: both are authorised to maintain the public order and to defend the realm. The true distinction between the regal monarch and the political and regal monarch is to be found instead in the methods which each may properly employ in the exercise of royal power. *De laudibus* unequivocally proclaims that the regal king cannot do *more* than his political and regal counterpart—he can only rightfully do the same things by different means.

Such comparison of the French with the English kingdom is especially valuable, Fortescue believes, in forming a judgement about whether both governmental systems 'are of equal merit, or whether one more richly deserves encomium than the other, not from my opinion, but from those points whereupon their rules differ'.[48] A shift from description to evaluation leads Fortescue to recommend the English polity for two reasons. First, he argues that the practices associated with English common law are 'more reasonable and effective for the discovery of truth' than French civil law.[49] Where evidence based on witnesses and torture will inevitably produce error, Fortescue remarks, the empanelling of jurors and other procedures unique to English courts result in sure and valid verdicts. In a variety of instances ranging from wardship to illegitimacy to the officers of the court, the common law of England can be demonstrated to be superior to the civil code of France. Insofar as each legal system reflects the particular form of government within its respective nation—common law a cooperative creation of king and subjects, civil law an emanation of the royal will alone—the comparative study of laws redounds to the differences in political structures.

The second element of Fortescue's evaluative comparison of French and English polities concerns the impact of each system on social and economic conditions. Specifically, Fortescue encourages his readers to 'consult your own experience of both governments; begin with the results of the merely regal government, such as that with which the king of France rules his subjects; then examine experience of the political and regal government, such as that with which the king of England rules over his subject people'.[50] In French territories, *De laudibus* reports, the king by virtue of his regal authority enjoys many privileges: his men are billetted and fed without charge by the populace at large;

he claims monopolies on certain essential commodities; he exacts without restriction goods, monies and military services from all the villages and towns of the realm. Consequently, France, in spite of its natural wealth, is a poor and miserable land, wherein most men are not properly fed or clothed and are denied access to even basic guarantees of due process of law.[51] The English king, by contrast, has neither privilege of purveyance nor right of monopoly and his government can in no way impose 'tallages, subsidies or any other burdens on his subjects, nor change the laws, without the concession or assent of his whole realm expressed in his parliament'. Thus, Englishmen consume the fruits of the earth in all their fullness and abundance, without fear of confiscation or recrimination. Subjects of England's monarchy cannot be despoiled of their goods through the will of the ruler and they cannot be abused in their persons by means of royal courts.[52] In its society and economy, England approaches the Garden of Paradise in comparison to conditions in France, at least on Fortescue's account. How then can we fail to prefer a form of government which defends and protects the populace and its property to a kingdom whose ruler 'is so overcome by his own passions or poverty and cannot keep his hands from dispoiling his subjects'?[53] While Fortescue insists that the regal king *might* refrain from oppressing those over whom he reigns, there is still nothing in the procedure by which he wields power to prevent him from exploiting his rank for private gain. But the temptations open to the regal monarch simply do not apply to the king whose authority is both regal and political. Although the capacity of each ruler to do good is precisely equivalent,[54] experience of France and England demonstrates that 'the power of the king ruling regally is more troublesome in practice, and less secure for himself and his people, so that it would be undesirable for a prudent king to change a political government for a merely regal one'.[55] In reaching this conclusion, which is at the core of *De laudibus legum anglie*, Fortescue has summoned up and refined the tools of comparative political analysis. That Fortescue's authority and model for such techniques of comparison should be derived from Aristotle's *Rhetoric*, rather than from the *Politics*, suggests a recognition of the limitations of Aristotelian political theory in coping with differences among the emerging 'national' governments of western Europe.

The obvious similarity in the three cases we have just surveyed is the inadequacy of Aristotle's *Politics* as a tool of political analysis suited to the late Middle Ages. This is a discovery with serious repercussions insofar as one of the cornerstones of current interpretation among historians of mediaeval political thought has been the 'revolutionary' impact attributed to the *Politics* after 1250. Our survey of Pierre d'Auvergne, Pierre Dubois, Marsiglio of Padua and John Fortescue—each a committed Aristotelian—reveals exactly how contentious is the claim that political authors of the late Middle Ages were unable to escape the basic doctrines and principles of Aristotle's social and political philosophy. Precisely because of the prevalence of the interpretive paradigm, then, scholars have failed to ask themselves: in what ways and for what reasons did mediaeval authors cite Aristotle's works on metaphysics, natural philosophy, language and the like as authority for political views? If we extrapolate from our case studies, we may conclude that when Aristotle's social and political ideas could not be of assistance in addressing problems endemic to feudal Europe, late mediaeval thinkers turned to and often distorted other texts within the Aristotelian corpus in order to establish an 'Aristotelian' provenance for their theories. Indeed, since the practice of lending authoritative weight to the discussion of uniquely mediaeval issues by citing Aristotle's non-social philosophy was common among some of the most prominent authors of the late Middle Ages, we may infer that political theorists of the time were not concerned with conforming their own thought to the teachings of the *Politics* and *Ethics*. More plausibly, the Philosopher's expressly political ideas were applied selectively whenever such concepts were (or could be made) relevant to the questions which were of interest to the mediaeval mind. But since feudal Europe was hardly ancient Greece, the value of Aristotle's political thought for the Middle Ages was somewhat confined by a change of historical context. In order to satisfy the demand for Aristotelian authority, while addressing problems associated with the circumstances of contemporary feudal society, late mediaeval political authors put the natural and speculative components of Aristotle's philosophy to work for them. Behind the facade of bookish citations so characteristic of political texts at the end of the Middle Ages we thus find lively real-world debates that touched on the political and social conditions of Western Europe prior to the sixteenth century.[56]

NOTES

1. The first charge is made by Donald Hanson, *From Kingdom to Commonwealth* (Cambridge, Mass.: Harvard University Press, 1970), pp. 12–13, 130 and Maude V. Clarke, *Medieval Representation and Consent* (New York: Russell & Russell, 1964), p. 5; the second charge is expressed by Conal Condren, 'Marsilius of Padua's argument from authority', *Political Theory* **5** (May 1977), 205–18.

2. For a classic instance of such intellectual dishonesty, see Hans Liebeschütz, 'John of Salisbury and pseudoplutarch', *Journal of the Warburg and Courtauld Institutes* **6** (1943), 33–9.

3. The leading figure in this regard is Walter Ullmann, in whose view 'the impact of Aristotle's theories of government revolutionized the thinking concerned with basic conceptions of society and its government, and in fact produced such a radical change that we are still not in the position to grasp its extent fully'; *Medieval Political Thought* (Hardmondsworth, Middlesex: Penguin, 1975), p. 167; cf. pp. 159, 167–73. Seldom in contemporary scholarship has Ullmann's thesis of an 'Aristotelian revolution' been challenged.

4. See Quentin Skinner, *The Foundations of Modern Political Thought*, 2 vols. (Cambridge: Cambridge University Press, 1978), Vol. I, pp. 49–50; Walter Ullmann, *The Medieval Foundations of Renaissance Humanism* (Ithaca: Cornell University Press, 1979), pp. 89–90, 94–5 and *passim*.

5. For another example of fidelity to Aristotle's appearance, but not his actual views, see Antony Black, *Guilds and Civil Society in European Political Thought from the Twelfth Century to the Present* (Ithaca: Cornell University Press, 1984), pp. 91–2.

6. For what follows, see Georges Duby, *The Early Growth of the European Economy*, trans. H.B. Clarke (Ithaca: Cornell University Press, 1974), esp. pp. 43, 168–77.

7. The distinction is explained in further detail by John Bell Henneman, *Royal Taxation in Fourteenth Century France* (Princeton: Princeton University Press, 1971), pp. 17–24.

8. The evidence is presented by Joseph R. Strayer, 'Consent to taxation under Philip the Fair', in J.R. Strayer and C.H. Taylor, *Studies in Early French Taxation* (Cambridge, Mass.: Harvard University Press, 1939), pp. 7, 95–7.

9. The sources of public revenue in the polis are surveyed by M.I. Finley in *Economy and Society in Ancient Greece* (Harmondsworth, Middlesex: Penguin, 1983), pp. 90–1, *The Ancient Economy* (Berkeley: University of California Press, 1973), pp. 163–4 and *Politics in the Ancient World* (Cambridge: Cambridge University Press, 1983), pp. 32–3.

10. Aristotle's most substantial discussion of direct taxation occurs when offering advice to prospective tyrants —hardly surprising when one realises that public taxes were thought throughout Greece to be the mark of tyranny. Aristotle counsels the tyrant to maintain his own position and to prevent civic disorder by taxing moderately and discretely. See *Politics*, trans. E. Barker (Oxford: Oxford University Press, 1958), 1314b.

11. The relevant passages occur in *Metaphysics*, 1013a–1014a and *Physics*, 194b–195b.

12. *Metaphysics*, 1014a; my translation.

13. The text of d'Auvergne's *quodlibet*, from which the following quotation and summary has been translated, was published by Elizabeth A.R. Brown as an appendix to 'Cessante causa and the taxes of the last Capetians: the political applications of a philosophical maxim', *Studia Gratiana (Post Scripta)* 15 (1972), 585–7.

14. Pierre Dubois, *De recuperatione terre sancte*, ed. C.V. Langlois (Paris: Picard, 1891), sec. 123; all translations from this text are mine.

15. *Ibid.*, sec. 124.

16. *Ibid.*, sec. 124.

17. *Ibid.*, sec. 128.

18. See *ibid.*, secs. 127, 130 and 131.

19. An expanded discussion of the themes in this paragraph may be found in Perry Anderson, *Passages from Antiquity to Feudalism* (London: NLB, 1974), pp. 147–53.

20. These themes run, for instance, throughout the Periclean funeral oration composed by Thucydides in *History of the Peoloponnesian War*, trans. R. Warner (Baltimore: Penguin, 1954), II, 34–46; see also *Politics*, 1252b.

21. As established by John Le Patourel, 'The king and the prince in fourteenth-century France', in J.R. Hale, J.R.L. Highfield and B. Smalley, Eds., *Europe in the Later Middle Ages* (Evanston, Ill.: Northwestern University Press, 1965), pp. 44–75.

22. Aristotle's insistence upon the supremacy and singularity of the polis is illustrated by his claim that the polis 'is prior to the individual', insofar as individuals (as well as households and villages) lack the self-sufficiency of the polis (*Politics*, 1253a). Logically speaking, the individual is merely a part, while the polis is the whole; as the whole is by definition prior to any of its parts, so the polis must be prior to the individual.

23. Aristotle, *On the Movement of Animals*, trans. E.S. Forester (Cambridge, Mass.: Harvard University Press, 1937), 700a–b.

24. *Ibid.*, 700b.

25. *Ibid.*, 703a–b.

26. Marsiglio of Padua, *Defensor Pacis*, ed. C.W. Previté-Orton (Oxford: Oxford University Press, 1926), I.17.2; all translations from this text are mine.

27. *Ibid.*, I.17.1.

28. *Ibid.*, I.17.3, I.17.5, I.17.6.

29. *Ibid.*, I.17.8. A general treatment of the organic theme in the *Defensor* is contained in Tilman Struve, *Die Entwicklung der Organologischen Staatsauffassung im Mittelalter* (Stuttgart: Hiersemann, 1978), pp. 257–88. But Struve fails to appreciate that the organic analogy in Marsiglio—and indeed, in numerous other mediaeval thinkers—is employed in order to redress various difficulties posed by feudal society. For the

examination of another mediaeval application of organic imagery to the feudal polity, see C.J. Nederman, 'The political significance of the organic metaphor in John of Salisbury's *Policraticus*', (*History of Political Thought*, forthcoming).

30. *Defensor Pacis*, I.17.11.
31. *Ibid.*, I.17.3, I.17.4.
32. As is illustrated by Marsiglio's admission that kingship is the most perfect form of rule and his detailed accounts of the forms of monarchy and how kings may be appointed (*ibid.*, I.10, I.16). To no other system of rule does Marsiglio devote such great attention.
33. See the survey by Thomas J. Renna, 'Aristotle and the French monarchy, 1260–1303', *Viator* **9** (1978), 309.
34. An amplification of these ideas may be found in Joseph R. Strayer, *On the Medieval Origins of the Modern State* (Princeton: Princeton University Press, 1970), pp. 42–51.
35. It is for this reason that students of comparative politics and law trace the origins of their disciplines back to the Greeks generally and to Aristotle in particular. See Harry Eckstein, 'A perspective on comparative politics, past and present', in H. Eckstein and D.E. Apter, eds., *Comparative Politics: A Reader* (New York: Free Press, 1963), p. 3; Paul Vinogradoff, *Outlines of Historical Jurisprudence*, 2 vols. (Oxford: Oxford University Press, 1920), Vol. I, p. 67.
36. *Politics*, 1276b.
37. Aristotle, *Rhetoric*, 1409a–b.
38. *Ibid.*, 1410a; my translation.
39. *Ibid.*, 1419b–1420b.
40. *Ibid.*, 1410a; my translation.
41. John Fortescue, *De laudibus legum anglie*, ed. S.B. Chrimes (Cambridge: Cambridge University Press, 1949), chap. 24.
42. *Ibid.*, chap. 34.
43. *Ibid.*, chap. 9.
44. *Ibid.*, chap. 9.
45. *Ibid.*, chap. 11.
46. *Ibid.*, chap. 12.
47. *Ibid.*, chap. 13.
48. *Ibid.*, chap. 19.
49. *Ibid.*, chap. 20.
50. *Ibid.*, chap. 34.
51. *Ibid.*, chap. 35.
52. *Ibid.*, chap. 36.
53. *Ibid.*, chap. 37.
54. *Ibid.*, chap. 14.
55. *Ibid.*, chap. 37.
56. The author wishes to thank his former colleague Dr. Malcolm Grieve, now of Dalhousie University, for helpful comments on and criticism of an earlier draft of this essay.

XVI

CONCILIARISM AND CONSTITUTIONALISM: JEAN GERSON AND MEDIEVAL POLITICAL THOUGHT

I

The obscurities which surround the origins and development of constitutionalism form a favourite topic of investigation and discussion among historians of political thought. In the past, a wide range of alternative sources have been cited to explain the emergence of constitutional ideas and practices, among them the institutions and philosophies of ancient Greece and Rome, the doctrines associated with Roman Law, and the civic humanism of Renaissance Europe. More recently, however, another interpretation of the genesis of constitutionalism seems to have achieved particular cachet. The substance of this view is that constitutional principles first arose in and were directly shaped by the ecclesiology of the Latin Middle Ages, in particular, by the conception of the supremacy of the General Council of the church over the pope. Such a position received its seminal statement in J.N. Figgis's *Studies of Political Thought from Gerson to Grotius: 1414-1625*, a set of lectures which are fast approaching the centenary of their initial delivery.[1] Figgis maintained that the essential elements of constitutionalism emerged out of the crisis in church government created by the Great Schism and were given earliest theoretical expression by the conciliarist authors of the late fourteenth and fifteenth centuries.[2] Thus, for Figgis the year 1414, which marked the settlement of the schism at the Council of Constance, ushered in the dawn of the constitutionalist age.[3] That a General Council could actually depose legitimately-elected popes and appoint its own candidate—and could do so on the basis of a theory of conciliar sovereignty—represented, according to Figgis, a definitive break with all previous ideas of government and its relation to the community over which it rules.

The thesis propounded by Figgis has been greatly expanded by later scholars in two important directions. First, where Figgis had drawn his conclusions based on brief and generalised observations about the figures associated with conciliarism, his successors have undertaken more thorough and detailed study of the major and minor contributors to the conciliar theory of Constance and its era. In particular, the scholarly literature has sought to examine the differences as well as the similarities which distinguish the various proponents of conciliar doctrines.[4] The second major aspect of the renovation of Figgis was Brian Tierney's discovery that the basic precepts of conciliar thought were themselves rooted in a tradition of canon law that dated as far back as the twelfth-century

Reprinted from Cary J. Nederman, 'Conciliarism and constitutionalism: Jean Gerson and medieval political thought', *History of European Ideas* Vol. 12, No. 2 (1990), pp. 189–209, by kind permission from Elsevier Science Ltd., The Boulevard, Langford Lane, Kidlington, Oxford, OX5 1GB, UK.

decretists.[5] While challenging Figgis's view that conciliarism was strictly a product of its time and place, Tierney has lent the weight of several centuries of legal and political convention to the main claim that constitutionalism had its genesis in the ecclesiological thought of the Latin Middle Ages.

Consequently, scholarship in the past few years has become comfortable with the idea of a direct intellectual lineage extending from modern constitutionalism back to a medieval ecclesiological forebear. In its broadest terms, this genealogy has been traced from the twelfth to the eighteenth centuries, or as Tierney has stated, 'from Gratian to Madison'.[6] But the more commonly held claim is that the one may detect echoes of the conciliarism of the fourteenth and fifteenth centuries in the parliamentarianism of the seventeenth century. Thus, for Francis Oakley, 'the road from Constance to 1688 was a direct one',[7] while for Antony Black 'conciliarist writings were a major source of precedent and, occasionally, inspiration for men of the sixteenth and seventeenth centuries'.[8] Nor have such claims been confined to specialists in the field of medieval political thought. Rather, general treatments of modern Western political theory now often ascribe to conciliar ideas (whether in the formulation of the earlier canonists or the later polemicists) a pivotol role in shaping constitutional notions of government.[9]

Yet it remains unclear exactly how the notion of constitutionalism itself is understood by advocates of the ecclesiological genesis of constitutional ideas. By and large, proponents of Figgis's interpretaton have been vague about the definition they impute to constitutionalism, or they have taken the meaning of the term to be unambiguous and self-evident. For instance, in Tierney's 1979 Wiles Lectures (published in 1982), he simply speaks of 'recurring patterns of constitutional thought',[10] and of a thematic 'evolution of Western constitutional thought... preoccupied with consent, legitimacy, community rights, and, beyond these generalities, with rather technical problems concerning the relationship between central and local government, representation, rights of resistance, collegiate sovereignty, the distribution of authority within a complex collegiate sovereign'.[11] Tierney is perhaps somewhat more explicit in his definition of constitutionalism in his 1966 Presidential Address to the Catholic Historical Association:

> I am using the word "constitutionalism" to signify simply the most basic, taken-for-granted ideas that are implied by the most familiar platitudes of our political discourse, by phrases like "government under law" or "government by consent". We mean, I take it, a system in which a citizen is guaranteed due process of law and in which law itself is not merely the arbitrary will of a despot but rather reflects the moral outlook of the whole society, at least in its broad principles. And "government by consent", of course, means to us ... that the machinery exists for eliciting a consensus of opinion, for formulating courses of action that all citizens are prepared to accept, even though with differing degrees of enthusiasm. The characteristic institutional machinery in modern constitutional states is the elected representative assembly with effect rights of consent to legislation and taxation.[12]

Black also speaks in terms of 'clusters' of ideas whose logical interrelation is left undetermined: 'The chief points on which the parliamentarians cited concilar theory and practice were the popular origin of political power, the at least occasional supremacy of the representative assembly over the prince, and ... the legitimacy of deposing a king'.[13] Such a loose approach to the essential elements of constitutionalism and their conceptual ordering begs many important questions. Is a constitutional structure constituted primarily by an institutional apparatus of consent and representation? Is it a function of the rule of law? Does it entail any particular notion of the relation between the rights of the individual and the power of the state? Without answers to questions like these, it proves difficult to evaluate with any precision the claim that the origins of constitutionalism derive from the principle of conciliar supremacy.

In spite of such uncertainties, it is possible to identify a pair of assumptions which appear to be necessary to all the various accounts of the impact of medieval conciliar ideas upon early modern constitutionalism. First, the followers of Figgis must maintain that the conciliar conception of government differs significantly from other strains of medieval political thought, especially from theories of the secular polity. Were this premise to be denied, there would be nothing particularly unique about conciliar thought to distinguish it from other medieval approaches to political rule, and thus there would be no basis for the claim that conciliarism *specifically* begat constitutional thought. Second, the body of scholarship under consideration must hold that the conciliar framework embraces essentially the same notion of constitutional rule as that adopted by modern thinkers. Otherwise, it would be senseless to talk about 'recurring patterns' of thought and the 'persistence' and 'continuity' of ideas, as well as the 'influence' of particular texts and thinkers—phrases which occur regularly in the work of Figgis and those who adhere to his views.[14] Should it be the case that the concepts and vocabulary of the conciliarists took on a different meaning in light of early modern constitutional experience, there would be no basis for assigning responsibility to conciliarism itself for any substantive intellectual contribution to the constitutionalist cause in the seventeenth century. In the absence of a commitment to both of these premises, therefore, any statement of the claim that early modern constitutional thought arose from conciliar ecclesiology would lack adequate justification.

It is the claim of the present paper, however, that neither of these assumptions is warranted. It will be argued, on the contrary, that the conciliar conception of the church stems from fundamentally the same principles as other medieval theories of government and thus that, insofar as 'constitutionalism' is present within conciliar doctrines, it is a version of constitutional rule which was typical of the Latin Middle Ages rather than of early modern Europe. In other words, I maintain both that conciliarism is more consistent with medieval political thought in general than has been allowed and that there is a decisive break between this medieval approach to government and a distinctively modern framework. The failure of many scholars to appreciate the essentially medieval quality of conciliar thought, and hence to distance conciliarism from modern constitutionalism, is perhaps the result of their tendency to plunder specific doctrines from texts without appropriate regard for the wider intellectual and political beliefs and concerns of their authors.

The extent to which it is erroneous to view modern constitutionalism as the culmination of conciliar ecclesiology is evident, for instance, from careful study of the theory of the General Council propounded by the late medieval theologian Jean Gerson. Since the publication of Figgis's *Studies*, Gerson has been acclaimed as one of the clearest cases of a conciliar author whose ideas pointed the way forward to constitutionalism. Gerson's conciliar credentials are spotless. He was personally active in promoting a conciliar solution to the Great Schism, and his writings were widely disseminated throughout the period of the Councils of Pisa and Constance.[15] Gerson was neither particularly original nor startlingly radical in his ecclesiology, however.[16] Rather, he was noted for adopting a 'moderate' view of church government in both theoretical and practical terms.[17] Yet, at the same time, Gerson's version of conciliarism received considerable attention well into the seventeenth century. Tierney speaks of him as 'a very influential transmitter of medieval constitutional thought into early modern times'.[18] So if Gerson's thought was both firmly rooted in the mainstream of later medieval conciliarism and also popular among seventeenth-century inheritors, Figgis's thesis would lead us to expect that his theoretical perspective should be more attuned to the basic precepts of modern constitutionalism than to the salient doctrines of preceding medieval political thought. In fact, however, we shall discover that Gerson's ecclesiology was firmly planted in the most characteristic political traditions of the Latin Middle Ages. Only by neglecting the intellectual foundations of Gerson's conciliarism is it possible to attribute distinctively modern constitutional ideas to his writings.

II

Much of the uncertainty surrounding the claim that the conciliarism of Gerson (and more broadly, of other advocates of the supremacy of the Council within the church) was constitutionalist in its bearing derives from significant ambiguities in the meaning of the term 'constitutionalism' itself.[19] For confusion arises from the fact that two distinct yet related definitions are commonly ascribed to constitutionalism, at least when the word carries a normative connotation.[20] In one of these senses, constitutionalism denotes 'a legal limitation on government' or 'the rule of law'.[21] This meaning of constitutionalism entails the incompatibility of constitutional rule with any doctrine or actual regime in which government is seen to depend upon the exercise of an arbitrary or unchecked will. In a constitutional system so conceived, the rulers are subject to the same legal dictates as individual citizens. In short, any government that submits itself to law (and that, concomitantly, can have law imposed upon it) qualifies in this sense as a constitutional regime.

But this cannot be what scholars have in mind when they say that conciliar ecclesiology provides an important source for later constitutional thought. If they did wish to say that conciliarism begat constitutionalism merely in the sense that conciliar theory advocated the legal restraint of rulership, then there would be nothing particularly unique about the doctrines of the conciliarists. For the idea that government must be limited by and subservient to law was widely upheld by medieval authors who were neither conciliarists nor even directly concerned with the political organisation of the Church. Rather, proponents of the position that conciliarism stands at the origins of secular constitutional theory would seem to construe constitutionalism according to a narrower definition which refers to principles characteristic specifically of the West in recent times. A century and a half ago, Hegel proclaimed that 'the development of the state' along genuinely constitutional lines 'is the achievement of the modern world'.[22] More recent scholars have confimed this interpretation by attributing the dissemination of constitutional doctrines solely to the seventeenth or eighteenth centuries.[23] The substance of the 'modern' definition of constitutionalism does not exclude the previous sense of the limitation of government through legal means and procedures. But it is argued that rule of law is an insufficient characterisation of the criteria of constitutional rule. Rather, the distinctively modern connotation of constitutionalism requires political rule to be organised on the basis of a more concrete set of features, including:

(1) an impersonal conception of government grounded in the office rather than the person of the ruler;[24]
(2) limitation of rulers through public control over the offices of state;[25]
(3) the guarantee of specific and imprescriptible rights to all persons or citizens;[26]
(4) individualised free consent to rulers and their official deeds.[27]

Viewed collectively, these principles supplement the rule of law so as to compose the core of modern constitutional theory. According to the uniquely modern sense of constitutionalism government is conducted within the confines of law by officials whose duties are determined in advance and carefully regulated, who hold office at the pleasure of the citizen body at large, and who must treat as sacrosanct certain forms of individual activity.

The extent to which this specifically modern conception of constitutional rule differs from commonly held medieval beliefs about the rule of law is very great indeed. During the Middle Ages, arguments for the requirement of rule according to law did not appeal to institutional mechanisms; instead they were rooted in a definite conception of law itself. In particular, regardless of the immediate source of the law, it was understood to be a manifestation of divinely-ordained precepts of justice. Legal positivism was simply not a feature of the medieval outlook.[28] Rather, human legal codes were deemed to be valid insofar as they were not arbitrary expressions of private will, but temporal applications of God-given decrees.[29] As a consequence, the Middle Ages treated obedience to the law as a moral obligation instead of merely as a legal or political duty. And this moral duty was no less incumbent upon rulers than upon their subjects.[30]

Medieval authors acknowledged, however, one significant difference between rulers and subjects, namely, that princes and the like were empowered to enforce law coercively over their inferiors—to judge justly and to execute judgment[31]— whereas there was no source of authority short of some superior competent to judge rulers. In other words, while rulership existed precisely in order to ensure that moral obligations were fulfilled and to penalise non-compliance ('to reward the good and to punish the evil'),[32] it remained uncertain whether anyone could impose an obligation upon a ruler who acknowledged no temporal superior. As Bracton expressed this paradox, the king is 'under God and under law, but not under man'.[33] Medieval solutions to the dilemma posed by the king who was subject to law yet without a master were couched in terms of a demonstrably personalised conception of governmental office in which the expectation of royal conformity to law is derived from the character traits of the individual ruler. As Aquinas declared, 'it is necessary that the man who is raised up to be king by those whom it concerns should be of such condition that it is unlikely that he would become a tyrant'.[34] Thus, Thomas and indeed the mainstream of medieval political thought devoted considerable effort to identifying the appropriate moral qualities for a ruler.[35] But more importantly, medieval authors were concerned to demonstrate that these personal features were deeply rooted and not subject to sudden change. This they commonly did by reference to the Aristotelian doctrine of *hexis* (translated into Latin as *habitus*), that is, the idea that virtue is a firm and unshakeable dispositional state acquired through repeated practice.[36] This notion was in circulation from at least the twelfth century[37] and was viewed as the foundation for the limits of a ruler's action by a range of theorists who otherwise had little in common.[38] The conclusion universally reached on the basis of the Aristotelian doctrine of *habitus* was that the ruler whose moral character was well-formed could always and forever be expected to judge in accordance with the law and to obey just statute in all things, precisely because his disposition towards virtue led him to conform his conduct to the justice inherent in the law. Hence, the ruler whose personal traits were inclined towards goodness would limit himself—his moral character was so imbued with the desire to do good that he could not intentionally will an illegal act.

At the same time, of course, medieval authors were perfectly aware that for a whole array of reasons a ruler might come to power whose character was not properly disposed towards virtue and thereby law. In other words, the king or prince might be transformed into a tyrant, a ruler who 'seeks his private interest' according to 'the desire of his will' and pure 'caprice', and who thus opposes law and justice.[39] Theorists of the Latin Middle Ages were widely concerned with the problem posed by the tyrant,[40] and made a variety of provisions for the eventuality of tyranny. Some advocated direct appeals to God,[41] some proposed that the corporate community or its representatives could censure or depose him,[42] others recommended ecclesiastical correction and reprimand,[43] a few even defended the option of tyrannicide.[44] But regardless of the solution suggested, a single factor ran through all medieval responses to tyranny. Theorists always sought to limit, direct or punish the ruler in a personal sense, as the bearer of certain subjective moral qualities, rather than to control the actual exercise of the powers of his office. There could be no grounds for restricting the authority of a ruler whose moral will was oriented towards the performance of just deeds. The reason that we can find no attempt to specify prospectively the valid activities of government is that office and its attendant powers were regarded to be inherently good, a gift from God.[45] Thus, if governmental authority was abused, the source of the abuse could only lie with the particular occupant of the office.[46] The exercise of power per se could never be bad, but only the person who misused his privileges. Whenever a medieval ruler was said to exceed the bounds of his authority or to require limitation, this did not mean that he had exercised certain powers to which he was not entitled as a legitimate incumbent of his office. Instead, the restriction of government pertained solely to the intent, the moral will, on the basis of which the office-holder conducted his duties. A good prince, one who lived up to the moral obligation to conform his actions to just legislation and hence to serve the public welfare, could not properly be opposed. The response to tyranny in the Middle Ages was thereby necessarily *ad hoc* (regardless of the form it took) because tyranny itself arose from the vicissitudes of the individual ruler's moral will and therefore could not be controlled or provided for in advance.

The impact of the moral conception of government typical of the Middle Ages upon the status of subjects was two-fold. First, subjects were assured of no fixed or independent rights in relation to the ruler. Rulers could do as they saw fit so long as they remained consistent with the dictates of justice. This was ordinarily interpreted to mean that government was authorised to do whatever was necessary for the promotion of the common good.[47] There was no legitimate defense from or redress for governmental actions done on the basis of a valid claim of the common benefit, even if such an act caused demonstrable harm to private interests or welfare. Even a theorist like John of Paris, who was well disposed towards a large role for private and individual pursuits,[48] readily admitted that the king's determinations for the public utility took ultimate precedence over any personal rights.[49] Where subjects enjoyed rights against their political masters, they only did so collectively, insofar as the corporate whole was endowed with a superior capacity to determine when its own common good has been violated.[50] In their private status, individual members of the community possessed no guarantee of standing or respect when faced with the genuine needs and welfare of the totality. Governments were seen to be unlimited in their capacity to defend the public advantage.

The other effect of the moral conception of rulership upon subjects pertains to the theoretical principle that rulers ought to receive the continuing consent of their subordinates. Often enough, this doctrine was advocated by medieval authors. It was ordinarily thought to encompass two factors: first, that rulers are appointed through an act of election; and second, that whosoever comes to power by means of election may be deposed or corrected by his electors. But these doctrines were given a distinct collectivist gloss. The act of election was viewed as the deed of the *totus populus* or *universitas*, that is, the corporate body acting in concert. Yet the actual mechanism through which the whole people or corporation renders its consent might be narrowly constituted or merely formal, as in the selection of the *rex Romanum* by the imperial electors on behalf of the entire Roman people or the 'recognition' of the king by those in attendance at a coronation ceremony.[51] By no stretch of the imagination was the consent implicit in election of an individualised nature; it was instead a 'unamimous' act of the entire community, the collectivity speaking with one voice.[52] Similarly, when medieval authors pointed out the structural parallel between election and deposition—that those with the authority to confer power must also have the authority to remove it—they conceived of the entire community acting with a single mind against its government.[53] The idea that individuals as individuals might have legitimate grounds to withdraw political consent would seem very strange to medieval political theorists, as indeed it later did to the French Huguenot authors of the sixteenth century.[54] The corporate community alone is authorised to depose its ruler and to replace him, since it is the unique bearer of the ultimate knowledge of its own good. And thus the safety and security of the public welfare forms the sole legitimate basis for the dissolution of a government.

III

It is beyond dispute that Jean Gerson was committed to the doctrine of limited papal rule conducted according to law. He stated flatly that 'spiritual [jurisdiction] should be exercised according to canonical laws towards the ultimate end of realizing beatitude', just as 'temporal [jurisdiction] should be exercised according to the civil laws'.[55] Like the secular prince, who executes and enforces the law but does not legislate, the pope is viewed as a judge whose determinations must occur on the basis of law.[56] Of course, the functions of papal jurisdiction are unique, constituted by 'the juridical power of excommunication or interdict by denial of ecclesiastical sacraments and the communion of faith to those who rebel against and disobey the church'.[57] The pope, in other words, is charged with primary jurisdiction for the maintenance of faith and morals among the body of Christian believers to be accomplished by the enforcement of church law. But the canons of the church are by no means coextensive with the whim of the papal incumbent. Gerson found abhorrent the application of the Roman Law doctrine 'Quod placuit principi legis habet vigorem' to the governance of the church.[58] Rather, church law was to be strictly the expression of divine decree and natural rectitude; those 'positive regulations' which demonstrably conflict with 'natural and divine law and the common utility... ought not to be observed'.[59] Gerson explains that canon law, because it is the creation of fallible humans, can be shunned on the grounds that it violates the so-called principle of equity, which he borrows from Aristotle's idea of *epikeia*.[60] But even the application of equity in order to measure or vary man-made law does not pertain to the pope (or indeed to any other individual). Equity is a capability vested uniquely in the whole church or its corporate representative, the General Council.[61] The pope, in short, is strictly bound to observe the statutes of the church, which are neither of his creation nor at his disposal.

Gerson's requirement that the papacy must govern in accordance with law does not, however, entail a denial of the papal plentitude of power, that is, the independence of the authority of the pope's office from any superior except God. Indeed, some affirmation of the pope's *plenitudo potestatis* was included in virtually all the canonistic and conciliar literature which has been cited as the source-material of modern constitutionalism.[62] Gerson remarks simply that 'the papal plenitude of power was granted by Christ in those things which are supernatural... [and] stands supreme'.[63] This principle is accepted universally throughout Gerson's writings, in spite of the fact that his arguments would perhaps have been rendered more coherent and consistent by its rejection.[64] In turn, the theoretical basis for the pope's indispensable *plenitudo potestatis* may be located in Gerson's analysis of the nature of ecclesiastical power in general. Gerson argues that all offices within the church have, formally speaking, been ordained directly by God.[65] In this sense, the powers pertaining to the pope cannot be curtailed or controlled by any human authority without violating the divine will. Rather, 'ecclesiastical power in its plenitude is formally and subjectively in the Roman pontiff alone... The plenitude of ecclesiastical power is the power of order and jurisdiction which was supernaturally given by Christ to Peter, as His direct and first King, for himself and for his successors to the end of time, for the edification of the church militant towards the achievement of eternal felicity'.[66] It is thereby erroneous to attribute to Gerson the position that 'the pope's apparent plenitude of power is in effect conceded to him as a matter of administrative convenience'.[67] To the contrary, Gerson believes that the papal *plenitudo potestatis* is of divine origin and is absolutely essential for the conduct of the church's main business, namely, the salvation of souls. In no way ought the pope to be construed as ancillary or derivative to the full spiritual life of the church.

At the same time, however, Gerson is aware that the doctrine of *plenitudo potestatis* has perpetuated an exaggerated vision of the pope's office. Consequently he allows that ecclesiastical power may also be understood to convey two other meanings: a 'material' or 'respective' sense, related to its assignment 'to particular persons by legitimate right'; and a sense connected to the 'exercise or execution' of power.[68] Materially speaking, the pope (or any ecclesiastical officer) must be chosen and consecrated, activities which appropriately inhere in the whole church. Thus, the church as the mystical body of Christian believers retains ultimate authority over the specific occupants of the papal office.[69] Analogously, the power of regulating the use to which particular persons put the rights attached to ecclesiastical government is to be found in the corporate church.[70] For papal jurisdiction exists not for its own sake, but instead in order to 'edify' the church, to serve the common good of salvation.[71] And should a given pope not aim at this end, the authority pertaining to the papal office is abused rather than rightly used. In short, Gerson believes that 'the regulation of the use' of papal power is confined to those circumstances in which 'it is liable to be turned into abuse'.[72] The church does not control the office; it instead supervises the conduct of the individual incumbent of the papacy. The regulatory role with which the church is endowed arises because of the uncertainties surrounding man's moral will: 'since the supreme pontiff ... is open to sin and may wish to turn his power to the destruction of the church', it is necessary for 'abuse of this sort to be repressed, limited and moderated' by the whole church.[73] A pope who reveals a vicious moral character, like a prince who proves to be evil, will govern for his own sake rather than for the utility of the church.[74] As a consequence, his personal qualities are inconsistent with the nature of his office, and he is thereby subject to correction, punishment and even deposition.

Yet, on the other hand, the pope whose behavior is appropriate to the office that he occupies is beyond any scrutiny; he is protected by his *plenitudo potestatis*. The pope can do whatever is demanded for the edification and welfare of the church without any limit or supervision. When its incumbent acts according to the precepts of faith and charity, the papacy must be totally free to exercise and impose its jurisdiction: 'We are able to do what we are able to do rightfully'.[75] Abuses of power are defined only in terms of actions arising from a morally bad will (the will of the tyrant) which places its private interests above the needs of the public. The 'limitation' of papal authority can only be applied to the use of the powers at their disposal by individual occupants, and never to the direct control of the office itself, which is a matter for divine determination. Gerson's attitude is summarised by his declaration: 'Papa fluit, papatus stabilis est' ('The pope changes but the papacy is stable').[76] It is solely the person and personality of the pope that fall within the perview of the entire church; the terms of his office cannot be altered or varied by any authority other than God Himself. The church must see to it that the exercise of ecclesiastical power is placed in the hands of men of good will; and the church may strip papal power from an individual who demonstrates by his judgments and actions that his personal character is malformed. Otherwise, the church must submit to the pope's *plenitudo potestatis*.

It is such fundamental moral considerations that also inform the relationship between the pope and the General Council. A number of canonistic sources had proposed that the formal deposition of a pope by a General Council was unnecessary or, at least, merely confirmatory. They argued that the pope in effect deposes himself by ruling the church according to an evil, instead of a good, will. Conciliar deposition is thereby to be regarded as a public proclamation of an accomplished fact—recognition of the vacancy of the Papal See, not the act by which the previous occupant was removed.[77] It has been taken as an important feature of Gerson's thought that he refused to conceive of the process of deposition in this fashion.[78] Rather, Gerson argued that just as a pope is only elevated to office when he has been formally elected and consecrated, so he can only be ousted from the papal throne by a public proceeding and final judgment within the context of a General Council.[79] Deposition is hence treated as an institutional act, instead of as a strict consequence of the pope's own moral disposition.[80] But Gerson also makes it clear that the reason popes are deposed by Councils stems from human frailty and imperfection. Insofar as an individual pope may fall into sin, he is susceptible to the judgment of Church and Council, 'to which he is subject in the same manner as one who is capable of erring to what can never err.'[81] In other words, because it is exercised by fallible humans, the papal will is 'accidentalis atque mutabilis',[82] whereas the will of the General Council is without moral defect and may therefore always be expected to reach the correct decision in matters of papal turpitude. The determinations of the Council are effectively the actions of a morally superior and incorruptible body. So long as the pope conducts his government in a manner consistent with a good moral will for the benefit of the whole church, he can never run afoul of the General Council. Therefore, at least in the realm of intentional action, it is only through vice and the attendant pursuit of private interests that a pope falls prey to the condemnation and punishment of the permanently righteous Council.

The 'perfection' of the General Council is perhaps one of the more problematic features of Gerson's thought. But his reasoning is strikingly similar to that of secular theorists of ultimate community supremacy during the Middle Ages. Gerson asserts that the general Council is thoroughly and invariably representative of the entire church.[83] The Council may thus be conceived as the sole and incontrovertible voice of the corporate mystical body of the church. When the Council speaks, its proclamations do not reflect the private concerns of its membership but the true needs and purposes of the total ecclesiastical corporation. The General Council does not have a will of its own; rather it expresses the genuine and singular will of the church community. At this juncture we encounter the corporatism that was an ingrained feature of medieval canonistic and conciliar writing.[84] As a mystical body, the church has only one will and only one set of interests; its common utility is to be found in the defense and dissemination of the orthodox faith and correct morals, a universal and self-consistent doctrine. The church, in sum, is the bearer of 'indeviable wisdom'[85] with regard to its own goals and ends. In view of its organisation, furthermore, the welfare of the corporate church is characteristically distinct from and superior to the private benefit of any of its particular members. Within the ecclesiastical setting, the communal church is the final arbiter of all matters touching upon the beliefs and conduct of the faithful.

By extension, the General Council derives its infallible status from the special and privileged access which the whole ecclesiastical community enjoys to the absolute knowledge of its own common good.[86] As representative of the church, the Council is simultaneously representative of that welfare of which the mystical body alone on earth is the ultimate judge. An individual will can never represent this common utility infallibly and without fail, for it is too easy a matter for a single person (or even small group) to be tempted by passion and led astray into sin. But the corporate structure of the General Council, insofar as it resembles the structure of the entire church, is not believed to be capable of entering into a similar path of immorality.[87] The perfect wisdom with which the church is endowed is explicitly transferred to the decrees of a General Council. And such perfection renders the Council functionally supreme in the determination of faith and morals, including the conduct of a pope who abuses the powers pertaining to his office.

In a sense, then, the pope does rule with the consent of the church manifested through its unique representative, the General Council.[88] But such consent is characteristically corporate, a function of a 'higher' ethical and religious consensus. Neither Gerson nor (so far as can be ascertained) any other proponent of conciliar supremacy stipulated that the General Council ought to canvas and reflect the actual, empirical wills of individual church members.[89] The Council is not beholden to particular interests within the church in the manner of an elected representative in a modern republic who is bound to be responsible and responsive to his constituency. For the Council is under the direct guidance of the Holy Spirit, and the church itself has only one genuine interest to be served: the perpetuation of a unified orthodoxy, about which there could be no legitimate difference of opinion. Therefore, the General Council concerns itself solely with matters arising from the identification and enforcement of catholic doctrine, that is, with the truer and higher purpose necessarily shared by all Christians.[90] In this, the faithful at large were effectively treated as mere subjects rather than full citizens; their actual participation as individual members of the church was not essential or important. The freedom of each Christian to consent to the Council and its work is reminiscent of Isaiah Berlin's idea of 'positive liberty'.[91] The advocate of positive liberty, like the proponent of consent within conciliar theory, claims that the criterion of free choice is adequately met when true human or spiritual goodness is realised and imposed upon individuals. We must never confuse the mystical body of the church with an aggregate of its particular members. In view of the inescapable demand for a single canon of beliefs, the General Council cannot be representative of nor even seek consultation with the diversity of real opinions and interests among individuals within the mundane church.

There would consequently appear to be no basis in Gerson's ecclesiology for the ascription of fundamental rights to individuals. It is true that Richard Tuck has recently discovered in Gerson's writings a 'theory of subjective rights', that is, the idea that each and every human being is endowed with the right to control his own life and property and, hence, to consent to any demands made upon him by government.[92] But to the extent that this doctrine appears in Gerson, it is a product of his moral theology rather than his ecclesiological theory. To attribute to Gerson's conciliarism a grounding in subjective rights, as has lately been proposed by Quentin Skinner,[93] is to misconstrue seriously the corporatist premises of the argument.[94] Even Tuck acknowledges an incompatibility between the 'potentially individualistic' implications of the theory of subjective rights and the 'crucial feature' of conciliar doctrine 'that a community was the source of political authority'.[95] Stated less circumspectly, Gerson's corporatism was intellectually hostile to the individual's standing as an individual. Thus, Gerson regards as dangerous and pernicious the doctrine that individual Christians might properly and legitimately resist the dictates of a pope. Such resistance pertains strictly to the General Council as corporate representative of the church.[96] On similar grounds, Gerson repeatedly challenges the view that it is possible for the entire church, excepting only one or a few individuals (worse yet, women!), for fall into heresy. To allow individual persons to allege a superior awareness of true doctrine, Gerson argues, is to make a mockery of the sacraments and to attack the divinely-ordained 'hierarchy of grades and offices' assigned for the common utility of the church.[97] The infusion of the Holy Spirit ensures that the institutional church will always enjoy the special knowledge of orthodoxy typical of the *corpus mysticum*. There is no notion in Gerson that the individual requires protection from the government of the church, thus no principle of individual rights. To the contrary, the corporate and ultimately conciliar organisation of the church exists to uphold values such as unity and order that are fundamentally opposed to individuality and independence.

IV

Based on the evidence of Gerson's ecclesiological writings, we are warranted in drawing two conclusions. First, Gerson was indeed a constitutionalist. He advocated government strictly in accordance with law; he denied to the ruler the despotic authority to propound or suspend the law; and he sought means by which to impose limitations effectively over the conduct of rulers. But the character of Gerson's constitutionalism was closely allied with more general, and not uniquely ecclesiological, tendencies within medieval political thought. Gerson's papal ruler retains an unlimited power to serve the good of the community. When the private will of the pope intrudes into his exercise of jurisdiction, so that use becomes abuse, however, the church or its conciliar representative may act to regulate, correct or depose him. The community is always the repository of final judgment with regard to the substance of its own welfare. Yet Gerson expects that a pope whose personal qualities dispose him to act on the basis of the moral and theological virtues will normally rule without consulting the body of the faithful. The General Council remains a fundamentally extraordinary institution, assembled to discuss and make determinations about difficult or unusual problems of faith and morals touching upon the corporate interests of the church.[98] It is representative precisely insofar as it gives concrete expression to the genuine common utility of the whole church, namely the unity of faith and morals.

Consequently, we may also conclude that Gerson's ecclesiological vision reflects none of the distinctive themes or patterns of thought which we associate with constitutionalism in its specifically modern sense. Gerson's analysis of papal government concentrates on the personal moral condition of the incumbent rather than the impersonal terms and provisions of the office itself. The quality of a given papal reign depends crucially upon the relative moral disposition of the pope himself. Nor does the papal office arise from any act on the part of the community. The duties of the papacy are assigned by divine ordination and are directed towards supernatural ends. Thus, the only real limitations on papal conduct are retrospective ones, that is, *ex post facto* admonition and punishment. Moreover, Gerson's theological concerns preclude the incorporation of any significant role for the individual within the governance of the church. A single catholic faith untroubled by heresy or schism is profoundly incompatible with the plurality of opinion and diversity of conduct implied by modern ideas of consent and individual rights. Gerson's appeal to corporate and hierarchical ideas of church government—a perspective widely shared among medieval canonist and conciliarist authors—ensured that the real views and wishes of individual Christians would carry less weight than an abstract conception of what they *ought* to consent to (or be made to consent to) in the name of true faith and good morals. That persons should enjoy determinate rights *against* the collective totality of the church and its officials and representatives, instead of *within* the mystical body, would have seemed a very odd doctrine indeed to Gerson.

An analysis of Gerson, then, reveals that neither of the crucial assumptions necessary for maintaining the conciliarist origins of modern constitutionalism apply to his work. Gerson's ecclesiology embraces a conception of government which is fundamentally in agreement with other philosophical and legal discussions of limited temporal rulership typical of the Latin Middle Ages. Conciliar theory as formulated by Gerson involved no great departure from principles which were widely accepted by medieval authors. Thus, Gerson cannot accurately be classified as a medieval precursor or founder of the doctrines of modern constitutionalism. Although both medieval and modern accounts of constitutional government are firmly committed to the rule of law, the corporatist and spiritual tenor of medieval constitutionalism contrasts markedly with the individualistic and secular tone of its modern successor.

The failure of Gerson to live up to the two assumptions underlying the Figgis thesis in turn suggests the validity of one of two conclusions about the relation between constitutionalism and conciliarism. On the one hand, it may be that scholars have been mistaken in treating Gerson's thought as typical of or central to the conciliarist movement. If this is so, then perhaps other advocates of the supremacy of the Council will still prove to be more 'modern' in their outlook than Gerson, and hence conciliarism may continue to be treated as an important intellectual influence on sixteenth- and seventeenth-century constitutionalist doctrines. The present essay offers no judgment on Gerson's congruence with or divergence from the conciliarism of his contemporaries, other than to point out that the denial to him of a central role in the formulation of conciliar theory

XVI

contradicts a standard claim within the existing body of scholarly literature. On the other hand, if Gerson's ideas are indeed as characteristic of conciliar thought as scholars have thus far supposed, then we may be justified in posing a challenge to other proponents of conciliarism similar to that which we have made to Gerson's reputation. In other words, it may eventuate that the alleged 'modernity' of conciliar ecclesiology in general is purely a function of the anachronistic ascription of more recent categories of thought to earlier texts without regard for differences of historical perspective, linguistic usage or political context. Such an anachronistic stance certainly explains Gerson's continued popularity into the seventeenth century as a political author. His early modern inheritors were unconcerned about fidelity to the broad contours of his thought. Instead, they reinterpreted his theories selectively and in accordance with their own particular problems and assumptions. This was not an uncommon practice when early modern thinkers drew upon medieval doctrines and texts.[99] But the fact that modern political authors plundered their medieval forebears for ideas and authoritative citations does not permit us to infer thereby the conceptual 'modernity' of the medieval sources themselves. Instead, we must distinguish between the meaning of ideas in their own terms and how such ideas were received and applied by succeeding generations. It is the refusal to acknowledge this distinction that seems to have stimulated most of the recent scholarly efforts to locate medieval conciliarism at the root of modern constitutionalism. Such a refusal, however, distorts both the nature of conciliarist thought and the true achievement of the early modern constitutionalists.

NOTES

Earlier versions of this essay were presented to the 1987 meeting of the Australasian Political Studies Association, and to colloquia at York University and the University of Canterbury. The author acknowledges the helpful suggestions of participants in these sessions, and is especially grateful to Dr Glenn Burgess for his insightful comments.

1. Figgis's book began as the Birkbeck Lectures, delivered in 1900; it was first published in 1907, printed in a second edition in 1916, and reprinted with an introduction by Garrett Mattingly under the title *Political Thought from Gerson to Grotius: 1414–1625, 7 Studies* (New York: Harper and Row, 1960).
2. The substance of Figgis's argument is contained in *Ibid.*, pp. 41–70.
3. For further analysis and appreciation of the contribution of Figgis, see Brian Tierney, *Religion, Law, and the Growth of Constitutional Thought, 1150–1650* (Cambridge: Cambridge University Press, 1982), pp. 2–6; and Francis Oakley, 'Figgis, Constance, and the Divines of Paris', *American Historical Review* 75 (1969), pp. 368–86.
4. Among these contributions to the study of conciliar theory may be included: Francis Oakley, *The Political Thought of Pierre d'Ailly* (New Haven: Yale University Press, 1964); Oakley, 'Legitimation by Consent: The Question of Medieval Roots', *Viator* 14 (1983), pp. 303–35; Oakley, *Natural Law, Conciliarism and Consent in the*

Middle Ages (London: Variorum Reprints, 1984); Paul E. Sigmund, Jr, *Nicholas of Cusa and Medieval Political Thought* (Cambridge, Mass.: Harvard University Press, 1963); John B. Morrall, *Gerson and the Great Schism* (Manchester: Manchester University Press, 1960); Antony J. Black, *Monarchy and Community: Political Ideas in the Later Conciliar Controversy, 1430–1450* (Cambridge: Cambridge University Press, 1970); Black, *Council and Commune: The Conciliar Movement and the Fifteenth Century Heritage* (London: Burns and Oates, 1979); and Black, 'Society and the Individual from the Middle Ages to Rousseau: Philosophy, Jurisprudence and Constitutional Theory', *History of Political Thought* 1 (Summer 1980), pp. 145–66.

5. Among Tierney's more significant studies are: 'The Canonists and the Mediaeval State', *Review of Politics* 15 (1953), pp. 378–89; *Foundations of the Conciliar Theory* (Cambridge: Cambridge University Press, 1955); 'Medieval Canon Law and Western Constitutionalism', *The Catholic Historical Review* 52 (April 1966), pp. 1–17; and *Religion, Law, and the Growth of Constitutional Thought*. Many of Tierney's other studies have been collected and published under the title *Church Law and Constitutional Thought in the Middle Ages* (London: Varorium Reprints, 1979).

6. Tierney, *Religion, Law, and the Growth of Constitutional Thought*, p. xi.

7. Oakley, 'On the Road from Constance to 1688: The Political Thought of John Major and George Buchanan', *Journal of British Studies* 1 (1962), p. 31. It should be noted that Oakley himself has revised his position in recent times, and now stresses important discontinuities between conciliar and modern constitutionalist ideas; see 'Legitimation by Consent', p. 323 (where he says that the path to full-fledged constitutionalism from conciliarism was 'not quite' a direct one) and 'Disobedience, Consent, Political Obligation: The Witness of Wessel Gansfort (*ca.* 1419–1489)', *History of Political Thought* 9 (Summer 1988), pp. 211–2.

8. Antony Black, 'The Conciliar Movement', in J.H. Burns, ed., *The Cambridge History of Medieval Political Thought* (Cambridge: Cambridge University Press, 1988), p. 587. For a similar position, see Zofia Rueger, 'Gerson, the Conciliar Movement and the Right of Resistance (1642–1644)', *Journal of the History of Ideas* 25 (October–December 1964), pp. 467–86.

9. For instance, Quentin Skinner, *The Foundations of Modern Political Thought*, 2 vols (Cambridge: Cambridge University Press, 1978), II, pp. 36–7, 114 and Andrew Vincent, *Theories of the State* (Oxford: Basil Blackwell, 1987), pp. 82, 86.

10. Tierney, *Religion, Law, and the Growth of Constitutional Thought*, p. viii.

11. *Ibid.*, p. 103.

12. Tierney, 'Medieval Canon Law and Western Constitutionalism', pp. 2–3.

13. Black, *Council and Commune*, p. 197.

14. For instance, see Figgis, *Political Thought from Gerson to Grotius*, pp. 26–8 and the passages from Tierney quoted at notes 10–12 above.

15. Gerson's career and contributions are reviewed by Morrall, *Gerson and the Great Schism* and Louis B. Pascoe, *Jean Gerson: Principles of Church Reform* (Leiden: Brill, 1973).

16. Oakley has argued that Gerson's ecclesiology is heavily indebted, for instance, to Pierre d'Ailley: 'Gerson and d'Ailley: An Admonition', *Speculum* 40 (January 1965), pp. 74–83.

17. Black, 'The Conciliar Movement', pp. 576, 580.

18. Tierney, *Religion, Law, and the Growth of Constitutional Thought*, p. 93. Gerson's particular popularity in the seventeenth century has also been stressed by Rueger, 'Gerson, the Conciliar Movement and the Right of Resistance', p. 486.

19. Giovanni Sartori addresses these confusions in 'Constitutionalism: A Preliminary Discussion', *American Political Science Review* 56 (1962), pp. 853–64 and in his 'Rejoinder' to W.H. Morris-Jones, *American Political Science Review* 59 (1965), pp. 441–4.

20. This excludes the essentially descriptive notion of constitutionalism as the regular pattern of behaviour according to which any regime governs, a definition which has been proposed by Kenneth Wheare, *Modern Constitutions* (Oxford: Oxford University Press, 1966).
21. Charles H. McIlwain, *Constitutionalism: Ancient and Modern* (Ithaca: Cornell University Press, 1947), pp. 21–2.
22. G.W.F. Hegel, *The Philosophy of Right*, trans. T.M. Knox (Oxford: Oxford University Press, 1967), sec. 273. Oakley has recently reviewed and defended the position espoused by Hegel; see 'Disobedience, Consent, Political Obligation', pp. 212–13.
23. Among them may be counted Francis Wormuth. *The Origins of Modern Constitutionalism* (New York: Harper, 1949), Sartori, 'Constitutionalism', pp. 859–60; and Donald W. Hanson, *From Kingdom to Commonwealth* (Cambridge, Mass.: Harvard University Press, 1970).
24. Skinner, *The Foundations of Modern Political Thought*, I, p. x.
25. Julian H. Franklin, *Constitutionalism and Resistance in the Sixteenth Century* (New York: Pegasus, 1969), p. 15; Franklin traces this notion to H.D. Hazeltine (p. 201 note 7).
26. Sartori, 'Constitutionalism', p. 855 and note 10.
27. Oakley, 'Legitimation by Consent', pp. 323–4, 329–30.
28. Ewart Lewis's refutation of the attribution of legal positivism to the *Defensor Pacis* holds good more broadly for medieval political theory; see 'The "Positivism" of Marsiglio of Padua', *Speculum* **38** (1963), pp. 541–82.
29. The medieval tradition of political thought would never dispute the statement of John of Salisbury, *Policraticus*, ed. C.C.J. Webb, 2 vols (1909; reprinted Frankfurt a.M.: Unveränderter Nachdruck, 1965), 777d that 'lex donum Dei est, aequitatis forma, norma iustitiae, divinae voluntatis imago'.
30. For elaboration of this basic doctrine, see Gaines Post, 'Bracton on Kingship', *Tulane Law Review* **42** (1968), pp. 519–54 and Cary J. Nederman, 'Bracton on Kingship Revisited', *History of Political Thought* 5 (Spring 1984), pp. 61–77.
31. William of Ockham expresses this view succinctly: 'Ad potestatem regalem . . . spectat regulariter de causis saecularibus iudicare et ea, quae ad iurisdictionem temporalem pertinent, exercere' (*An Princeps*, Chap. 2 in H.S. Offler, ed., *Opera Politica*, v. I (Manchester: Manchester University Press, 1974), p. 234).
32. Ockham's *Octo Quaestiones* provides a complete list of the duties associated with temporal jurisdiction: 'Ad principantem, de quo est sermo, multa pertineant, videlicet iura sua unicuique tribuere et servare, leges condere necessarias atque iustas, iudices inferiores et alios officiales constituere, quales artes et a quibus in communitate sibi subiecta debeant exerceri, omnium virtutum actus praecipere et alia multa: tamen ad hoc videtur principalissime institutus, et corrigat et puniat delinquentes' (in Offler, ed., *Opera Politica*, I, pp. 109–10).
33. Henry de Bracton, *De Legibus et Consuetudinibus Angliae*, ed. S.E. Thorne, 4 vols (Cambridge, Mass.: Harvard University Press, 1968–1974), II, p. 304: 'Non sub homine, sed sub Deo et sub lege'.
34. St. Thomas Aquinas, *De Regno*: 'Est necessarium ut talis conditionis homo ab illis, ad quos hoc spectat officium, promoveatur in regem, quod non sit probabile in tyrannidem declinare' (in A.P. d'Entrèves, ed., *Aquinas: Selected Political Writings* (Oxford: Blackwell, 1948), p. 28).
35. More thorough discussion of this theme may be found in: Lester K. Born, 'The Perfect Prince: A Study in Thirteenth- and Fourteenth-Century Ideals', *Speculum* 3 (1928), pp. 470–504; Wilhelm Berges, *Die Fürstenspiegel des Hohen und Spätmittelalters* (Stuttgart: Hiersemann, 1938), and Harry R. Dosher, *The Concept of the Ideal Prince in French Political Thought, 800–1760* (Chapel Hill: Unpublished dissertation,

University of North Carolina, 1969), pp. 43–138.

36. Aristotle, *Nicomachean Ethics*, 1103a–b, 1105a–1106a. Some philosophical puzzles posed by Aristotle's concept of *hexis* have been discussed by William Bondeson, 'Aristotle on Responsibility for One's Character and the Possibility of Character Change', *Phronesis* **19** (1974), pp. 59–65.

37. As has been established by Cary J. Nederman, 'Nature, Ethics and the Doctrine of *Habitus*: Aristotelian Moral Psychology in the Twelfth Century', *Traditio* (Forthcoming 1990).

38. John of Salisbury, Bracton and Marsiglio of Padua come immediately to mind: on John, see Cary J. Nederman and J. Brückmann, 'Aristotelianism in John of Salisbury's *Policraticus*', *Journal of the History of Philosophy* **21** (April 1983), pp. 218–23 and Cary J. Nederman, 'Aristotelian Ethics and John of Salisbury's Letters', *Viator* **18** (1987), pp. 161–73; for Bracton, see Nederman, 'Bracton on Kingship Revisited', pp. 69–76; and for Marsiglio, see Jeannine Quillet, *La Philosophie Politique de Marsile de Padoue* (Paris: J. Vrin, 1970), pp. 153–60.

39. Aquinas, *De Regno*, p. 16: 'Tyrannus, contempto communi bono, quaerit privatum... A iure disceditur, nec firmari quidquam potest, quod positum est in alterius voluntate, ne dicam libidine'.

40. For a survey of these concerns, see Friedrich Schoenstedt, *Studien zum Begriff des Tyrannen und zum Problem des Tyrannenmordes im Spätmittelalter insbesondere in Frankreich* (Würzburg: Buchdruckerei R. Mayr, 1938) and Johannes Spörl, 'Gedanken zum Widerstandsrecht und Tyrannenmord in Mittelalter', in B. Pfister and G. Hildmann, *Widerstandsrecht und Grenzen zur Staatsgewalt* (Berlin: Duncker und Humblot, 1956), pp. 11–32.

41. Aquinas, *De Regno*, pp. 32, 34.

42. Bracton, *De Legibus*, II, p. 110; and Marsiglio of Padua, *Defensor Pacis*, ed. C.W. Previté-Orton (Cambridge: Cambridge University Press, 1928), I.15.2, I.18.1–3.

43. James of Viterbo, *De Regimine Christiano*, ed. H.X. Arquillière (Paris: Gabriel Beauchesne, 1926), II.7.

44. John of Salisbury, *Policraticus*, 512c–d, 792c and passim. For a detailed examination of this concept, see Cary J. Nederman, 'A Duty to Kill: John of Salisbury's Theory of Tyrannicide', *Review of Politics* **50** (Summer 1988), pp. 365–389.

45. As John of Salisbury expresses the matter, 'Omnis autem potestas bona, quoniam ab eo est a quo solo omnia et sola sunt bona. Utenti tamen interdum bona non est aut patienti sed mala, licet quod ad universitatem sit bona, illo faciente qui bene utitur malis nostris... Est enim tirannis a Deo concessae homini potestatis abusus (*Policraticus*, 785d–786a).

46. It is in this vein that Ockham concludes, 'Abusus verae potestatis aut iurisdictionis vel dominium veram protestatem minime tollit' (*An Princeps* 2, p. 235).

47. For the explicit equation of justice with the common good, see John of Salisbury, *Policraticus* 515a–b and 621c; Ockham, *An Princeps* 9, pp. 259–60; and Aquinas, *De Regno*, pp. 6, 8.

48. On the substance of John of Paris's doctrine, see Janet Coleman, '*Dominium* in Thirteenth- and Fourteenth-Century Political Thought and its Seventeenth-Century Heirs: John of Paris and Locke', *Political Studies* **33** (1985), pp. 73–100.

49. John of Paris, *De Potestate Regia et Papali*, ed. F. Bleienstein (Stuttgart: Klett Verlag, 1969), p. 98.

50. This theme is addressed by Michael Wilks, 'Corporation and Representation in the *Defensor Pacis*', *Studia Gratiana (Post Scripta)* **15** (1972), pp. 253–92 and Black, 'Society and the Individual From the Middle Ages to Rousseau', pp. 146–59.

51. Further discussion of these ideas may be found in Michael Wilks, *The Problem of Sovereignty in the Later Middle Ages* (Cambridge: Cambridge University Press, 1963),

pp. 196-9, 239-46; Quillet, *La Philosophie Politique de Marsile de Padoue*, pp. 83-99; Jeannine Quillet, '*Universitas populi* et Représentation au XIVe Siècle', *Miscellanea Mediaevalia*, 8 (1971), pp. 186-200; and Walter Ullmann, *Principles of Government and Politics in the Middle Ages* (London: Methuen, 1961), pp. 145-7.

52. *Ibid.*, p. 146. Exactly this doctrine of election is described by John of Salisbury at *Policraticus*, 549a.

53. As in the case of Marsiglio of Padua, *Defensor Pacis*, I.18.1: 'Correctiones aut totaliter mutationes principatuum ad legislatorem pertinere quaemadmodum institutiones ipsorum'.

54. See Philippe du Plessis-Mornay (?), *Vindiciae Contra Tyrannos* in Franklin, *Constitutionalism and Resistance in the Sixteenth Century*, p. 154.

55. Jean Gerson, *De Potestate Ecclesiastica* in P. Glorieux, ed. *Oeuvres Complètes*, vol. 6 (Paris: Desclée, 1965), p. 216: 'Temporalis execetur secundum leges civiles ad finem quietae conversationis humanae pro hac vita. Spiritualis autem exercetur secundum leges canonicas ad finem principalem beatitudinis consequendae'.

56. Gerson's repeated comparison between the organisation of secular and spiritual governments has been highlighted by Skinner, *The Foundations of Modern Political Thought*, II, pp: 114-5.

57. Gerson, *De Potestate Ecclesiastica*, p. 216: '... juridica potestas excommunicandi vel interdicendi ab ecclesiasticis sacramentis et communione fidelium rebelles et inobedientes Ecclesiae'.

58. *Ibid.*, p. 218. The pope should not suppose law to be a bridle on his liberty, Gerson insists, since 'non esse servitutem obedire legibus' (*Ibid.*, p. 239).

59. Jean Gerson, *Tractatus de Unitate Ecclesiae* in Glorieux, ed., *Oeuvres Complètes*, vol. 6, p. 139: '... nec in praejudicium juris divini et naturalis et boni communis est aliquatenus observanda'.

60. Gerson describes 'epikeia' and 'lex superior' in *De Auferibilitate Sponsi*: P. Glorieux, ed., *Ouvres Complètes*, vol. 3 (Paris: Desclée, 1962), p. 301.

61. Gerson, *Tractatus de Unitate Ecclesiae*, p. 138: 'Summarie et de bona grossaque aequitate potest procedere concilium istud generale in quo residebit sufficiens auctoritas judicialis utendi epikeia, id est interpretandi omnia jura postiva, et ad finem celeriorem et salubriorum habendae unionis eadem adaptandi, aut si opus fuerit relinquendi'. On the background to this conception of *epikeia*, see Morrall, *Gerson and the Great Schism*, pp. 121-1.

62. As is acknowledged by Tierney, *Foundations of the Conciliar Theory*, pp. 141-8, 188-9 and passim.

63. Gerson, *In Recessu Regis Romanorum* in P. Glorieux, ed., *Oeuvres Complètes*, vol. 5 (Paris: Desclée, 1963), p. 479: '... Plenitudo potestatis paplis collata est a Christo in his quae supra naturam sunt... supremo stat'.

64. Some of the confusions created by Gerson's maintenance of papal supremacy are addressed by Tierney, *Religion, Law, and the Growth of Constitutional Thought*, p. 94.

65. Gerson, *De Potestate Ecclesiastica*, p. 226: '... ecclesiasticum potestatem... est immediate a Deo homine Christo sic quod a nullo altero fuit instituta. Nec congregatio totius universitatis hominum secluso Christo potuisset sibi potestatem hanc instituere'.

66. *Ibid.*, pp. 227-8: 'Potestas ecclesiastica in sua plenitudine est formaliter et subjective in solo Romano Pontifico... Plenitudo potestatis ecclesiasticae est potestas ordinis et jurisdictionis quae a Christo collata supernaturaliter Petro sicut vicario suo et monarchae primo pro se et suis successioribus legitimis usque in finem saeculi ad successioribus legitimis usque in finem saeculi ad aedificationem Ecclesiae militantis pro consecutione felicitatis aeternae'.

67. Skinner, *The Foundations of Modern Political Thought*, II, p. 116.

68. Gerson, *De Potestate Ecclesiastica*, p. 220: 'Potestas ecclesiastica considerari potest et debet... alio modo materialiter seu respective prout applicatur ad hanc vel illam personam jure legitimo; quod communiter fit per consecrationem et electionem... Consideratur tertio modo quoad exercitium vel executionem'.

69. *Ibid.*, p. 223.

70. *Ibid.*, p. 232: 'Potestas ecclesiastica in sua plenitudine est in Ecclesia sicut in fine et sicut in regulante applicationem et usum hujusmodi plenitudinis ecclesiasticae per seipsam vel per generale concilium eam sufficienter et legitime repraesentans'. Also cf. *Ibid.*, p. 226.

71. Gerson, *De Auferbilitate Sponsi*, p. 300: 'Nullum quippe statum, nullum gradum dignitatis, nullum ministrationis genus dedit Deus nisi in aedificationem suam et utilitatem communem'.

72. Gerson, *De Potestate Ecclesiastica*, p. 232: 'Potest etiam dici in Ecclesia vel in concilio haec plenitudo ecclesiasticae potestatis... quoad usum regulandum, si fortassis in abusum verti quereretur'. Gerson draws similar conclusions elsewhere. For example, *In Recessu Regis Romanorum*, pp. 477-8: 'Concilium generale quamvis non possit nec debeat plenitudinem potestatis papalis commissam a Christo Petro et successioribus ejus tollere vel minuere, sed legibus et statutis limitare in aedificationem Ecclesiae'. Also see *De Potestate Ecclesiastica*, p. 217: 'Ecclesia potest condere leges obligantes et regulantes etiam ipsum papam, tam quoad personam quam respectu usus suae potestatis; non sic e contra potest papa judicare totam Ecclesiam vel usum suae potestatis limitare'.

73. *Ibid.*, p. 233: 'Cum igitur Summus Pontifex... sit peccabilis et possit hanc potestatem in destructionem Ecclesiae velle convertere... abusus hujusmodi potestatis reprimi, dirigi atque moderari'.

74. Gerson, *De Auferibilitate Sponsi*, p. 301: 'Nolumus tamen impugnare quin summus pontifex habeat potestatem regitivam et auctoritativam respectu omnium hominum... non pro se tantummodo sed magis ad utilitatem Ecclesiae'.

75. Gerson, *De Potestate Ecclesiastica*, p. 221: 'Id possumus quod de jure possumus'. Gerson is speaking in this context of the powers associated with ecclesiastical office in general; he argues that while, in a factual sense, such powers may be used 'sive bene sive male', in a normative sense ecclesiastical rights are only said to be truly valid when they are used in accordance with right. Medieval authors commonly made a similar point about secular offices to the effect that 'nihil enim aliud potest rex in terris, cum sit dei minister et vicarius, nisi id solum quod de jure potest' (Bracton, *De Legibus*, II. p. 305).

76. Jean Gerson, *Propositio Facit Coram Anglicis* in Glorieux, ed., *Oeuvres Complètes*, vol. 6, p. 132.

77. Tierney, *Foundations of the Conciliar Theory*, pp. 60-7.

78. Tierney, *Religion, Law, and the Growth of Constitutional Thought*, p. 94.

79. Gerson, *De Auferibilitate Sponsi*, p. 309: 'Et haec unio videtur absolute sufficere ad hoc quod aliquis rite prius in papam electus maneat caput Ecclesiae quosque fuerit per sententiam definitivam depositus'.

80. This claim has two implications. First, it allows Gerson to assert that a pope may be deposed for troubles which are not strictly his fault but which endanger the health of the church, such as incarceration by infidels or physical infirmity (*Ibid.*, pp. 310-1). Second, by insisting upon a formal judicial process of deposition, Gerson can assert that unproved charges of unconfessed occult crimes are insufficient to dethrone a reigning pope *de facto* (*Ibid.*, p. 308). But both provisos still pertain to the personal circumstances and condition of the papal incumbent rather than to the powers of the office per se.

81. Gerson, *Tractatus de Unitate Ecclesiae*, p. 140: '... tota Ecclesia cui similiter subjectus

est tamquam deviabilis indeviabili'.

82. *Ibid.*, p. 137.

83. Gerson, *In Recessu Regis Romanorum*, p. 479, presents a classic summary description of the General Council: 'Concilium generale est congregatio legitima auctoritate facta ad aliquem locum ex omni statu hierarchico totius Ecclesiae catholicae, nulla fideli persona quae audiri requirat exclusa, ad salubriter tractandum et ordinandum ea quae debitum regimen ejudem Ecclesiae in fide et moribus respiciunt' (repeated in *De Potestate Ecclesiastica*, p. 240).

84. As has been emphasised by Tierney, *Foundations of the Conciliar Thoery*, pp. 106–53 and passim and *Religion, Law, and the Growth of Constitutional Thought*, pp. 13–28.

85. Gerson, *De Potestate Ecclesiastica*, p. 233: '... finalis resolutio ad hanc sapientiam fiet ad Ecclesiam ubi est sapientia indeviabilis vel ad generale concilium'.

86. For the early development of this argument, see Brian Tierney, *Origins of Papal Infallibility* (Leiden: E.J. Brill, 1972), pp. 46–9 and passim.

87. Gerson, *De Potestate Ecclesiastica*, p. 240: '... potestas universalis Ecclesiae vel generalis concilii legitime congregati dici possit major in amplitudine vel extensione, major in infallibili directione, major in morum reformatione, in capite et in membris, major in coercitiva potestate, major in causarum fidei difficilium ultimata decisione, major denique quia copiosior'.

88. Gerson, *In Recessu Regis Romanorum*, p. 479, declares that the General Council 'praeterea legitimus et securus, nec suspectus rationabiliter ab aliquibus christianis cum procedat omnium vel quasi omnium communi consensu vel assensu'.

89. On this notion of consent as corporate *consensus*, see Paul E. Sigmund, Jr, 'Cusanus' *Concordantia*: A Re-interpretation', *Political Studies* 10 (June 1962), pp. 187–8.

90. Gerson, *In Recessu Regis Romanorum*, pp. 478–9: 'Est autem generale concilium politia talis composita, habens suam directionem magis ex assistentia speciali Spiritus Sancti et promissione Jesu Christi quam ex natura vel humana sola industria. Hinc est illud quod praediximus, quod ipsum est saluberrima et efficacissima regula ad regimen totius Ecclesiae tranquillium vel conservandum vel reformandum vel inveniendum, tamquam supremus et sufficiens legislator universalis et potens epiekes'.

91. Isaiah Berlin, 'Two Concepts of Liberty' in *Four Essays on Liberty* (Oxford: Oxford University Press, 1969), pp. 16–9.

92. Richard Tuck, *Natural Rights Theories: The Origins and Development* (Cambridge: Cambridge University Press, 1979), pp. 25–31.

93. Skinner, *The Foundations of Modern Political Thought*, II, p. 117.

94. This has previously been stressed by Oakley, 'Legitimation by Consent', p. 330 note 91. See also, Brian Tierney's critique of Tuck's interpretation of Gerson in 'Tuck on Rights: Some Medieval Problems', *History of Political Thought* 4 (Winter 1983), pp. 437–40.

95. Tuck, *Natural Rights Theories*, p. 30.

96. Gerson, *De Auferibilitate Sponsi*, pp. 304–5.

97. *Ibid.*, p. 298: 'Auferibilis non est sponsus Ecclesiae Christus ab Ecclesia sponsa sua et filiis ejus sic quod remaneat Ecclesia in sola muliere, immo nec in solis mulieribus omnibus, immo nec in laicis solis, lege stante et non facta divinitus nova institutione. Da oppositum, tunc Ecclesia deficiere posset in suis gradibus et officiis hierarchis, in suis etiam sacrementis usque in finem. Patet hoc, praesupponendo quod sacerdos a non sacerdote et episcopus a non episcopo nequit instituti, immo nec a tota multitudine laicorum aut mulierum simul congregata, si per casum mortui essent omnes sacerdotes'. For a similar claim, see Gerson, *Propositio Facit Coram Anglicis*, p. 132.

98. It remains unclear whether Gerson accepted the terms of the 1417 decree *Frequens*, stemming from the Council of Constance, which required the meeting of ecclesiastical

General Councils at fixed intervals. Morrall suggests that the 'germ' of the decree is already present in Gerson's 1415 sermon *Ambulate dum lucem habetis* (*Gerson and the Great Schism*, p. 97). But even if Gerson believed that the Councils should meet regularly, he did not conceive them as the effective day-to-day administrators of ecclestiastical business. Instead, the function of the Council was still to address the 'special' questions posed by the determination of orthodoxy.

99. For another example of similar early modern reinterpretation of medieval political ideas, see Cary J. Nederman, 'Bracton on Kingship First Visited: The Idea of Sovereignty and Bractonian Political Thought in Seventeenth-Century England', *Political Science* **40** (July 1988), pp. 49–66.

HUMANISM AND EMPIRE: AENEAS SYLVIUS PICCOLOMINI, CICERO AND THE IMPERIAL IDEAL*

ABSTRACT. *The paper argues that the* De ortu et auctoritate imperii Romani *of Aeneas Sylvius Piccolomini (1446) has been unjustifiably ignored by historians of quattrocento humanist political thought simply because of its adherence to the ideal of universal imperial government. At present, when* De ortu *is addressed at all, it is considered merely as an anachronistic product of a 'medieval' mentality. It is shown, however, that Aeneas, by working within a demonstrably Ciceronian framework, actually articulates a philosophically coherent defence of a single universal empire by exploiting a conceptual ambiguity in Cicero's own presentation of the foundations of social and political association. Aeneas suggests that Cicero's account of the communal nature of human beings, so far from sanctioning republican civic institutions, actually justifies the imposition of universal empire. A study of Piccolomini's political thought thus points to a greater diversity within the political viewpoints associated with humanism than current scholarship on the subject acknowledges. Moreover, it reveals the level of philosophical sophistication to which renaissance defences of empire could aspire.*

One of the more enigmatic figures connected with the history of political thought in the fifteenth century is Aeneas Sylvius Piccolomini. In virtue of his biography, one would expect Aeneas' political ideas to embody the values and doctrines associated with *quattrocento* Italy.[1] The recipient of a fine humanist education, Aeneas was an almost exact contemporary of Palmieri, Valla and Patrizi, and enjoyed a similar reputation for his writings; his letters, in particular, compare favourably in their style as well as their substance with the best of humanist literature.[2] A man of action and faith as well as letters, his career included lengthy service to Emperor Frederick III as a secretary and diplomat, appointment to the bishoprics of Trieste and Siena, and ultimately elevation to the papal seat in 1458 as Pius II.[3] He is widely regarded to be both

---

* An earlier and abbreviated version of this paper was read at the Second Conference of the International Society for the Study of European Ideas, Leuven, Belgium, September 1990. The author wishes to thank Professor Walter Nicgorski for his helpful comments on that draft.

[1] Brian Pullan describes Aeneas' career and contributions as a virtual archetype of the humanist experience in the fifteenth century (*A history of early renaissance Italy* [London, 1973], p. 182).

[2] Piccolomini's accomplishments have been surveyed most recently by Guido Kisch, *Enea Silvio Piccolomini und die Jurisprudenz* (Basel, 1967) and Berthe Widmer, *Enea Silvio Piccolomini in der sittlichen und politischen Entscheidung* (Basel, 1963).

[3] The standard biography of Aeneas is by Georg Voigt, *Enea Silvio Piccolomini als Papst Pius der zweite und sein Zeitalter* (3 vols., 1857–1863; reprinted Berlin, 1967). A more abbreviated account

500

the first 'humanist pope' and a leading disseminator of the Italian renaissance to northern Europe.[4]

Yet Aeneas' name consistently fails to appear in recent surveys of renaissance political thought.[5] Instead, when his political writings are addressed, such discussion usually occurs within the context of preceding, essentially 'medieval', intellectual traditions.[6] The reason for this, simply stated, is that Aeneas' main treatises on politics are almost exclusively concerned with defending and promoting a universalist, imperial and even absolutist ideal of government under the banner of the Holy Roman Empire. Consequently, his political thought is treated (at least implicitly) as an anachronistic reversion to the mental constructs and categories of the Latin middle ages rather than as the reflection of an authentically renaissance perspective on politics.

Explanations of the incongruity between Aeneas' renaissance learning and his 'medieval' political values vary. For some scholars, this divergence is an indication of his opportunism or lack of personal integrity.[7] By contrast, other commentators have emphasized a process of maturation and intellectual evolution on Aeneas' part that led him away from his early humanism and towards the adoption of a 'medieval world-view'.[8] But one assumption runs through all of these accounts: that renaissance humanism was somehow conceptually incompatible with the advocacy of an imperial ideal. The

---

of Aeneas's career, albeit concentrating on his activities on the papal throne, is provided by R. J. Mitchell, *The laurels and the tiara: Pope Pius II 1458–1464* (London, 1962).

[4] The former judgement is addressed by Peter Partner, *Renaissance Rome 1500–1559* (Berkeley, 1976), p. 14 and John F. D'Amico, *Renaissance humanism in papal Rome* (Baltimore, 1983), p. 8; the latter may be found in Noel L. Brann, 'Humanism in Germany', in A. Rabil, Jr. (ed.), *Renaissance humanism: foundations, forms and legacy* (3 vols.; Philadelphia, 1988), II, 126–7 and Rado L. Lencek, 'Humanism in the Slavic cultural tradition', in ibid. II, 348–9.

[5] For example, his political ideas receive no attention from Hans Baron, *The crisis of the early Italian renaissance* (2nd edn; Princeton, 1966); Jerrold Seigel, *Rhetoric and philosophy in renaissance humanism: the union of eloquence and wisdom, Petrarch to Valla* (Princeton, 1968); Quentin Skinner, *The foundations of modern political thought* (2 vols.; Cambridge, 1978); Hans Baron, *In search of Florentine civic humanism: essays on the transition from medieval to modern thought* (2 vols.; Princeton, 1988); Quentin Skinner, 'Political philosophy', in C. B. Schmitt and Q. Skinner (eds.), *The Cambridge history of renaissance philosophy* (Cambridge, 1988), pp. 408–30; and Richard Tuck, 'Humanism and political thought', in A. Goodman and A. MacKay (eds.), *The impact of humanism on western Europe* (London, 1990), pp. 43–65.

[6] See Ewart Lewis, *Medieval political ideas* (London, 1954), pp. 157–8 and passim; John B. Toews, 'The view of empire in Aeneas Sylvius Piccolomini (Pope Pius II)', *Traditio*, XXIV (1968), 471–87; Heinrich Schmidinger, *Romana regia potestas: Staats- und Reichsdenken bei Engelbert von Admont und Enea Silvio Piccolomini* (Basel and Stuttgart, 1978); and David Luscombe, 'The state of nature and the origin of the state', in N. Kretzmann, A. Kenny and J. Pinborg (eds.), *The Cambridge history of later medieval philosophy* (Cambridge, 1982), pp. 763–4. Even this interpretation is not entirely uniform, however; for instance, Piccolomini's work is not cited at all in J. H. Burns (ed.), *The Cambridge history of medieval political thought* (Cambridge, 1988).

[7] This was the judgement of Voigt's seminal study and it has persisted into the present century; see Paul Joachimsen, 'Der Humanismus und die Entwicklung des deutschen Geistes', *Deutsche Vierteljahrsschrift für Literaturwissenschaft*, VIII (1930), 435.

[8] John Gordon Rowe, 'The tragedy of Aeneas Sylvius Piccolomini (Pope Pius II): an interpretation', *Church History*, XXX (September 1961), 290–3; and Toews, 'The view of empire in Aeneas Sylvius Piccolomini', 472–4 and passim.

existing scholarship never seriously entertains the possibility that Aeneas might simultaneously promote some conception of imperial rule while retaining a commitment to humanist precepts. Such an assumption apparently rests on the belief that *quattrocento* humanism enjoyed an inherent connection with urban political culture and even republican values, i.e. that humanism was essentially 'civic' in nature.[9] Even among scholars who have explicitly questioned Hans Baron's so-called 'civic humanist' thesis and his virtual equation of humanism with Florentine experience,[10] there have been negligible efforts to re-evaluate, let alone sever, the general relationship between *quattrocento* humanism and the political climate of the Italian cities.[11]

One reason why no examination of this sort has occurred may stem from the classical source materials which stimulated and supported the early Italian renaissance. In particular, the humanist political theory of the period has been most closely associated with the theoretical doctrines propounded, as well as the personal example set, by the Roman archenemy of the imperial form of government, Cicero.[12] Current scholarship seems to take largely for granted that, because Ciceronian thought was fashioned in such intimate relation to the social and political convictions of Rome and its republic, the humanist devotion to Cicero was necessarily coextensive with a firm dedication to his basic philosophical and personal values. There is little evidence to support such a contention, however. As the example of the reception of Aristotle's philosophy in both the middle ages and renaissance suggests,[13] identification with a given classical authority or source by no means guaranteed acceptance of any specific doctrine or intellectual programme. Moreover, it is becoming increasingly clear that renaissance thought cannot be distinguished from its medieval predecessor simply on the basis of 'the rediscovery of Cicero',[14] that

[9] This is stated most forcefully, of course, by Hans Baron in *The crisis of the early Italian renaissance*. For elaboration and defence of the basic hypothesis, see J. G. A. Pocock, *The Machiavellian Moment: Florentine political thought and the Atlantic republican tradition* (Princeton, 1975), esp. pp. 49–80 and Baron, *In search of Florentine civic humanism*, esp. II, 194–211.

[10] For example, Paul O. Kristeller, 'The moral thought of renaissance humanism', in *Renaissance thought II: papers on humanism and the arts* (New York, 1965), pp. 46–7 and passim; Paul O. Kristeller, *Renaissance thought and its sources* (ed.) M. Mooney (New York, 1979), pp. 243–4 and passim; Jerrold E. Seigel, '"Civic humanism" or Ciceronian rhetoric? The culture of Petrarch and Bruni', *Past and Present*, XXXIV (1966), 3–48; and Seigel, *Rhetoric and philosophy in renaissance humanism*.

[11] See the survey by Albert Rabil, Jr. of the major contributions to the debate: 'The significance of "civic humanism" in the interpretation of the Italian renaissance', in Rabil (ed.), *Renaissance humanism*, pp. 141–74.

[12] Tuck, 'Humanism and political thought', pp. 51–63; Baron, *In search of Florentine civic humanism*, I, 113–33; Seigel, *Philosophy and rhetoric in renaissance humanism*, pp. 3–4.

[13] The dilemma posed by the very notion of a single, coherent definition of medieval or renaissance 'Aristotelianism' has engendered a growing body of literature; some aspects of the problem are treated by F. Edward Cranz, 'Aristotelianism in medieval political theory: a study of the reception of the politics' (Unpublished Ph.D. thesis, Harvard University, 1940); Charles B. Schmitt, *Aristotle and the renaissance* (Cambridge, Mass., 1983), pp. 10–33; Edward Grant, 'Ways to interpret the terms "Aristotelian" and "Aristotelianism" in medieval and renaissance natural philosophy', *History of Science*, XXV (1987), 335–58; and Cary J. Nederman, 'Aristotle as authority: alternative aristotelian sources of late medieval political theory', *History of European ideas*, VIII (1987), 31–44. [14] Baron, *The crisis of the early Italian renaissance*, p. 121.

is, the recovery of a more 'genuine' or 'accurate' appreciation of Cicero's intellectual and political career.[15] It seems implausible to take refuge in the claim that renaissance Ciceronianism was distinctively characterized by 'fervent advocacy' of an 'authentically classical perspective'.[16] Indeed, it does not seem unreasonable to suggest that, just as essentially Ciceronian doctrines were employed during the middle ages to support many different regime types and units of political association (including kingdoms and empire as well as cities), so in the *quattrocento* Ciceronian thought could equally be used to bolster non-urban as well as urban forms of rule.

All of this has a direct bearing on our estimation of the political ideas of Aeneas Sylvius Piccolomini. The main body of Aeneas' political thought may be found within two treatises, the *Pentalogus de rebus ecclesiae et imperii* of 1443 and *De ortu et auctoritate imperii Romani*, composed three years later. The first of these is primarily a practical book of advice to the emperor containing recommendations for the reunification of Europe and the reconquest of the Holy Lands.[17] Consequently, the *Pentalogus* is of interest to the modern reader for more purely historical rather than theoretical reasons. By contrast, one may detect in *De ortu* the presence of a coherent philosophical argument of demonstrably Ciceronian provenance.[18] Scholars have seldom acknowledged a Ciceronian component within *De ortu*, let alone investigated the significance and depth of Cicero's impact upon Aeneas' political theory.[19]

Once the assumption of an inherent connection between humanist Ciceronianism and Italian urban culture is set aside, however, it becomes possible to recognize how Aeneas could draw upon his humanist immersion in

[15] The continuity of facets of Ciceronianism in medieval and Renaissance political thought has lately been stressed by Quentin Skinner, 'Ambrogio Lorenzetti: the artist as political philosopher', *Proceedings of the British Academy*, LXXII (1986), 1–56; Cary J. Nederman, 'Nature, sin and the origins of society: the Ciceronian tradition in medieval political thought', *Journal of the History of Ideas*, XLIX (January 1988), 3–26; and Tuck, 'Humanism and political thought', pp. 48–50. This is not to deny all difference between Ciceronian thought in the middle ages and renaissance, as Tuck stresses (pp. 50–1), a subject which I address in a paper, 'Reason, speech and the foundation of political society: conflicting Ciceronianisms in medieval and renaissance thought', presented to the American Political Science Association, Washington, DC, September 1991.

[16] Skinner, *The foundations of modern political thought*, I, 88; also see Seigel, *Rhetoric and philosophy in renaissance humanism*, p. 30. This is a position which Skinner himself has surrendered in favour of the view posited in 'Ambrogio Lorenzetti.'

[17] The text of the *Pentalogus* was edited by B. Pez, *Thesaurus antecdotorum novissimus* (Augsburg, 1721), III, 637–744. On its dating and substance, see H. J. Hallauer, *Der Pentalogus des Aeneas Silvius Piccolomini* (Unpublished dissertation, University of Cologne, 1951).

[18] We shall employ the text of *De ortu et auctoritate imperii Romani* edited by R. Wolkan, *Der Briefwechsel des Eneas Silvius Piccolomini* in *Fontes rerum austriacarum*, LXII (1912), 6–24. The text and a German translation are also available in Gerhard Kallen, *Aeneas Silvius Piccolomini als Publizist in der epistola De ortu et auctoritate imperii Romani* (Cologne, 1939), pp. 52–100.

[19] Within the main twentieth-century discussions of *De ortu*, Cicero is accorded no special place among the sources upon which Aeneas relied, and his name often appears only in a list alongside other classical and Christian authorities. See Alfred Muesel, *Enea Silvio als Publizist* (Breslau, 1905), pp. 36–8; Felice Battaglia, 'Il pensiero politico di Enea Silvio Piccolomini', in *Enea Silvio Piccolomini e Francesco Patrizi: due politici senesi del quattrocento* (Siena, 1936), pp. 9, 30, 44; Kallen, *Aeneas Silvius Piccolomini als Publizist*, p. 29; and Schmidinger, *Romana regia potestas*, p. 21. Toews, 'The view of empire in Aeneas Sylvius Piccolomini', does not mention Cicero at all.

Cicero's thought in order to promote the ideals and values of an imperial regime. It may be argued, in fact, that Aeneas more nearly approaches the philosophical core of Cicero's own thought – and is, therefore, truer to the Ciceronian theoretical framework – than were *quattrocento* figures such as Leonardo Bruni who are ordinarily upheld as paragons of Ciceronianism.[20] For Aeneas recognizes that Cicero's own work embraced an unresolved tension between what might be termed 'nationalism' (or more properly, if less elegantly, 'civism') and a 'supernationalism' or 'transnationalism' which might be used as the foundation for a theory of universal empire.[21] Even if Cicero himself resisted the implications of this tension, later authors identified and applied it within the context of their own theoretical projects.[22] On Aeneas' account, nationalism constitutes a stimulus for the disintegration of the principles of mutual association and common benefit upon which society itself is built. Nationalism is incompatible with the rational foundations of social and political life which stem from human nature, a claim which arises directly out of Aeneas' adherence to Ciceronian premises. Thus, in Aeneas' view, national sovereignty and particularism cannot be reconciled with human nature itself. By contrast, only a world empire performs the functions necessary for the maintenance of social bonds among human beings, and is therefore uniquely consistent with the natural endowment of mankind.

To the extent that Aeneas' work seeks to develop and refine a set of philosophical precepts derived from the writings of Cicero, the alleged incongruity between his humanist intellectual commitments, on the one hand, and his 'medieval world-view', on the other, becomes considerably less tenable. Admittedly, *De ortu* occasionally relies upon a traditional medieval model of the divine ordination of the Roman emperor and his successors.[23] But such remarks are largely tangential to the main features of Aeneas' argument; they augment his position rather than provide its premises. If we instead view his theory as essentially Ciceronian in orientation, however, we may more readily understand how a dedicated humanist could without self-contradiction arrive at an ostensibly anachronistic, 'medieval' view of political life.

In order to appreciate the extent of the Ciceronian dimension within *De ortu*'s vindication of a universal world empire governed by an emperor with absolute power over his subjects, it is necessary to rehearse several elements of Cicero's own teachings. In his mature philosophical writings, Cicero articulated the Stoic-derived view that human beings are most essentially

[20] Bruni's status as the paradigmatic renaissance Ciceronian is championed especially by Baron, *In search of Florentine civic humanism*, I, 121–3 and passim.

[21] This tension has recently been highlighted by Walter Nicgorski, 'Cicero on the functions and limits of Roman nationalism', presented to the Second Conference of the International Society for the Study of European Ideas, Leuven, Belgium, September 1990. This paper will be integrated into a larger study of Cicero's political theory which Professor Nicgorski is presently completing.

[22] A clear example has been documented by Cary J. Nederman, 'Nature, justice and duty in the *Defensor pacis*: Marsiglio of Padua's Ciceronian impulse', *Political Theory*, xviii (November 1990), 615–37.

[23] The features of this model are examined in depth by Lewis, *Medieval political ideas*, pp. 430–66.

504

rational creatures and that their natural powers of reason constitute the precondition for all social intercourse and political community.[24] In *De finibus*, he declares that 'among the many points of difference between man and the beasts, the greatest difference is that nature has bestowed on man the gift of reason...It is reason that...has prompted the individual, starting from friendship and family affection, to expand his interests, forming social ties first with his fellow citizens and later with all mankind'.[25] Similarly, he states in *De officiis*, 'The natural power of reason associates men with other men both through speech and through social life'.[26] Reason itself is the bearer of the communal bond; human beings congregate because reason reveals to them the advantages which stem from co-operation. Cicero explains at great length that when rational creatures work together, discernible benefits abound: protection from the elements and the improvement of productive capacities, no less than the pleasures of social intercourse and the advantages of economic exchange. Reason teaches that persons can live a materially more satisfactory existence in a community than under the conditions of solitude.[27]

But Cicero also recognizes that rational self-interest is insufficient as the basis for a stable and harmonious society. He remarks that 'just as we obtain great utility from consent and co-operation among men, so there is no pestilence as detestable as that which men have wrought upon men'.[28] If self-interest alone were at the heart of social relations, then no community would endure, since men would only co-operate when it suited them and they would always try to take advantage of or even oppose their fellows whenever personal gain dictated that course. Natural reason seeks to resolve this dilemma in two ways: first, through the discovery and dissemination of the virtues, especially justice; and second, by means of the appointment of governors and the formulation of laws whose purpose is to maintain social order by imposing justice upon the community.

Cicero maintains that society, and hence our very capacity to conceive of a public welfare, depends on the cultivation of virtue. He observes that 'since, therefore, one may have no doubt how men may be both most helpful and most harmful to men, I state that virtue exists for this reason: to reconcile the minds of men and to bind them to each one's aid'.[29] The mark of a harmonious communal setting is the presence of virtue as an ingrained feature of its organization. Cicero singles out and concentrates upon justice, identifying it as the virtue most crucial to the perpetuation of human association. He insists that 'the society of humans amongst themselves and the quasi-communal life are maintained' solely on the basis of adherence to just precepts.[30] The absolute prerequisite of social organization is the presence of a commonly recognized and respected principle of justice.

The Ciceronian conception of justice becomes more fully comprehensible

---

[24] For a more extensive treatment of the following themes in Cicero, see Neal Wood, *Cicero's social and political thought: an introduction* (Berkeley, 1988), pp. 78–89.

[25] Cicero, *De finibus*, ed. H. Rackham (London, 1931), II.xiv.45.

[26] Cicero, *De officiis*, ed. W. Miller (Cambridge, Mass., 1913), I.iv.12.

[27] Ibid. II.iii.12–iv.15.   [28] Ibid. II.v.16.   [29] Ibid. II.v.17.   [30] Ibid. I.vii.20.

when viewed in light of the doctrine of natural law. Cicero holds that nature imposes upon us a certain code or measure of conduct, constituted in particular by the requirement to promote the ends and interests of human society. This idea he expresses by reference to natural law. The commission of an injury (such as theft or fraud) constitutes a violation of natural law precisely because it 'is necessarily disruptive of that which is most in accordance with nature, the generation of human society'.[31] It is in order to prevent perpetual endangerment to the bonds of society that the law of nature is afforded prescriptive force. Cicero contends that recognition of the dictates of justice emerges 'much more effectively from natural reason itself, which is law for human beings and divinity alike'.[32] To know what accords with the law of nature, and hence what behaviour is required by justice, one reasons about the common good. Our duty on the basis of natural law is always to act in the general welfare when there exists a conflict between private benefit and the general interests of society. Because by 'nature there are interests that all have in common', Cicero asserts that 'we are all subject to one and the same natural law' and that 'we are certainly forbidden to harm another person on the basis of natural law'.[33] The Ciceronian doctrine of natural law codifies and authorizes the obligation stemming from justice to value social fellowship above all else.

It is one matter to identify such an obligation, of course, and quite another to enforce it effectively. This is why reason also induces the creation of political power to supplement and actualize the sociability natural to human beings. For since the impulse to associate may be diverted by the harm which individuals are capable of causing to one another, Cicero contends that no assurance exists that social relations will continue if left to themselves. In order to remedy the abuses which would have occurred in primitive society, he explains, kings were first appointed and, later, laws were established. He views early monarchy as a popular institution, created in order to ensure the equity which justice requires: 'Hence, since the multitude was oppressed by those who had greater power, they appealed to one person of outstanding virtue; it was he who, when he prevented injuries against inferiors, succeeded in establishing equity in equal rights of the lesser with the greater men'.[34] Cicero regards political power to be necessary only insofar as some human beings prove incapable of submitting themselves to the justice which forms the core of the social bond. The function of political institutions is to impose the dictates of justice on every member of the community without regard for their wealth, status or other extraneous considerations. This required rulers who possessed the greatest personal virtue: 'Those were formerly selected for rulership who were most just in the opinion of the multitude'.[35] Such highly esteemed moral character was especially necessary in early times because government was conducted without reference to statutory law. Instead, kings ruled on the basis of their direct access to and knowledge of the laws of nature upon which equitable social order was grounded.

---

[31] Ibid. III.v.21–2.   [32] Ibid. III.v.23.   [33] Ibid. III.vi.27.   [34] Ibid. II.xii.41.
[35] Ibid. II.xii.41.

But Cicero also recognizes that entrusting unlimited political power to kings was a precarious enterprise. Primitive kingship functioned effectively so long as 'a just and good man' occupied the throne. When communities failed to generate such a ruler, however, 'laws were invented which would speak to everyone at the same time with the same voice ... The reason for constitutional laws is the same as that for kings. For equitable right is always sought'.[36] A legal system was substituted for personalized political rule, but the fundamental purpose of both was identical: to guarantee that justice is done and hence that the community is safeguarded. In this sense, the civic law, like the good ruler, must conform to the natural law and the dictates of justice. The special character of civil law, as distinct from natural law, stems from its applicability to persons as citizens rather than as members of the human species. But civil law ought neither to violate the precepts of natural law nor to exempt citizens from their social duties. As Cicero says, 'Civil law is not always the same as universal [that is, natural] law; still, universal law should be the same as civil law'.[37] The statutes of communities must embrace and cohere with the requirements of what Cicero describes as 'veri iuris': civil law is not the product of arbitrary human determination, but reflects a framework engendered by reason. Even when positive law does not prohibit acts which are injurious, no one may engage in such conduct precisely because it is 'still forbidden by natural law'.[38] In sum, since the purpose of human law is to bring social arrangements into line with the percepts of justice, civil statutes are both subordinate to natural law and lend support to it. Hence, whether in a personalized or an impersonal form, political power is not in itself natural in Cicero's account, but is authorized by nature (or by the imperfect realization of human nature). Reason invents the various manifestations of political power in order to serve the naturally associative inclinations of mankind.

Lingering within Cicero's presentation of human association, however, is a measure of tension between the universal foundations of human society and the narrower sphere for the application of political power. On the one hand, he forwards the claim that 'we must respect, defend and maintain the common bonds and fellowship that obtain within the whole human race'.[39] Cicero asserts that human society transcends regional or national configurations: it is instead a universal manifestation of human nature. *De officiis* declares that 'nature prescribes that men will seek to promote the interests of other men, regardless of who they are, simply because they are fellow men'.[40] Yet Cicero recognizes that this general bond of sociability may seem remote when compared with relationships based on shared language, citizenship, kinship, friendship and so forth.[41] Human beings do indeed congregate into more intimate units such as nations and cities, a fact which is reflected in the many differences that arise between civil law and natural law.[42] The universality of justice congruent with the natural human propensity towards association is

---

[36] Ibid. II.xii.41–2. [37] Ibid. III.xvii.69. [38] Ibid. III.xvii.69.
[39] Ibid. I.xli.149. [40] Ibid. III.vi.27. [41] Ibid. I.xvii.53–8.
[42] Ibid. III.xvii.69.

not matched in Cicero's thought by the arrangement of the political power designed to enforce such justice. The law of nature, which underpins the perpetuation of harmonious social relations, extends to all human beings, yet Cicero upholds the legitimacy of particularistic political entities which seem to detract from the affirmation of the natural fellowship of mankind.

This ambiguity in the Ciceronian framework is effectively exploited by Aeneas Sylvius Piccolomini in his demonstration of the consistency of universal empire with reason, nature and justice. He unequivocally asserts that Roman dominion 'takes its origin from the rational faculty of human nature itself, which is the best guide of how to live and which all must obey'.[43] Where traditional medieval defences of the empire had concentrated upon theological or moral justifications,[44] Aeneas sought to construct imperial foundations upon the experience of human nature (construed in Stoic/Ciceronian fashion).[45] Of course, his Christian commitments compel him to acknowledge the sinful condition of post-lapsarian man. But this does not intrude into his account of the origins of human social and political relations. Aeneas observes that 'once our first parents had been driven out of the paradise of delights', men were condemned to 'roaming the fields and woods like beasts and preserving their existence with the meat of wild animals.'[46] Thus, the Fall induced among men a solitary existence, bereft of whatever forms of association might have existed in paradise – in sum, a state of primeval isolation.

Such a pre-social world corresponds to the description of the 'original' circumstances of mankind sketched by Cicero in his rhetorical works in order to explain the role played by oratory in uniting dispersed individuals.[47] But Aeneas never appeals directly in De ortu to men's linguistic faculties. Rather, adopting the essentially Stoic framework of the mature Cicero, who made speech consequent upon rationality, he identifies reason as the unique source of man's social tendencies.

Man observed – since God created him to share in His rational faculty – that to draw man together with man for the maximally good life, a society would be of great necessity. Therefore, those who had previously lived their lives separate from one

---

[43] De ortu, p. 7. The phrasing of this statement is unmistakably Ciceronian in character; cf. De finibus, II.11.34.

[44] These justifications included: the contemporaneity of Christ's birth and Augustus' rule; the anaology between God as the single ruler of the universe and the emperor as the single ruler of the earth; and the reliance of the unity of Christian faith upon the unity of political power. Perhaps the classic medieval defence of the Empire was offered by Dante, De monarchia, trans. H. W. Schneider (Indianapolis, 1949).

[45] This does not mean, of course, that Piccolomini excludes God as either a proximate or an immediate cause of the Empire. De ortu contains some of the same religious justifications for Roman domination that one finds in the medieval tradition; and it also accepts (as did the medievals) that nature itself was ultimately beholden to God. Yet De ortu keeps the theological bases for the Roman empire conceptually distinct from the naturalistic ones.

[46] Piccolomini, De ortu, p. 7.

[47] Cicero, De inventione, ed. H. M. Hubbell (Cambridge Mass., 1949), I.i.1–ii.3 and De oratore, ed. E. W. Sutton and H. Rackham (Cambridge, Mass., 1942), I.viii.33–4, I.ix.36.

another in the forests, like wild animals, whether at nature's behest or by the will of God who directs all nature, came together in the same place, established societies, built houses, surrounded their communities with walls, discovered practical skills, and, when one man ministered to the convenience of another, the civic way of life was astonishingly pleasing for individuals, and the companionship of neighbours and friends, which had previously not been known, seemed exceedingly sweet.[48]

Aeneas here recapitulates the main points emphasized by Cicero in *De officiis*: natural reason impels people to discover the myriad of advantages which social co-operation affords to them. The material interests of each are best served in the context of communal relations.

But Piccolomini also shares with Cicero a pronounced doubt about the permanence of such a primitive social arrangement founded solely on reason and nature. He explicitly cites the dictum of *De officiis* that 'just as many advantageous things are acquired by man for his fellow man, so there is no evil which is not brought about by man for his fellow man'.[49] He proceeds to describe a condition of existence not so far removed from a Hobbesian state of nature, in which neither wealth and possessions, nor families, nor even personal safety can be assured, and which hence knows no social bond. Aeneas ascribes this breakdown of communal harmony to the vice of 'cupidity', which could 'not suffer the justice of a pure society to endure inviolate for long'.[50] The very rational self-interest which stimulates men to join together into a community thus proves to be the ultimate enemy of social relations. In such a context, justice may too readily be ignored even when it is acknowledged to govern the communal order. Individuals cannot be counted upon to exercise self-restraint and moderation in a consistent fashion, and thereby to respect the rights of their fellows.

The 'justice of a pure society' thus needs to be complemented by what Aeneas terms 'civil justice', which performs the function of 'guarding the bonds of human society'.[51] Such civil justice is essentially equivalent to the exercise of political power: it encompasses the authority to punish the unjust and to uphold the dictates of justice upon which all social cooperation is founded. Again, Aeneas finds his warrant for this in Cicero's thought. He repeats almost verbatim the passage of *De officiis* which asserts that primitive kingship arose in order to shield the rights of weaker men from injury by the stronger. Throughout his writings he insists that the sole basis for the rule of the king is justice: 'There would have been no need for a king, nor would it have been necessary to entrust to anyone the distinction of such great rank, to be preferred to all others, to be honoured ahead of all, and to instruct all, for any reason other than that there was a need for an individual who would watch over public affairs and administer justice'.[52] If justice could have been

---

[48] Piccolomini, *De ortu*, pp. 7–8.   [49] Ibid. p. 8.   [50] Ibid. p. 8.   [51] Ibid. p. 8.

[52] Ibid. p. 8. Aeneas expands upon the centrality of justice to the function of kingship in his letter of 1 June 1444 to Wilhelm von Stein: 'Sed nesciunt hii stulti atque dementes, equitatem plus in principe locum habere quam rigorum. Quod si non juri scripto cesar nonnunquam obtemperet, satis est, quia sequitur equitatem, apud philosophos late descriptam...' (A. R. Baca [ed.], *Selected letters of Aeneas Sylvius Piccolomini* [Northridge, Calif., 1969], p. 102.

maintained by men in a purely social setting, political power would never have been conferred upon kings in the first place (a fact which guides the subsequent imposition of political power over communities for Aeneas). The king is regarded in Ciceronian terms as the personification of justice: his moral character outshines that of his fellows, and so he does not require law as the foundation of his rule, since his judgements are so rooted in a sense of justice and equity that they enjoy the force of law.[53] Hence, the introduction of royal government represents an extension of the principles of natural reason: 'Nature disposed matters so that the variety of impulses of private men would be moderated by the just governance of kings'.[54] Kingship accords with nature inasmuch as it permits human beings to live that sociable existence towards which they are naturally inclined but with which the vice of cupidity interferes. For this reason, kings are never excused from the duty to enforce the precepts of justice.

Thus far, Aeneas has worked along strictly Ciceronian lines. But he begins to diverge from this path when he addresses the disintegration of primitive kingship. It may be recalled that Cicero premised the replacement of such rulers on the acquisition of the crown by persons of evil character; a system of law was replaced to combat the vicissitudes of arbitrary personal government. As described by Cicero, this process is entirely contingent. So long as a succession of good men occupy the throne, there is no reason for kingship to be supplanted by the rule of law. By contrast, Aeneas thinks that he detects an inherent weakness in political arrangements associated with kingship, regardless of the moral qualities of a particular royal incumbent. He points out that the creation of the king was not a unique or isolated event: 'It occurred not only among one people but among many peoples'.[55] Thus, we confront a plurality of territorial units. As these kingdoms defined and expanded their geographical boundaries or spheres of jurisdiction, they inevitably came into conflict. And since there was no means of arbitration amongst such coequal powers, the resolution of disputes between them occurred by means of armed engagements.

Two points flow from Aeneas' observation. First, it is clear that the ensuing conflicts between royal powers are directly the function of an inescapable structural limitation endemic to localized or regional kingship *per se*. It is not morally corrupt rulers alone who are held responsible for clashes over lands and rights. Instead, any king who is performing his proper duties will, Aeneas supposes, inevitably enter into contention with another king and will be compelled to turn to warfare.[56] This suggests a second consequence: the political model of an independent network of kingships is incompatible with the very purpose for which civil justice was instituted, namely, the maintenance of harmonious relations among human beings. As Aeneas remarks, 'In the din and rage of battles, republic was unable to meet together with republic, nor territory with territory, and that sweetest commerce of

[53] Piccolomini, *De ortu*, p. 8.   [54] Ibid. p. 9.   [55] Ibid. p. 8.   [56] Ibid. pp. 8–9.

human society was obstructed'.[57] The decentralized distribution of royal power ultimately produces an effect which is exactly contrary to that intended. Empowered as the agent of social harmony, kingship proves to be its enemy, confounding rather than reinforcing the associative propensities within human nature. Sociability is deemed in Ciceronian fashion to be a universal human attribute. The particularity of royal regimes runs afoul of this universality of nature and the ordained end of political power will thereby never be achieved.

It is on this score that Piccolomini renders explicit the tension which lurks beneath Cicero's own account of social and political organization. For he confronts a question with which Cicero had declined to deal: are certain political forms more or less consistent with the purpose of political power as the upholder of justice and social order? Aeneas' answer is that the universality of human society founded upon justice requires the concomitant universality of political rule, that is, a single world empire. Nature itself authorizes such a universal arrangement of political power: 'The beneficent providence of human nature [namely, reason], which strives by its very nature towards the best, not wishing present or future circumstances to be badly disposed, was at hand. Therefore under its influence, it was resolved that individual rulers should be brought back under a single will, which the Greeks call monarchy and we call empire'.[58] In empire alone does political power finally attain a form consistent with the universalistic tendencies of sociability implicit within human nature. Rational reflection about the common good will inevitably lead us to acknowledge that imperial rule is necessary for the maintenance of the basic principles of human association.

Aeneas only moves beyond a naturalistic Ciceronian perspective when he attempts to justify the specific claim of the Roman emperors and their heirs to global predominance. At that point, the tone of his argument shifts markedly, emphasizing instead a combination of historical and religious factors. He recounts the failure of various pre-Roman empires and of the Roman republic. He asserts in teleological fashion that these other nations and forms of government were a kind of prelude to the best regime – the imperial system founded by Julius Caesar and consolidated by Augustus.[59] The superiority of the rule of a single man over the entire world is confirmed by the deeds and words of Jesus, as well as by the teachings of the church, all of which accord to the Roman empire special rights and prerogatives.[60] Although Aeneas sometimes implies that nature itself has sanctioned the authority of the Roman rulers and their Frankish and German successors,[61] his ultimate conclusion about the relation between the natural basis of imperial power, on the one hand, and the historico-religious foundation of specifically Roman dominion, on the other, is more subtly stated: 'Since natural reason itself showed that a single ruler was required – one who would resolve disputes, administer justice, watch over the peoples in peace, and preside over all temporal matters – it is

---

[57] Ibid. p. 9. [58] Ibid. p. 9. [59] Ibid. pp. 9–10. [60] Ibid. pp. 10–13.
[61] For example, at ibid. pp. 9, 10 and 13.

clear that the dignity of this task is fit for the Roman king, who, it is agreed, has had this task in his keeping for a long time'.[62] Reason instructs us in the necessity of the rule of one imperial authority over all human affairs; historical experience and divine intervention indicate to us that this authority should be vested in the Roman emperor. Thus, Aeneas implicitly recognizes that the Ciceronian framework has an essentially philosophical bearing: it can tell us which arrangement of political power is best (and why), but not which historical configuration must be obeyed. To justify the latter, other criteria of a non-philosophical sort (such as tradition and divine ordination) must be invoked.

The Ciceronian dimension does not thereafter disappear from Aeneas' argument, however. Rather, he returns to a fundamentally naturalistic approach when he addresses the central theme of *De ortu*, namely, the explicit critique of the claims of national regimes and their defenders to be independent of imperial control. He observes that one of two grounds are ordinarily advanced for such an exemption from subjection to the empire: either liberty has been conceded by the superior authority of an emperor or it has been earned by meritorious virtue.[63] In both instances, the case for autonomy rests on a readiness to shatter the bonds of human sociability, the maintenance of which is the primary purpose of the exercise of political power. Even admitting that an emperor might have ceded some of his prerogatives to inferior governments, still all such grants are cancelled because of their incompatibility with the natural law dictates of universal justice:

Since, as we have shown previously, it is agreed that empire was established in accordance with the law of nature and that monarchy is necessary to the preservation of peace and the administration of justice, it is certain that concessions of the sort which confer power upon a multitude of authorities have no validity. For discord is born of this, robbery frequently occurs, murder in various forms and countless numbers is committed, since once the peace has been upset wars spring up everywhere, because there is no individual greater than all others who could impose a limit on discord with the rule of law. If we were living under one head, if we owed obedience to a single person, if we recognized only one supreme ruler in temporal affairs, the best sort of peace would flourish everywhere on earth and we would all enjoy sweet harmony.[64]

Society itself crumbles when divided by concessions of liberty, reverting to those conditions which obtained in the past before the multitude of kingdoms was replaced by a single world empire. But since political power is pointless or arbitrary unless it contributes to the promotion of communal intercourse, such reversion cannot be justified by even the most thoroughly documented and complete grant of freedom given by an emperor to a nation or its rulers.

Similar considerations exclude merit as a legitimate rationale for the assertion of national sovereignty. Aeneas allows that during the dark days of empire, certain men may have recovered imperial territories from barbarian domination and thereby claimed hegemony over a given province as the reward for their courage and skill. He does not deny that such a liberator and

---

[62] Ibid. p. 14.   [63] Ibid. pp. 14–15.   [64] Ibid. p. 15.

his heirs should be permitted to serve in the role of imperial vicar in these reclaimed lands. But the authority enjoyed by those who recover imperial territories is at best that of a protectorate; *de facto* possession and rule does not confer *de jure* lordship (*dominium*). Indeed, if such *dominium* were claimed, these men would be thieves and usurpers rather than defenders of the empire. No merit of persons or families can displace the fact that political power must be exercised according to a universal plan if it is be employed in a manner congruent with the legitimate standards of reason and justice. The application of authority independent of the emperor by even the most virtuous individual 'shatters the dignity of monarchical power, produces schism within the empire, and takes away all the harmony of human society'.[65] The emperor is thus obliged to assert his imperial rights over any lesser ruler who believes that he has earned autonomous power over a realm because of his own good deeds or those of his ancestors. If the division of the empire into national units is not to be destructive of social order, the governors of nations must acknowledge their lack of sovereignty and their primary duty to defer and submit to their imperial master.

In this way, a Ciceronian conception of the natural foundations of society, when purged of some of its internal ambiguities and tensions, yielded the philosophical premises for a critique of national and civic government. The validity of this conclusion is in no way undermined by Piccolomini's further devotion to an absolutistic model of imperial rule according to which the emperor's will has the force of law and he also enjoys the rights to appropriate the private property of his subjects. Indeed, while these doctrines may be utterly anathema to the views espoused by Cicero,[66] Aeneas' account suggests that the two perspectives may not be so incompatible, at least logically, as they would seem at first glance. For he endeavours to elucidate the imperial powers of appropriation and legislation in terms consonant with Ciceronian teachings. In the instance of the emperor's claim upon the goods of his subjects – which is in any case limited to 'when necessity demands it for the republic'[67] – Aeneas connects his position with Cicero's remark in both *De finibus* and *De officiis* that our duties extend beyond ourselves to the political community of which we are a member.[68] *De ortu* proclaims that 'if a citizen will give everything he possesses for his safety, by how much more will he do this for the sake of the republic, for which we ought to develop our wealth no less than for ourselves'.[69] Inasmuch as the 'republic' in question can only be the empire, because it is the only legitimate political structure, Aeneas posits the duty of all persons to surrender their material goods without objection to the emperor when

---

[65] Ibid. p. 16.

[66] The distance in this regard may be judged by the diametrical opposition of their judgements of the significance of Julius Caesar. For Cicero, Caesar was a hated tyrant, an enslaver of his people (*De officiis*, II.vii.23 and III.xxi.83–5); for Aeneas, Julius was the glorious founder of the imperial majesty of Rome (*De ortu*, p. 10). For a full appreciation of the significance of the evaluation of Caesar's and Cicero's reputations in renaissance political thought, see Baron, *The crisis of the early Italian renaissance*, pp. 94–166 passim.   [67] Piccolomini, *De ortu*, p. 18.

[68] Cicero, *De officiis*, I.vii.22 and *De finibus*, II.xiv.45.   [69] Piccolomini, *De ortu*, p. 18.

required for the common welfare. He repeatedly stresses the obligation of individuals to prefer the benefit of the community to any private gain. Since Cicero himself pointed out in *De officiis* that the overriding interests of the individual in the maintenance of society authorize any sacrifice necessary for the public good,[70] Aeneas' citation of Cicero in this regard is perhaps not wholly inappropriate.

The theory of legislation in *De ortu* perhaps affords still clearer insight into Aeneas' extension of Ciceronian ideas to support imperial absolutism. He accepts that under ordinary circumstances the emperor should regard himself as bound by the same laws which he enforces over his subjects, restating the traditional *digna vox* formula.[71] Yet Aeneas also insists that the main purpose of imperial rule prohibits the permanent enforced submission of the emperor to statutory law. The reason is that the empire and emperor exist not for the sake of imposing law, but in order to disseminate justice. Justice composes the essential fabric of society, and in its absence communal disorder necessarily ensues. But what, then, of the case (envisaged by Cicero himself) in which justice and statutory law conflict? Aeneas declares that it is precisely our ability to raise this question which indicates the need for the emperor to stand above law and to dedicate himself to 'equity, that which is just beyond the scope of written law. If a law instructs one course and justice argues some other course, it is right that the emperor tempers the force of law with the check of equity; it falls to the emperor alone to interpose an interpretation between the letter of the law and the spirit of justice...'.[72] Relying upon an awareness of the historicity of law, the growth of which was central to renaissance humanism,[73] Aeneas explains that statutes 'which were once just have been rendered unjust, ineffective, harsh or iniquitous'.[74] Consequently, he regards it to be necessary for the emperor to possess the authorization to abrogate or change the law when such incongruities emerge. The emperor is not granted *carte blanche* to legislate arbitrarily or for personal gain. Rather, he acts at times above the law in order to secure that end for which his office and political power generally were instituted: to uphold the harmonious order of society by enforcing justice. Since it is not always assured that 'the legal' is coextensive with 'the just', the emperor as the agent of the universal bonds of community must be permitted to exercise his discretion in revising or dismissing unjust decrees. To deny him this authority would be to imperil the perpetuation of human association itself. Once again, Ciceronian premises can be seen to underpin a political doctrine which admittedly shares little with Cicero's own vision of politics.

Paul O. Kristeller has pointed out that the humanism of the Italian renaissance

[70] Cicero, *De officiis*, III.v.25–vi.26.

[71] Piccolomini, *De ortu*, pp. 20 and 21. The formula is derived from *Codex* I.14.4.

[72] Piccolomini, *De ortu*, p. 20. This statement may be compared to his remarks in his letter to Wilhelm von Stein, 1 June 1444 (Baca [ed.], pp. 101–2).

[73] See Donald R. Kelley, *Foundations of modern historical scholarship* (New York, 1970), pp. 19–50.

[74] Piccolomini, *De ortu*, p. 20.

was by no means a monolithic phenomenon nor one which necessarily implied a particular set of political doctrines or values. Responding to some of the excesses of the Baron thesis, Kristeller argues that

> it would be quite mistaken to identify Renaissance humanism as a whole with... Florentine civic humanism. There was a good deal of 'despotic' humanism even in fifteenth-century Italy, and it would be quite impossible to include under the heading of 'civic humanism' the entire political literature of the Renaissance period, let alone the large body of humanist literature that was not concerned with political problems at all.[75]

Although Kristeller does not cite Aeneas Sylvius Piccolomini expressly, *De ortu* offers an illustration (albeit a rather extreme one) of the diversity which was possible within humanist political thought. Indeed, one might speak of Aeneas as the founder, or at least a leading exponent, of a strain of *quattrocento* humanism that was imperial in character. Such 'imperial' humanism is related to, although still distinct from, the 'despotic' humanism to which Kristeller alludes. Where such renaissance defences of despotism were still associated with essentially urban institutions and identities, 'imperial' humanism found its inspiration in the other great political formation of antiquity, empire. Thinkers like Aeneas not only found warrant for universal empire in ancient history and literature, but they adapted and applied the philosophical lessons of the classical age (even, as the case of *De ortu* reveals, non-imperial doctrines) to the enhancement of the imperial ideal.[76] To exclude such imperial theories from the range of humanist political literature on the largely *a priori* grounds that the promotion of the Holy Roman Empire was an inherently medieval mode of thought thus seems indefensible. We are justified in rejecting as a false dichotomy the distinction which has been repeatedly drawn within the scholarship on Aeneas between his renaissance humanist inclinations and his 'medieval', imperial political propensities.

Recognition of the humanist flavour of Aeneas' argument in *De ortu* also helps us to resolve an outstanding debate about the so-called 'originality' of his work. The range of scholarly opinion about the extent of Aeneas' novelty has varied widely: Felice Battaglia once credited *De ortu* with originating the modern concept of sovereignty,[77] while Lewis regarded it as merely a useful summary of conventional arguments favouring the Roman empire.[78] Most commentators have tended to share the judgement of John B. Toews that *De*

---

[75] Paul O. Kristeller, 'Humanism and moral philosophy', in Rabil (ed.), *Renaissance humanism*, II, 289. Similar views are cited by Rabil, 'The significance of 'civic humanism', in the interpretation of the Italian renaissance', pp. 155–6.

[76] In this way, 'imperial' humanism has detectable echoes in what John D'Amico has identified as the 'Roman' version of Ciceronianism, which constituted 'the chief means of expressing Roman humanism's authoritarian and imperial associations...Roman humanists neglected the political side of Cicero's life and teachings...they preferred to look at Cicero as the great Latin stylist rather than as a politician and defender of the Republic' (*Renaissance humanism in papal Rome*, pp. 126, 125).

[77] Battaglia, 'Il pensiero politico di Enea Silvio Piccolomini', pp. 33–4 and passim.

[78] Lewis, *Medieval political ideas*, p. 465.

ortu shows 'little originality of thought' and depends heavily upon ancient and contemporary sources.[79] But the present examination suggests that much of the 'novelty' of *De ortu* stems from Aeneas' subtle extension and recasting of the theoretical framework provided by Cicero in directions which the Roman himself had not envisaged. Aeneas' Ciceronianism is a vital one inasmuch as it treats Cicero's ideas as materials to be transformed and fashioned according to their inner logic as well as external political exigencies. This reshaping of Cicero's thought (or indeed, of any other classical source) to suit current concerns and rigorous philosophical standards was by no means unique to Aeneas. Renaissance humanism in general was not merely a passive repository of classical learning, but a creative force for the synthesis and application of ancient values and ideals to confront modern issues and experiences. The specific contribution of Aeneas' *De ortu* was to wrest the substance (if not the intent) of Cicero's political thought away from the exclusive control of urban and republican authors; hence, he revitalized and advanced a debate which had commenced in the fourteenth century about the proper relation between the Roman emperor and the political communities of Europe (and beyond) by translating the terms of such controversy into a Ciceronian language accessible to *quattrocento* humanists of all orientations.[80] If this does not place Aeneas Sylvius Piccolomini quite in the front rank of fifteenth-century political thinkers, it should at least cause scholars to reconsider the continued exclusion of *De ortu* from the canon of texts to which they refer when recounting the development of political humanism in the early renaissance.

One further conclusion is merited. Our identification of a significant Ciceronian component within the argument of *De ortu* hints at the futility of interpretations of Aeneas' career which appeal to an unresolved tension or tragic conflict between 'medieval' and 'renaissance' elements of his experience.[81] Unlike many of his modern interpreters, Aeneas does not seem to have divided his mental world into 'medieval' and 'renaissance' elements. Hence, no necessary inconsistency was implied by his persistent commitment to humanist learning while simultaneously also upholding imperial, papalist and crusader ideals. Our study of *De ortu* has established that dedication to *quattrocento* humanism was not incompatible with advocacy of a theory of empire. Might similar conclusions be forthcoming with regard to the other so-called 'medieval' features of his activity and intellect?[82] Perhaps the imposition of fixed conceptual and historical categories upon the fifteenth century is primarily responsible for the enigma which presently characterizes the thought and career of Aeneas Sylvius Piccolomini.

---

[79] Toews, 'The view of empire in Aeneas Sylvius Piccolomini', p. 476 n. 17.

[80] For the fourteenth-century background, see Joseph P. Canning, *The political thought of Baldus de Ubaldus* (Cambridge, 1987).

[81] Rowe, 'The tragedy of Aeneas Sylvius Piccolomini', pp. 301–3.

[82] This was indeed noted by J. B. Morrall, 'Pius II: humanist and crusader', *History Today* (January 1958), pp. 33–4.

INDEX